Beaches,
Ruins, Resorts

Beaches, Ruins, Resorts

The Politics of Tourism in the Arab World

Waleed Hazbun

University of Minnesota Press   Minneapolis / London

Portions of the Introduction were previously published as "Globalization, Reterritorialization, and the Political Economy of Tourism Development in the Middle East," *Geopolitics* 9, no. 2 (2004): 310–41, http://www.informaworld .com; reprinted with permission of Taylor and Francis. Portions of chapters 3 and 4 previously appeared as "Mapping the Landscape of the 'New Middle East': The Politics of Tourism Development and the Peace Process in Jordan," in *Transitions in Contemporary Jordan, 1989–2000,* ed. George Joffé (London: Hurst, 2001), 330–45; reprinted with permission of Hurst Publishers. An earlier version of chapter 5 was previously published as "Explaining the Arab Middle East Tourism Paradox," *Arab World Geographer* 9, no. 3 (2006): 201–14; reprinted with permission from *AWG—The Arab World Geographer,* Toronto, Canada.

Published by the University of Minnesota Press
111 Third Avenue South, Suite 290
Minneapolis, MN 55401-2520
http://www.upress.umn.edu

Library of Congress Cataloging-in-Publication Data

Hazbun, Waleed.
    Beaches, ruins, resorts : the politics of tourism in the Arab world /
Waleed Hazbun.
        p.   cm.
    Includes bibliographical references and index.
    ISBN 978-0-8166-5491-8 (hc : alk. paper) — ISBN 978-0-8166-5492-5
(pb : alk. paper)
    1. Tourism—Political aspects—Middle East.   2. Geopolitics—Middle East.
I. Title.
    G155.M66H39 2008
    338.4'79156—dc22

                                                                        2008028419

Printed in the United States of America on acid-free paper

The University of Minnesota is an equal-opportunity educator and employer.

15 14 13 12 11 10 09 08   10 9 8 7 6 5 4 3 2 1

Contents

Abbreviations

ACOR	American Center for Oriental Research
AFT	Agence Foncière Touristique
ARA	Aqaba Regional Authority
ASEZ	Aqaba Special Economic Zone
COFITOUR	Compagnie Financière et Touristique
CRSN	Committee for Resisting Submission and Normalization
CTKD	Consortium Tuniso-Koweitien de Développement
DOA	Department of Antiquities (Jordan)
EIU	Economist Intelligence Unit
EU	European Union
GCC	Gulf Cooperation Council
IFC	International Finance Corporation
IMF	International Monetary Fund
IPE	international political economy
ISI	import-substitution industrialization
JD	Jordanian dinar
JICA	Japan International Cooperation Agency
JTB	Jordan Tourism Board
JTI	Jordan Tourism Investments
JVA	Jordan Valley Authority
MEMTTA	Middle East–Mediterranean Travel and Tourism Association

MENA	Middle East and North Africa
MOP	Ministry of Planning (Jordan)
MOTA	Ministry of Tourism and Antiquities (Jordan)
MTI	Movement de la Tendance Islamique
NGO	nongovernmental organization
ONAT	Office National de l'Artisanat Tunisien
ONTT	Office National du Tourisme et Thermaliseme; *later renamed* Office National du Tourisme Tunisien
PFLP	Popular Front for the Liberation of Palestine
PLO	Palestine Liberation Organization
PNT	Petra National Trust
PRPC	Petra Regional Planning Council
QIZ	Qualified Industrial Zone (Jordan)
REDWG	Regional Economic Development Working Group
RSCN	Royal Society for the Conservation of Nature
SHTT	Société Hôtelière et Touristique
SPN	Society for the Protection of Nature
TD	Tunisian dinar
TNC	transnational corporation
UAE	United Arab Emirates
UN	United Nations
UNESCO	United Nations Educational, Scientific, and Cultural Organization
UNWTO	World Tourism Organization (a UN agency)
USAID	U.S. Agency for International Development

Introduction: Tourism, Territory, and the Politics of Globalization

For readers who associate the Arab world with images of political violence, authoritarian rule, and hostility to foreigners, a book about the politics of tourism might be expected to focus on how airplane hijackings, attacks against tourists, and restrictions on foreign visitors have hindered the rise of a leisure tourism industry. This book tells a different story. It investigates how, despite these many challenges, international tourism has become one of the most prevalent aspects of globalization transforming the Arab world. In doing so, this book challenges common portrayals of Arab states and societies as disconnected from globalization and culturally inclined to resist its effects.

The study of international tourism development offers a lens through which one can gain an original perspective on the political economy and international relations of the Arab world. In the chapters to come, I follow the journeys of Europeans seeking Mediterranean beaches and classical ruins, the first Israelis crossing into Jordan as leisure tourists, and diverse visitors discovering the trendsetting resort hotels and shopping malls of Dubai. In the process, I trace the region's incorporation into the networks of the global tourism economy and explore how the increasing transnational flows of tourists, tourism receipts, and investment capital have shaped economic development, state building, and international relations. At the same time, I also show how tourism development and tourism flows have often been crafted to serve state interests.

With a focus on how local tourism spaces are created, I argue that tourism development has allowed states to promote integration into the global economy while simultaneously expanding control over their domestic economies and societies. Viewing international tourism development as a transnational process, I also expose the critical role that tourism played in the peace process between Israel and Jordan and the efforts of Tunisia to foster greater economic integration with Europe. Additionally, I explain why, through all the post–9/11 turmoil across the region, the tourism economies of the Arab world have witnessed rapid expansion, with the cities of the Persian Gulf States becoming key nodes in regional and global networks of travel.

Tourism Development and "Itineraries of Globalization"

As the first major study of the political economy of international tourism development in the Middle East, this book fills gaps in both the field of international political economy (IPE) and Middle East studies. International tourism has long played a critical role in the expansion of the postwar global economy. Growing at an average annual rate of 6.5 percent since 1950, international tourism arrivals worldwide topped 800 million in 2005, generating over $680 billion in tourism receipts that year.[1] Today international tourism drives vast transnational flows of people, commodities, and capital that circulate in globally coordinated production networks governed by large transnational firms such as airlines, tour operators, and hotel management companies. Not only is the volume of these flows massive, but more critically, international travel and tourism are also closely tied to patterns of economic and social change in localities across the globe. The expansion and transformation of international tourism, in short, has exhibited many of the core features of what we have come to refer to as globalization. While the literary critic Jonathan Culler has aptly suggested that "there are few clearer indicators of shifting lines of force within the economic order than changes in the flow of tourists,"[2] the political implications of tourism have nevertheless been overlooked by IPE scholars and the vast literature on globalization.

An exploration of tourism also provides a new lens through which to view the changing political economy and geopolitics of the Middle East. International tourism was one of the first sectors in the region to be integrated into the markets and flows of the post–World War II international economy. In recent decades, tourism has been a leading source of hard currency, embraced by policy makers and entrepreneurs as an engine of economic growth and a means to promote economic liberalization and global economic integration. While regional conflicts and political instability often disrupt tourism flows across the region, tourism also plays an important role in state efforts to promote domestic stability and order and to reshape external relations.

Ever since modernizing Arab regimes first sought to promote national economic development after gaining independence, tourism boosters have argued that the region's sunny beaches, picturesque deserts, biblical locales, architectural ruins, "exotic" cultures, and native hospitality should be used to generate new sources of wealth. The results reshaped coastal landscapes, cultural heritage sites, and built environments. The lure of tourism income and investment capital led to the construction of massive tourism complexes and encouraged state and private agencies to develop a range of new attractions such as restored antiquities sites, heritage museums, and nature parks. Funded by international investors, local capital, and abundant petrodollars, the region has experienced a series of hotel-building booms, which produced blocks of generic whitewashed hotels along sunny beaches in North Africa, renovated clusters of old buildings in Damascus into boutique hotels, and gave rise to a wave of new luxury palaces in Amman, Beirut, and Dubai. The now iconic image of the Burj al Arab, the luxury hotel shaped like a massive sail, symbolizes Dubai's emergence as a leading tourism destination for the global jet set. Expanding flows of international travelers—drawn to world heritage sites like Jordan's rock-carved city of Petra or to the cosmopolitan cultural scene in Beirut—have helped represent the Middle East as an emerging destination within the circuits of global travel.

Although largely ignored by scholars of Middle Eastern political economy and international relations,[3] tourism not only constitutes a critical feature of economic development but also shapes many aspects of international relations. Tourism development influences the political, economic, and cultural relations between societies by promoting new patterns of border crossing and transnational flows. Many Middle Eastern states seeking foreign investment but hindered by their location in what is often viewed as an unstable and crisis-prone region use tourism development to project an external image of stability, prosperity, and economic openness. During the Arab-Israeli peace process of the early 1990s, tourism development was expected to serve as a vehicle for regional economic cooperation leading to the formation of the "New Middle East" connected by economic flows rather than, as in the past, separated by militarized frontiers. Tourism even played a role in initial American visions for integrating postwar Iraq into the global economy. As the *New York Times* reported, after a trip to Iraq in the late summer of 2003, U.S. secretary of defense Donald H. Rumsfeld "observed that Iraq could not rely on its oil revenues alone to rebuild its decrepit infrastructure but must plan to develop industries like tourism that would benefit from national and historic treasures like the ruins of the ancient city of Babylon."[4] Since the oil boom of the early 1970s, Gulf states have expanded their regional influence through massive investments in hotel development and tourist spending. More recently, many of these states have become major tourist destinations with lavish hotel complexes and airline networks. As a result, the rise of oil incomes in the post–9/11 era led to the recentering of regional Arab economic flows around the investment and purchasing power of the oil-rich Gulf states.

These trends, however, suggest many urgent questions. The post-1945 economic boom in the advanced industrial states gave rise to a new wave of mass tourism that allowed even the lower-middle classes to partake in international leisure travel. With this explosion of tourism as a global industry, many local and international critics have questioned if tourism economies and their social relations in the Third World too closely resemble colonial-era structures and processes. Many worry that tourism development is at best land speculation and unlikely to generate sustainable growth with broad societal benefits and at worst a form of cultural prostitution. During the hotel boom launched by the first wave of petrodollar investment in the 1970s, Edward Said asked a gathering of Arab intellectuals, "Don't you wish you could wake up one day and read that plans are afoot to build a great Arab library instead of a new hotel?"[5]

State agencies and tourism developers are often challenged by the changing dynamics of the global tourism economy—from the shifting tastes of tourists to the operational choices of transnational airlines and hotel management firms. Tourism development also creates unexpected political challenges and transformations by engaging a new set of local and transnational actors in struggles to define the scope of state powers over the economy, society, and landscape. In addition, the massive size and prominence of the tourism industry make it a highly politicized sector. As tourism generates negative social and environmental consequences, it mobilizes a range of local and regional opponents. Local communities, environmental activists, and Islamist movements challenge the tourism development efforts of state and private actors. Political opposition to economic liberalization and global integration often takes the form of ideological discourses, social mobilization, and even terrorist violence against tourists, the tourism industry, and the infrastructure of tourist travel. Especially in the post–9/11 era—after the attacks of September 11, 2001, and a series of bombings in Indonesia, Tunisia, Egypt, and Jordan—the international tourism economy remains at the center of questions about global security, inequality, and the governance of transportation networks that sustain the flows of globalization.

The politics of tourism development thus provide a critical lens through which to view wider struggles over economic development and the position of the Middle East within globalization and the changing global order. To explore a broad range of these experiences in depth, I examine tourism development from three vantage points. The first centers on how the North African state of Tunisia, beginning in the 1960s, transformed its shores to gain a position within the Mediterranean economy for mass beach tourism. Tourism development remains a pillar of the Tunisian economy, as the state relies on it to project images of openness and stability in its effort to attract foreign investment, promote economic liberalization, and seek closer integration of its economy into European and North American markets. My second vantage point is Jordan, located at the center of the volatile geopolitics of the Middle East. With a territory rich in religious and cultural heritage sites, Jordan has long struggled to build a vibrant tourism industry. Like other Middle Eastern states, Jordan turned to tourism development during the late 1980s when regional economies were hit by the decline of oil incomes, worker remittances, and access to foreign aid. The rise of the Arab-Israeli peace process in the 1990s helped launch a vast, internationally backed tourism development drive in Jordan that was expected to reap the dividends of peace and lead to expanded regional economic cooperation. My third vantage point investigates the post–9/11 trends that have led to the expansion of regional tourism and, more generally, the recentering of Arab economic flows around the Gulf oil economies. It includes a case study of tourism development in Dubai, a member of the United Arab Emirates (UAE), and shows how other locations have replicated similar development strategies and spatial patterns. While showing how these trends reflect the increasing agency of actors in the Middle East to shape the regional and global networks of the tourism economy, I also note the limits of this model of globalization and explore emerging alternative styles of travel and strategies of tourism development.

As shown in Table 1, as a group, international tourist arrivals in Tunisia, Jordan, and the UAE have grown at faster-than-average rates, steadily increasing their share of world totals between 1980 and 2003. Tunisia's numbers for 1990 in Tables 1 and 2 reflect its earlier development of a mass tourism economy, but its relative size has been eroded by the expansion of tourism in Jordan and the UAE since. A notable feature of Table 2 is the jump in the group's share of tourism receipts after 2000, a period marked by regional political turmoil and several attacks targeting the tourism sector. As discussed in chapter 5, I refer to this phenomenon as the "Middle East tourism paradox." Figure 1 displays how tourism represents a significant share of gross domestic product (GDP) in several Arab economies, with Dubai, Jordan, and Tunisia having the highest percentages as of 2000.

Table 1. International tourism arrivals (in thousands)

	1980	1990	2000	2003
Tunisia	1,602	3,224	5,057	6,378
Jordan	393	437	1,427	2,353
UAE	300	973	3,907	5,871
Subtotal	2,295	4,634	10,391	14,602
World	287,781	457,306	698,793	694,600
Subtotal share	0.8%	1.0%	1.5%	2.1%

Source: World Tourism Organization. Note: 1980 data for UAE are for Dubai only.

Table 2. International tourism receipts (nominal million $US)

	1990	1995	2000	2005
Tunisia	948	1,393	1,496	2,063
Jordan	512	660	722	1,441
UAE	315	632	1,063	2,233
Subtotal	1,775	2,685	3,281	5,737
World	263,357	406,200	475,772	682,700
Subtotal share	0.67%	0.66%	0.69%	0.84%

Source: World Tourism Organization

Each of the three studies is set in a different context for tourism development and depicts different dynamics operating within the world of policy makers, private firms, and various societal actors who seek to meet the challenges and opportunities of global integration. Together they survey a range of what I refer to as the *itineraries of globalization* being pursued across the region. By framing this book around the notion of itineraries, I can investigate diverse understandings and projections of globalization rather than measure each experience against a common index. Despite the academic debate about the measurable reality of globalization, the concept plays a powerful role in shaping the goals and agendas of policy makers, entrepreneurs, social activists, and tourists in the Middle East and elsewhere. In other words, for my purposes, globalization is defined as what these actors make of it.

To better understand the construction of these itineraries, this Introduction develops a political-economy approach focused on the territorial aspects of transnational flows. Like other facets of globalization, the development and spread of international tourism

Egypt	4.4
Israel	2.8
Jordan	**8.5**
Morocco	6.1
Syria	2.6
Tunisia	**7.7**
UAE	1.5
Dubai	**12.0**

Figure 1. International tourism receipts as percentage of GDP in 2000. *Sources:* World Tourism Organization; World Bank; Sampler and Eigner, *Sand to Silicon,* 17. *Note:* Dubai data are for 2001.

are products of networks that sustain flows of people, capital, and commerce across national territories. While defined by actors and processes in multiple locations, these transnational networks help shape patterns of economic development, identity formation, and political control in particular localities. The key to understanding these impacts is to analyze the changing territorial dynamics of these processes.

Most studies of globalization focus on processes that generate *deterritorialization,* where territorial features (such as distance, borders, and location) become less salient across a seemingly homogeneous space. Deterritorialization often erodes the territorially based regulatory capability of states and challenges territorially based social formations and identities. Globalization, however, should also be understood as generating *reterritorialization* in which such territorial features become more salient. In its economic forms, reterritorialization entails the development of nodes within global networks that generate spatially defined economic benefits for firms and property owners. The political significance of economic reterritorialization is that it can increase the power and regulatory influence of state agencies, private firms, and societal actors who control such spaces. In its political forms, reterritorialization consists of policies and ideologies that enhance territorial identities and promote rebordering to limit transnational flows.

Using this framework, I show how tourism development has often been used as a means to integrate Arab economies into increasingly competitive and volatile global markets. This occurs because many states and firms view tourism development as the most feasible means to promote economic reterritorialization and thus expand their control over capital flows, markets, and territory while also promoting globalization. I demonstrate how struggles within each state or locality over patterns of development can determine how and if a territory becomes integrated into regional and global networks and transnational flows. Thus the politics of globalization can be understood better as struggles between rival local actors within spaces shaped by the transnationally produced effects of deterritorialization and reterritorialization than as a global confrontation between globalizing processes and local forms of resistance. This framework posits globalization as a heterogeneous process across time and space. It is best suited to capturing how the patterns of tourism development across the Middle East are often defined by authorities that are able to assert control over local spaces and territory but not over globe-spanning networks.

The International Political Economy of Tourism

The origins of the international tourism economy and its expansion across the Middle East can be traced back to what is often called the first era of globalization during the second half of the nineteenth century. Beginning in the 1840s, the British firm Thomas Cook & Son helped convert travel, often undertaken for the purposes of business, religion, and education, into a leisure commodity.[6] By prearranging to provide the transportation, accommodation, and other needs of many travelers as a group, Thomas Cook was able to decrease the costs and risks of leisure travel and lay the foundations for the rise of organized popular tourism. These efforts created a tourist market in the transportation and accommodation sectors, leading first to the development of an infrastructure for tourist travel across Europe and eventually to the proliferation of tourism-related businesses that sought to commercialize all aspects of the travel experience. As travel became cheaper and more convenient, the practice of leisure tourism spread throughout the upper-middle classes of the industrializing societies of Europe and North America, who could now easily travel independently of organized groups. After the opening of the Suez Canal in 1869, at a time when the firm was losing some of its competitive advantages and market share in a growing industry, Thomas Cook's son, John Mason Cook, led the expansion of the company's operations into the Middle East. He soon established a vertically integrated tourism business based on the firm's control of Nile transportation, several hotels, and hundreds of agents, guides, porters, and servants across Egypt and the Holy Land. Following in the footsteps of Thomas Cook & Son, more firms—called tour operators—sprang up, accelerating the development of mass tourism globally by aggregating ever-larger numbers of tourists and negotiating contracts for the large-scale supply of transportation, lodging, and other services by local providers. The result was an overall reduction in the cost of tourism that further expanded its market.

The latest phase of the development of the international tourism economy began at the end of World War II. The United States became an early proponent of reopening European borders to tourist flows and encouraged American tourism to France as a means to inject the economy with dollars and begin economic reconstruction before Marshall Plan funds were mobilized.[7] The eventual reduction of travel barriers across Europe, the postwar economic boom, and the establishment of international travel and tourism networks— including airline routes and international hotel chains—led to the development of tourism as one of the largest sectors of the global economy. By one estimate, in 2008 international and domestic tourism will directly and indirectly generate over $5.9 trillion, accounting for about 10 percent of gross world product and employing 238 million people worldwide.[8]

While anthropologists, economists, and geographers have since explored the social, economic, and spatial aspects of this industry, political scientists have barely begun to examine the political implications of tourism.[9] As Lisa Martin, a leading IPE scholar, notes, previous calls "for political scientists to take the subject seriously have appeared, to little effect."[10] The limited scholarly attention given to the topic of international tourism by political scientists stands in contrast to the claim made in 1966 by Somerset Waters, a member of the U.S. Department of Commerce's Travel Industry Advisory Committee. He suggested that "perhaps history will show that in the mid-period of the twentieth century, tourism exceeded all other influences in creating an impact on world economic, cultural, and social behavior."[11] Waters's seemingly far-fetched suggestion was motivated by the phenomenal growth of international tourism in the early postwar years. Between 1950 and 1965, international tourist arrivals expanded from 25 million to over 112 million, while foreign travel expenditures grew at an average annual rate of 12 percent. In the 1950s and 1960s, the rapid expansion of global tourism was spurred on by industrial growth in the North Atlantic economies, the development of the welfare state, and the rise of middle- and working-class leisure time and mass consumerism. Tourism development was generally understood to help southern European states in their postwar efforts to modernize their economies by diversifying their sources of foreign exchange and by generating job growth in underdeveloped regions.[12] In ten years' time, international tourists were expected to be spending $40 billion per year, leading Waters to conclude that more than foreign aid or manufactured exports, "tourism may play *the key* role in the future in providing the underdeveloped nations with a much needed new source of foreign exchange required for economic development."[13]

While the vast majority of tourist activity consists of travel within and between the industrialized states, it is also clear that international tourism has shaped patterns of economic, cultural, and social change in many if not most developing nations, where the political implications of these impacts might be greater. The international tourism economy has largely been driven by the growth of a linked set of firms and organizations and the rise of leisure travel as a form of mass consumerism. The operations of airlines, tour operators, and hotel management firms account for the bulk of the global tourism industry.[14] Within each destination, the tourism industry incorporates a heterogeneous array of local actors—from hotel owners and travel agents to street vendors and tour guides—who contribute to the process of tourism development by turning spatially defined experiences into commodities and providing visitors with goods, services, and information. Though tourism is often referred to as the largest sector of the global economy, the exact size of the sector is impossible to determine, as it has no clearly defined boundaries. It is the nationality, motivation, and experience of the consumer, rather than that of the producer, that defines any economic activity as tourism. While some firms might operate within the space of a tourism enclave where all consumers are foreign tourists, firms outside such spaces might routinely provide goods and services to both visitors and local residents. Moreover, while a foreign tourist's consumption of goods and services is defined as an export, similar purchases made by a resident engaged in domestic leisure tourism are not. The amorphous nature of the sector often complicates both policy formulation and scholarship about tourism.

Its massive size and global impacts notwithstanding, it is not (yet) possible to speak of the international political economy of tourism as a distinct subfield with an established literature. Thus, rather than presenting a survey of an existing literature, I draw on research about tourism and related matters from a range of disciplinary approaches to define some of the building blocks needed to develop an IPE-of-tourism subfield and research agenda. This effort is organized around two key questions. Both questions address issues central to the field of international political economy that are critical for understanding the effects of tourism development in the Middle East. The first question relates to the relative power of state agencies, private firms, and international markets in shaping the politics of tourism development. In other words, are local patterns of development shaped more by an economy's (usually subordinate) position in the global economic system or by the autonomous actions of state agencies and other local actors? The second question addresses the political effects of transnational flows: do cross-border flows promote economic and political integration and facilitate cooperation, or do these flows generate asymmetrical economic and cultural relations that foster political conflict?

The Global Tourism Economy and the Politics of Development

In the 1960s and 1970s, governments across the developing world, backed by agencies such as the World Bank and the U.S. Agency for International Development (USAID), pushed tourism as a means to promote market-based economic growth and provide capital for industrialization.[15] These efforts were largely inspired by models derived from modernization theory and development economics in that they focused on large-scale, capital-intensive infrastructure projects. Like many other development efforts, the results often did not meet expectations. Much of the early literature focused on measuring the smaller-than-expected economic benefits and the larger-than-expected social and environmental costs.[16] For example, while modernization approaches had emphasized how most of each dollar spent by tourists was respent over and over again locally, creating the "multiplier effect," other scholars began to measure how the need for imported goods, expatriate labor, and payments to foreign firms led to a large share of the foreign currency gained by tourism being "leaked" back out.

The first studies to explore the international political economy of tourism appeared in the 1970s, when a few scholars studying the rise of transnational corporations (TNCs) ventured to incorporate tourism firms into these frameworks. Many of these studies were influenced by theories of dependency and underdevelopment and challenged modernization theory.[17] One important model viewed the global tourism economy in terms of an "international division of leisure" where less-developed countries came to represent a "pleasure periphery" for European and North American tourists.[18] At the center of this model was the notion that developing countries, due to constraints on capital, technology, marketing, and market size, were unable to reap major economic rewards from tourism development. As a result, the model's proponents argued, when developing countries opened their territory, larger TNCs from developed states would come to dominate the most lucrative elements of the industry (airlines, hotels, tour operators). And as more territories opened up, the bargaining power of local governments and firms only decreased.

The concerns of these studies still influence scholars who explore international tourism development as a form of (exploitative) global capitalism.[19] Some, focusing on smaller island economies, suggest that tourism represents a form of neocolonialism often supported by the policies of international development organizations like the World Bank.[20] By the 1990s, however, paralleling the work of others who saw the dependency approach as too deterministic, a new wave of scholarship showed how tourism could be promoted like other forms of export-oriented development if carefully planned while noting the benefits of local, community-organized alternatives to mass tourism development.[21] These studies contributed to a debate about tourism development and its relationship to privatization and neoliberal economic policies, which many developing countries implemented in the 1980s and 1990s as part of structural adjustment programs. These approaches, however, tend to focus on national development strategies or microcontexts,[22] treating the nature of the international tourism economy as an exogenous factor.

To bridge the gap, this book builds on innovative efforts to view the international tourism economy through the framework of global commodity chain analysis.[23] The commodity chain approach helps explain how the most lucrative segments of the international tourism economy are often dominated by the large TNCs. It also demonstrates how firms based in developing countries, often with government support, have been able to capture a growing share of industry profits when large business concerns develop their own set of local tourism-related firms or when small local firms succeed in exploiting specialized niche markets.

While the global commodity chain approach usefully maps the global tourism economy as a set of connected service sector businesses, the approach pays too little attention to the diverse spatial and cultural dynamics that shape the markets for demand and the conditions of the production and commodification of tourism. I develop an approach that begins with the notion that tourism development is best defined as the commodification of experiences of place. The experience of place and value of the product is shaped by changing transportation technologies, ways of seeing, cultural lenses, and processes of commodification, all led by diverse actors such as government agencies, local entrepreneurs, TNCs, and NGOs. The task of developing an international political economy of tourism thus requires a framework that sees tourism in each location not as a product of a global economic system driven by a single capitalist logic but as shaped by ever-changing networks connecting heterogeneous local actors through international transportation systems to travelers from other parts of the world.[24] Local actors in developing states, such as state agencies and private firms, generally are not able to reshape the structure of the global tourism economy. The transnational networks that shaped these economies are mostly based outside their own borders, and owing to the relatively small share of global flows to the Middle East, these states and firms based in the region have limited influence on the global markets that shape the behavior of TNCs. Under certain circumstances, however, their control over local territorial resources can be used to shape local experiences and reposition their tourism products within certain networks of the global tourism economy.

Tourism as a Transnational Process

Another critical facet of tourism barely explored by existing political-economy approaches is the way it operates as a vehicle for transnational flows of people, capital, commodities, and images. The process of tourism development and the experience of tourist travel shape people's experiences of, and relationships to, places and territory. Travel, like other aspects of globalization, often plays tricks with our sense of geography. Historically, at each moment when the globe was viewed as becoming "smaller" due to faster and more extensive travel and communications, there were those who heralded the "end of geography." Some described it as the development of interdependence and the erosion of the political, economic, and cultural differences that sustain global conflict and inequality. To take one example, in the 1940s the rise of international aviation allowed civilians to travel rapidly across the globe, as Wendell Willkie did in 1942. This moment of rapid space-time compression helped give rise to the "one-world movement" that supported the creation of a federal system of world government.[25] At the same time, however, others have countered that making the world "smaller" does not result in making it more homogeneous or prone to cooperation across borders. More intense interactions can generate new geographies of enmity and conflict. Samuel Huntington, for example, views contemporary global politics as fragmented between territories separated by their civilizational differences.[26] From a quite different perspective, Edward Said argues that the expansion of travel and communications in the age of empire helped generate "imagined geographies" that folded distance into difference, demarcating "the same" from "the other."[27] From either view, the ability to traverse distance and space only heightens the saliency of differences and provides the basis for conflict and exploitation.

While scholars of tourism have explored both these effects individually, they have yet to develop integrated theories that explain both effects within the same framework. At the broadest level, international travel and tourism are sometimes portrayed as vehicles for promoting cross-cultural understanding and cosmopolitan identities. Prominent advocates of this line of thinking include the UNESCO World Heritage Committee and the International Institute for Peace through Tourism. Arend Lijphart, for one, viewed tourism flows as one form of cross-border interaction that contributes to the development of interdependence between states and might help foster regional integration.[28] Others have focused on how bilateral tourism flows have shaped diplomatic ties between states. In the early postwar period, for example, U.S. policy makers hoped that increased travel to Europe would prompt Americans to view themselves as connected to Europe as part of the Atlantic community and support funding of the Marshall Plan.[29] Another example is the impact of U.S. tourism to Israel, promoted by the Israeli government and private organizations in both countries. These flows have helped sustain support at the societal level for closer strategic ties.[30] While these examples are cases of drawing strategically allied states closer together, some have suggested that tourism can act as a vehicle for increasing understanding and cooperation between societies separated by mutually suspicious

governments with hostile relations.[31] Such advocates of the "contact model" of cultural change claim that "tourism operates at the
most basic level of track-two diplomacy by spreading information
about personalities, beliefs, aspirations, perspectives, culture and
politics of the citizens of one country to the citizens of another."[32]

In contrast to these liberal views of interdependence and cosmopolitanism, scholars drawing on realist and statist notions of
state power have noted how the global structure of tourism flows
reflects the interests of the most powerful states in the international
system. For example, they argue that the structure of air transport
networks, the regimes that govern them, and the increasing liberalization of air travel reflect the relative power of states in the international system.[33] The denial of tourism flows can also be used as a
political weapon to isolate states and deny them the hard currency
tourism provides.[34] This vulnerability can also be exploited by militant groups to advance their objectives through the disruption of
patterns of interdependence and cooperation.[35] At the same time,
national governments, as well as various ethnic, religious, and political groups, often shape tourist attractions and itineraries to serve
their own goals, interests, and political narratives (rather than cosmopolitan ones). Other scholars, drawing on dependency theory
and postcolonial approaches, have observed that international
tourism development is often driven by, or results in, constructions
of "otherness," which emphasize the differences and inequality
between guest and host societies.[36] The experience of travel, even
when part of programs seeking to promote cross-border understanding, can result in reinforcing (often hierarchical) notions of
national identity and difference.[37] Tensions between host societies
and guests can be exacerbated when tourism is viewed as promoting the homogenization of culture, or what Ben Barber refers to
as "McWorld."[38] In these cases, transnational tourism and capital
flows are often challenged by local social and political movements,
including religious extremists and terrorist networks.

These tendencies of integration and conflict illustrate how transnational tourism flows and the organization of the global tourism
industry can shape political, economic, and cultural relations between states. Most explorations into the transnational effects of
tourism, however, either present a narrow case study with limited
relevance for other contexts or else portray tourism as a universal
process promoting similar integrative and conflictive effects wher-

ever it develops. In contrast, I draw on the work of scholars such as Arjun Appadurai and James Rosenau to explore the dynamics of tourism's seemingly contradictory effects by focusing on the issue of territoriality.[39] As Rosenau writes, "tourism" and "religious pilgrimages, migrations, professional meetings, and cultural exchanges . . . are part and parcel of the process whereby ideas and individuals transgress national boundaries and fashion networks of interaction that ignore or otherwise spread well beyond the principles of territoriality even as they may also heighten people's sense of attachment to their local community."[40] Rosenau emphasizes how globalization leads to integrative, boundary-dissolving behavior as well as fostering movements that assert local (territorially based) identity and autonomy leading to fragmentation. He awkwardly terms the resulting consequences "fragmegration."[41]

Such a framework, however, does not help us explain the nature of political, economic, and cultural forms produced within any particular territory or allow us to understand how notions of territory are not limited to attachments to the "local." Instead I suggest that within each territory, political, economic, and cultural forms are produced by interactions between local agents and transnational flows. In the process, notions of place, territoriality, and even "the local" are constructed and reconstructed. Studying these networks is a means to map the heterogeneous processes of globalization as they are shaped by international tourism and other activities in each context.

Mapping the Territorial Effects of Globalization

To explain both the political economy of tourism development and the effects of transnational tourism flows, this book emphasizes the role of territoriality within the context of transnational networks. I develop a framework that suggests what might be called the *territorial paradox of globalization*. Rather than diminishing the importance of geography, processes of globalization unevenly generate deterritorialization and reterritorialization at different scales and locations, resulting in the heightened importance of territory, location, and boundaries.

Many portrayals of globalization overemphasize the process of deterritorialization. They highlight the diffusion of new technologies,

expansion of markets, and policy changes, which have made distance and national barriers easier and cheaper to traverse and have
led to the increased transnational mobility of capital, commodities, and people.[42] In this view, diverse local or territorially bound
actors and institutions across the globe are expected to face more
similar environments resulting in pressures to adopt more similar
behaviors. Much of the literature regarding the developing world
views globalization as a pressure on states to adopt neoliberal economic policies as their territories become integrated into the global
economy. Noting these trends but often debating their extent,
many scholars of international relations and international political
economy stress the importance of nonterritorial forces and agents
such as global norms, identity, transnational NGOs, and international organizations.[43]

In contrast, scholars adopting territorial approaches challenge
the notion that globalization, by making the world "smaller," makes
geography less important.[44] Unlike neorealists, statists, and other
globalization skeptics,[45] such scholars do not limit their understanding of territory to the nation-state unit and the national economic sphere. Instead, while highlighting the challenges posed to
the nation-state's regulatory capabilities and hegemony over identity formation, territorial approaches explore the continuing but
changing importance of territory, boundaries, and location as ex-
planatory variables operating at multiple scales.[46] As John Agnew
explains: "Rather than the 'end' of geography, globalization entails
its reformation away from an economic mapping of the world in
terms of state territories toward a more complex mosaic of states,
regions, global city-regions, and localities differently integrated
into the global economy."[47] In studies of global production networks, such approaches seek to explain how actors within transnational networks "constitute and are re-constituted by economic,
social and political arrangements of the places they inhabit."[48]

At the same time, many of these geographers also emphasize
that globalization is not simply a material effect or a product of
markets, technological change, and policy shifts; it also involves
ideational, discursive, and cultural factors that are part of the process of reconfiguring global space. As a result, Gearóid Ó Tuathail
argues, "The geography of the world is not a product of nature but
a product of histories of struggle between competing authorities
over the power to organize, occupy, and administer space."[49] Ideas

about geography, or what I refer to as "geopolitical imaginaries," are thus critical to struggles over space. It is through these imaginaries that policy makers, academics, businesspeople, the general public, and others understand the terrain of global politics and the international political economy. Recognizing the role of geopolitical imaginaries helps explain how, within the same territory, different actors can "read" the impact of globalization and its political implications differently.

In my framework, deterritorialization is not a universal process but the effect of the formation of specific networks across particular spaces within a particular geopolitical imaginary. Within this space, the differences between the territories (such as distance, local characteristics of place, and national context) are of diminishing relative importance to the agents of the network. While deterritorialization has primarily been viewed as a process driven by economic forces, in my usage, deterritorialization has distinct economic, cultural, and political forms.

A common example of *economic deterritorialization* is the "global factory" defined by production networks in which "footloose" firms are driven by increased competition to shift locations of production in search of lower labor costs, weaker regulatory frameworks, and lighter tax burdens. This process generally erodes the territorially based regulatory capabilities of political authorities and harms stationary actors such as workers while benefiting firms and investors with mobile assets and influence over global markets and their rules of operations. Similarly, *cultural deterritorialization* refers to the homogenization of culture in which differences between local cultures are diminished as multiple locations adopt more common (shared or imposed) "global" cultural forms. We can also define *political deterritorialization* as processes or policies that decrease the saliency of boundaries, distance, and territorial specificities as means of regulation, control, and identification.

To understand the politics of any form of deterritorialization, one needs to examine the situation and perspectives of the competing authorities seeking to reorganize space and those affected by it. For some actors, deterritorialization may be experienced as a form of external domination or threat to their identity, security, or economic well-being. For others, economic deterritorialization may enable access to larger markets and enable more cost-efficient forms of production, while political deterritorialization may assist the creation of new transnational or diasporic identities and solidarity that reduce the saliency of, or overwrite, existing borders and mappings of territorial attachments.

Deterritorialization, however, is only one aspect of globalization. As Ó Tuathail notes, "every deterritorialization creates the conditions for a *reterritorialization*."[50] In this process, "newly imagined visions of state, territory, and community are projected in an effort to restabilize and reterritorialize identity and global flux."[51] In other words, deterritorialization, by disrupting territorial patterns of identity, economic regulation, or political authority, often provokes counterefforts to reassert and redefine the saliency of territory, geography, distance, and borders. Processes of political and cultural reterritorialization include the rebordering of national economies to prevent "threatening" inflows (of immigrants, illegal drugs, goods from low-wage countries), the rise of substate and suprastate regionalisms, and the efforts of states and other actors to (re)assert various forms of territorial attachment and control, including movements advocating political separatism and cultural autonomy. The presence of these trends, even when limited in scope, generates new geopolitical imaginaries or other lenses for understanding the impact of globalization.

Deterritorialization and reterritorialization are best understood as relative processes. Indeed, some forms of deterritorialization can simultaneously be experienced as reterritorialization. For example, the formation of the European Union has decreased internal boundaries and promoted a common European identity and economic space, but at the same time it has heightened the territorial distinctions between Europe and the regions outside its external boundaries.

A common goal of political reterritorialization is to forge protected economic spaces by controlling flows to limit economic deterritorialization. The incorporation of places into transnational networks and flows, however, does not necessarily produce economic deterritorialization and erode the regulatory power of territorial authorities. Rather, some aspects of economic globalization are characterized by processes in which territorial features—such as location, characteristics of place, and proximity to inputs, other firms, and markets—become more important. I refer to this process as *economic reterritorialization*.[52] It describes cases where the set of locations that offer benefits decline or the relative benefits

offered by some locations increase. For example, even as globalization enables more firms to increase their access to resources and
distribute their products across greater distances, they may cluster
in specific locations to capture spatially defined economic benefits.
These benefits can be analyzed in terms of rents and positive external economies.[53]

Nodes of transnational production networks often develop
as firms cluster in specific localities to exploit access to well-
developed infrastructure networks, concentrated pools of skilled
labor and specialized service firms, regional specialization, locational branding, and closer interfirm relationships that require
geographic proximity. Economic reterritorialization has characterized many forms of economic activity driving globalization, such
as the emergence of high-tech clusters and regional economies in
Europe, North America, and East Asia.[54] So-called global cities
have played a critical role as nodes in the global economy by hosting financial districts and the command centers of transnational
firms that are operating within expanding networks of global markets and capital flows.[55] Creative and design-intensive industries,
which service transnational firms with global markets, also often
cluster in particular urban areas noted for their local facilities, services, and quality-of-life features.[56] Moreover, urban spaces have
been transformed by tourism and entertainment-based downtown
revitalization efforts.[57] Economic reterritorialization can also operate on a wider regional scale when economic benefits are created
not by trade protection and discrimination but as a consequence of
similar positive attributes across the whole territory.

The Territorial Politics of Globalization

The political significance of the concept of economic reterritorialization lies in its ability to increase the political power and regulatory influence of state, societal, and transnational agents who
are able to exert control over territorial assets and the reterritorialization process.[58] As David Harvey explains, "If capitalists
become increasingly sensitive to the spatially differentiated qualities of which the world's geography is composed, then it is possible
for the peoples and powers that command those spaces to alter
them in such a way as to be more or less attractive to highly mobile capital."[59] As a result, he concludes, "The active production of

places with special qualities becomes an important stake in spatial competition between localities, cities, regions, and nations."[60]

Building on this notion, I suggest that as a territory is subject to economic deterritorialization, spatial competition results in the refashioning of local conditions to match benefits and characteristics available elsewhere. These adjustments generally occur along an index common across the space of deterritorialization. Typical examples include lowering labor costs and regulatory standards. States, firms, and other actors will generally seek to promote aspects of deterritorialization that they can shape or benefit from while resisting aspects they view as eroding their control over territory or threatening their territorial identities and interests. When multiple processes of deterritorialization driven by the same networks affect the actors in both positive and negative ways, they must weigh the relative trade-offs or seek to unbundle them.

In contrast, to the degree that localities are able to promote economic reterritorialization by providing locational benefits and distinguishing their territory from other places, they will be better able to shape and control local patterns of development and flows of capital. Viewing aspects of globalization in terms of economic reterritorialization offers a tool to analyze modes and scales of territorial regulation over global economic flows and understand the role of the state, as well as the roles of local and global nonstate actors, in supporting and challenging these modes. Economic reterritorialization is often viewed as the most feasible means for territorially confined actors (such as local political authorities and nonmobile capital and labor) to influence the processes of globalization affecting their territories, societies, and national economies. But it also heightens territorial conflict over the management and exploitation of the economic benefits at stake. Depending on the configuration of control over the reterritorialization process and the spaces that generate economic benefit, economic reterritorialization can lead to either the expansion of state control, or the increased political power of local societal actors, or the dominance of private capital (including local and transnational corporations) over the local economy. When control over such spaces is fragmented between actors with rival interests, the process of economic reterritorialization is often impeded.

The study of globalization requires that we understand that the politics of deterritorialization and reterritorialization operate simultaneously in each location, often interacting with each other. When the expansion of transnational networks produces economic or cultural deterritorialization, they often spawn processes and discourses of political reterritorialization. Territorially confined actors and authorities are more likely to support expanded flows across their territories and resist calls for political reterritorialization when the networks that sustain those flows help generate economic or cultural reterritorialization. At the same time, economic reterritorialization often leads rival local authorities to compete against each other for territorial benefits. As such, the politics of globalization are often a product of struggles at the local level. Within each locality, such struggles are likely to play an important role in how and if that territory becomes integrated into regional and global networks. As a result, as states seek to define their own itineraries of globalization, they must navigate between the macro (or national) benefits of integration and the micro (or local and sectorial) impacts of integration.

One implication of this framework is that territories are more likely to become integrated through globalization when the expanded flows across them do not eliminate the salience of local authorities, economies, and cultures through deterritorialization but rather weave and connect diverse localities across distances while promoting economic reterritorialization. An increasingly globalized political economy is likely to become more heterogeneous and consist of an overlapping patchwork of various forms of both deterritorialization and reterritorialization. The politics of globalization cannot be reduced simply to a struggle between local and global forces or between globalizers and antiglobalizers. Nor can the globe be easily divided between spaces of globalization and territories disconnected from globalization. All actors simultaneously seek to selectively promote processes of deterritorialization and reterritorialization in an effort to exert power over territories, flows, and the networks that connect them.

The Framework Applied: Political Geographies of Tourism

This transnational network approach to the study of globalization provides an alternative framework through which to understand the politics of globalization in the Arab world. Across the region, people, states, private firms, and various organizations have developed complex reactions and coping strategies to gain control and authority over how transnational flows and global processes impact them. Like elsewhere, the process of becoming increasingly enmeshed in the networks of the international economy has led to internal conflicts. On the one hand are those who fear that integration will lead to social dislocation, external dependence, and the erosion of local control. On the other hand are those who seek to take advantage of the new opportunities and urge their societies and economies to reform and adapt to the changing global environment. The resulting nature of political, economic, and cultural patterns across the region is less a product of a generalized resistance to globalization or of states failing to promote economic liberalization than the result of specific struggles between state, societal, and international forces over transnational flows and national territory.

Other scholars have studied the affect of transnational flows such as oil incomes, foreign aid, labor remittances, and media communications.[61] In this book, I build on these efforts by investigating how Arab states have been integrating their economies into the global production networks and transnational flows of people, capital, and commodities associated with international tourism development. In doing so, I assess the ever-increasing impact of these flows while elaborating a theory about the territorial dimensions of globalization. With its many configurations, a focus on tourism allows us to explore within the same sector various facets of deterritorialization and reterritorialization in their economic, cultural, and political forms. Moreover, tourism development has provided Arab economies with a way to promote economic reterritorialization, which explains much of tourism's increasing prominence as a national development strategy.

Critical questions about the political economy of tourism development and the transnational effects of tourism can be addressed by mapping how specific territories across the Middle East were incorporated into the networks of the global tourism industry and the shifting territorial nature of these tourism economies. These networks and their spread are shaped by various actors including global markets, technologies, government policies, and cultural tastes. Each of the following studies explores a different context, drawing on a range of political-economy tools (including development economics, product cycle models, commodity chain analysis, and Regulation theory) to outline the structure of the local tourism economy and its relationship to the global tourism economy. In each case, actors in host territories are generally viewed as having limited influence over the construction of transnational tourism networks and the regimes and norms that govern them. For example, the global demand for international tourism is primarily shaped by economic conditions, cultural tastes, and public policies in guest societies (i.e., where the tourists depart from). Most aspects of the networks that sustain the transnational mobility of tourists are shaped by the policies of states and TNCs located outside the host territories. Drawing on the territorial approach outlined earlier, I argue that actors in host territories are able to gain agency over transnational tourism flows by exerting territorially based powers at the national and local levels. These powers include control over border crossings, policies that shape the development of tourism sites, and regulation of the local behavior of firms in the tourism sector. In the chapters to come, I explore how state agencies, private firms, and local communities engage in spatial competition against rival destinations to attract tourists, tourist spending, media attention, and investment capital. This form of spatial competition requires, at its core, the commodification of experiences of place. This process entails a range of activities from the commercialization of tourist sites (providing tourist services near a historic monument or charging an entry fee) to the construction of "artificial" destinations, such as theme parks. In the process, these actors shape, as well as must respond to, the changing territorial nature (i.e., deterritorializing or reterritorializing) of tourism development.

Tourism development generates economic deterritorialization when locations replicate similar experiences of place found elsewhere to capture part of an existing market for a standardized product. Mass beach tourism as developed along the Mediterranean in the postwar era with the rise of mass consumerism in Europe represents one of the most prominent examples of economic deterritorialization in the tourism sector. I argue that mass beach tourism was critical to the development of the so-called international division of leisure in the 1960s that incorporated locations such as Tunisia. The rise of dependency-oriented approaches occurred at a unique moment when the rapid expansion of mass beach tourism dominated the international tourism economy. Within such an economy, local agents are forced to struggle with trade-offs between increased flows and loss of territorial control. The intensity of this trade-off is shaped by the position of local actors within the structure of the transnational tourism economy, in which tourists and tour operators view rival destinations as interchangeable. As developing countries sought to promote mass beach tourism, local developers were forced to cater to foreign markets rather than local tastes. Developers gain little advantage from local knowledge and their ability to craft "hybrid" products that mix aspects of local, nontourist experiences of place with more general forms expected by tourists. Instead states that seek to gain influence over deterritorializing forms of tourism development must develop institutions that can more effectively, and more cheaply, mass-produce commodified experiences of place. Such forms of tourism development, however, threaten to spread cultural deterritorialization as diverse locations fashion themselves as spaces in which local cultural specificities are replaced by homogenized forms of "staged authenticity" tailored to tourist expectations.[62] These effects often mobilize processes of political reterritorialization that seek to limit tourism flows or confine them to enclave spaces. In the Middle East, such discourses and policies are usually generated by leftists, nationalists, and Islamist critics of Western-oriented mass tourism and foreign investment.

While much of the literature on the political economy of tourism focuses on aspects of economic and cultural deterritorialization, this book highlights how tourism development can also result in patterns of economic and cultural reterritorialization.[63] Tourism economies are constructed by mobile consumers visiting locations that are developed by spatially fixed deployments of capital, a process that results in a complex system for generating locational rents and external economies.[64] In general, the relative ability of tourism spaces to generate such benefits reflects their attractiveness to tourists and tourism firms, their incomparableness, and their international renown. In the Middle East, some of the locations of highest value include the pyramids in Egypt, the ruins of Petra in Jordan, and the towns of Jerusalem and Bethlehem in Israel/Palestine. While such sites have attracted visitors for centuries, tourism destinations are made, not found. New tourism spaces are constantly being developed through the commodification of places, natural geographies, and regionally specific cultural experiences and practices. These efforts to fashion tourism spaces often seek to invent or exploit the rise of new tourism markets and trends such as nature tourism, ecotourism, and heritage tourism. While connected to global transportation structures, such forms of tourism development require local and international expert knowledge to produce particular experiences of the place based on archaeological ruins, desert tours, museum displays, or mythical and imagined narratives. Moreover, to draw visitors, tourism promoters must usually develop and propagate "place-myths."[65] As John Urry notes, the ways that tourists imagine and experience place are not unmediated but usually "self-consciously organized by [tourism] professionals" such as writers of guidebooks, tour operators, regional tourism boards, and local residents turned tourism promoters.[66]

The production of tourism space allows its owners to extract rents from the developers of tourism facilities. In turn, these private or state-owned tourism facilities are able to extract rents from tourists. Additionally, the spatial fixity of tourism sites generates positive external economies in the surrounding spaces made available for tourism development. To enhance and localize the generation of these external economies, states and other actors provide public goods such as marketing, infrastructure, and tourism site development. Moreover, the clustering of tourists and tourism firms around a site or within a multifunction resort, such as a theme park, allows the tourism developer to intensify the generation of economic externalities in the same space and thus capture more income. This dynamic explains why tourism patterns have increasingly exhibited spatial concentration in the form of enclave tourism complexes and urban "tourism bubbles."[67] Locational economies are also generated near or within the central nodes of other networks, such as business districts or well-traveled spaces such as airports, shopping centers, and national landmarks.

Forms of tourism development that generate economic reterritorialization can increase the political influence of state, societal, and transnational agents that are able to exert control over the specific territorially defined resources and institutions that drive the reterritorialization process. In contrast to certain aspects of tourism development, such as beach tourism, that promote cultural deterritorialization, these forms of tourism development often redefine the cultural politics of tourism by promoting cultural reterritorialization. For example, economically reterritorializing forms of tourism development can provide opportunities for local and national communities to project their own identities, practices, and values. They can also help generate income and provide incentives for the revival of indigenous rituals and forms of artistic expression.

When characterized by economic reterritorialization, however, tourism development can also lead to more intense struggles between various local, state, and transnational actors—from private landowners and tourist firms to indigenous communities and archaeologists—with rival objectives and interests in the development of territorial resources and the symbolic representation of territorially based identities and cultures. The consequences of economic reterritorialization depend on the cartography of control over the reterritorialization process. When state agencies own the tourism spaces or otherwise control the process, they enhance their power over societal actors while encouraging transnational flows and economic liberalization. In contrast, when local communities, foreign private firms, or transnational NGOs control land, media flows, and the skills needed for tourism development, they gain influence over the process. In some cases, territorial control will be fragmented between many actors, leading to conflict over the processes and the proceeds of the rents and positive external economies; conflict in turn might impede economic reterritorialization.

Deterritorialization and reterritorialization are relative concepts and must be viewed in relationship to each other. The political geography of tourism development is often complex and multifaceted, with rival actors seeking to refashion spaces to integrate them into various networks of deterritorialization and reterritorialization. Tourism spaces can lose their value when tourism flows are constrained by political reterritorialization, as experienced in the United States as a consequence of increased security concerns after 9/11. And the replication of similar strategies of economic reterritorialization can even result in *re-deterritorialization,* for example, when certain shopping mall or theme park designs, which drew visitors when their first exemplars seemed to represent innovative spaces, blend into a bland homogeneity as they become commonplace.[68] Alternatively, to the degree that tourism development is able to produce hybrid tourism products, developers can create a heterogeneous landscape that appeals to and exploits broad markets for recognizable global products while maintaining local features that provide for local tourist and nontourist forms of consumption.

The notions of reterritorialization and deterritorialization provide tools to explore what Rosenau identifies as the integrative, boundary-transgressing aspects of tourism and travel, as well as the fragmentative aspects that result from assertions of local (territorially based) identity and political autonomy.[69] These aspects correspond roughly to the rival views of tourism as either promoting integration, understanding, and cooperation between societies or generating conflict based on cultural differences. As suggested by the territorial paradoxes of globalization, the impact of tourism depends on the structure and geography of each specific tourism economy. Economic deterritorialization, while expanding transnational flows between societies, is likely to foster discourses and movements of political reterritorialization leading to fragmentation. In contrast, societies that sustain transnational flows that promote economic reterritorialization within each state are more likely to sustain moves toward greater integration, cooperation, and pluralism rather than provoking forms of political and cultural reterritorialization.

The Itinerary Ahead

The chapters of this book map political geographies of tourism development and transnational tourism flows in three contexts centered around the destinations of Tunisia, Jordan, and Dubai. In each location, state authorities have promoted tourism development as an engine of economic growth and as part of a strategy of global economic integration. At the same time, each setting represents a differing political context with its own geography of tourism resources and a different relationship to the global tourism economy. These studies, however, are not parallel case studies. Instead they offer three vantage points from which to survey a wide range of diverse experiences of tourism development, transnational networks of tourism, and itineraries of globalization. The chapters progress chronologically and move eastward from the rise of mass beach tourism in Tunisia in the 1960s, to the efforts to develop a cultural tourism sector in Jordan during the rise and fall of the New Middle East in the 1990s, and finally to the post–9/11 expansion of regional Arab tourism leading to a recentering of Middle

Eastern tourism economies around the oil-rich Gulf states. These cases were chosen because they allow an examination of the widest range of geopolitical contexts, patterns of state building, and features of local and global tourism markets while helping to elaborate separate elements of a territorial approach to understanding the political economy of globalization.

Chapter 1 explores the incorporation of the small North African state of Tunisia into the Mediterranean mass beach tourism economy dominated by large European tour operators. The Tunisian president Habib Bourguiba viewed international tourism as a means to promote greater openness and closer ties to Europe and other Western states. Although Tunisia experienced an explosion of tourism growth in the 1960s and 1970s, I show how the country's position within these expanding global tourism networks was soon defined by the "international division of leisure" while mass beach tourism also generated economic and cultural deterritorialization. These processes led to an erosion of the state's limited abilities to regulate the process of tourism development and to the rise of leftist and Islamist critics who sought to curtail Tunisia's openness to these flows. To face the challenges of deterritorialization, Tunisia developed institutions for tourism planning, financing, and land management, which allowed the state to establish territorial control over the production and regulation of tourism spaces across its territories. The result was the establishment of a system of regulation with which the state could better coordinate the local provision of tourism supply to match the patterns and styles of global demand.

Chapter 2 begins by outlining the spatial and social consequences of Tunisia's laissez-faire *infitah* (economic opening) policies of the 1970s and early 1980s. The erosion of territorial control over economic development and transnational flows helped push the country toward economic and political crisis. Instability threatened in the wake of a series of hotel bombings by militant Islamists targeting Bourguiba's hometown, but order was restored in November 1987, when prime minister Zine El Abidine Ben Ali, a former army officer, removed the senile leader from power. Tourism development subsequently played a major role in Ben Ali's efforts to integrate Tunisia's economy into global markets while simultaneously consolidating the power of the state over the economy and society. The Tunisian state has used tourism to develop new means of extending state control over space, capital, and social transformation while promoting closer economic integration into European markets and transnational flows. Responding to shifts in the global tourism economy, these patterns of development concentrated tourist activity within enclave spaces and relied more heavily on creating place-specific forms of cultural, heritage, and nature tourism. While the state projected images of "openness" to foreign tourists and investors, it used its territorial control over tourism spaces to expand authoritarian control over society and the economy to create what I call the paradoxical nature of globalization in Tunisia.

The focus then shifts to the Hashemite Kingdom of Jordan, a state carved out by the British at the end of World War I. Since 1945, tourism development in Jordan and other states of the Levant rich in archaeological ruins and cultural heritage sites has been challenged by the region's fragmented geopolitics, which have deterred long-haul visitors and limited the possibilities of regional travel. Chapter 3 examines the connections between tourism economies and geopolitics, as well as the role that geopolitical imaginaries can play in reshaping both. At the center of this study is the signing in 1994 of the Israel-Jordan peace treaty, the product of a U.S.-backed effort to transform the region's geopolitics, promote neoliberal economics, and develop transnational links of economic cooperation and interdependence to form the New Middle East. Regional tourism development was widely viewed as the first sector in which regional linkages would be formed and economic cooperation would begin. The resulting tourism boom was also expected to jump-start the expansion of the tourism sector and help realize the dividends of peace. I argue that without the expectation of tourism development, the notion of the New Middle East would not have been imaginable. Moreover, tourism development played a pivotal role in the efforts of the Jordanian regime to "sell the peace," as tourism was the only means to suggest that peace could rapidly generate broad-based economic benefits for Jordanian society. If it were not for these efforts to promote tourism development, domestic opposition to the treaty, the normalization of relations with Israel, and U.S. efforts to promote the New Middle East would have mobilized faster and more broadly.

Chapter 4, however, exposes the unexpected consequences of the New Middle East. It explores how within Jordan, fragmented control over the territory and institutions governing tourism development led to a period of rapid "rent seeking" by rival private interests competing for a share of windfall rents rather than the creation of locational rents and externalities. State plans to extend centralized control over the tourism development process in an effort to promote economic reterritorialization were met by private-sector entrepreneurs and indigenous communities able to assert local territorial control over these resources. In the end, only a limited number of firms were able to successfully realize the promotion of economic reterritorialization within enclave tourism spaces under their control. The resulting failure of tourism development to meet popular expectations helped to generate an ideological counterdiscourse of political reterritorialization in reaction to cross-border flows between Israel and Jordan made possible by the peace process. This reaction was one factor in fostering the rise of the powerful "antinormalization" social movement that has since challenged the Jordanian regime's efforts to expand ties with Israel and integrate Jordan into the global economy.

Chapter 5 surveys patterns of tourism development in the era marred by the 9/11 attacks, the U.S. invasion of Iraq, regional tensions across the Persian Gulf, and a wave of terrorist attacks against tourism-related targets. In this final chapter, I explore the trends that have resulted in the unexpected expansion of Arab tourism economies since 2001. These include the resurgence of intraregional tourism, shifting business practices and development strategies, and the impact of petrodollars. More broadly, I suggest that these patterns represent the emergence of economic reterritorialization at the regional scale. During this period, Dubai became one of the fastest-growing tourist destinations and established itself as a node within regional and global economic and tourist networks. Drawing on insights developed in previous chapters, I explain how Dubai's success in tourism development has been guided domestically by a regime of territorial control and externally by the city's ability to enmesh itself in a dense set of transnational networks.

While showing how these trends reflect the increasing agency of actors in the Arab world to shape the regional and global networks of the tourism economy, the final chapter also notes the limits of this model of globalization and explores emerging alternative styles of travel and strategies of tourism development. These trends suggest that the region will continue to promote tourism as an engine of economic growth and vehicle for globalization and transnational integration, but these models of globalization are limited to connecting the new enclave spaces within the Arab world to global economic networks. Such trends, however, are not the only ones. I conclude by considering alternative modes of tourism development and emergent itineraries and styles of travel, such as Islamic tourism, and the travelogue of the Egyptian playwright Ali Salem about his drive through Israel at the height of hopes for the New Middle East. These itineraries suggest alternative geopolitical imaginaries for the Middle East and show how tourism and cross-border travel can serve as vehicles to connect territories and their populations in ways that generate more pluralist, heterogeneous geographies.

1. Fordism on the Beach: Tunisia and the International Division of Leisure

The Mediterranean Sea has long defined a space connecting the societies of Europe and North Africa.[1] The most recent phase of this relationship has been characterized by European dominance over an economic sphere into which the Arab states have sought to become integrated. Gregory White refers to these states as being "on the outside of Europe looking in."[2] As Alan Richards and John Waterbury note, it was the small North African state of Tunisia that "pioneered the 'opening up' *(infitah)* approach" toward increased economic integration in the late 1960s.[3] While these scholars and others have recounted Tunisia's experience with economic liberalization, this chapter and the next explore the role that international tourism development played in defining Tunisia's integration into transnational markets and economic flows. When Tunisia gained independence in 1956, its political elite viewed tourism development as a vehicle to promote modernization and closer economic ties to Europe. The country's resulting integration into the networks of the international tourism economy represented one of the most pronounced forms of economic deterritorialization to hit any part of the Arab world. In fact, the politics of international tourism development in Tunisia in the 1960s and 1970s prefigured late-twentieth-century debates about the politics of globalization. Mass tourism across the Mediterranean became an economic sector where transnational flows of people and capital met few national

1

Figure 2. Map of Tunisia, 2007. Copyright 2007 by World Trade Press. All rights reserved.

barriers, where production processes were globally organized, and where the local private sector produced services that had to compete in a global marketplace. State authorities were unable either to manage the demand for tourism or to regulate the agents, flows, and markets of transnational tourism networks outside the nation's borders. And in contrast to inward-oriented development strategies, they could not promote tourism development by using protectionist barriers, Keynesian fiscal policies, and price controls.

Many critics of tourism development in the 1960s and 1970s argued that the structure of the international tourism economy "ensures that Third World destinations have a largely passive and dependent role in the international system."[4] Louis Turner viewed this structure in terms of an "international division of leisure," declaring that "it cannot be over-stressed that tourism is a thoroughly deceptive industry. . . . This is not to say that Third World governments cannot take steps to improve the returns from tourism, but one sometimes wonders if they should be encouraged to be in the industry in the first place."[5] Likewise, most Tunisian scholars of tourism development argued that the sector was not serving the nation's interests but rather was dominated by the interests of international capital and the needs of the middle classes of industrialized states.[6] Many leftist intellectuals, religious traditionalists, and conservative nationalists feared that transforming Tunisian shores into a space for Western leisure consumption represented a form of economic and cultural neocolonialism. These concerns became more pressing in the early 1970s as Tunisia became the first Arab state to adopt *infitah* policies and open its economy to more transnational economic flows.

This chapter contextualizes these claims and other arguments made by tourism scholars influenced by dependency theory by showing how the terms of Tunisia's incorporation into this international division of leisure were shaped by the specific territorial dynamics of mass beach tourism. Tunisian territory was integrated into this economy based on its ability to supply an increasingly standardized and place-substitutable product. Fordist industrialization and the rise of mass consumerism in postwar Europe produced the homogenized culture of mass beach tourism that was sustaining the expansion of the Mediterranean tourism economy and facilitating Tunisia's incorporation into it as an inexpensive destination.[7] Tunisia, however, had to compete with other Mediterranean destinations that were expanding the global supply of beach tourism as European tour operators were encouraging downward pressures on price. In the early 1970s, after recognizing the limitations of Tunisia's position within the international division of leisure and the negative effects of cultural deterritorialization, Tunisian authorities launched a series of tourism-planning and infrastructure-building projects that allowed the country to more efficiently mass-produce the supply of beach tourism. Developing what I call a new regime of regulation, Tunisian officials built a centralized system to govern capital, labor, and space within the tourism sector.[8] This capacity-building effort established centralized state control over the tourism development process through the management of domestic territory and space. Tunisia improved its ability to exploit transnational flows of people and capital and promote tourism development as a key element of state building and national economic development. As a result, the hotel-building boom of the 1970s, including the construction of the country's first integrated tourism complex, became a visual manifestation of the flood of petrodollars that washed over the region as states like Tunisia turned away from Arab socialism and opened their economies to foreign investment.

Establishing a Position in the Mediterranean Tourism Economy, 1956–73

Tunisia gained independence from France in 1956 after an anticolonial struggle waged through episodes of popular mobilization organized by the nationalist Neo-Destour (New Constitution) party. The movement was led by a pragmatic French-educated lawyer, Habib Bourguiba, who would serve as the new nation's president for the next three decades. After capturing the state and consolidating its power, the country's new political elite, drawn from the rural towns along the *sahel* (central eastern coast), pursued the objective of using the centralized state structures it inherited to reverse the socioeconomic effects of colonialism by promoting industrialization.[9] At first, Tunisia adopted a "liberal approach" in the hope of encouraging Europeans to maintain their sizable investments. The policy failed. The economy suffered massive capital flight and the departure of its French bourgeoisie. Soon the Tunisian government moved to create a national currency, exchange controls, and an indigenous banking system.[10] These policies began the process through which the state established control over transnational flows and sought to develop the national economy through state-led import-substitution industrialization (ISI).

For most Third World nationalists concerned with decolonization and industrialization, the international tourism economy offered little of what they desired. In *The Wretched of the Earth*, Frantz Fanon turned "the industry into a metaphor for the brothelization of the Third World at the hands of Western leisure imperialists."[11] Tourism in Tunisia had long catered to a European elite and from the nineteenth century to the early twentieth served as a hunting playground, winter retreat, and peripheral stop on the Grand Tour. European upper-class travel to Tunisia was facilitated by entrepreneurs such as the firm of Thomas Cook & Son, which first included Tunisia as part of a North African tour in 1895. More critically, while British and German travelers also visited Tunisia, in the early twentieth century, tourism was organized under French rule as a means to advance its colonial project. The French protectorate government created institutions to promote tourism, such as the Office du Tourisme Tunisien.[12] Tourism functioned, along with colonial exhibitions, to "foster identification by French citizens with 'their' empire" and encourage Europeans to settle the territories.[13] The notion that tourism could promote economic development and modernization in Tunisia was first formulated by the French as a means to advance their *mission civilisatrice*. Not only did these tourist itineraries help promote exoticized images of Tunisian peoples and landscapes, but French efforts to promote heritage preservation and teach young Tunisians to produce traditional crafts worked as a vehicle to traditionalize indigenous culture while highlighting the identification of French colonial forms with modernity. The colonial tourism economy, however, declined by the late 1930s owing to economic crises and political turmoil in Europe.

The Regime's Vision for Tourism Development

In the same way that the nationalist elites sought to replace Tunisia's colonial economy, state officials took charge of building a tourism industry to serve the nationalist project. Several leading international tourism experts visited Tunisia in the years after independence, and most supported the idea of using state planning to develop a tourism industry. When one visiting French economist advised against it, warning that tourism development would draw capital away from other sectors, the government organized a panel that rejected his findings.[14] President Bourguiba played a critical role in shaping Tunisia's tourism development policy, defending the

sector with "a lot of panache."[15] Bourguiba viewed tourism development as a means to realize his postcolonial vision, an alternative to those shaped by the radical nationalist ideas sweeping much
of the Arab world and driving the Algerian war for independence.
Rather than combating the regional influence of former colonial
powers, Bourguiba sought to create what he often referred to as a
more "open country," meaning one turned toward the West. He
argued that the "reorientation of Tunisia toward the West would
represent progress and prosperity, the very objectives that an independent Tunisia aspired to."[16] In his view, attracting tourists from
Europe and North America would help promote economic modernization domestically while projecting images of modernity and
openness internationally. During his visit to the island of Jerba in
November 1958, Bourguiba declared, "There is an economic activity that particularly interests Jerba, as well as other privileged
regions of the Republic: It's tourism."[17]

State-led tourism development began in 1959 with the establishment of a parastatal corporation, the Société Hôtelière et
Touristique (SHTT). While the SHTT began by building a few
large luxury hotels such as the Miramar in Hammamet (southwest of Nabeul) and Ulysse Palace in Jerba, many hotel construction projects were meant to illustrate the new prestige of the regime
and serve as symbols of modernity by catering to party and trade
union officials and their conferences. On the tree-lined main boulevard of the French-built section of the capital, the government
built a twenty-story glass-clad skyscraper. The towering Hotel
Africa, managed by the French firm Le Meridian, marked the city's
skyline and represented the regime's aspirations to modernize the
country. The headquarters of the SHTT was located in Monastir,
Bourguiba's birthplace, a town within the home region of much
of the Neo-Destour elite. Other developments were set inland in
towns such as Gafsa, Kairouan, and Kasserine following the state's
policy to promote regional balance by spreading out the distribution of government spending, prestige, and jobs.[18]

In the early 1960s, tourism began to play a larger role in the
state's project for national development. This new role was part of
the overall shift in the state-led effort to promote economic development in Tunisia led by Ahmed Ben Salah, who helped to initi-
ate an ambitious "development decade" (1961–71) based on "socialist" style central planning. Reflecting this effort, in 1964 the

Neo-Destour changed its name to the Parti Socialiste Destourien (PSD). Ben Salah said at the time that "it is . . . highly essential to consider investments in tourism as a means to expand the country's economy and to use the benefits derived from this sector to create and consolidate the foundations of a new Tunisia."[19] Thus a decade after European settlers had fled Tunisia with their capital and investments, a new tourism policy was enacted to draw European currency back in the form of tourism spending (and later investment). The SHTT never planned to build and manage the entire sector but only to create a model for profitable investments that would then attract local private capital. The challenge for early tourism developers in Tunisia was to create supply with little control over the size and shape of demand. The task was complicated by the uncertain condition of infrastructure for water, communications, and power, the availability of skilled labor, and the nature of amenities and attractions.

Standardizing the Product

While previous forms of tourism development in Tunisia may be faulted for serving the colonial project, they nevertheless were built around territorially specific experiences of place. Under French political control, state authorities and private firms promoted Tunisia's classical heritage, natural environments, and traditional crafts. In the 1960s, visitors could explore the ruins of Carthage, the nearly intact Roman coliseum at El Jem, and the Grand Mosque and carpet factories at Kairouan. Some did, but these sites had yet to be developed and commercialized. Tunisia's first efforts were directed at building luxury hotels to make the country a resort destination for European and American tourists. These efforts failed, since Tunisia could not easily compete against other destinations as a high-class "Riviera." A British journalist observed at the time: "The government is rapidly building new hotels. The trouble is that most are rather expensive—prices are almost as high as in France—and as yet there are few cheaper hotels suitable for tourists."[20]

These efforts were soon sidelined as state authorities redirected their attention toward the largest and fastest-growing segment of the international tourism economy at the time, mass beach tourism. The rise of the international mass tourism economy was a product of the economic boom across Western Europe from 1945 to 1973 that led to the rise and expansion of mass consumerism.[21] Within this system of national Fordism, rising incomes and social welfare legislation for paid vacation time led to the rise of leisure tourism as a mass phenomenon. Fordism was also responsible for the homogenization of consumer tastes around standardized products like mass beach tourism.[22] In this era, the dominant form of tourism across Europe became beach tourism, where leisure activities centered on the sun, sand, and sea.

In the 1960s, beaches across the Mediterranean became sites of mass production. Driven by increasingly homogenized consumer tastes, cheaper mass-produced building materials, and the business strategies of international hotel chains, beach resorts took advantage of economies of scale and could be built in a wide range of coastal locations. The architecture of beach hotels was relatively cheap to design and easy to replicate. As beach tourism became increasingly standardized—a white concrete hotel along the beach with buffet meal and optional leisure activities—it also became increasingly substitutable from place to place. As developments in hotel architecture, airline capacity, and labor legislation were decreasing the price of tourism supply while increasing the volume of tourism demand, the expanding markets needed to be coordinated, as in Fordist mass production. European tour operators accelerated the development of mass tourism by aggregating ever-larger numbers of tourists and negotiating contracts for the large-scale supply of charter flights, lodging, and other services by local providers. The result was to reduce the overall cost of tourism and to increase the demand for it. As mass beach tourism locations were highly interchangeable, tour operators could book holidays at whatever location could offer them the lowest rate, thus creating more pressure on hotel developers and managers to supply more volume at cheaper cost.

As these developments were taking place around the Mediterranean, the SHTT transformed Tunisia into a major beach resort destination for tourists from advanced industrial economies. This program started off modestly in 1964 with preliminary tourism studies commissioned under the office for national economic development. During the first comprehensive four-year development plan (1965–68), state authorities began planning and managing the tourist sector by setting growth targets for both the public and private sectors.[23] By 1966 the SHTT completed the Tanit chain of hotels in the major resort areas of Hammamet, Jerba, and Monastir. In contrast to the SHTT's earlier luxury "palaces," the new hotels were large-capacity two-star "vacation villages" with between five and six hundred beds each.[24] As Bergaoui notes, "The idea was to build hotels with a minimum level of comfort but plenty of space."[25] Some of the last major projects built and managed by the SHTT, the Tanit hotels redefined what would become the basis of the standardized Tunisian tourism product: large midrange hotels that were cheap to build using mostly locally produced materials.[26] These large beach hotels catered to the cheaper package tours being offered in the mid-1960s, driven by the expansion of the charter airlines.[27] By 1966 about 70 percent of tourists visiting the country came on group tours. Another 14 percent bought inclusive air and hotel packages

Figure 3. A luggage sticker from a beach hotel at Hammamet. Author's collection.

from travel agents, while only about 15 percent of visitors (mostly French) made their own arrangements and traveled independently.[28] The seasonality of the tourism product became more pronounced with a high season between June and September, peaking in July and August. The vast majority were northern Europeans, with the bulk being French, German, and British.

Mobilizing Private Capital, Expanding the Tourism Sector

As the tourism product was increasingly being standardized and global demand for mass tourism continued to rise, tourism officials needed to mobilize more capital in the sector to expand national hotel capacity. In 1966, under the auspices of the United Nations, the Tunisian state commissioned a Czechoslovak firm to design a private-sector planning model for tourism.[29] The SHTT projects provided the catalyst for this by demonstrating the potential profitability of investments in the sector. At the same time, the new SHTT hotels provided the model for future developments in terms of both the type of hotels and their location, thereby initiating mass tourism development in three zones. Tourism development would remain focused nearly exclusively on these zones until the 1990s. These were Nabeul-Hammamet, Sousse-Monastir, and Jerba. The share of bed capacity across the country in these three zones expanded from 46 percent in 1965 to 74 percent in 1972.[30]

In September 1966, to meet the need for increased supply, the state established a series of incentives for the private sector that included subsidizing the cost of feasibility studies for hotel development, helping to secure loans from local banks, and granting rebates on the duties paid on imported equipment.[31] Private-sector investments quickly outpaced SHTT spending. With government encouragement, this effort was led by commercial families such as the Fourati, Khéchine, and Miled, who had been in the business of making and selling carpets from their home region of Kairouan (located inland from the Sousse-Monastir tourism zone).[32] Members of these families, who often got their start by working in the state-owned hotels,[33] set out to develop the first privately owned hotel chains in Tunisia. They were assisted by the state-owned bank, the Société Tunisienne de Banque (STB), which was directing 62 percent of its medium-term loans toward tourism. While the SHTT controlled over 90 percent of national bed capacity in 1962, with the expansion of private-sector investment, by 1968 about 83 percent was privately owned.[34]

In 1969, a few years after the expansion of private investment in tourism began, Ben Salah's "socialist experiment" came to an abrupt halt owing to a poor agricultural season, growing internal and external political opposition to his policies, and state authorities exceeding their ability to directly control production.[35] Hédi Nouira, who was made prime minister at the end of 1970, launched Tunisia's *infitah* (economic opening) program, supported by the notion that "Tunisia's growth and prosperity depended on tightening economic links with Europe."[36] In this first phase of economic liberalization, the state legitimated the development of a new class of industrialist entrepreneurs and began encouraging private investment in small-scale export-oriented industry. While the state continued to control and invest in heavy industry, the lighter industrial sectors, such as textiles, were given generous tax breaks, easy credit, and protection.[37] For a time, Tunisia became an important location within global commodity chains, with European clothing labels subcontracting manufacturing work to Tunisian firms.

Before the *infitah* spurred this wave of light manufacturing, the period of the second development plan (1969–72) marked the transition of tourism development—as the Tunisian geographer Noureddine Sethom describes it—from the "artisan" to the "industrial" phase.[38] In this period, the process of tourism development took on a well-defined, replicable pattern as Tunisian authorities sought to shape the supply of tourism to match the standardization and economies of scale that guided how European tour operators organized the demand for tourism. As each tour operator sought to expand its volume to gain economies of scale and lower its prices, operators sought access to more supply. Meanwhile, in Tunisia, the expansion of supply required the mobilization of state as well as local and international private capital.

As the tourism product became increasingly standardized, mass produced, and rigidly packaged, these changes were reflected in hotel architecture. The share of hotel capacity in nonluxury midrange hotels expanded from 29 percent in 1968 to 68 percent in 1972.[39] By 1973, 56 percent of Tunisia's hotels were located in costal tourist zones from Nabeul to Jerba but they held 79 percent of its bed capacity. The average hotel size grew from 55 beds per hotel in 1962 to 191 by 1972. Between 1963 and 1970, the average capacity of new hotels each year was between 100 and 350, but by the early 1970s it ranged from 300 to 500 beds. Between 1969 and 1972, the average real investment per hotel nearly doubled while the cost per bed dropped.[40] To encourage the private sector to invest in tourism, the state subsidized the cost of equipment and ensured that the state-owned banks provided substantial portions of the capital needed for increasingly large and costly hotels.

Meanwhile, tourism resorts along the northern shores of the Mediterranean were becoming more crowded. The crowding decreased their attractiveness just as labor costs were rising because of economic growth in these regions. At the same time, increased competition between European tour operators squeezed profit margins, leading them to search for new destinations that could be developed at lower building and labor costs. These forces led to the international division of leisure.[41] This phenomenon mimicked what some described as the new international division of labor in manufacturing, where the ability to standardize mass production pushed firms to seek alternative locations with lower wage levels and production costs. This reorganization of production left firms in the advanced industrial economies to specialize in production with higher skill, capital, and technological requirements.[42]

Tour operators thrive on economies of scale, but unlike most other transnational corporations they often do not require large amounts of start-up capital because they do not need to own assets and can generally take in a deposit from clients before they pay suppliers. In the 1960s, with the expansion of the tourism market and the low cost of entry into the tour operator business, competition increased and drove prices lower. Profit margins by the early 1970s became razor thin, which encouraged the development of even larger economies of scale, often accomplished through mergers with failing firms.[43] Increasingly, tourism providers improved their efficiency and lowered their costs by creating dedicated systems of Fordist production such as specialized charter flights and large beach hotels with stripped-down generic services (such as buffet meals). In many destinations, multinational hotel chains emerged to provide accommodation services. These firms often did not build or own hotels directly but managed operations, providing local investors with an internationally recognized "brand." As

European tour operators expanded their volume of sales in the early 1970s, they found themselves in constant need of more accommodation capacity. Many began offering cash advances to local hotels interested in expanding their bed capacity and bought ownership stakes in hotels.

Tunisian authorities recognized the need to expand local capacity to meet the needs of tour operators. In 1969 the state incentives given to the local private sector were extended to foreign capitalists.[44] In the 1960s, foreign sources accounted for little more than 3 percent of total investment in the tourism sector.[45] In 1970, to further attract investment and expand hotel capacity in Tunisia, the World Bank's private investment arm, the International Finance Corporation (IFC), announced plans for the Compagnie Financière et Touristique, or COFITOUR, to begin soliciting external capital from European, Arab, and American banks and financial institutions—including American Express—for tourism projects. The IFC developed a model for a new type of assistance to Third World states that could spur "economic growth though broad assistance to a single industry of high development potential."[46] The IFC, at the time, "said the plan is expected to have a 'considerable and quick' impact in Tunisia."[47] The COFITOUR helped organize financing and partnerships for the new large-scale tourism and transportation projects, as well as feasibility studies and technical assistance. By the early 1970s, the share of investment in the tourism sector from foreign sources expanded to 10 percent.[48]

As tourism development became both highly standardized and increasingly competitive, large transnational tourism corporations sought to expand their profits by increasing the scale of operations, thus expanding to new destinations, as well as vertically integrating by increasing their stake in hotel ownership.[49] This strategy allowed them to gain a larger share of the profits along the commodity chain and provide access to expanded supply. The impact of international capital was most visible along the Hammamet-Nabeul shoreline, a fifty-kilometer drive south from Tunis. In Hammamet, the German tour operator Neckerman built the Phénicia Hotel with 720 beds, while the American transnational conglomerate ITT built a Sheraton.[50] Club Med established a new vacation village in Nabeul with 1,200 beds.[51] By 1973 American and European corporations owned one-third of the bed capacity in the Hammamet tourism zone.[52] These new foreign-backed hotels often displaced the smaller, older ones and required more management expertise than the traditional basic hotels. Soon Club Med, Le Meridian, Novotel, and Hilton were managing hotels and vacation villages across the country.[53] The widespread presence of European and American investment in hotel building, of brand-name TNCs managing hotel operations, and of ever larger European tour operators organizing tourists to Tunisia created a situation where the flows of capital between firms, often subsidiaries of the same corporation, could escape regulation by local authorities. This situation raised suspicions of transfer pricing and other techniques to limit the local economic benefit.[54] At the same time, hotel developers required more and more land and resources such as water. They began transforming the social character of the community, disarticulating the urban focus of the town's layout as hotels stretched farther down the coast.[55]

Regardless of the negative consequences of tourism development, less than a decade after Tunisian authorities began to build a tourism industry, they could claim success in launching a booming economic sector that had become an indispensable aspect of the national economy. As the early phase of the *infitah* policies that opened the economy to more imports was increasing the country's balance-of-payments gap, tourism receipts became the economy's leading foreign-currency earner. The sector grew from covering 10 percent of the gap between merchandised exports and imports in 1964 to covering 95 percent of the much larger gap in 1972.[56] As in other developing countries, Tunisia's socialist planning targets for industrialization proved to be too ambitious. In contrast, Tunisia generally surpassed its tourism targets. From 1969 to 1972, capacity grew from 30,000 to 46,000 beds, the number of visitors grew from 373,000 to 780,000, and investment expanded from TD 14.9 million to TD 23.7 million per year.[57] These numbers highlight, however, how the pace and direction of the expansion of tourism supply in Tunisia was less a result of state planning models than a product of the massive expansion of the global tourism market and the desire of private capital to invest in a sector with seemingly low-risk returns. These numbers also suggest how the Tunisian economy lacked any institutional mechanism to regulate the supply and demand of tourism or to coordinate the balance between them.

The Limits of Tunisia's Position in the International Division of Leisure, 1973–74

The lack of a mechanism to regulate tourism supply and demand became evident in 1973 and 1974 when, after a decade of rapid growth, the Tunisian tourism sector experienced its first major crisis. In 1973 arrivals and real receipts both fell for the first time since the launching of the sector. A year after witnessing a 16 percent increase in tourist nights, the sector suffered a 13 percent drop, and occupancy rates fell from 58 percent to 44 percent.[58] This episode marks a rupture in the tourism development process, exposing the fragile structure of the industry and the pressing need for the state to develop a regulatory regime over tourism development. Additionally, though not necessarily clear at the time, this period also marks the peak maturity of the product cycle for mass beach resort tourism as demand became saturated in the traditional European markets.[59] This shift in the global tourism economy would have profound effects on Tunisia and Mediterranean destinations, forcing these sectors to find ways to diversify the products they offered. I discuss these longer-term consequences in chapter 2.

The crisis of 1973–74 was caused by many factors. An official report by the Tunisian tourism office pointed to the weak European economy, higher airline ticket prices, the 1973 Arab-Israeli war and oil crisis, currency devaluation in sending countries, and potential tourists' psychological reactions to these developments.[60] These factors, though, mostly account for the decline in international tourism for the 1974 season. To explain the initial drop during the season beginning in the summer of 1973, we must look elsewhere. Sethom states: "The explanation appears evident: the Tunisian market was the object of a veritable boycott on the part of German clients."[61] In 1970–71 the West German tour operator Neckerman had reserved 4,600 beds for the tourist season for use by the 45,000 clients it brought annually to Tunisia.[62] This contract alone filled one out of every seven beds in the country. But in an interview with the Tunisian daily *La Presse* conducted during the summer of 1973, the director of the recently formed Office National du Tourisme et Thermaliseme (ONTT) "accused the foreign tour operators and Neckerman in particular, [of] organizing a veritable 'sabotage of the Tunisian market' [by] directing their clients toward other destinations."[63] A year before the crisis, a national commission was assigned to study the evolution of the tourism sector over the

1961–71 "development decade." The commission's report, released in May 1972, described the consequences of state policies for the local sector and its future. The report noted that prices were being defined by external conditions and did not reflect in any direct way local market costs.[64] In 1973 some tourism officials worried about the downward pressure on prices and the strain it put on the profitability of hotels. As prices held steady, costs for many hotel operators were rising almost 10 percent a year.[65] In their negotiations with the German tour operators, tourism officials appear to have tried to raise hotel rates, but the highly standardized product could not attract a premium. As Turner explains, Tunisia fell out of favor in 1973 and 1974 "because tourists resented paying astronomical prices for food and drinks and got bored with the lack of entertainment facilities."[66]

As a result, in 1975 Tunisia was forced to lower its overall rates "to avoid the collapse of a sector which had become absolutely indispensable for the economy of the country."[67] This experience illustrates the limited capability of state officials to regulate and promote tourism within the increasingly competitive global marketplace. It also exposed the dependence of the economy on international tourism demand and the organized power of the European tour operators, who controlled virtually all the tourism infrastructure from the clients' homes to their landing at the airport in Tunisia. Tunisian officials had inserted the country into the global tourism economy by offering a less-expensive standard commodity. The process of planning, development, and marketing was still unorganized, and the state brought limited skills and tools to the massive coordination efforts needed to plan, finance, and promote the sector. Local hotel development was being impeded by the lack of order and coordination. For example, in 1972 the lack of cement and other difficulties encountered by developers prevented the completion of an additional 8,000 beds.[68] More critically, insufficient infrastructure, low quality of service, and lack of personnel training also limited the ability of Tunisia to compete with other destinations.[69]

Cultural Deterritorialization along the Mediterranean Shore

While the tourism crisis of 1973 can be blamed in part on inadequate planning and organization within Tunisia, its broader causes were shaped by patterns of tourism development across the Mediterranean. In the early 1970s, many other destinations around the Mediterranean were developing mass beach tourism facilities. When excess capacity of a similar product existed at other resort destinations, tour operators gained additional leverage over Tunisian hotels. The Tunisian authorities had secured a position in the market by defining and marketing the country as a competitive destination in negotiations between international tour operators, charter airline companies, and local hotels. As an internal SHTT report dated February 1972 explained, the state's goal had been to "grant to the tour operators very attractive prices . . . in order to capture a relatively significant share of clients and permit Tunisia to solidly establish itself in the international market relative to the other countries in the Mediterranean basin."[70] The local hotel operators had little choice but to accept these prices because filling their large hotels depended on securing international contracts that reserved large allotments of their capacity over long durations. These contracts made large-scale mass tourism development in Tunisia possible because they reduced the risks of building hotels with large capacities. Hotels could not rely on the local market or reservations made by local travel agents with independent travelers to secure a profitable hotel occupancy rate.

Tunisia's incorporation into the international division of leisure cannot be understood without considering how the standardization and deterritorialization of tourism led to demand being price sensitive while not discriminating about destination. With downward pressures on price, the ability of hotels to cover their expenses and loan payments declined. The power of the European tour operators only increased as they grew in size and developed more vertical and horizontal integration across the global tourism industry.[71] Just as global supply was increasing to match the growth in global demand, the hotel sector in Tunisia began to lose what bargaining power it once had because meanwhile hotel development had expanded not only in Spain and Italy but also in new, lower-cost destinations such as Morocco, Yugoslavia, Bulgaria, and Romania. In these markets, the trend toward "group tours was accelerating" while the brand of tourism on offer remained "the classic combination of sun, sand, and sea."[72]

In *The Golden Hordes* (1975), Louis Turner and John Ash described "the rapid conversion of the whole of the Mediterranean coast into the Pleasure Periphery of Europe" (100). While Turner and Ash launched a broad and lasting indictment of all forms of tourism, viewed in retrospect, their book came out just as the international tourism economy was beginning an era of transition. In many ways, the early 1970s constituted a unique moment in the history of postwar tourism, when the beach tourism market was at the peak of mass standardization and place substitutability:

> To judge from the tour operators' brochures, the product being demanded by the consumer is a fortnight's holiday in a modern white concrete hotel with a swimming pool and a bar, the whole bathed in sunlight under a cloudless sky. Little or no concern is shown about the country in which the resort is situated, and it may be inferred that the international tourism passenger is quite indifferent to the nature or status of that country.[73]

Tunisian tourism promoters and their publicity materials often sought to present Tunisia as a highly accessible beach resort destination that offered a slightly "exotic" cultural element compared to the standard Mediterranean beach experience. To the degree that the tourism product featured an exotic element, it represented a minimal variation on a highly standardized product. Tourists on package tours to the Mediterranean were generally not looking to experience indigenous culture and heritage. The exotic flavoring added little to the ability of Tunisia to bargain with tour operators for higher prices. Moreover, marketing Tunisia as an exotic destination may have had drawbacks. In the early 1980s, for example, "An ONTT survey observed that further expansion in the British tourist market was hampered by Tunisia's image as an exotic Middle Eastern—rather than Mediterranean—destination."[74] At the same time, tourism officials did not seem interested in developing cultural and heritage tourism. While investigating the possibilities for regional development, an American researcher was discouraged by a Tunisian official from considering the development of regional or rural tourism in the country: "The large majority (90%) of the European tourists are interested in what she calls the three S's (sand, sea, sun), i.e., Tunisian beaches. The European tourists have more than enough 'cultural' and archeological sites in their respective countries."[75] Thus the percentage of tourists who came to Tunisia especially for these sites and willing to pay a premium for them was extremely limited.

For those on tours to the beach resorts, the experience of the country's cultural heritage usually amounted to little more than brief organized trips to traditional markets, staged cultural shows, or the purchase of "indigenous" crafts. As Orvar Löfgren describes, across the Mediterranean tour operators manufactured forms of "local" cultural content in virtually the same manner in each location, such that there was "a constant standardization of cultural difference."[76] Tourists on package tours to Turkey and Tunisia might not be able to distinguish between local cultures, while handicrafts made in India might be sold as "local crafts" on the beach in Morocco. While travelers to Tunisia interested in finding examples of artisan crafts, the product of both long tradition and individual creativity, could search them out, most visitors on package tours could not afford such items. If they bought souvenirs, they made do with poor-quality crafts often mass-produced in state-managed factories.

As mass beach tourism became the dominant cultural and economic model for tourism in the developing world, the experience of international tourism likely played a role in erasing the specificity of cultures and locations in the non-Western world. To an increasing number of tourists from Europe and North America, these diverse local cultures became simply members of a larger geocultural grouping of the nonmodern developing world. Löfgren notes that "in many Northern European settings the Mediterranean simply became 'the South' and this south stretched easily to include other sun destinations like Gambia and Thailand. 'South' became the territorialization of a certain kind of holiday, rather than a fixed geographical region."[77]

Constructing a "Factory" for Tourism Development, 1973–81

By the early 1970s, the Tunisian shorelines around Hammamet, Sousse, and the island of Jerba were lined with hotel developments poorly integrated into the local fabric. In the wake of such rapid, unplanned hotel growth, the water, power, and transportation infrastructures of these regions were stretched to the point of exhaustion. These factors not only threatened to diminish the attractiveness of the Tunisian tourism product to potential tourists but also hampered the ability of hotel developers and hotel managers to expand capacity and thus improve the product by creating more amenities and a more-appealing built environment. Meanwhile the costs of inputs were often higher than anticipated by hotel managers, exacerbated by inflation caused by the increased demand in tourism material, supplies, and labor.[78] Tunisian tourism authorities soon came "to fully grasp the difficulties threatening this industry," such as "the uncertainty of the profitability of investments in hotels," which required "considerable amounts of capital and are highly dependent on a fluctuating demand."[79] While unable to shape global tourism demand or the activity of the large European tour operators, the Tunisian authorities did control domestic territorial resources. Tourism officials thus developed new mechanisms to more efficiently mass-produce tourism space and created more stable conditions for entrepreneurs in the sector. As a result, the state could plan the growth of the sector more successfully while coordinating the supply of tourism in Tunisia with global demand.

Organizing the Mass Production of Tourism Space

The crisis of 1973–74 made it apparent to tourism officials that they had limited power to influence price negotiations with international tour operators and needed to develop alternative means to expand their regulatory power over the tourism economy. This lack of relative power can be understood in part as a product of the deterritorialized nature of tourism development in this era. In formulating his critique of dependency theory, Peter Evans notes that the relative power of state authorities over foreign capital increases to the degree that capital investments are territorially rooted or "sunk assets," such as when a firm makes the fixed capital investments needed to begin heavy industrial production or raw material extraction.[80] By the same logic, TNCs in a sector such as light manufacturing with lower fixed costs, limited requirements for skilled labor, and a large number of alternative locations for investment—in other words, where economic activity is highly deterritorialized—have relatively more power in their bargaining with the state. States, however, can encourage more sunk-asset investment by foreign capital by making such investment a condition for special access to profitable opportunities in the local market. The more certain these opportunities are, the more likely a firm will be to commit to making fixed-asset investments. Moreover,

Evans also explains that states can promote local capital accumulation and "create space" for local firms by protecting segments of the local markets from external competition or insisting that foreign corporations develop more backward and forward linkages to local firms.

In the early 1970s, under its *infitah* program, Tunisia sought to encourage private and foreign investment in sectors such as light manufacturing and textile subcontracting. Part of the program's early success in fostering a new class of small Tunisian industrialists relied on extensive protection of the local market that accorded these firms profitable opportunities.[81] To follow a similar strategy in the tourism sector required the state to more efficiently produce tourism spaces in Tunisia to limit the internally generated risks and obstacles that local developers had increasingly been facing. By developing these opportunities, the state could begin to encourage larger investments that would be more territorially rooted as sunk assets, thereby enhancing the bargaining power of the state vis-à-vis these firms.

In the mid-1970s, Tunisia began to promote a new regime for the mass production of tourism supply, and "with the new policy, tourism [became] . . . subject to continuous improvement but always within the limits of a fundamental principle, that is, the deliberate choice of tourism as one of the country's leading industries."[82] Besides providing the equivalent of public goods for tourism firms—such as transportation infrastructure and overseas marketing—this new regime standardized the development process by sharply defining the product and mapping out a template for developers in the sector. The policy resulted in reducing the state's direct control over the sector, as the state's tourism assets were the first to be privatized. This policy nevertheless increased the state's indirect management of the overall tourism economy, giving it more power to shape Tunisia's location within the global tourism economy.

At the center of the institutional capacity-building effort was the expansion of the ONTT, now renamed the Office National du Tourisme Tunisien. The ONTT was formally created in 1971 with the purpose of elaborating and executing state tourism policy in the context of national development planning.[83] It was soon charged with the task of planning and managing Tunisia's tourism resources to maximize the benefits for the national economy while avoiding the degradation of Tunisia's physical resources, which might compromise the possibilities for future development.[84] The ONTT was also given the task of managing and coordinating the activities of the diverse public and private actors in the sector, such as travel agencies and tour guides. Its functions were further defined and elaborated in 1973 in regard to planning, financing, and regulating hotel building and the development of tourism complexes.[85]

A central task of the ONTT was the collection and analysis of data to give planners better tools to model the tourism economy. As James C. Scott observes, states must rely on representations of society, the economy, and territory to monitor and direct social and economic transformations.[86] The process of state building requires that bureaucratic agencies make society legible and measurable by developing indexes and templates for state use. Organizational charts, balance sheets, and gross national product flows all help states monitor and govern firms and their national economy as a discrete system.[87] The nature of standardized mass tourism provides clear units of production and measures of demand that can be read against highly legible indexes. For example, measuring visitor bed nights and hotel capacities generates hotel occupancy figures, a good index of the profitability of hotels in the sector. A government report noted that the data the ONTT compiled "will gradually enable experts to adjust the supply to the demand, and perhaps, through a more rational advertising policy, adjust demand to the supply as well."[88] By tracking the national origin of tourists and eventually conducting surveys of visitors' impressions of their stay and the external "image" of Tunisia, ONTT studies of source markets helped guide and monitor promotional efforts to increase demand. As these capacities were being developed, the minister of the national economy observed that in the 1960s, "We were offering tourists sun and sand. Now we need a new promotional approach. Tourism has to be sold and marketed like any other product and people have to be trained to market that product."[89] While still modest compared to the efforts of larger tourist destinations in southern Europe, beginning in 1972 Tunisia was increasingly able to influence its target markets through promotional campaigns in external markets and increased efforts by ONTT representatives stationed abroad.[90] During the fourth national plan (1973–76), the state allocated TD 4 million for external promotion, and in the fifth national plan (1977–81) TD 5 million.[91]

Ten years of an expanding volume of tourist flows had not been matched with adequate infrastructure development, which strained the existing systems for water, power, and roads. The existing pattern of uncoordinated hotel development haphazardly ate up land, resulting in "a privatization of the seashore" that diminished the potential economic value of inland spaces by blocking access to the beach.[92] Moreover, the linear configuration of hotels stretched along the coast made infrastructure development costly. In 1971 the ONTT asked the World Bank to develop a plan for expanding Tunisia's coastal tourism development.[93] The firm ItalConsult was commissioned to design an infrastructure plan to be put into action during the course of the fourth national plan from 1973 to 1976. Its implementation was financed by long-term loans from the World Bank, USAID, and a German bank.[94] The plan defined and demarcated tourist zones and created a system of development planning and management of these spaces. The new tourism zones consisted of strips of coastal land in Tunis-North, Tunis-South, Nabeul-Hammamet, Sousse-Monastir, and Jerba-Zarzis. The state established planning codes for the use of space and resources to avoid further beach erosion. In the various zones, target densities were established to keep beaches from becoming too crowded as well as to control the total amount of additional coastal territory consumed by hotel development.

The ItalConsult plan also established a network of roads, additional water resources, electrical connections, and telecommunications lines.[95] Focused on supplying the tourist zones, the design of this infrastructure project eliminated the existing gaps in the national system and provided a better basis for future development. Not only did these zones help guide tourism planning, but the tourism spaces they defined became marked-off enclaves, centrally managed by the state but also tightly integrated into global economic and cultural flows.

Tunisia's three international airports were located near the dominant tourism zones. These included one at Tunis (serving the Tunis and Hammamet regions), one on the island of Jerba (built in 1964), and one at Monastir (built in 1969). As the share of tourists arriving by air expanded to 80 percent in 1971, a new terminal was built at the Tunis-Carthage airport.[96] Between 1970 and 1979, nonresident air arrivals would multiply fourfold to over one million visitors per year, and the airports at Monastir and Jerba became the important arrival points for international tourists.[97]

Before 1972 no special set of rules had governed tourism development, leading to imbalances in resource and infrastructure demand, uncontrolled land speculation, unprofitable hotels, and hotel developments built too close to the beach and without adjoining facilities. In 1973 the Agence Foncière Touristique (AFT), a land management agency, was established to govern the newly defined tourist zones and to help meet the ONTT targets for the expansion of tourism capacity as outlined in the four-year (and soon five-year) national development plans. The AFT's goals included ending land speculation and rationalizing the hotel development process. All land transfers concerning tourist facilities would now be conducted through AFT authorities. The agency set out to buy up the land in the tourist zones. It was given the power to either "buy it amicably, to invoke its right to expropriate at a determined price, or to confiscate outright in the interest of the public good."[98] The AFT often resold the land it bought at a lower price, effectively subsidizing hotel building. Between 1974 and 1980, the AFT made 1,500 acquisitions amounting to 800 hectares (1 hectare equals 10,000 square meters) of land at an average price of TD 0.480 per square meter.[99] By 1981 the AFT had resold 450 hectares to the private sector at an average price of TD 0.425 per square meter.[100]

The AFT also established a procedure for governing the process of developing new hotels. A developer chose a desired plot from those designated by the AFT for tourist development, then requested the rights from the ONTT to develop the lot at an approved quality rating and bed capacity. These parameters were guided by the ONTT development plans. The developer was then required to draw up a floor plan and design the overall architecture for the hotel following the ONTT's codes and standards for the designated class and size of hotel. Beginning in 1973, the ONTT established a five-star hotel classification scheme that specified detailed requirements for each level, including features such as room size, hallway layout, and restaurant capacity.[101] The developer was also required to conduct feasibility studies and present a financing plan to the ONTT for approval before work began.[102]

Another major deficiency of the tourism sector was its lack of trained personnel.[103] Before 1970, though some senior staff were educated abroad, there was no formal training system other than learning on the job. A 1971 employment survey found a drastic lack of trained personnel staffing the hotels, which by 1972 employed over eighteen thousand. One-fifth of all employees had no formal education, and only one-third had attended secondary school. Training was needed to efficiently and effectively run the hotels as well as to maintain their value, improve their quality, and eventually reshape the tourism product. Each planning zone included space for a tourism school with an eventual capacity of about 250. In 1973 the total capacity of these schools was only nine hundred, and plans were established to expand the Monastir school and build new ones in Nabeul and Jerba.[104] By the mid-1970s, the sector had eight thousand full-time employees who had received proper training, though this figure still represented under one-half the number of Tunisians working in the sector.[105]

The state also supported hotel development in other ways. From 1965 to 1973 alone, the total value of direct state support to hotel developers in the form of tax breaks on duties, interest payments, subsidies for architectural costs, and infrastructure spending amounted to TD 9.5 million, equivalent to a 10 percent subsidy.[106] In addition, parastatal banks provided the backbone for investment in the sector. Between 1961 and 1980, the Banque Nationale de Développement Economique de Tunisie (BDET) advanced TD 65 million in long- and medium-term credit for tourism development. From its creation in 1969 through 1985, the COFITOUR (which later became the Banque Nationale de Développement Touristique, or BNDT) financed a total of 330 tourism projects amounting to TD 210 million.[107]

The result of these efforts was the creation of what Scott calls a "geometric order" that allowed the state's project of tourism development to be imagined and centrally planned as a whole using tools of miniaturization and mapmaking.[108] Another result of creating "homogenous, geometrical, uniform property" units out of the coastline was to increase "its convenience as a standardized commodity for the market."[109] In other words, the state now had the tools to commodify the primary asset of the tourism product and, with territorial control over these spaces, control the extraction of rents.

Tourism and the National Economy

The new regime of centralized policy formation, extensive infrastructure outlays, and regulatory institutions laid the foundations for transforming the tourism development process in Tunisia.

While the mass tourism product was vulnerable to foreign exchange swings and economic stagnation in Europe, the new tourism regime allowed Tunisia to continue to generate critically needed hard currency while extending state control over what would prove to be one of the nation's most valuable economic resources for decades to come. In 1972 the minister of the national economy declared that tourism would become "one of the principal pillars of the Tunisian economy."[110] By the end of the decade, receipts represented over 7 percent of GNP, and the sector directly employed over 28,600 workers, often at an average wage higher than those in the rapidly growing textile industry.[111] In addition, tourism indirectly promoted increased employment in other sectors such as construction, agriculture, and handicrafts. According to Ahmed Smaoui, a leading tourism official:

> Tourism in Tunisia has helped to create and strengthen a clearly defined class of entrepreneurs. Many of these were originally merchants, farmers, and owners of small handicrafts factories who have initiated tourism projects. They had a little capital to start with, but thanks to the system of credit and state aid and the facilities granted for land purchase they have found themselves catapulted into the position of heads of large-scale businesses.[112]

Moreover, for many Tunisians, "tourism and its symbols, such as the jumbo jet and luxury hotels, elicited an image of studied modernity and of much sought-after development."[113] The hotels with "an easily recognizable similarity with the 'modern' international style of architecture" were "in the eyes of the local people . . . true symbols of the life-style of the highly industrialized, developed, countries."[114] And for those who could now afford to visit them, these hotels represented new leisure spaces liberated from conservative social norms.

The success of tourism development in the 1970s hinged on the formation of a quasi-Fordist mode of mass production. After recovering from the dip in 1974, arrivals from France, the United Kingdom, and Scandinavia increased. To continue this growth, Tunisia had to offer cut-rate prices to draw increased demand. For example, as the Economist Intelligence Unit (EIU) reported, "Tunisia's tourist officials see in the UK market increased proof of their conviction that attention to cost and the development of the right package tour to fit the individual market conditions can overcome austere economic conditions abroad."[115] Providing low-cost tourism products required that the development and production system become hyperstandardized and be able to reap larger economies of scale. The average capacity of new hotels rapidly increased from 219 beds in 1968 to 511 in 1975.[116] A 1974 ONTT study found that the rate of return on capital investment varied geometrically with increased size: 2 percent for hotels with under 200 beds, 8.3 percent for those with 400 beds, and 18 percent for those with 600.[117]

While targeted government policies had given external capital the necessary incentives to invest in the tourism sector since the late 1960s, by the mid-1970s the economic and territorial contexts for investment and development had been transformed. Tourism development had become a cookie-cutter-style operation churning out huge, nearly identical white boxes with blue trim along the sandy coastlines, all guided by a series of government institutions. However, the development of large-scale hotel projects would progressively require larger sums of capital. In the first wave of mass tourism hotel development (1966–71), the average additional bed cost TD 10,500 (all figures in 1987 dinars). In the decade between 1972 and 1982, it rose to TD 13,000, and between 1983 and 1989 it reached TD 22,000.[118] Even in the 1970s, most local entrepreneurs were investing in small-scale light-industrial or food-processing plants requiring smaller capital costs. The new scale and style of development thus required more concerted efforts by the state to solicit external investment.

Petrodollars and the Beginnings of the Economic Reterritorialization of Tourism Development

In the aftermath of the 1973 Arab-Israeli war, the oil boycott led to a rapid rise in prices, resulting in a massive expansion of income for the oil-exporting states of the Middle East that lasted into the 1980s. This oil price shock (followed by another in the early 1980s) contributed to the disruption of the postwar era of economic expansion across the North Atlantic. It destabilized the existing Fordist systems of mass production and set in motion a transformation of international tourism markets. While economic recession and higher transportation costs weakened the growth in demand for international tourism in the North Atlantic markets, the oil crisis had a profound impact on reshaping the political economy of tourism development in the Arab world. The crisis came at a difficult time for international airlines, just after they had expanded their fleets with new Boeing 747 "Jumbo Jets." Pioneer carriers like TWA and Pan Am sought to avoid bankruptcy by selling parts of their fleets to the now spendthrift oil states. As a result, "the glittering new airports of the Middle East, filled with the half-empty jumbos of Iran Air, Saudia or Gulf Air, became the most showy signs of the huge transfer of wealth; and Saudia, which TWA had set up less than thirty years earlier, was now richer than its old master."[119]

In the wake of the 1973–74 tourism crisis in Tunisia and economic recession in Europe, European and American direct investment in the tourism sector dropped off. Transnational tourism companies retreated from direct ownership of foreign assets such as hotels and limited their activities to tour operations and hotel management. While it took another three decades before a few of the smaller Gulf states developed their own large-scale tourism and airline sectors, in the mid- and late 1970s they began recycling a significant portion of their petrodollars through tourism development around the Arab world. This new source of capital provided funding for much larger, more luxurious hotel and resort projects. While small compared to the size of the mass tourism market, the possibilities for luxury-oriented development across the region expanded with a new wave of business travelers and tourists from the oil-rich states. Coming just as the Tunisian state had established a new regime for tourism development, these new projects channeled capital through a system highly regulated by state and public-sector officials. The new infrastructure works, policy-making institution, and hotel planning system gave the state new bargaining powers when it came to foreign investment.

Real estate was a favored sector for Arab investors and state-owned development funds from the Gulf. In 1976 the Tunisian government signed a TD 30 million tourism development deal with the Consortium Koweitien d'Investissement Immobilier (CKII).[120] The result was the creation of the Consortium Tuniso-Koweitien de Développement (CTKD) with 60 percent Arab capital and 40 percent from the Tunisian state and public banks. The CTKD began by building the Dar An-Andalous hotel in Port El Kantaoui. In the early 1980s, the CTKD went on to build a chain of grand four-

and five-star resorts from Tabarka to Jerba under the Abou Nawas brand name.[121] There were other channels of oil money, such as the Compagnie Touristique Arabe, founded in 1981 by the well-connected Saudi businessman Ghaith Pharaon. It was able to mobilize TD 120 million for the construction of projects in Gammarth and Monastir. The Société de Tourism et de Congrès, with 40 percent Kuwaiti capital, was formed with the intention to build an international convention center in Tunis. Other tourism ventures financed by capital from the Gulf would include the Fonds Saoudien de Développement Economique, the Société Tuniso-Saoudienne d'Investissement et de Développement (STUSID), and the Banque Tuniso-Qatari.[122] Foreign investment in the tourism sector expanded in the early 1970s with the *infitah* but declined after the 1973 crisis. Beginning in 1977 as petrodollar-financed investments came online, the share of external investment in the tourism sector rapidly climbed (see Figure 4).

While tourism growth rates would never again match the sustained rapid climbs of the 1960s and early 1970s, the mature Tunisian market continued to grow significantly after 1974. As noted earlier, this growth was achieved by a deliberate pricing policy that sought to hold down rates. The result was a reduction in the receipts per night (in 1987 TDs) from about TD 42 in 1973 to under TD 35 in 1975. The real value of the average receipt per bed night would not regain its 1973 level until 1978 but then sank back down during the decline of global demand caused by the second oil shock (see Table 3).[123] As the structure of the Mediterranean tourism economy allowed global competition to drive down prices and squeeze profit margins, Tunisian tourism maintained its integration by efficiently providing a low-cost destination. The tourists that Tunisia attracted had limited means or interest in spending

Years	% of total investment
1962–69	3.4
1970–72	10.1
1973–76	1.9
1977–80	11.7
1982–86	32.0

Figure 4. Foreign investment in the tourism sector. Office National du Tourisme Tunisien, *Le VIIème Plan*, 30; Signoles, *L'Espace Tunisien*, 879.

Table 3. Value of the Tunisian tourism product, 1973–81

Year	Tourist bed nights		Tourist receipts per bed night	
	Nights	Change	TD	Change
1973	5,882,497	–13%	42.1	12%
1974	5,636,385	–4%	39.5	–6%
1975	8,652,556	54%	34.9	–12%
1976	8,898,029	3%	36.4	4%
1977	8,117,577	–9%	39.9	10%
1978	8,804,945	8%	42.2	6%
1979	11,170,943	27%	38.9	–8%
1980	12,097,984	8%	37.7	–3%
1981	12,507,186	3%	37.2	–1%

Source: ONTT. Note: Receipts are expressed in constant 1987 TDs.

more income on extra goods and services. As a result of this model, there was little scope for extracting more rent or generating positive external economies. It was soon apparent to officials in the tourism sector that their development policies had led them into a low-equilibrium trap where the product had to continue to undercut prices at other destinations. The alternative was to establish new products, new markets, and a new image.

The rapid expansion of the Tunisian model of package tourism had resulted in a landscape dominated by midrange three-star hotels that looked like simple concrete blocks or "tourist cages," as one researcher called them, lined up in tourism zones along the coast.[124] The operations of the highly standardized package tourism systems had tourists "recruited en mass by travel agencies, shuttled over on charter flights, transferred in a group by motor coach from the airport, and then left in their hotel."[125] Once they arrived at their hotels, however, these tourists generally remained stationary, spending on average twenty-two hours a day there: "This includes four hours on the beach, three hours at the pool, and fifteen hours within the actual hotel."[126] As one study found, "Most visitors to Tunisia, and to Sousse in particular, are middle-income tourists, many of them cannot afford to make excursions inland, or even to lay out the fares to go from their hotel to the center of town. . . . 65 percent of the tourists do not visit it at all!"[127]

In the wake of the 1973 tourism crisis, public authorities not only saw the need for better planning, infrastructure, and organization within the sector but also came realize the eventual limits of the mass beach tourism product cycle and Tunisia's position within it. In a 1974 interview, M. Ayari, minister of the national economy, suggested that "to regain the momentum of the '60s, the challenge . . . is to 'diversify' Tunisian tourism." With the help of local and foreign consultants, in 1977 authorities began to study the marketing of Tunisian tourism. The term "diversify" appeared in all subsequent tourism reports and planning documents, but how the term was operationalized evolved and became more elaborate over the years. The first strategy pursued was based on the judgment that the linear model of development, where long strings of hotels were spaced along stretches of otherwise undeveloped coastline, needed to be replaced by a "nuclear model."[128] Tunisia decided to imitate features of development that were appearing along the more dense French and Spanish coasts, such as the integrated tourism complex.[129]

The layout of the integrated complex is defined by clustering a number of hotels close together within a landscaped campus surrounded by amenities (such as golfing, boating, restaurants, and nightclubs) as well as boutique shops and special services (such as clothiers and travel agencies). This model has a number of advantages over the linear model. First, the design of the complex as a whole can be planned centrally, and a single developer or development authority can coordinate its implementation. Second, compactness limits the environmental damage caused by tourism and makes the building of infrastructure and facilities more cost-effective. As an enclave space located away from local communities, the design can also limit the negative social and cultural impacts of tourism. Third, the nuclear model promotes the generation of territorial rents and positive economic externalities, as it gives tourists easy access to other activities such as sports, recreation, shopping, and entertainment.

The Birth of the Station Intégrée in Tunisia: Port El Kantaoui

The diversification policy outlined in the fourth and fifth national development plans set out a new strategy for the promotion of larger clusters of hotels, vacation villages, and the flagship of the integrated tourism complexes: Port El Kantaoui, located north of the town of Sousse. The idea for this new tourism complex was based on an ItalConsult feasibility study and plan for the Sousse-North region completed in 1971. The development of the project was initiated by the establishment of the Société d'Études et de Développement de Sousse-Nord in 1974.[130] This consortium was organized by the COFITOUR and financed mainly by state capital, the Abu Dhabi Fund for Arab Economic Development, COFITOUR, the IFC, and the Arab Bank International (Cairo).[131] The Tunisian government took charge of developing the infrastructure and purchasing over three hundred hectares of land, amounting to 22 percent of the cost of the project.[132] The consortium then planned the hotel zones and eventually recruited large hotel promoters, such as the Kuwaiti-Tunisian Abou Nawas, to develop the numerous hotels for the project.[133]

The site for the complex is well outside Sousse, past the string of hotels trailing north along the coast. This more isolated location allowed the complex to be constructed in undeveloped open space with no constraints to its design. The land, at the time zoned for agriculture, was expropriated from the local landowners, who were compensated about TD 0.5 per square meter.[134] Its design is centered on a landscaped artificial marina, which the ONTT calls "the premier garden-port of the Mediterranean."[135] The promotional literature for Port El Kantaoui describes the project as "built like a real Tunisian village, whitewashed houses, arches and arcades," with "the charm of a typical small port."[136] The walkway along the marina is lined with restaurants, cafés, a nightclub, and various tourist shops, such as an artisan handicraft shop, a bank, food stores, a car rental agency, an art gallery, and a hair salon.[137] The total space for the sixty-five commercial units is five thousand square meters.[138] Clustered immediately around this center are time-share condominiums. This core represents the nucleus of the larger complex, which eventually stretched 5.5 kilometers down the coast to occupy 310 landscaped hectares with twelve hotels of various classes offering a total capacity of 15,000 beds. Behind the marina is an area with 500 deluxe villas and beach houses, adding another 1,000 beds to the resort's capacity. Inland from the beach among the hotels are an American-designed golf course and fifty tennis courts. A tourism school with accommodations for the local staff is also attached to the resort. The complex as a whole employs over 6,000 people.

Figure 5. A postcard of Tunisia's first integrated tourism complex at Port El Kantaoui. Author's collection.

Port El Kantaoui represents what the ONTT had planned to be the new face of Tunisian tourism over the 1980s and 1990s, which entailed transforming the economic, territorial, and political dynamics of tourism development (explored in chapter 2). This project was the first of several larger, more capital-intensive projects. These included efforts to build more luxury accommodations, promote increased income generation by making available better-quality recreational and commercial activities, and support higher-class branding efforts by Tunisian and Arab firms such as CTKD's Abou Nawas. When Port El Kantaoui opened its first hotel and apartments in 1979, the five-star hotel rooms were not sold as part of discounted package deals but were available only at the higher individual booking rates.[139] The complex also sought to hold business conferences and attract wealthy visitors to lease apartments and villas as second homes. The layout of Port El Kantaoui, with its high-class hotel accommodations, marina, commercial complex, golf course, and beach club, represented an effort to design a tourism space that would generate more territorially based rents and positive externalities because of its upscale image and auxiliary activities. One sign of its success was that while in the 1970s the land for the project was expropriated at about TD 0.5 per square meter by the state, by 1984 land near Sousse would sell for over TD 22 per square meter.[140] The marina area, the condos next to them, and several of the hotels are adorned with carved stone facades, decorative ironwork, and touches of the color green. Tourism officials proudly refer to this architecture as being built in an "authentic" Andalusian style. While the architecture stands out from the white-washed "cages" of the typical international-style hotels that cover the rest of the coastline, the complex nevertheless is one of "stark outlines and detachment from the surrounding countryside."[141]

While some travel writers have criticized the resort as "artificial, soulless, even anemic,"[142] others have described it as "artificial, but quite attractive," noting that "the main attraction of Port El Kantaoui is the picturesque aspect of the harbor, fringed with palm trees, cafes and restaurants, and the 'village' lying behind. The gleaming white walls are graced with colorful bougainvillea and jasmine. Behind the harbor are cobbled lanes of boutiques and cafes."[143] The effort to construct an atmospheric tourism space marks a critical move toward economic and cultural reterritorialization. The attempt to mimic an Andalusian style and create a sense of place has the strange irony of evoking both contemporary Spanish tourist destinations (which Port El Kantaoui was built to compete against) and the Islamic-Andalusian history and culture of Spain from which segments of Tunisian society—most notably its urban artisans, elite political and intellectual classes, and Jewish community—trace their roots. This tourism project, however, only palely reflects the depth of cultural and historical resources that Tunisia could draw on in reshaping the image of its territory.

This new direction of development relied heavily on funding from the Gulf. By the mid-1980s, one-quarter of all investment for the project came from foreign sources such as Kuwait and Saudi Arabia.[144] Supported by both investment and visitors from the Arab Gulf, developments like Port El Kantaoui—which became a model for other projects at Gammarth, Hammamet-Sud, and Tabarka—defined a new mechanism to expand the state's capability to regulate capital, space, and tourist flows. While the SHTT had stopped building and managing hotels in the 1970s, the rise of the integrated complex set out a larger and more defined role for the state in planning, financing, building, and managing these projects. They were built on large tracts of government-owned land on which the state was responsible for building a centrally planned infrastructure network. The integrated complex established more tasks within the tourism development process that the state controlled and directly regulated. It made developers more dependent on, and vulnerable to, state authorities, since they defined the context of each hotel project and remained responsible for the overall complex. Moreover, the state maintained ownership of shares in these projects, directly through government institutions or indirectly through public development banks. Integrated complexes introduced a new phase of centralized enclave development supervised by state planning and regulation agencies. Port El Kantaoui also represented the formation of stronger political connections between tourism development and centralized state power. This connection is reflected in the location of the complex in the Sahel, near the cluster of towns from which many of the nationalist leaders hailed. The completion of Port El Kantaoui, however, marked the beginning of a new era of challenges for the political elite and the ability of the state to manage the further integration of Tunisia into the global economy.

2. Images of Openness, Spaces of Control: Tourism in Tunisia's New Era

By the late 1970s, Tunisia had successfully established an external image as a stable, relatively liberal Arab state. Western media coverage typically focused on President Habib Bourguiba's staunch support of women's rights, investment in social development, friendly relations with Western powers, and openness to both foreign investment and tourists. The role of tourism in building the country's image was exemplified by a profile published in *National Geographic* magazine in 1980 titled "Tunisia: Sea, Sand, Success."[1] These images, however, failed to represent what would become day-to-day experiences for many Tunisians by the mid-1980s: social dislocation, economic hardship, labor unrest, and growing disenchantment with Bourguiba's authoritarian rule.

While Tunisia's *infitah* of the 1970s led to the rise of a private manufacturing sector and allowed consumers greater access to imported goods, the promotion of economic growth based on external markets and capital flows also eroded the state's territorial control over the economic system, limiting its ability to regulate the process of economic change and its social effects. By the mid-1980s, a political crisis of regulation emerged when declines in oil revenues, remittances, export manufacturing, and tourism receipts left the state unable to sustain consumer subsidies and external borrowing.[2]

Tunisia's reliance on tourism now proved a double liability. It made the national economy vulnerable to economic decline in Europe, political instability in other parts of the Arab world, and the changing markets of the global tourism sector. Tourism also provided a ripe target for the Islamist movement that quickly became the leading political force challenging the secular authoritarian state. Islamists replaced the Left as the primary critics of economic integration, drawing support from Tunisians suffering social dislocation caused by rapid economic change, and suggesting an alternative vision for Tunisia focused on what the Islamists saw as its authentic Islamic heritage.

The endgame of this political crisis was launched in the wake of a series of hotel bombings in the summer of 1987 blamed on militant Islamists. On November 7, 1987, Prime Minister Zine El Abidine Ben Ali deposed the nation's aging and increasingly erratic leader by having him declared medically unfit. Assuming the presidency, Ben Ali pledged to create a new era based on political pluralism, an end to corruption, and economic growth through economic modernization and closer integration into the global economy.

While bringing stability and prosperity back to the country, Ben Ali's Tunisia has challenged many early post–Cold War assumptions about how market reform and global economic integration would eventually create pressures for more accountable government, open societies, and democratization.[3] The Tunisian state has been able to advance economic liberalization and embrace globalization while constructing little more than a facade of political openness. While tourism development represents only one aspect of Ben Ali's strategy for national development, the tourism sector contributed to his consolidation of power by assisting Tunisia's economic recovery in the early post-coup era. The new patterns of tourism development emphasizing economic and cultural reterritorialization helped the state maintain an outward image of stability and openness to both tourists and investors while promoting an increasingly authoritarian form of state control over society and politics. Tourism development in Tunisia's new era represents a pioneering effort to successfully forge a strategy of "paradoxical globalization," a highly filtered form of openness in which expanded state control over domestic space is achieved through global economic integration.

Shifting Transnational Flows and the Erosion of State Control, 1981–87

As the Tunisian state under Bourguiba developed institutions to regulate capital flows and development in the tourism sector in the 1970s, the economy's growing reliance on external market forces was eroding the state's territorial control over other aspects of national economic development. In contrast to the early postcolonial phase of state building, by the 1980s Tunisian society was being reshaped by international markets and transnational flows leading to regional inequality, unsustainable urbanization, labor discontent, and growing Islamist reaction against external cultural influences.

The Territorial Consequences of *Infitah*

The economic liberalization policies of the 1970s led to a period of sustained economic growth based on foreign investment, the rise of small-scale export-oriented manufacturing firms, and mass tourism development. These incomes were supplemented by modest oil exports. Meanwhile trade liberalization, growing consumer demand, and the manufacturing sector's need for capital goods and inputs from abroad drove up the volume of Tunisian imports. The increased openness of the economy is reflected in the rise between 1970 and 1980 of total exports and imports as a share of GNP from 50 percent to 88 percent.[4] Higher oil prices and the availability of international credit allowed the Tunisian state to expand investment and employment in the loss-generating state sector and to subsidize consumer goods.[5]

At the same time, the state's limited regulatory control over the spatial consequences of its *infitah* policies exacerbated the political challenges of regional disparities, rapid urbanization, and domestic and transnational labor migration. For example, much of the early success of the *infitah* was based on growth in the textile sector. Export-led manufacturing growth in the 1970s in part resulted from Tunisia's ability to capture opportunities within the new international division of labor in which manufacturing firms that used simple mass-production technologies were moved from Europe to countries with lower wages, such as Tunisia.[6] Encouraged by Law 1972-38, which granted offshore status to foreign firms established in Tunisia for export, German, French, and Italian capital rushed in to set up textile and clothing factories.[7] European firms also subcontracted work to small-scale Tunisian firms that had been established with state encouragement.[8] Between 1974 and 1980, textile and clothing exports to the countries of the Organisation for Economic Co-operation and Development (OECD) grew 832 percent.[9]

During the next six years, however, such exports grew only 35 percent.[10] As Hakim Ben Hammouda argues, the shift in Tunisian manufacturing from a focus on the internal market to participation in a highly deterritorialized economy eroded the state's ability to regulate production and consumption in the sector.[11] Factors that the state could not regulate, such as slack demand in Europe and the loss to Asia of Tunisia's comparative advantage in labor costs, contributed to the decline of its exports.[12] The 1980s also saw the "relocalization" of production as firms moved more manufacturing back to Europe owing to protectionist measures and increased automation in labor-intensive industries.[13] At the same time, foreign direct investment "delocalized" away from Tunisia owing to the inability of the Tunisian textile sector to expand the skills of its workforce, keep up with technological change, and compete with the growing adoption of flexible production systems in the global industry.[14]

With investment allocations shaped more by private firms, foreign investment, and subcontracts with European companies, the state lost territorial control over the location of investment and job creation. In contrast to government efforts in the 1960s to establish industrial growth poles in interior locations, during the 1970s over 90 percent of the investment and jobs created in the export sector took place in the littoral regions.[15] As a result, the economic geography of Tunisia was divided in two, with Tunis and the *sahel* benefiting from new public and private investments while the southern and central regions remained impoverished.[16]

This pattern of investment accentuated the unequal dispersal of employment opportunities, resulting in job seekers migrating to densely populated northeast Tunisia.[17] Market forces drove up rents and land prices, overwhelming state social policy. By the late 1980s, roughly 21 percent of the population of greater Tunis lived in *bidonvilles* (shantytowns).[18] Housing and social welfare problems were exacerbated by the elimination of subsidies and public-sector jobs owing to structural adjustment in the 1980s. As a result, the urban populations in the *medina* of Tunis and the surrounding *bidonvilles* and popular neighborhoods developed survival strategies such as unlicensed building and the expansion of informal and black-market economic activity. This was aided by a new form of *commerce à la valise* driven by the consumer goods brought back during the seasonal visits of Tunisians working abroad.[19] The informal economy can be viewed as a safety valve for generating household income.[20] Its expansion, however, also means that more of the population is experiencing life outside the state's social contract, based on the provision of economic benefits in exchange for political acquiescence.[21] These high concentrations of urban poor and unemployed soon functioned as recruiting grounds for the Islamist movements in the 1980s. Islamist groups expanded their base of support by providing social services and establishing patronage networks to assist those classes increasingly marginalized by the state and national economy.[22]

Toward Political Crisis

The political effects of these socioeconomic changes became most evident when Tunisia's major sources of income, including tourism, declined. By the early 1980s, in the wake of the second oil shock and protectionist policies in Europe, the nature and movement of transnational flows in the international economy shifted, and the income sources that Tunisia developed in the 1970s became increasingly volatile. When they dropped sharply in the mid-1980s, they contributed to a political and economic crisis for the regime. Tunisia became less able to draw capital inflows, adjust its economy to changing market environments, and provide for the social needs of its population. The authoritarian state's ability to maintain its social contract soon came under threat.

In late 1983 Prime Minister Muhammad Mzali was forced to cut consumer subsidies, doubling the price of bread by the end of the year. Tunisia was plunged into almost two weeks of bread riots and violent clashes with government forces.[23] Villagers from the impoverished south and southwest, who were hardest hit by the price increases, mobilized first. They were joined by students and the unemployed from the slums of Tunis's *medina* and suburbs, who felt increasingly alienated from the state and the once-inclusive political system.[24] The protests were aided by the burgeoning Islamist movements that developed from within these communities and came to dominate politics on university campuses.[25] In their efforts to suppress the demonstrations, looting, and destruction of public property, the Tunisian security forces killed at least 150 and wounded thousands of others. At the end of the riots, Bourguiba announced that the price increases would be rescinded, but the regime remained on shaky ground.

In the following year, oil revenues and worker remittances crashed, and unemployment rates surged as high as 40 to 50 percent among workers under twenty-five.[26] Bourguiba replaced Mzali with the hard-line Richard Sfar, a finance specialist. Under Sfar the government turned to the IMF in the summer of 1986 for a structural adjustment loan. Implementing structural adjustment by eliminating subsidies, privatizing the public sector, and liberalizing trade while dealing with the social and political consequences of these changes quickly became the central challenge for the state.[27]

The Limits of Mass Tourism Development in Tunisia

Although it was only one element of the economic challenges facing the regime in the mid-1980s, the tourism economy's vulnerability to external forces exemplifies Tunisia's crisis of regulation. As the country headed toward economic and political crisis, the government's reliance on its tourism sector increased. Not only was tourism a leading source of hard currency; it was also a major creator of jobs. Government officials calculated that the sector directly and indirectly supported about a half million of the country's 6.5 million population.[28] The sixth national plan for 1982–86 had declared that "tourism activity constitutes one of the priorities," noting that tourism should "contribute in a large way to the realization of the objectives of the plan."[29] The plan called for building forty thousand new hotel beds and doubling the ONTT's promotion budget.

By the mid-1980s, however, the tourism industry had failed to make up for the loss of jobs and income in other sectors. The SHTT-owned hotels were suffering major losses and running high debts.[30] Tourism demand grew by an average of only 1.4 percent per year, well below the government's expectation of 5.6 percent growth. Moreover, the regulatory regime built in the 1970s to control expanding flows of tourists and investment could not cope with the shifting markets of the 1980s.

Table 4 summarizes the weakness of the tourism sector in the early 1980s. In addition to any effect that the 1984 riots might have had, the decline of tourism in this period is often blamed on regional conflicts with little relationship to Tunisian politics. These include the 1985 Israeli bombing raid on the headquarters of the Palestine Liberation Organization (PLO) near Tunis, the 1986 U.S. bombing of neighboring Libya, and the wave of terrorist attacks launched against Israeli targets in Europe.[31] The decline in European visitors, however, predated these events. A somber ONTT report in 1986 noted weak tourism numbers from 1983 to 1985 owing to declines in economic growth in Europe that led European countries to promote restrictive monetary policies and protectionist measures to combat budget deficits.[32] These countries also encouraged domestic tourism to avoid the loss of currency abroad.

While Tunisia suffered from these events, structural changes in the Mediterranean tourism economy were in the process of reshaping the longer-term fate of tourism development in the country. The end of the era of Keynesian Fordism in the 1970s and the emergence in the 1980s and 1990s of new post-Fordist production systems based on flexible labor markets transformed the structure of tourism demand. Leisure patterns became more fragmented and eventually led to new forms of tourist activity.[33] As part of the same broad transformation, the global production system of sun, sand, and sea mass tourism was experiencing its own crisis of sorts.

On the demand side, the market for mass beach tourism in northern European economies became increasingly saturated. The

Table 4. Decline of Tunisian tourism, 1982–86

Year	Receipts (1,000s)	Change	Bed nights	Change	Receipts/ night TD	Change
1982	462,908	0%	11,160,209	–11%	41.5	12%
1983	483,478	4%	10,330,408	–7%	46.8	13%
1984	414,484	–14%	10,251,787	–1%	40.4	–14%
1985	459,071	11%	12,671,218	24%	36.2	–10%
1986	415,285	–10%	12,549,689	–1%	33.1	–9%

Source: ONTT. Note: Receipts are expressed in constant 1987 TDs.

rapid expansion of supply at decreasing prices had allowed an ever-widening segment of these societies to experience the standardized sun, sand, and sea holiday. Beaches became overcrowded and coastal resorts overdeveloped. The mass beach market in Europe could no longer be expected to grow at the rates witnessed in the 1950s and 1960s. The beginning of the 1980s also saw a waning of sun lust.[34] People became increasingly aware of the health risks of sun exposure.[35] The new generation of middle-class travelers who came of age after 1968 were less interested in reproducing the consumption habits of their parents. Tourism patterns were also being reshaped by a growing awareness of the negative social and environmental impacts of mass tourism development.[36] Overall, more of the traveling public sought new cultural and environmental experiences. Rather than spend leisure time sunning on the beach, many engaged in sports or explored nature and the wilderness on their own terms. More travelers sought self-reflective or meaningful experiences by engaging art, history, and culture.[37] These trends led to the diversification and segmentation of tourism markets shaped by the rise of ecotourism and adventure travel and the expansion of cultural, heritage, and urban tourism markets.

The waning of the era of mass beach tourism was also driven by changes on the supply side. As price competition in the sector drove down the firms' narrow profit margins, the "cycle of low prices and low investment" resulted in an erosion of the beach experiences offered.[38] Many resorts on the Mediterranean had become worn out and were in desperate need of "reinvention." Changes in tourist demand required them to refashion and diversify the content of their products and services by, for example, adding more leisure activities (such as golfing and boating), shopping outlets, and theme-park attractions, as well as providing higher-quality service and facilities.[39] Meanwhile many tour operators within the mass beach tourism sector could not survive the cutthroat discounting and shrank or folded.[40]

Because these changes occurred over a number of seasons and at different times in different places, it would be an oversimplification to suggest that there was ever a generalized "crisis of mass tourism." As markets shifted, many tour operators found new clients and suppliers, and some beach resorts remodeled their facilities. The transition, however, was most jarring for the developers of tourism spaces in places like Tunisia where the tourism infrastructure was so dedicated to low-cost tourism. Tunisia, in particular, had created an image that was hard to revise. In many ways, the large, boxy hotel complexes that lined the Tunisian coast faced a challenge similar to the one faced by the Fordist manufacturing plants that dotted the American Midwest in the era of deindustrialization.

As Figure 6 outlines, while tourism in Tunisia grew at exceptional rates from 1965 to 1975, outpacing the Mediterranean as a whole, in the late 1970s the annual rate of growth, measured in bed nights, slowed to the Mediterranean average of 6 percent. By the early 1980s, Tunisia's growth rate had dropped below the Mediterranean average to less than 2 percent. The slower rates of growth, coupled with the image of Tunisia as a discount sun, sand, and sea destination, prodded Tunisia to sink its prices ever lower to remain a competitive destination.[41] Like other resorts in decline, Tunisia fell prey to the vicious cycle where "the growing habit of selling four star hotels for the price of two" led to a situation where "services tend to deteriorate fast."[42] The years of mass tourism also took their toll on environmental and social conditions. An ONTT report citing the poor state of public hygiene and crime concluded that "in the tourist regions and communities, the physical and human environment does not contribute to the amelioration of the image of Tunisia."[43]

By the mid-1980s, the "sea, sand, success" image of Tunisia presented in *National Geographic* was under threat. The nation's tourist image was suffering from regional conflict, domestic political struggles, and a product viewed as worn out, dated, and increasingly polluted. The last thing the regime needed was the rise of an ideological critique of its tourism development strategy and a violent attack directed at its hotels and tourists.

Years	Mediterranean	Tunisia
1965–70	8.8%	27%
1970–75	5%	20%
1975–80	6%	6%
1980–85	3%	1.8%

Figure 6. The rise and decline of mass tourism in terms of average annual growth in bed nights, 1965–85. *Source:* Office National du Tourisme Tunisien, *Le VIIème Plan*, 24–25.

The Islamist Challenge and the Fall of the First Republic

The decline of the tourism sector contributed to the overall economic crisis, but Tunisia's reliance on mass tourism also generated other challenges for the Bourguiba regime. Tourism had brought many positive benefits to society by creating employment and entrepreneurial opportunities, but by the 1980s, many Tunisians grew concerned about the social and cultural impact of the beach tourism economy, which had come to dominate large sections of the coastline and flooded the country with millions of visitors each year. Many beach-oriented tourism activities—such as excessive consumption of alcohol and nude sunbathing—were widely viewed as alien to Tunisian culture and socially undesirable.[44] As many young Tunisians found work at tourism resorts, they had to negotiate between "the society of their parents, restricted and monitored, and the one of their work lives that turns on semi-nude beaches and brilliant nightlife."[45] Another social consequence of tourism development was the *bezness* scene, where foreign women came to Tunisia for liaisons with local men, usually in exchange for material gifts.[46] These issues generated widely shared concerns, often expressed privately, across the population, even among its social elite, who were most at home with European leisure culture. Criticism of the tourism industry occasionally showed up in more public expressions, such popular media and films. Ridha Behi's film *Soleil des hyènes* (1977) makes a searing attack on the impact of tourism development on a rural North African fishing village as a German firm builds a tourism complex.[47] The film shows how local villagers and their economy are marginalized by the hotel and the local elites who collude with the Germans. Many of the economic benefits of the hotel, such as the jobs that men gained during its construction, are minimal or quickly disappear. Such commentaries, however, had limited impact on tourism policy, as they failed to gain wide circulation in the state-controlled media and film sector. In any case, Behi's film or the writings of indigenous academics critical of the state's tourism development strategies generally did not call for abandoning tourism development but emphasized other means for development and the need for planning and regulation of the sector.[48]

A more threatening challenge emerged in the late 1970s from the religious and socially conservative elements of Tunisian society who had long opposed Bourguiba's secularization efforts and his vision for Western-oriented modernization. Together with other Islamists, Rashid Ghannouchi formed a political organization with the goal of re-Islamizing Tunisian society. This movement was fueled by the decline of socioeconomic conditions, growing disenchantment with the failings of the nationalist regime and the Left, and popular identification with the country's Arabic and Islamic heritage rather than the Mediterranean identity or Franco-Tunisian synthesis that appealed more to the country's Westernized elite. The Islamist movement presented an ideological critique of the state's tourism development strategy. It sought not only to redirect the economy away from reliance on the tourism sector but also to promote an alternative construction of Tunisia's identity and external image. As Lisa Anderson notes, Islamists "have found their support in those social categories that benefited least from government largesse," while they cast their "claims against the government . . . in terms of personal (religious) identity and moral outrage . . . rather than interpretations of economic interest."[49] Mass beach tourism oriented to European desires proved an especially ripe target for Islamist tracts against Westernizing and secularizing government policies and social trends toward consumerism and materialism. Bourguiba had sought to define Tunisia as a Mediterranean society, situated historically and in the current era as a crossroads of multiple civilizations. He emphasized Tunisia's connection to ancient Rome and the Phoenicians, directed the country's vision of modernity toward France and Europe, and marginalized the importance of Islam as a religion and source of identity and moral guidance. This construction of national identity not only was tied up with his vision for modernizing the country but also corresponded to efforts to project a tourist-friendly image for Tunisia.

Islamists rejected Bourguiba's model, calling it a failure that led the regime's narrow elite toward greater despotism. Rashid Ghannouchi countered Bourguiba by noting that "Tunisians are not tourists who live in a hotel."[50] Ghannouchi challenged the Westernizing orientation of the state's tourism program and image, claiming, "All that remains of the previous identities is a few perished traces whose residuals are found in some touristic Tunisian cities."[51] In leaflets and pamphlets, Islamists openly called for the "resuscitation of the Islamic personality of Tunisia so that it can recover its role as a great home of Islamic civilization in Africa and put an end to the situation of dependency, alienation and decay."[52] While never presenting a coherent alternative framework for economic development, Islamists declared their opposition to "the cultural colonization of our Islamic world by Westernization" and lamented that "our economy is based on producing things that we don't need, with cheap labor, for the West, and on tourism."[53]

In 1981 Ghannouchi and his colleagues formed the Movement de la Tendance Islamique (MTI) and sought formal recognition as an opposition party as the regime began experimenting with multiparty elections. As the state faced broader economic and political challenges, the Islamists launched numerous public demonstrations. Many led to confrontations with the police. Rather than legalizing an Islamist party, the government attempted to suppress the MTI by arresting much of its leadership.[54] Meanwhile, in July of that year, the Club Med resort at Korba (north of Nabeul) was ransacked following a cultural event where Jewish tourists sang the Israeli anthem *Hatikvah*. The attack was never viewed as being perpetrated by the MTI, but it nevertheless threatened to tarnish the image that Tunisian government officials sought to project of a country tolerant of both its remaining Jewish minority and its Jewish visitors, which included groups who made an annual pilgrimage to Jerba.

In the wake of the 1984 bread riots, as Mzali sought to restore stability and the credibility of his government, he convinced Bourguiba to grant the MTI leaders a presidential amnesty after they sent the president a letter affirming their commitment to the rule of law. The MTI was granted semilegal status and publicly confirmed its commitment to democratic principles. With the rising influence of the Islamists as well as religious conservatives, Tunisian authorities found they had to "walk a fairly narrow path between pleasing the tourists—and some Tunisians—and respecting religious traditions and the mosque."[55] Tensions with the regime grew as the Islamists expanded their political mobilization efforts, gaining a broader middle-class following while challenging the regime as it struggled to cope with ongoing economic crises. The MTI grew frustrated as the government failed to recognize it as a legal political party, and it appears that some within the party began formulating a strategy to displace Bourguiba, possibly through a coup led by the group's underground military wing.[56] In March 1987, when the French arrested six Tunisian militants with purported ties to Iran, Tunisia broke off relations with Iran in an effort to discredit the MTI and claim that the movement was an Iranian revolutionary export.

On the night of Sunday, August 2, 1987, several bombs detonated simultaneously at four hotels in Monastir and Sousse, at the heart of Tunisia's main tourism region. The bombs at Monastir struck Bourguiba's hometown on the day before his birthday in the midst of a monthlong official celebration praising Bourguiba's rule. Thirteen people, including tourists from Britain and Italy, were injured in the attack. In a communiqué to media outlets in Paris, the militant Djihad Islamique en Tunisie, which included former members of the MTI, claimed responsibility.[57] The government, however, refused to consider the claim, and a few days later, state television broadcast a videotaped confession by Mehriz Boudagga in which he confessed to leading the group that placed the handmade bombs as a "protest against scantily-clad tourists."[58] He also claimed that he was following instructions sent from the MTI hierarchy.[59] While the human-rights community was critical of the trial, with some claiming that Boudagga's confession was a result of torture, Minister of Justice Sadok Chaabane later recounted that at the trial "the judge found that there were many circumstances indicating that the leadership [of the MTI] was advocating damage to tourists to damage the economy and to incite the anger of religious leaders against tourists."[60]

Bourguiba ordered his interior minister Ben Ali, who had led the government's security forces during the 1984 bread riots, to crack down on the MTI and find those responsible. Mohamed Elhachmi Hamdi, a former MTI activist, notes that "the entire state apparatus was mobilized in the battle."[61] The MTI denied responsibility for the attacks and responded with demonstrations and an information campaign targeting the local and international media. Ninety Islamist activists, ranging from the two fingered as the planters of the bombs to prominent leaders of the MTI—including Ghannouchi—were put on trial. When the verdict was announced in September 1987, the two directly tied to the bombing and five others tried in absentia were given death sentences. The others were given various prison and hard-labor sentences. During the trial, Ghannouchi reconfirmed his commitment to democratic principles but was sentenced to life in prison.

Bourguiba, acting ever more erratic, was furious. He viewed the Islamists as an affront to his lifelong efforts of secular state building and modernization. Five days later, he appointed Ben Ali, a for-mer general and interior minister, to the position of prime minister and demanded that he retry the Islamists and give them death sen-tences. After attempting to convince Bourguiba to change his mind, Ben Ali took advantage of a recent change in the constitution. On the night of November 6, Ben Ali gathered a panel of doctors and experts to attest that the eighty-four-year-old Bourguiba was men-tally incapacitated and unable to fulfill his duties as president.

Tunisians woke on Saturday, November 7, 1987, to a message from Ben Ali announcing that he was assuming the presidency and command of the armed forces. The new president's first state-ment included pledges to increase political pluralism, end corrup-tion, and revamp the political system. At the same time, in contrast to Bourguiba's modern secular style, Ben Ali began his statement with the now commonplace Quranic expression of invocation and emphasized the Arab and Islamic character of the state. Ben Ali had established Tunisia's second republic and quickly set about rebuilding the power of the state while accelerating Tunisia's pro-gram of economic liberalization, external integration, and tourism development.

Restoring Stability: The Uses of Tourism in Ben Ali's Consolidation of Power

Across much of the political spectrum in Tunisia, Ben Ali's "medi-cal coup" was viewed with relief. Ben Ali's assumption of power, referred to as Le Changement (the Change), ended the uncertainty caused by Bourguiba's poor health and erratic behavior. It also seemed to put the country on a new path. The new president skill-fully defused the crisis with the Islamist movement by commuting some of the harsh sentences passed against the MTI members and made visible moves to reverse some of Bourguiba's policies of state secularization, for example, by having the call to prayer broadcast on government media. One of Ben Ali's first major political accom-plishments was to gather members of Tunisia's fractured and diverse civil society (excluding, however, the MTI) for open discussions leading to the signing of a "National Pact" on the first anniversary of Le Changement. Much of Tunisian society and many academic observers were hopeful about the prospects for democratization. A year after unprecedented criticism of the Tunisian government by the U.S. Congress, American observers were now optimistically noting that "a friendly country has been saved from probable chaos and set on the road to pluralism and economic openness."[62]

Tourism as Stability and Openness

A collapse of the tourism sector in the wake of the 1987 hotel bombings would have been devastating to the regime. A year before the coup, the seventh tourism development plan (1987–91) announced: "Today, the development of tourism in Tunisia has become an economic necessity to which there is little alternative. As a generator of foreign exchange, added value, and employment, the Tunisian tourism industry must be considered as a priority becoming one of the assets upholding the external equilibrium of the Tunisian economy."[63] Meanwhile, at the time of the coup, Tunisia was implementing the 1986 economic stabilization plan that many feared would exacerbate economic hardships and social tensions before economic growth could return to Tunisia. While Ben Ali defused the political crisis by displacing Bourguiba and making moves toward political liberalization, the revival of tourism played a critical role in his consolidation of power and Tunisia's ability to promote economic development and again project images of stability and openness.

Ben Ali discussed his interest in promoting tourism development at his first council of ministers meeting, only five days into the new era. He created a secretariat of state for tourism and appointed Ahmed Smaoui, an experienced tourism official, to head it. Within a year of taking office, Ben Ali created the freestanding Ministry of Tourism and Handicrafts and chose Mohamed Jegham as the country's first tourism minister. Jegham's experience in developing Tunisia's first major tourism resort complex, Port El Kantaoui, and his close ties to Ben Ali helped further increase the political profile and administrative clout of the tourism sector.

Through luck, good timing, and some rapid policy maneuvers, the year after Ben Ali assumed the presidency was a record tourism season. It was by far the largest Tunisia had ever seen, with tourism receipts totaling over TD 1 billion and representing almost 29 percent of all exports and over 13 percent of GNP.[64] Hotel occupancy rates reached 95 percent during the high season and averaged 62.3 percent for the year, up from around 45 percent for three of the previous five years. According to government estimates, the sector employed 45,000 and indirectly created jobs for nearly another 100,000. The income, revenues, and hard currency generated by the tourism recovery helped finance consumer subsidies, delayed the need to take another IMF loan, and sustained the economy through the transitional phase between the initial 1986 stabilization program and the more extensive liberalization and structural adjustment plan implemented in the mid-1990s.[65] Furthermore, the successful season set a course toward promoting tourism as a motor for development and projecting a positive image for the new regime.

Much of the success of the tourism season was due to exogenous factors such as the resumption of economic growth in northern Europe and the recent devaluation of the dinar. Nevertheless the new Ministry of Tourism publicly announced that tourism expanded significantly in 1988 because "the advent of 7 November ameliorated the external political image of Tunisia as well as gave confidence to tourism promoters and foreign visitors."[66] The success of the tourism season helped to consolidate the legitimacy and stability of the new regime by allowing Le Changement to appear to quickly make good on its promises to restart national economic development. In contrast to the dire warnings before the bomb blasts, in 1988 the EIU reported that "political and terrorist incidents in and around Tunisia do not seriously affect Tunisia's image as an attractive and relatively safe holiday location in the same mold of Spain, Greece, and Italy."[67] Even after the 1987 bomb blasts injured British and Italian tourists, Europeans continued to visit Tunisia in record numbers.

One policy possibly responsible for mitigating the negative effects of the bomb blasts was a new marketing campaign in Europe, planned before the coup, that sought to define Tunisia as a Mediterranean, rather than a Middle Eastern, destination.[68] This rebranding was coupled with limiting international media coverage of the bombing events and replacing such images three months later with those of a new political leader bent on returning order to the country while opening it up politically. At the same time, Ben Ali opened the door for a rapprochement between Tunisia and Libya, leading to the reopening of the border eight years after the Libyan-backed Gafsa insurrection. A majority of the increase in tourist arrivals to Tunisia in 1988 and much of the gain in tourism revenues were due to the opening of the border with Libya, which led to four thousand Libyan visitors a day "filling up hotels in the Sfax area."[69]

The return of political stability and the state's policy measures in the first year after the November 7 coup gave local and foreign investors and professionals in tourism reasons to expect the sector would now grow faster and generate stable profits. These measures included immediate steps to kick-start the tourism sector as well as signs from Ben Ali that the sector would receive active government involvement. Ahmed Smaoui, director of the ONTT, promoted investment in the tourism sector aided by the new tourism investment code enacted in 1986, which granted additional tax breaks to private investors.[70] International lending agencies and private investors were also encouraged by the successful privatization of the state's tourism assets.[71] Investment in the sector jumped from a low of TD 63 million in 1987 to TD 109 million in 1989 and soared to over TD 250 million by 1992.

Tourism as an Engine of Economic Growth

In a speech in May 1989, Tourism Minister Jegham outlined a new vision for how tourism could play a more vital role in national development and become an engine of economic growth.[72] He noted that tourism "can generate development in different sectors of production and services and play a fundamental role at the level of improving the basic infrastructure of the country as well as its urban fabric." To accomplish these development goals, Tunisia would have to diversify its tourism product by creating new sorts of tourism experiences. Such an effort would require greater exploitation of untouched swathes of Tunisian territory, such as the southern desert, the expanded tourist commodification of its culture, and the development of additional leisure activities such as hunting and boating. This direction signaled a shift from a heavy reliance on forms of tourism characterized by economic deterritorialization toward seeking to promote economic and cultural reterritorialization. The new policy envisioned the building of more theaters, museums, cinemas, and cultural and sporting centers, as well as improving and promoting archaeological sites to create new attractions. Together with product diversification, Tunisia would have to vastly upgrade the quality and amenities of its coastal tourism resorts, such that, in Jegham's words, Tunisia would eventually have "integrated tourism complexes that cause a stir across the Mediterranean and the world." These tasks would demand substantial financial resources and "a considerable effort, equally on the part of promoters, the banks, and the state to attain these objectives."[73]

Jegham's Ministry of Tourism governed the existing tourism-related institutions, including the ONTT, the Agence Foncière Touristique (AFT), and the Office National de l'Artisanat Tunisien (ONAT). Building on these institutions, tourism development would be directed and controlled by a growing number of state councils, institutions, and land management policies. In the 1990s tourism bureaucracies expanded their access to resources and influence within the wider circles of state power. In particular, the government expanded the ONTT's promotional budget, allowing the ONTT to station additional representatives abroad and launch more sophisticated marketing campaigns in foreign media markets.

As Hédi Mechri, a respected economic journalist, announced in 1989, "The blue gold [tourism] has dethroned the black gold [oil] and all the others."[74] Mechri reflected both government and private-sector views when he observed, "This infatuation [for tourism development] represents the new national spirit. . . . It constitutes henceforth the motor and the locomotive of the Tunisian economy."[75] The logic of the new policy direction was supported by trends in international tourism growth. In aggregate numbers, the period from 1987 to 1990 saw a revival of global tourism, with arrivals growing an average of 8 percent each year and receipts expanding by 20 percent per year.[76] This expansion reflected the reduction of cross-national barriers and costs of international travel caused by the decline of oil prices and the end of the Cold War. The expansion of business and leisure travel generated by the newly industrialized economies of East Asia also added to the figures. The director of marketing at the ONTT noted that "the expanding globalization of tourist activities, [and] the lowering of barriers, geographic as well as cultural, due to technological developments,"[77] were opening new markets for Tunisian tourism. He suggested that Tunisia should commit itself to a new promotional strategy with the goal of "seriously conquering" markets in North America, the Middle East, and Japan. While in the late 1980s and into the 1990s the value of the basic packaged beach vacation was declining in the markets of the advanced industrial economies, the emerging middle classes of East Europe offered a new market to exploit. Meanwhile travelers from across the advanced industrial economies increasingly sought out new cultural, heritage, and nature-based tourism experiences, for which Tunisia had considerable untapped resources. The new vision for tourism development was codified in the eighth national development plan, covering 1992 to 1996.[78] The national development strategy stated that "tourism has become an important industry generating a flow of foreign currency enabling a consolidation of Tunisia's policy of openness with regard to the outside world."[79]

Strategies of External Integration and Internal Control

In announcing his assumption of power, Ben Ali declared, "We have chosen, with firm conviction, to open our country to the outside world."[80] After consolidating power, he guided an overhaul of the Tunisian economy through the next two development plans, the seventh plan (1987–91) and the eighth plan (1992–96). The seventh plan focused on achieving macroeconomic stability, and the eighth sought to promote foreign investment, privatization, financial liberalization, and "closer integration of Tunisian trade into world, and especially European, markets."[81] As the World Bank would note about its *bon élève*, "In the mid-1980s Tunisia made the strategic choice to become a modern, market-oriented, and internationally integrated economy."[82]

Economic liberalization and integration under Ben Ali did not simply extend the *infitah* policies of the 1970s, which had contributed to the erosion of state control over the economy. Rather, Ben Ali proceeded by developing strategies to manage markets and development such that local and foreign private firms had the ability to find profitable opportunities while remaining dependent on state actions and policies. As Robert J. King argues, "The Tunisian state has encouraged market forces, but only through a bureaucratic-corporatist containment. . . . [It] liberalizes through its [own] institutions."[83] For example, many investment projects required special entitlements from the state and involved large sunk costs that increased the dependence of private capital on the state. Bradford Dillman notes that "foreign investors need to cooperate with state officials if they want the special entitlements that will allow their investments to reach fruition."[84] And in contrast to other states promoting economic globalization and visits by Western tourists, Tunisia has obstructed the rise of "brand-name" international franchises and as of 2008 remained without a single McDonald's restaurant.[85]

At the same time, the regime has been willing to forgo more fluid forms of investment, such as portfolio capital. As Clement Henry notes, Tunisia remains an "information-shy regime," constantly calibrating its economic policies to help its firms compete in global markets while remaining cautious of policies and technologies (such as the Internet) that might allow the private sector and the broader population to mobilize a more autonomous civil society.[86]

While many economic liberalization and structural adjustment policies have negative social consequences for vulnerable segments of society, Ben Ali's regime has skillfully sought to counter these. As Guilain Denoeux explains: "The regime has been shown capable of correcting a part of the important disequilibriums that had become apparent under Bourguiba, not only between social classes, but between cities and the countryside, between coastal and interior regions, and between the northeast of the country and the south and southwest."[87] One of the regime's tactics has been to create a national solidarity fund, commonly referred to by the account number 2626 to which donations to the fund are sent. This fund is used to support needy families, low-income housing, and development projects in the poor and underdeveloped "shadow zone" of Tunisia. Besides the highly personalized patronage effects of the aid, the image of state legitimacy is furthered by Ben Ali's frequent visits to these zones, creating numerous public-relations and photo opportunities for propagation by the national media.

New Regimes of Tourism Development, Image Making, and Territorial Control

Although tourism is only one element of the regime's strategy to open the nation to transnational flows while maintaining and expanding state control over society and economy, it has played a critical role as a site for the development of such means of rule. Following Ben Ali's consolidation of power in 1988, state officials continued to advocate a greater role for tourism development in shaping the ongoing structural transformation of the rules, institutions, and techniques used to govern territory and population. Accomplishing these tasks, in the context of changes in the global tourism economy, required that the tourism product continually be enhanced and further diversified. The state would have to promote new forms of tourism development—in particular, those that rely more heavily on place-specific cultural, heritage, and natural resources that could generate economic and cultural reterritorialization. These efforts also included the development and expansion of tourism complexes, such as Port El Kantaoui, which created enclave spaces that generate territorially based rents and positive external economies for the firms operating in them. State control over transnational networks and flows associated with tourism (from tourist spending to media reports and images of the country) relies on the ability of state agencies to govern territory and images of territory. As a result of these strategies, tourism development functions as a means to increase state power and widen state legitimacy. This has been done by more effectively mitigating regional disparities, by creating new private-sector and middle-class partners to bolster the state's fragmented political support, and by increasing state control over the construction and manipulation of icons, symbols, and cultural practices that shape the national identity of the state and its citizens.

Expanding Tourism Development into the South

Ben Ali demonstrated his commitment to diversifying Tunisian tourism at his first meeting of the council of ministers on November 12, 1987. He instructed state agencies to develop tourism in the southeast and offer incentives to investors to establish hotels and other facilities throughout the region.[88] Ben Ali seemed well aware that tourism development would be one of the fastest methods to create jobs and economic opportunities in the country's poorer rural regions.[89] Moreover, tourism in this desert area, home to many natural and cultural tourism resources, could augment the image of Tunisia by catering to an expanding market of tourists looking for new experiences.

The southwest quadrant of Tunisia is where the boundary of its national territory cuts into the northern edge of the Sahara. Inland from the eastern coast, the landscape consists of semidesert plains that merge into sand dunes and rocky hills. The desert is dotted with green patches of palm groves surrounding the numerous oases, including Tozeur, located along the large salt lake of Chott el Jerid. Regional development since the colonial era has mostly been limited to the mining operation at Gafsa, where a wage-labor force has long helped foster a labor movement. While state policies in the 1960s sought to create poles of development in several interior towns, the private sector expressed little interest in investing in this underdeveloped region. As a result, the region was progressively more marginalized.

The eighth national tourism development plan for 1992 to 1996 noted the need to create "thematic tourism products" and called, in particular, for making desert tourism *"le must"* of Tunisian tourism.[90] Tourist development in the south was Tunisia's first major effort to develop a market segment based on the commodification of a highly distinctive experience of place. The ONTT defined the new product, *le tourisme saharien,* to evoke romantic images of the desert popularized in Western books and films.[91] The label helps to exoticize the tourism product without demanding that the tourist have prior knowledge of Tunisia's cultural past or of the specific complex histories of the region. The ONTT brochure notes that the region now provides comfortable modern accommodations and welcomes "visitors who are eager to experience feelings of disorientation and exoticism."[92] Saharan tourism development also sought to promote opportunities for smaller-scale regional entrepreneurs. The government opened up parts of the desert near the Algerian border, otherwise considered a security zone, to certified firms so they could take tourists on four-wheel-drive "adventures" through the sand dunes. State agencies also developed new types of policies and promotional efforts that have since become common in other efforts to diversify the tourist product and its image. The eighth tourism development plan additionally called for "the adoption of architecture and decoration inspired by the local traditions and [the use of] motifs and materials from the region."[93] In contrast to the experience of development in many other parts of the country, tourism planners in the south have sought to maintain the traditional quality and characteristics of buildings and markets of old city centers so that they remain a draw for tourists.

To allow the Sahara to be programmed as part of international

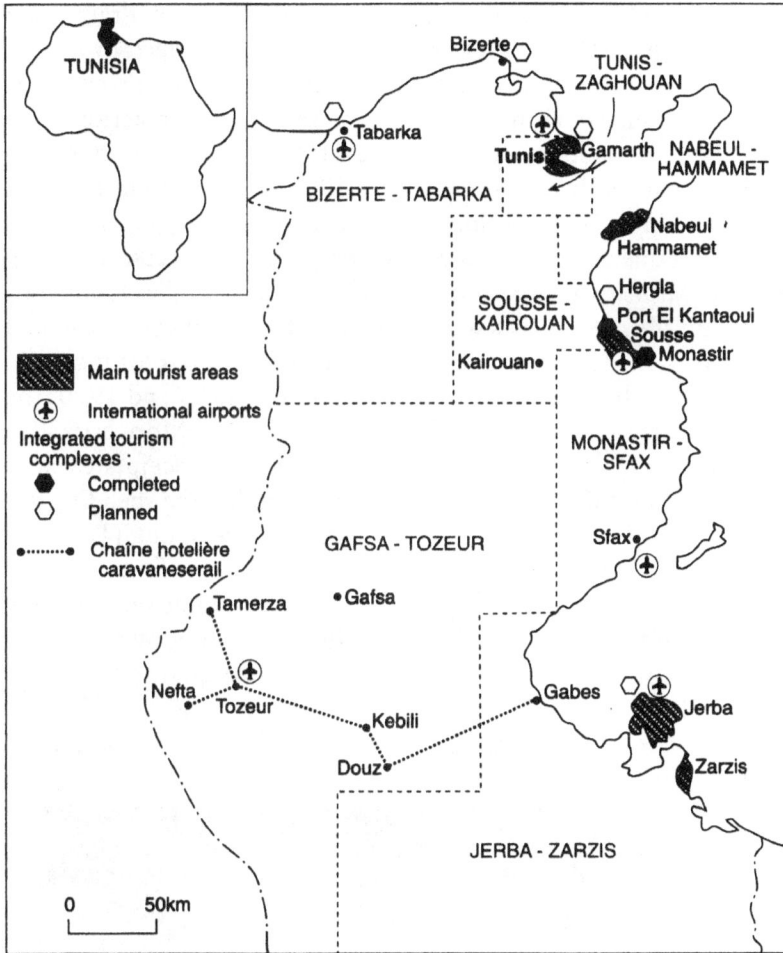

Figure 7. Map of regional tourism planning in Tunisia, 1992. Reprinted from Gant and Smith, "Tourism and National Development Planning in Tunisia"; reprinted with permission from Elsevier.

tours, a government building effort upgraded the airport at Tozuer for international flights and improved road access to the smaller towns. In 1989 the ONTT initiated a project to create the Chaîne Hôtelière Caravanesérail throughout southern Tunisia.[94] The state also built electricity connections for hotels and provided them with wells to supply their water needs.[95] On the edge of major towns across the Gafsa-Tozeur region, the AFT created *zones touristiques* with views of the outlying scenery in which the state agency acquired land to sell to hotel developers at much cheaper rates than other regions.[96] Hotel development was also encouraged by a large package of incentives, which demonstrated the state's commitment to seeing tourism flourish in the region. The reaction from local hotel developers was strong. By 1990, the region's hotel capacity expanded by two-thirds.[97] By 1991, in addition to the joint Tunisian–Arab Gulf development funds, almost 15 percent of the total investment in the sector was from foreign sources, including tour operators such as Neckerman, Thomson, Nouvelles Frontières, and Club Med.[98] Tourists were quick to take advantage of one- and two-day visits to the region, such that "while the total nights in residence declined nationally by 3% between 1988 and 1990, the Tozeur-Gafsa region recorded a 33% increase."[99] More critically, between 1987 and 1994, not only did tourism receipts expand from TD 14 million to almost TD 50 million, but the spending per tourist arrival also grew from TD 37 per night to about TD 64 per night.[100] Investment continued to expand, and in the first decade of growth, the region's hotel capacity "evolved in number and quality, passing from about 3,000 beds in 1987, consisting essentially of small hotels, to 10,000 in 1998, consisting of quality hotels offering all the facilities and features needed for long stays."[101] The region's share of national bed capacity climbed from 3 percent in

Figure 8. The Tamerza Palace hotel in southwestern Tunisia. Photograph by Patrick Frilet/hemis.fr.

1987 to 6 percent by 1995. According to the ONTT, tourism in the south generated 3,600 jobs directly and about 8,000 indirectly.

The growth of tourism in the south also increased the demand for locally produced handicrafts and agricultural products. The distinctive motifs found in crafts such as carpets and baskets help to define the new "brand" for Tunisian tourism. The local purchase of agricultural goods by visitors limits the profits skimmed off by distributors and bypasses protectionist efforts faced when exporting the same products. In particular, the sale of Tozeur's special variety of dates, called *deglet nur,* or "dates of light," contributes "to the continued well-being of oasis agriculture and may be more lucrative than export production which is becoming more difficult."[102] Some even claim that "the development of tourism in the south has not only halted the urban drift, it is attracting many young people back from the cities."[103] Mohamed Essayem, head of the southwest tourism sector, suggests, "With income from tourism . . . we have been able to win the war against desertification and multiply the agricultural output."[104] At the same time, however, tourism development will likely subject the region to many of the social impacts and economic distortions typically caused by tourists and shifting employment patterns.[105] These consequences might someday generate political reverberations domestically, but in the meantime the region continues to generate a positive and appealing external image for the country.

Tunisia in Film: Image Making and Tourism Marketing

After its initial spurt in the late 1980s, tourism development in the Tozeur region grew apace of that in Tunisia nationally. By 1997 the Saharan component came to play a broader role in fashioning a distinct place image for Tunisia in its marketing efforts. In November 1996 the movie *The English Patient* was released in the United States and soon became an international blockbuster. One of the major storylines is set in Egypt in the late 1930s. These scenes, however, were shot predominantly in locations throughout Tunisia. While numerous movies had been filmed in Tunisia (including Monty Python's *Life of Brian* and Spielberg's *Raiders of the Lost Ark*), *The English Patient* featured the stunning sand dunes of southern Tunisia while evoking, maybe better than any other film, the romantic, disorienting psychology commonly associated with the desert in European and American popular culture.

After the film won nine Academy Awards, the ONTT made a point of broadcasting the fact that the film was shot in Tunisia.[106] It began running ads in Europe with photos of the stars from the film kissing passionately next to a panoramic view of a sand dune landscape under the title *"The English Patient: A Tenth Oscar for the Tunisian Desert?"*[107] In the United Kingdom, the Dynamo Promotional Marketing agency was hired by the ONTT to "update its image" and ran ads with the tagline "More from the Mediterranean."[108] The ONTT and Dynamo worked with Foresight, the promoter of the film in the UK, to include a revised ONTT logo on *The English Patient* ads along with details for entering a sweepstakes offering a trip for two to Tunisia for a "desert excursion into *The English Patient* country." Some tour operators did more than use *The English Patient* as a marketing hook by organizing fan-oriented tours of the shooting locations. That year bookings from the UK and Ireland were up 30 percent, and the Tunisian Tourist Board was voted the "Best in the UK" by the trade magazine *Travel Weekly*. These techniques were later replicated for other national premieres of *The English Patient* as well as used for other films shot in Tunisia. The timing of the film's European release and the Academy Awards broadcast together with the successful marketing campaign helped Tunisian tourism rebound after declines in real tourist receipts of 5 percent in 1995 and 1 percent in 1996 to achieve a 10 percent growth in 1997.

As popular as *The English Patient* was at the time, the most celebrated and popular films shot in Tunisia remain those of the *Star Wars* saga. George Lucas, the creator and executive producer of the movies, had first come to Tunisia in 1976 to shoot the original *Star Wars* feature (later retitled *Episode IV: A New Hope*). Both the sand dunes and aspects of vernacular architecture and dress from the southern desert regions were used to create Tatooine, the distant home world of Luke Skywalker. In Tunisia, the marketing experience of *The English Patient* was soon followed by the filming of the *Star Wars* prequel *Episode I: The Phantom Menace*. Many European tour operators running *The English Patient* tours were able to quickly convert them into *Star Wars* tours when *The Phantom Menace* was released.[109] Roads built by the film crew to facilitate access to the locations of several shoots and even many of the papier-mâché sets such as the one for "Mos Espa," the spaceport from *The Phantom Menace*, were left standing "due to the popularity of the *Star Wars* films and what the Tunisian tourist board sees as an opportunity for business."[110] Even before the making of the prequel films, a generation of fans has visited Tunisia and trekked to the south to make a circuit of *Star Wars* filming locations. While *Star Wars* tourism is a small niche market, many destinations in the Tunisian south, such as the troglodyte underground dwellings at Matmata, are usually identified in the tourism literature by their association with the *Star Wars* films. In other words, the films have helped in fashioning Tunisia's place-myth for contemporary tourists who have little knowledge of the culture and history of the indigenous communities in the Tunisian south.

The Expansion of Tourism Complexes

While the development of Saharan tourism allowed Tunisia to begin to diversify its tourist image and spread the benefits of tourism, the main focus of the state's efforts in the 1990s consisted of extending and replicating the model of the integrated tourism complex first developed at Port El Kantaoui. The tourism complex became the framework through which Tunisian tourism was diversified and expanded while the state continued to exert influence over patterns of development and the overall product and its external image. Tunisia was seeking to refashion its image from a cheap mass beach tourism destination into a more sophisticated, upmarket Mediterranean destination that could better compete with the tourism complexes along the northern side of the Mediterranean. As Radhouane Ben Salah, president of the Tunisian Hotel Federation, explains, "We are looking for the jet-set."[111]

Integrated tourism complexes were key to the revitalization of beach resorts in southern Europe and the Mediterranean islands. By the 1990s, complexes along the northern Mediterranean grew in size and sophistication, so that Port El Kantaoui looked small and dated in comparison. These new complexes were self-contained spaces that offered many specialized facilities, services, and experiences. These typically included larger, more luxurious hotel complexes with gourmet restaurants, extensive athletic and sporting facilities, health spas, boutiques, specialty shops, conference facilities, and a variety of entertainment establishments. Some even included medical facilities and cultural institutions such as museums. In contrast, the standardized beach resort of the 1960s and 1970s offered stripped-down, generic features such as dining halls serving buffet meals and hotel disco rooms blaring canned music. In a Fordist manner, those mass-produced features allowed resorts to capture economies of scale and offer lower prices to gain more volume. Several scholars have suggested that the transformation of the mass tourism markets in the late 1970s represented something of a "crisis of Fordism" in which vertically integrated firms found themselves unable to sustain their business model as tourists sought differentiated and specialized experiences, characterized by "post-Fordist consumption" and more segmented markets.[112] However, as Rebecca Torres argues, tourism complexes—like many large firms—have been able to adapt to these shifting markets.[113] In addition to continuing to supply standard beach tourism experiences, within or near their complexes, small firms supplement these larger-scale experiences with diverse, small-scale "post-Fordist" offerings such as specialized tours to archaeological sites or facilities for medical treatment, which cater to only a small segment of visitors. As a result, these resorts can be viewed as "neo-Fordist" forms of tourism, like theme park attractions, which can mass-customize diverse visitor experiences within the same space.

This broad range of experiences is facilitated by the way the integrated complex turns the spatial logic of mass beach tourism inside out. Simple beach hotels are focused outward, toward the sea, as their touristic value is based on their proximity to the beach. By controlling this limited resource, they extract rents from tourists who value the experience of sand, sun, and sea. The integrated complex, in contrast, is mostly focused inward. While proximity to the beach and other tourist attractions may be important, the added value is constructed in large part by the quality and variety of features and services provided within the enclave of the resort itself. This shift in focus alters the territorial dynamics of tourism development. In the linear beach model, each new developer generally finds a location down the coast from existing developments in a recognized tourist zone. In contrast, integrated complexes require that all elements be decided on ahead of time, giving the planner considerable power to extract rents from potential developers and service providers seeking the locational value accorded to the facilities within the complex. Even when projects are undertaken by private developers, state control over territorial resources, planning processes, and financing sources gives a range of state agencies considerable ability to shape the nature of these projects. The creation of tourism complexes has the potential to create and extract rents, but with the integration of auxiliary services and activities, the complexes also generate positive external economies from the flow of tourists in the hotels. While the income generated from these flows may be termed "externalities" from the point of view of each firm, the developer of the complex might also own (and possibly also manage) these firms or rent space to others and thus indirectly capture the benefits created. As Tim Mitchell explains in the context of changes in patterns of tourism development in Egypt:

> Managers seek to increase their profit by channeling more and more tourist expenditure within their own establishments. The grand Egyptian hotels that used to provide little more than accommodation and a dining room have been replaced by complexes that offer three or four restaurants, several bars, shopping arcades, a swimming pool and fitness club, cruises and excursions, business facilities, and evening lectures and entertainment.[114]

Moreover, the self-contained nature of the complexes helps to isolate the negative social, cultural, and environmental impacts. Creating more distinct and isolated enclave spaces for tourism became important as the government, in an effort to appease conservative religious and cultural attitudes, began restricting alcohol sales, gambling by Tunisian nationals, and the opening times of cafés during Ramadan. In addition, the ability to generate positive external economies within its own self-contained space enables a complex to be built in a diverse range of locations—including those that have yet to draw international tourists—allowing the state to create tourism-related employment in underdeveloped regions. The complexes provided the backbone of the effort to expand hotel capacity. By 2001 Ben Ali oversaw the doubling of Tunisian capacity since 1987. With a concerted focus on luxury hotels, by 2002 half of all capacity and bed nights was in the four- to five-star range.

The effort to promote regional development is best exemplified by the building of the most isolated complex located in the northwestern coastal town of Tabarka, which sits close to the Algerian border. The northwest region is one of the least developed regions of Tunisia. The government built a new airport and invested heavily in other infrastructure works, such as roads and water supply. Like Port El Kantaoui, the Montazah Tabarka project is a self-contained *zone touristique* that was planned to include a number of more expensive hotels amounting to ten thousand beds, a yachting harbor, a golf course, and facilities for diving and fishing. The project is a joint venture between the state and the Kuwait Development bank, and tourism planners also envisioned that the complex would be an "economic and political pole" anchoring regional ecological and cultural tourism activities and providing hotel jobs as well as work for local handicraft manufacturers.[115]

Another major tourism project of the 1990s was Cap-Gammarth, situated on a cape just past the wealthy suburbs on the far north side of Tunis, where many foreigners live and well-to-do Tunisians have summer villas.[116] After many years of delay, the project was revived by a Saudi businessman. The initial design of the complex included a large five-star hotel, an apartment hotel, a health and sports center, a beach club, a casino, and a Las Vegas–style theater for live shows. The project is a joint venture of Tunisian, Kuwaiti, and Saudi Arabian investors and was initially managed by the American Cleopatra's World casino and resort operator. By 2000 several hotels were built, and a Tunisian-Singaporean venture was adding a conference center and a sports and leisure complex with a golf course and marina. The expansion of Cap-Gammarth was also to include a film center and a large nature park. Gammarth was built in proximity to Tunis, which until the 1990s had played a limited role in national tourism development planning.

Since the 1960s, the bulk of tourism remained the packaged beach type, though Tunis did attract a small share of culturally oriented tourists. These numbers, however, remained too small for the government to devote much time and effort toward heritage preservation and museum development. While tourists often visited the city—especially to see the medina, Carthage ruins, Sidi Bou Said, and the Bardo Museum—most would quickly move on to other locations. In was only in the late 1990s that the government sought to adequately protect the ruins of ancient Carthage (located in a suburb of Tunis) from erosion and encroachment, begin a new wave of excavations, and renovate the Carthage archaeological park.[117]

The Gammarth project was an effort to promote a tourism complex within the Tunis region that could expand the role of the capital in tourism development as well as attract higher-spending tourists by providing an exclusive vacation stop for those visiting Tunis as part of a leisure holiday or business trip. Moreover, the

Gammarth complex is also close enough to the capital to function as a business hotel and conference center or host parties held by local business and government elites. As hotels with golf courses were built, Tunisia entered the niche market for golf tourism. While adding a more sophisticated "country club" image to the tourism product, this also attracts business and conference tourism and allows Tunisia to better welcome prospective foreign investors, especially those from North America. The efforts to appeal to *haut de gamme* tourism increased as the tourism economy recovered from the impact of 9/11, the April 2002 attack on the old synagogue on Jerba, and the U.S. invasion of Iraq. In 2004 the minister of tourism declared that *hotels de charme* are a priority, and cosmopolitan gourmet restaurants began to appear in Tunis and elsewhere.[118]

The third major project built during the 1990s was the massive Yasmine-Hammamet complex. The tourism zone Hammamet-Sud is located ten kilometers down the coast from the main center of Hammamet and its long string of hotels spread along the beach. With an understanding of the aesthetic and environmental damage inflicted by the poor planning, run-down hotels, and dirty beaches that marred the Hammamet-Nebeul region, the development of Hammamet-Sud was part of a program to reshape the built environment of the region with "the goal of creating an integrated and harmonious tourism zone."[119] Yasmine-Hammamet, planned to be Tunisia's largest tourism complex with over forty hotels and hundreds of apartment units, will have the capacity to accommodate up to thirty thousand residents and visitors.[120] As one travel writer notes, stretched along the boulevards of the complex are "47 Las Vegas–style themed hotels. Here you can stay in mock-Roman opulence, in a pseudo-Greek temple or a Moorish theme park with hookah pipes and Turkish baths, all safely controlled by security guards and electronic gates."[121] The complex also includes a shopping center, marina, golf course, and clubhouse. Cleopatra's World was tapped to run a hotel-entertainment center with a theater and casino capable of hosting large gatherings and concerts. The state-of-the-art conference center was intended to host large international gatherings. With the hope that the venture would launch Tunisia into the deluxe tourism circuit of the global jet set, the first units built were five-star "palaces," some of the most luxurious ever built in Tunisia, with most of the other hotels expected to be four or five stars.[122] Targeting upscale tourists is an attempt to create on the

southern shore of the Mediterranean a French Riviera–style destination. In 2004 the Médina casino was inaugurated with a gathering of the "European, Arab, and African jet set," complete with
diplomats and movie stars. The developer's ambition is to make
Tunisia a destination known for quality facilities and "shine a light
on Tunisian tourism and glorify the image of the country."[123]

The complex is also notable for its efforts to develop cultural
and entertainment features not yet found across North Africa. Its
Médina Mediterranea commercial and entertainment complex is
built, according to its designer, in the style of an Arab *medina,*
with architectural re-creations that trace the history of Tunisia
and the Mediterranean from the Punic era through Arabo-Islamic
and Andalusian influences. Much of the project is the brainchild of
Abdelwahab Ben Ayed, who dreamed of reconstructing a medieval
city "with active souks, authentic artisan workshops, multicolored
fondouks that could transport [tourists] out of familiar surround-
ings and allow them to rediscover with the Tunisians their identity."[124] For a small admission fee, the Médina presents a pseudo-
public space filled with music, film, and other artistic activities. There
is also a religious museum that incorporates Christian, Muslim,
and Jewish teachings, as well as the family-oriented Carthagoland,

Figure 9. Entrance to the Médina Mediterranea complex at Yasmine-
Hammamet. Photograph by Isabelle Simon/Sipa Press.

a Disney-like theme park replete with educational activities. Ben Ayed notes, "We wish to make Tunisia a center for cultural and tourist radiance for all the Mediterranean. . . . Let us not forget that Hannibal wanted to link together all the circumference of the Mediterranean."[125] The Médina Mediterranea represents a neo-Fordist form of tourism development that can be centrally managed and controlled within the space of a tourism enclave well integrated into transnational flows of capital, peoples, and images.

Tourism and the Uses of Culture

Under Ben Ali, the regime also began articulating the view that developing cultural resources is necessary to counter the threat of cultural globalization. Mohammed Ghannouchi, a minister in charge of foreign investment, stated, "Culture is key to coping with any external crises or challenges our country may face."[126]

While the lack of cultural tourism had allowed the sector to languish, Tunisia has more recently begun showing great concern for its cultural heritage with the formation of groups like the Association Sauvegarde de la Medina, which gained outside funding to conserve sections of the Tunis *medina*.[127] In the 1990s, the government passed laws to protect and conserve cultural heritage, and in 1997 it created the Agence de Mise en Valeur du Patrimoine et de la Promotion Culturelle (APPC) "with the objective of enhancing historic and archeological sites for tourism development."[128] Not only would developing these resources expand the country's ability to tap into a growing segment of the global tourism economy that generally produces higher revenues, but cultural tourism could also bring income to smaller inland towns and create jobs for a wider range of Tunisians such as craftsmen, artists, and guides.

The advocates of cultural and heritage tourism see it as a means to combat the threats of cultural globalization. By valuing cultural heritage in this way, more funds and effort are put into heritage conservation, which helps limit the impact of uncontrolled tourism and other forms of development near sensitive sites. In 2001 the World Bank granted Tunisia a loan to protect several of its cultural heritage sites (including archaeological ruins, museums, and religious centers) and better prepare them for tourism. The government increased its cultural affairs spending to over 1 percent of its total budget. The state built a new national library, revamped and opened new museums, and organized more exhibitions and festivals.[129] These cultural programs can serve to augment the country's tourist image, but they are also part of creating a greater public awareness of the state's vision of Tunisian cultural heritage, especially though school tours.

While many of these projects seek to expand tourism revenues and protect cultural resources with tourism value, these projects also represent a dovetailing of tourism development and image making with national identity formation and mythmaking. The effort to promote the Carthaginian military commander Hannibal, who marched his army over the Alps into Italy during the Second Punic War, as a national "mascot" best exemplifies this convergence.[130] As highlighted in the Carthagoland theme park and ONTT brochures and advertisements, Hannibal has become an important element of the Tunisian "brand" used to mark a distinctive, territorially rooted identification for the nation's external image. At the same time, on the domestic front, the promotion of Hannibal as a national hero and icon has been stage-managed by the government, in part as a means to counter efforts by Islamists to encourage Tunisians to identify exclusively with Islam and the Arab world. The image of Hannibal is used to promote a diverse, pluralistic Tunisian identity with a seemingly authentic local resonance, though Tunisians have not typically embraced Hannibal as a nationalist figure or direct ancestor.

Official efforts to project this "modern" identity and external image, however, often amount to state-managed forms of cultural production. They sometimes generate opposition from historians, archaeologists, and cultural heritage preservationists who view the state as intruding into their realms of professional knowledge.[131] One way to contain the erosion of state control over the process of mythmaking is to develop state-sponsored institutions and scholars. In addition to the development of Hannibal-related memorials, most notably at Carthage, a central element of this effort is the formation of officially sanctioned Hannibal Clubs dedicated to understanding and promoting the legacy of the figure. Hannibal Clubs have also been established overseas, generally with the help of the local Tunisian embassy, and used as a context to recruit and celebrate friends of Tunisia. The clubs often seek to present Hannibal not as a nationalist military leader (who, in the end, provoked Rome's crushing defeat of Carthage) but as a figure of world history who represents universal values and can help promote cultural bridges, trade, and tourism. In establishing the Hannibal Club USA, Ambassador Noureddine Mejdoub, an artist himself, emphasized that Hannibal's legacy was not war and conquest but the "promotion of commercial relations around the shores of Mediterranean."[132]

Efforts to promote commercial relations around the Mediterranean took an ambitious turn in the 1990s with the development of the Oslo peace process and the U.S.-backed effort to promote the economic integration of Israel into the Middle East (explored in chapter 3). The Tunisian government has long affirmed that Muslim Tunisia maintained relatively tolerant relations with its Jewish community. Many Tunisian-born Jews, however, have felt that postcolonial Tunisia, especially after 1967, failed to fully integrate its Jewish community into what came to be defined as an Arab state.[133] The Oslo process and the seeming decline of the Arab-Israeli conflict opened a new window of opportunity between Tunisia and Israel, states with no formal diplomatic relations. Tunisian officials soon began making an effort to encourage and facilitate visits by Israelis and Jews with Tunisian roots. In 1993 the Tunisian foreign minister even expressed to a visiting Jewish leader from the United States that he thought there was "a major tourist market for American Jews anxious to uncover ancient Jewish roots in exotic Tunisia."[134]

External Openness, Internal Control: The Paradoxes of Tunisian Globalization

While images of a "clash of civilizations" and discussions about the Arab world's failure to embrace economic globalization have come to frame much of the Euro-American media coverage of the region, two decades after Ben Ali came to power and set the country on a new course, Tunisia is often presented as the region's economic success story, the place where efforts to realize European-style modernization have found their most fertile terrain.[135] In a recent travelogue, the iconoclastic political commentator Christopher Hitchens recounts the country's socioeconomic achievements, which include a high rate of home ownership, legal rights for women, and a globally competitive, externally oriented economy.[136] Hitchens briefly notes that President Zine El Abidine Ben Ali would soon celebrate his twentieth year of unchallenged rule and that Ben Ali's election victories claiming over 90 percent of the vote make the writer nervous. But these concerns are soon pushed aside as Hitchens praises Ben Ali's "guiding . . . hand." In his portrayal of Tunisia as "an enclave of development . . . menaced by the harsh extremists of a desert religion" that plague other Arab states, Hitchens likens Ben Ali's rule to an African version of Gaullism and credits it for creating an "outwardly happy and thriving society."

Hitchens's essay resembles American Cold War–era approaches to understanding the region. He evaluates political change in Ben Ali's Tunisia in terms of the regime's efforts to promote manifestations of modernity in the face of what Hitchens views as the antimodern threat of Islamic extremism. Such an approach effectively condones increasing authoritarian forms of rule while reflecting the broader post–9/11 abandonment of the early post–Cold War narrative, found on both the left and the right, of how market reform and external economic integration generate pressures for political liberalization and democratization. More troubling, the essay, based on Hitchens's visit to Tunisia and its tourist sites, functions to sustain Tunisia's external image of openness and obscure its internal regime of authoritarian control. Such a reading hints at the broader role that international tourism has come to play in Tunisian state building under Ben Ali. It is part of an adept strategy by the regime for advancing economic liberalization and embracing globalization while constructing little more than a facade of political openness.

Under Ben Ali, Tunisia has become ever more open to, and integrated with, the networks of the global economy. By generating flows of tourists and capital across the Mediterranean, the state's tourism development efforts have played a critical role in shaping this process. Increased marketing and efforts to diversify the Tunisian tourism product helped to expand tourism revenues by over 60 percent (in real terms) between 1990 and 2000.[137] While embracing Tunisia's Arab and Islamic character, Ben Ali has simultaneously sought to define Tunisia's path toward globalization as a bridging of distances across the Mediterranean through economic flows as well as the projection of a pluralistic, Mediterranean-based cultural identity. The result of these efforts is well represented by a visit to the postmodern Médina Mediterranea, where diverse elements of Tunisia's Mediterranean identities are brought together within a space exposed to the gaze of international tourists and sustained by the flows of the hard currency they bring. This space of "openness," however, is like the pseudo-public space of a theme park or shopping mall. It is a space of control, one that is politically managed rather than defined by the actions and interests of autonomous agents. In other words, representations of Tunisia's external openness, programs of economic liberalization, and its embrace of global integration belie the domestic regime of control that directs integration processes. As discussed in chapters 4 and 5, this paradoxical form of openness also characterizes patterns of development in Egypt, Jordan, Lebanon, and the Gulf as they also seek to use tourism development as a means to promote global economic integration though the construction of enclave spaces where state authorities maintain the ability to manage the transnational flows of people, capital, and images.

It was soon after Ben Ali consolidated the power of his regime that the moment of internal political openness and pluralism ended. By the early 1990s, political liberalization and reform were abandoned in an all-out effort to crush the Islamist movement after the outbreak of clashes with Islamist activists. These confrontations began in the context of Algeria's descent into civil war. Tunisia's external orientation made the economy especially vulnerable to being tarnished by any association with the violence next door. Civil freedoms and civil society were soon sacrificed to this internal war. The regime banked on the middle classes, the Left, women's rights activists, and the trade union movements to support the government and marginalize the Islamist challenge from mainstream support.[138] Meanwhile Ben Ali moved aside the old guard of the Parti Socialiste Destourien (PSD) and renamed it the Rassemblement Constitutionnel Démocratique (RCD) while expanding its base through a recruitment drive. While periodic elections continued to take place, they occurred in an environment where Ben Ali's forces had eliminated all traces of autonomy and divergence in the trade union leadership, the existing opposition political parties, the press, and all other civil society organizations, such as the Ligue Tunisienne des Droits de l'Homme.

Moreover, state control over society was expanded through the introduction of a *mukhabarat* (security police) state where the number of police increased from 20,000 during Bourguiba's last days to 80,000 ten years later.[139] Unlike other police states with closed economic systems in the region, throughout Tunisia's period of political deliberalization, the regime has continued to articulate a discourse of pluralism, democracy, and openness that supplements its cosmopolitan tourist image.[140] Tunisia can support an image of "openness" by reference to its maintenance of progressive personal-status laws, social programs such as the 2626 efforts, its enthusiastic support for negotiating free trade agreements with the European Union (and later the United States), and its constant expansion of tourist visitors and investment capital. At the same time, however, the state's authoritarian power is likely to be far more stable than in other Arab states more often referred to as police states in the Western media.

Not long after Ben Ali's regime of authoritarian control was established in the early 1990s, the European Union (EU) embarked on a process with its southern neighbors across the sea to forge a series of cooperation agreements seeking to create a zone of peace and prosperity. The EU states had a particular interest in promoting economic development to help stem the tide of (illegal) immigration. Many were also concerned that poor economic conditions would create an environment conducive to a militant Islamist movement. Following the EU-Mediterranean Barcelona declaration in 1995, Tunisia became the first state to sign an "association agreement" with the EU. It marked a new phase of development as Tunisia committed to economic reform, a full embrace of economic globalization, and a complete dismantling of tariff barriers by 2010. To ready Tunisian businesses, the state instituted a *mise à niveau* program in which firms receive government support to upgrade and modernize in order to successfully compete internationally. While many small, labor-intensive firms emerged in the 1970s, by the 1990s Tunisian firms were no longer able to achieve comparative advantages through lower wages and needed to increase skill and technology levels. Firms had to create internationally competitive goods or else provide the subcontracting operations needed by European firms in the high-tech, business services, and flexible-manufacturing sectors. In 2005 Slim Tatli, the manager of the industrial *mise à niveau* program, was appointed secretary of state at the tourism ministry and charged with developing a *mise à niveau* program for the hotel sector to be funded by Arab and French development agencies.

The *mise à niveau* program, however, represents another expression of the country's paradoxical globalization. It promotes economic integration and external openness, but via a process managed by state agencies. The result is a highly filtered form of openness in which, to avoid the effects of the 1970s *infitah,* the nation prioritizes maintaining social order over private-sector autonomy and the spread of new ideas and methods. In the program, assistance generally comes at the price of closer monitoring and dependence on, and direction from, state institutions. As Jean-Pierre Cassarino argues, "For the private sector the program represents a selective adjustment. . . . Its purpose is not to rescue business concerns as a whole, but to buttress the ability of a select number of private firms to survive international competition, by modernizing and optimizing their production lines, developing vocational training, and promoting their export capacity."[141] The state has encouraged the development of Tunisian conglomerates by a set of captains of industry because they can best gain economies of scale and acquire new production technologies needed for surviving increased trade liberalization. Politically, Cassarino explains, "by mobilizing the 'Captains' of these corporate groups, it enhances its control over economic liberalization, in the interest of securing social order."[142] After listing some of the captains of Tunisian industry, Cassarino notes, "It has to be said, however, that the most emblematic figure of the 'Captains' is perhaps 'Aziz Milad, who manages one of the most profitable private export-businesses in Tunisia, namely Tunisian Travel Service (TTS)."[143]

These trade-offs are ones that businessmen and entrepreneurs in Tunisia are generally willing to make.[144] The result, however, is that as Tunisia becomes more closely integrated into European and American marketplaces, its political economy remains constricted by the surveillance of an increasingly authoritarian state. Although Tunisia had long been considered one of the most open states in the Arab world, with a rich history as a meeting point for intellectual and cultural flows across the Mediterranean, by 2000 the *Economist* was suggesting that "with the exception of Syria and Libya, Tunisia has the most closed society on the Mediterranean."[145] These forms of control are evident in the tourism sector, where hotel operators are required to be sure that any meeting held in their facilities has been approved by the proper authorities. The ubiquitous police lining the roads and highways and intersections keep a close eye on travelers and will often redirect cars that are not tourist vehicles away from tourist complexes. Many tourists don't seem to mind. Especially in the wake of the wave of attacks against tourists in Egypt in the 1990s, and the 2002 bombing of a synagogue in Jerba, tourists are likely to welcome the added security. Tourists who stay within the confines of their seemingly cosmopolitan enclaves or do not wander off from their group tours might not even notice. As an American travel writer noted in an essay for *Condé Nast Traveler* touting Tunisia's makeover as a luxury destination for cultural tourists, "Largely invisible to tourists, the police-state machinery is impressively efficient."[146] Nor have these political changes yet hampered the country's external image of openness, modernity, and cosmopolitanism. As long as visitors such as Christopher Hitchens—impressed by the country's "stylish females," "clean streets," and "efficient taxis"—continue to view the Tunisian "success story" in terms of "an enclave of development . . . menaced by the harsh extremists of a desert religion,"[147] tourism development and tourist flows in Tunisia will continue to sustain the country's march along the path of paradoxical globalization.

3. The Geopolitics of Tourism and the Making of the New Middle East

While a tourism map of the Levant indicates a region replete with religious and cultural heritage sites, picturesque landscapes, and magnificent archaeological ruins, its tourism industries have long been hampered by regional conflict, political instability, and inward-oriented authoritarian states. As elsewhere, tourism development in the region is inextricably linked with its geopolitics. Since the 1948 Arab-Israeli war, not only have tourist flows between Israel and the Arab world been impeded by the ongoing conflict, but even regional flows between Arab states often suffer from geopolitical rivalries. The 1967 war dealt a devastating blow to Jordan as Israel took over what had been Jordan's main Holy Land attractions in Jerusalem and the West Bank. In Lebanon, the 1975–90 civil war and Israeli invasions in 1978 and 1982 further shattered the market for the regional circuit tours organized out of Beirut. Previously, cosmopolitan Beirut attracted both Arab and Western tourists who knew the country as the leisure "playground" of the Middle East.[1]

I begin this chapter by tracing the efforts of Jordan to develop a tourism sector within the context of the geopolitically fragmented Middle East. To explain the connections between tourism and geopolitics, I examine the ways in which the fragmentation of tourism economies across the Levant reflects a realist-territorial geopolitical imaginary that has shaped international relations and

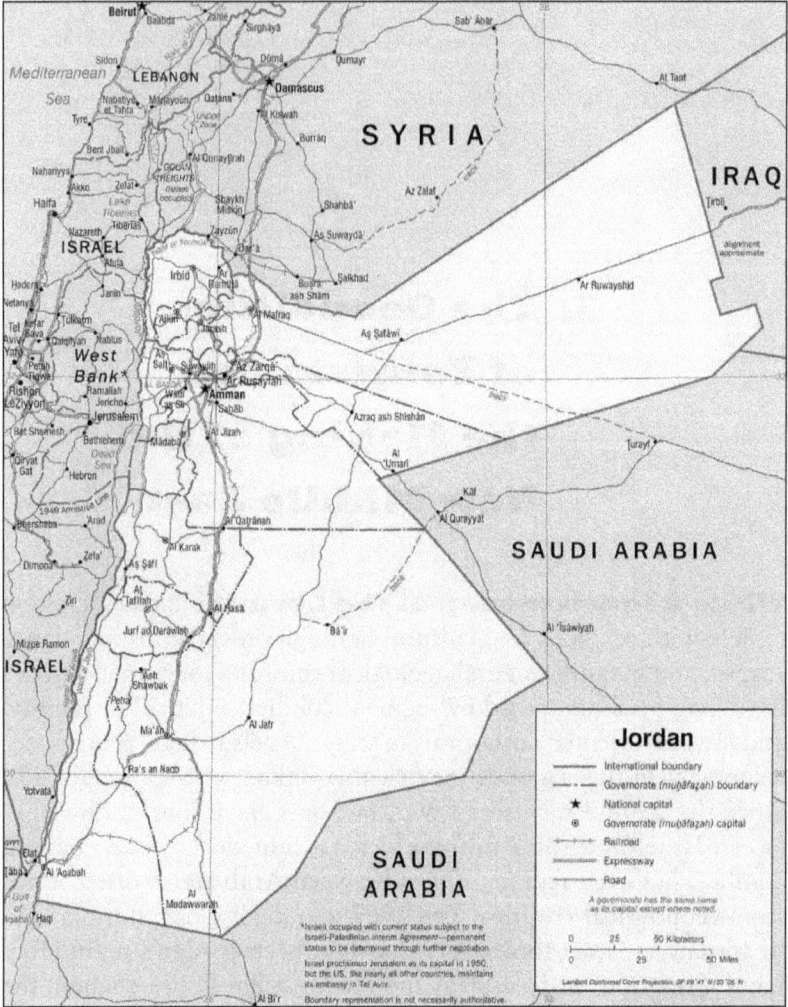

Figure 10. Map of Jordan, 2004. CIA map courtesy of the University of Texas Libraries, University of Texas at Austin.

state building within the region. As noted in the introduction, geopolitical imaginaries describe how actors "read" the impact of transnational flows and their political implications differently. The realist-territorial imaginary is defined by states that are concerned primarily with defensible borders, power accumulation, and potential threats posed by other states in a system of anarchy. A cohesive national identity, rooted to national territory, is considered essential to maintaining state legitimacy and domestic political order, while inward flows are viewed as a potential liability unless they serve to augment relative power. Syrian policy after the 1967 war and the 1970 crisis in Jordan exemplified this geopolitical imaginary when it closed its airspace to Jordanian flights and even banned American, British, and West German tourists not traveling on official government tours.[2] The regime also refused to detain and extradite the hijackers of Western airliners. Eventually Syria lifted the travel ban, not because it was seeking economic ties or friendly relations with these countries but because the regime decided it needed tourism as a source of hard currency. As the *New York Times* put it, the Baathist regime in Syria was not trying "to be nice"; rather, Defense Minister Hafez al Assad wanted "to buy new toys for his army."[3] Even when Israel and Egypt signed a peace treaty that opened their border to flows of goods, people, and ideas, the two states continued to define their policies and behavior toward each other, including those related to tourism development and tourism flows, through the realist-territorial geopolitical imaginary resulting in a territorial dispute and the politicization of tourism flows.

In Jordan, while international tourism flows were hampered by regional politics, tourism policy often operated domestically as a tool for state building by helping the Hashemite monarchy define a national identity for the country and support its own claim to rule.

The reemergence of the Arab-Israeli peace process in the early 1990s, however, radically transformed the country's tourism development efforts. In the wake of the Oslo Accords between Israel and the PLO in 1993, Israel and Jordan signed a peace treaty and negotiated a pathbreaking regional framework for economic cooperation and tourism development. Jordan and Israel opened their border to tourist traffic and planned joint projects in an effort to remake the regional tourism economy. Supported by international aid, Jordan sought to transform its tourism industry into an engine for national economic development as part of its promotion of economic liberalization and global economic integration. Increasingly, the government and private entrepreneurs worked to convert more of Jordan's cultural heritage and natural landscapes into commodities for the international tourism economy.

At first glance, this shift in tourism development strategy may simply appear as a *consequence* of the shift in geopolitics, the product of the new policies Jordan chose to maximize its security and economic interests. I argue, however, that tourism development was a *constituent* element of this geopolitical transformation and that the politics of tourism remain a critical, yet unexplored, factor in shaping the peace process and its ultimate consequences. The geopolitical transition of the peace process marked the rise of a new imaginary that came to frame the behavior of policy makers, strategists, and businesspeople in Israel, the United States, and Jordan. Proponents of the vision of the so-called New Middle East argued that peace between Israel and the Arab states could generate mutual economic benefits that would solidify closer interstate relations by forging shared material and strategic interests between the governments and their respective private sectors and societies. While most Arab states and societies remained skeptical of this vision, under American guidance the New Middle East defined the framework for an Israeli-Jordanian peace treaty in 1994 and a multilateral program of regional economic cooperation. For Jordan, the New Middle East offered an itinerary for securing economic and strategic support from the United States, promoting national economic development, and realizing prosperity for its people within a new regional geopolitical environment. In Jordan's effort to transform its economy while promoting regional and global integration, the New Middle East functioned in the way that Mark Blyth suggests: "Economic ideas make it possible for agents to [seemingly] reduce uncertainty by acting as interpretive frameworks that describe and systematically account for the working of the economy."[4]

While much has been written about the politics of the Arab-Israeli peace process, I highlight the critical role that tourism played in Jordan's peacemaking and the rise (and eventual fall) of the New Middle East. In short, without tourism, the notion of the New Middle East would not have been imaginable. Most observers and participants in the peace process expected the first phase of the New Middle East to be realized quickly in the tourism sector, demonstrating its benefits and feasibility. Even those skeptical of the New Middle East vision were able to envision the rise of regional economic cooperation within the tourism sector and assumed a boom would follow a peace treaty. Promoted by Jordanian officials, private investors, and the international community, the idea that the peace treaty and normalization of relations with Israel would result in rapid and broad-based economic dividends from tourism development allowed King Hussein to move Jordan toward peace with Israel in 1994 in the face of much latent domestic opposition. Without the imagined potential of tourism development, domestic opposition would have mobilized faster and more broadly to challenge the treaty and U.S. efforts to promote a New Middle East.

In tracing the emergence of the New Middle East, this chapter and the next consider not only the role of state elites and those socialized through state-to-state interactions but also the actions and discourses of societal and transnational actors such as private businesses, social movements, and NGOs. At any moment, states and societies are guided by multiple, often conflicting geopolitical imaginaries that compete to shape political discourse and public policy. Even within authoritarian states, such rival imaginaries can constrain the behavior of state elites and even redefine patterns of transnational ties. In contrast to the case of Tunisia, state building in Jordan has resulted in a regime that does not wield full, centralized control over its population or territorial control over its land. Examining geopolitical imaginaries presents an alternative theory for explaining when and why states do not act as unitary actors, but rather their policies are defined by state leaders who must "balance" (or seek to counter) both external and internal threats to their power.[5] While neorealists tend to view the existence of rival societal and state interests as a product of incomplete state building, ethnic diversity, or despotic power, such conditions are also the product of an open public sphere. Marc Lynch shows that to the degree that a domestic public sphere is supported by an open media, representative institutions, and public debate, societal forces will more likely advocate their own definitions of the national interest, challenge state actions that violate this definition, and through their own independent actions (such as business contacts or boycotts) seek to define the nature of the country's relationship to other states.[6] Thus, within an open public sphere, if a regime seeks to adopt a new geopolitical imaginary and redefine the nation's interests and identities, it must publicly defend that transformation while facing challenges from societal actors motivated by rival imaginaries.

Transnational flows—such as those associated with tourism, tourism development, and the international tourism economy—influence geopolitical imaginaries and the policies they generate. While the prospects for tourism development were critical to the rise of the New Middle East, the effort to "remap" Jordan's position in the Middle East and the flows it launched helped to generate an unexpected dynamic that gave rise to a geopolitical imaginary at odds with the state's vision. As I discuss in the following chapter, a powerful discourse of political reterritorialization developed in reaction to cross-border tourism-related flows that heightened local awareness of cross-border differences and potential threats to local and national territorial identities and political and economic interests.

Tourism Development in a Geopolitically Fragmented Middle East

Before the creation and bordering of modern nation-states in the region, Western travelers imagined the Levant as a single region, associated with ancient civilizations and the Judeo-Christian Holy Land, to be toured as a circuit. While the itineraries of most Western tourists and pilgrims in the nineteenth century centered on sites such as Bethlehem and Jerusalem, early modern travelers, explorers, and pilgrims occasionally journeyed east across the river Jordan. There they visited the spectacular Roman ruins of Jerash in northern Jordan or biblically related locales such as Mount Nebo, where Moses is said to have looked out to the promised land. With the publication of the explorer Johann Ludwig Burckhardt's account of his discovery of the rock-carved city of Petra, tourists began traveling to southern Jordan.[7] By the first decade of the twentieth century, Thomas Cook & Son was running tours, organized as elaborate camping parties, to Petra and "hitherto inaccessible regions east of the Jordan."[8] Nevertheless, during the first half of the twentieth century, Petra remained an out-of-the-way adventure requiring a considerable trek across sometimes dangerous terrain controlled by the Bedouin.

Travel through the region was facilitated somewhat after Transjordan, as the state was initially called, was established by Britain as a political entity following World War I. This territory east of the river Jordan was originally designated part of Britain's League of Nations' mandate for Palestine, but then a separate mandate was invented to create an Arab buffer state. With the help of a military that was trained, financed, and led by the British, the country's first ruler, Emir Abdullah, was able to subdue and co-opt the Bedouin tribes. By the 1920s, Thomas Cook had established a permanent tourist camp inside Petra.[9] The main impediments for Western travelers, however, remained safety and lack of information, requiring them to pay heavily for guides and protection.

Jordan as the Holy Land:
Tourism Development before 1967

In the 1948 Arab-Israeli war, Transjordan captured East Jerusalem and central Palestine, which it gave the name "West Bank" (of the river Jordan) as it claimed sovereignty over it and its population. Shortly thereafter King Abdullah was assassinated in Jerusalem by a disgruntled Palestinian. With the annexation of the West Bank, the newly independent state gained not only land and population but considerable tourism assets as well. The government of the state, now renamed the Hashemite Kingdom of Jordan, not only sought "to suppress or erase all reference to Palestine" but also appropriated "certain Palestinian symbols, such as the Dome of the Rock and traditional embroidery, and [claimed] them as Jordanian."[10] While Jordan sought to consolidate legitimacy and order over a majority Palestinian population within what it defined as an Arab Hashemite state, these policies can also be viewed as part of Jordan's effort to project its touristic identity as the territory of the biblical Holy Land to Western tourists.[11] Visits to biblical sites in central Palestine became the main attraction for (non-Arab) tourists to Jordan.

In the 1950s, Jordan made little progress in developing its tourism sector. While Jordan's prime tourism assets were located on the West Bank, the Jordanian state heavily favored the promotion of economic development on the East Bank. Even on the East Bank, much of the tourism sector was dominated by the petty bourgeoisie of Palestinian origin, which the state refrained from regulating or assisting. In any case, the 1956 Suez crisis, the destabilizing effects of Nasser's regional influence, and the simultaneous challenge of the nationalist opposition in Jordan impeded both tourism flows and national economic development efforts.

The expansion of tourism development in Jordan began only once King Hussein, in the face of a possible coup attempt, brought the era of liberal politics to an end, imposed martial law, and consolidated his own power. This effort coincided with the American assumption in the late 1950s of the burden of supporting (with economic aid, military assistance, and covert funding) the pro-Western monarchy. With clandestine help from the CIA, the American-based Trans-Ocean Airlines established Jordan's first airline, known at one time as "Air Jordan of the Holy Land."[12] The United States also began to support cultural tourism development in Jordan. The U.S. Agency for International Development (USAID) notes that "one of the best remembered gifts of the United States to Jordan since the Point Four program started in 1952 was the erection [in 1958] of a fallen column located at the Treasury [al Khazneh] at the end of Petra's siq."[13] As part of American development aid and technical assistance efforts, a Beirut-based American tourism adviser prepared "A Tourism Plan of Action for Jordan" in 1959. The report criticized the lack of institutional capacity, noting that the existing tourism authority "does not answer [the] need" for "a strong central development authority" and "should be abolished."[14]

In the early 1960s, as Jordan was implementing its first five-year plan for integrated economic development, the government established state-owned tourist facilities. In Amman, the government built a luxury hotel managed by Inter-Continental. It also established a modest thirty-five-room rest house near the entrance of the Petra Archaeological Park, which received 20,000 to 30,000 visitors a year. As tourism flows to Jordan expanded, increasing fivefold from 1960 to 1966, tourism receipts came to provide the kingdom with its largest source of foreign currency and a substantial amount of state tax revenue.[15] By 1966 tourism receipts represented over 6 percent of GNP.[16] In his 1962 autobiography, the young King Hussein devoted much of his one slim chapter on economic affairs to discussing the tourism potential of the country. He focused on the untapped opportunities for tourism on the East Bank and went so far as to exclaim, "I believe that when our tourist program really starts properly . . . the tourist income to Jordan may well equal the fabulous oil revenues of other Arab states."[17]

Tourism, Nation Building, the Rise of a Rentier Economy after 1967

The 1967 Arab-Israeli war resulted in the effective collapse of Jordan's tourism economy, shattering existing hopes for tourism development. In addition to the violence and regional instability unleashed by the war, the Israeli occupation of the West Bank robbed Jordan of its most vital tourism assets, representing 90 percent of its tourism sector. The Israeli occupation of the West Bank also shifted regional tourism flows. Most tourists seeking to visit the Holy Land would now pass though Israeli territory and tourist firms. While not free of bureaucratic hassles, an "open crossing" policy with Israel allowed tourists to visit the West Bank sites from Jordan, while Jordan continued to claim sovereignty over the territory. (Meanwhile the war further fragmented the Palestinian community and hampered its mobility across the Jordan river.) Tourism flows to Jordan, however, would not soon return to pre-1967 levels. The territorial redefinition of Jordan also brought about a shift in tourism policy, which increasingly focused on the ancient ruins and other attractions on the East Bank. In the wake of the war, the United States provided Jordan with a large economic aid package, and USAID commissioned the U.S. National Park Service to develop master plans for Amman, Jerash, and Petra, though little effort was made to realize the visions presented in the documents.

The shift to emphasize Jordan as a national destination, rather than as one connected to Holy Land sites west of the river Jordan, was gradual. King Hussein still struggled to assert control over the people and political future of the West Bank and the Palestinian communities of both banks. Conflict grew between the state and the PLO leadership, its radical-leftist factions, and the growing *fadayeen* guerrilla movement operating on Jordanian soil, all of which led to a violent showdown in September 1970. Not only did the fighting hurt the tourism economy, but internationally the most searing images of this era have remained those crafted by the leftist Popular Front for the Liberation of Palestine (PFLP) when it staged a multiple airplane hijacking, landing three European and American airliners at a former British landing strip outside Amman, which they referred to as "the Aerodrome of Revolution."[18] The group evacuated the passengers, held fifty-four of them hostage for two weeks, and created a spectacular media event by blowing up the planes on the tarmac. Hijacking attempts, tensions with Syria—which imposed a blockade of Jordan in 1971 and 1972—and the Arab-Israeli war of 1973 would continue to constrain Jordan's air links and depress growth of the tourism sector.[19]

It was only with the oil boom of the mid-1970s that the number of visitors to Jordan began to expand robustly, with tourism revenues growing from 5 percent of GNP in 1973 to 19 percent by the late 1970s.[20] Most of this growth in tourism consisted of visits by

Arabs from the Gulf who spent their summers in Jordan, especially after the outbreak of civil war in Lebanon in 1975.[21] These visitors were not, however, the focus of tourism development efforts. Much of the remaining tourist traffic consisted of Americans and Europeans visiting Jordan as part of multicountry tours, and thus the bed nights per visitor remained low. The oil-based income boom also led to increased public and private investment in the tourism sector. In Amman, a slew of new hotels sprang up in the late 1970s and early 1980s, some supported with indirect government financing.[22] While many of the smaller hotels were owned and operated by Palestinian-Jordanian businessmen, the most notable addition to the hotel landscape was the opening in 1982 of the American-style Amman Marriott Hotel financed by wealthy East Bank merchant families. The result, however, was a petrodollar-financed glut of hotel capacity. To make matters worse, the instability and seasonality of tourist demand made it "difficult to mount a satisfactory operation without losing money."[23] By the mid-1980s, this glut also "discouraged the private sector from investing in accommodations and has discouraged the government from further investment and improvement" in tourism.[24] For its part, the government-owned Inter-Continental Hotel expanded its capacity, and the state also built the larger-than-needed Queen Alia International Airport and other infrastructure projects. These projects were not directed at promoting tourist flows, nor were they needed to meet the general increase in business, media, and migrant traffic. Their main purpose seems to have been to provide a vehicle for government patronage and display the new wealth of the kingdom, supported by rentier incomes including aid, labor remittances, and investments from the oil-rich Gulf states. While the new airport did facilitate the development of a stopover market for travelers to Iraq and the other Gulf states, the Gulf states soon developed their own airline capacities to match their growing importance in the global economy.[25]

Following the stability and wealth enjoyed by Jordan in the late 1970s and 1980s, the state adopted policies promoting a new national identity, shifting away from suppressing or usurping well-established religious and cultural symbols from the West Bank toward establishing and emphasizing cultural symbols, practices, and places on the East Bank. This shift was also a response to the growing assertion of East Bank identity that was unleashed by the

1970 showdown with Palestinian guerrillas, which made evident the failure of the integration of the two banks into a Pan-Jordanian identity. While continuing to suppress Palestinian nationalism, the Hashemite state still claimed sovereignty over the West Bank and ruled a population on the East Bank widely understood to contain a majority of citizens with Palestinian roots. At the same time, the state's efforts at nation building within the tourism sector neither rejected nor excluded Palestinian cultural references, though these locations, handicrafts, and clothes were labeled as "Jordanian." State efforts increasingly focused on legitimating the Hashemite monarchy's rule and constructing a Jordanian national identity centered on Jordan's East Bank territory and people.

In the 1970s, Jordan expanded marketing campaigns offering "the Bedouins and Petra as the true representatives of Modern Jordan."[26] To forge deeper territorial roots for Jordanian identity within the East Bank, the government also sponsored archaeological research, history displays, and tourist literature to promote the connection of the ancient Nabateans, builders of Petra, to the current inhabitants of Jordan.[27] This strategy follows Benedict Anderson's argument that postcolonial states often graft their own purposes onto techniques first used by colonial states. These allow the state to "imagine its dominion—the nature of the human beings it ruled, the geography of its domain, and the legitimacy of its ancestry."[28] The city of Petra was marketed as both a tourist destination and a symbol for Jordan as a whole. Due to its remote location in southern Jordan, Petra was only gradually made more accessible to tourists. The construction of the Desert Highway helped cut down the travel time to Petra, but in the mid-1980s the town's hotel capacity was limited to one hundred rooms. In the early 1980s, with World Bank matching funds provided as part of an antiquities-focused tourism development project, the government built the Petra Forum Hotel, providing, for the first time, luxury-class hotel accommodations near Petra. While owned by the state, the hotel was managed by the Forum hotel company, a subsidiary of the Inter-Continental hotel chain. In December 1985 the Jordan's international tourism profile increased when the Petra Archaeological Park was inscribed on UNESCO's World Heritage list, signifying both its importance as a cultural monument of worldwide significance and the need for the world community to help conserve and protect the site from natural and human erosion.

Figure 11. Tourists take in the facade of El Khazneh (The Treasury) at Petra. Photograph by Michelle Woodward.

The expansion of tourism income in the late 1970s and early 1980s offset Jordan's growing volume of imports but did not provoke a concerted tourism development effort by the state. Jordan faced the dilemma of how to escape from what economists call a "low equilibrium trap."[29] In contrast to Tunisia, Jordan did not have the opportunity to pursue tourism development within a market with a rapid growth of the demand for a product it could readily offer. While Arab tourists periodically filled hotels and rented apartments, they did not patronize the country's tourism infrastructure or visit government-controlled tourist sites. As for non-Arab tourism, Jordan received only a limited number of visitors interested and wealthy enough to visit what was a relatively high-cost destination with limited tourist attractions and facilities. At the same time, the total volume of tourist expenditure was too low to warrant the state investing in costly, large-scale projects to develop public goods and services and make tourist sites more accessible and attractive. Meanwhile the small firms operating in the sector (mostly owned by Palestinian Jordanians) were unable to capture economies of scale, so the price of tourism products remained relatively high and subject to high rent extraction, which limited the scope for growth in tourist demand. In 1984 the Jordanian economist Fahd Fanik complained: "Apparently, tourism is not sufficiently appreciated by our decision makers, and accordingly is not given a high position in the scale of priorities."[30] Fanik also noted that "many think of the high volume of foreign receipts as a contribution to the national income, and conclude that the tourist sector is too large to need further support from the government."[31] A 1986 report by an American consultancy concurred, observing that "little purposeful action has been taken by the Jordanian government to direct significant economic resources to the sector."[32] The consultants recommended "greater emphasis on tourism needs to be reflected in a corresponding elevation of the position of the tourism sector within the government hierarchy."[33] The report also noted that Jordan's marketing was "passive" and that "Jordan is still little known and does not project a touristic image to the travel industry."[34]

The Crisis of the Rentier State

The government's interest in tourism development expanded in the mid-1980s as the country faced the erosion of its other sources of rentier income. As oil prices declined from their peak in the early 1980s, the oil-based Gulf economies began to contract. While these states struggled to adjust to declining incomes, Jordan saw the pillars of its own economy collapse. In only two years, between 1982 and 1984, Arab grant aid was cut in half, with most states reneging on payments promised as part of an Arab League effort to support Jordan's refusal to join Egypt in the U.S.-sponsored Camp David process in the late 1970s.[35] Total foreign aid as a share of GNP dropped from 45 percent in 1979 to 8 percent by 1988.[36] In addition, the oil economies could no longer absorb more Jordanian expatriate labor, and Jordan was soon faced with having to find jobs for returning workers in addition to all the new graduates produced by its expanded educational system. Between 1984 and 1989, remittances dropped from $1.2 billion to $623 million.[37] Meanwhile, between 1979 and 1988, tourism receipts as a share of GNP dropped from 19 percent to 9 percent.

By 1988 these pressures forced Jordan to devalue its currency, dropping a total of 45 percent against the dollar, and to implement emergency measures to control luxury imports and foreign currency transactions, freeze investment in large public-sector projects, and raise customs duties.[38] This era marked a transition for the Jordanian middle class when many of their income sources evaporated, the value of their wealth diminished, and the cost of imported products soared. No longer able to tap external rents or expand its debts, the state was compelled to implement an IMF-directed economic austerity program in the spring of 1989. The resulting price rises led to rioting not in the Palestinian population centers around Amman but in the southern town of Ma'an, long viewed as a government stronghold, and the northern town of Salt. During these riots, "local townspeople threw rocks, looted, and chanted slogans against the al-Rifai government's alleged mismanagement of the economy."[39] The riots engulfed the East Bank townspeople who had long been the core backers of the monarchy but also had reaped the least from the boom of the 1970s and the growth of consumerism.

It was in this context that Jordan began a controlled political opening that included submitting the lower house of parliament to elections in 1989 and, later, the legalization of opposition parties.[40] Most commentators have stressed how this process was driven by declines in rentier incomes and used to temper the critical political reaction to the austerity measures.[41] The reinstitution of competitive elections and the drawing up of the National Charter can be viewed as an attempt to develop a new political framework for relations between state and society, which throughout the 1970s and 1980s had relied on rentier incomes and large state expenditures to finance the military, public sector, and consumer subsidies. The National Charter, adopted in 1991, represents the first effort to craft a broadly inclusive consensus statement on the rules of the game in the era of political liberalization. After the 1989 elections, the elected lower house of parliament and a more liberal media environment opened spaces for the opposition to contest state policies. With fewer material rewards to dole out as patronage, the regime sought to shift the function of the state in society from primarily a nexus of material patronage to a space seemingly open for political contention, diverting political opposition away from directly challenging the Hashemite monarchy. This space, however, operated under highly constricted rules, which the regime continually manipulated to co-opt and divide the opposition.[42] Meanwhile these institutions allowed the state to forge a new set of political ties to a support base including tribal East Bank elements and the minority groups who long backed the king.

Political liberalization, however, did nothing to solve Jordan's economic problems, nor did it give the state new policy options. As Laurie Brand notes, "While budget cutting threatened one part of the government formula—the support of the Transjordanian bureaucracy and army—revenue raising threatened the other—the state's demand for political acquiescence from the important and largely Palestinian bourgeoisie in exchange for few extractive (taxation) demands."[43] By 1989 both ends of the ruling formula had suffered significant erosion. Jordan was now in a position where national security and domestic stability hinged crucially on promoting economic development, but the resources available to the state for managing the productive side of the economy were too limited to ensure regime stability. Jordan needed a means to promote economic growth and job creation, in other words, a postrentier strategy of development.

One element of this new postrentier strategy was the development of tourism. The devaluation of the Jordanian dinar had made Jordan a more competitive destination, and government agencies, backed by U.S. aid, became more interested in encouraging the sector. While a ministry of tourism was soon founded, a USAID review of the sector in 1990 noted "the absence of a national strategy; lack of reliable tourism statistics, lack of coordination between the private and public sector, narrowly focused and badly coordinated marketing; inadequate services across the sector; and inadequate tourism infrastructure."[44] The most tangible results in the tourism sector were a product of USAID's work with the American Center for Oriental Research (ACOR) and local Jordanian entrepreneurs. Privately managed rest houses, financed by USAID, were built in Pella and Umm Qeis, providing adequate facilities to make these archaeological sites in the northwest corner of the country possible stops for packaged tour groups.[45] In 1989 Jordan saw noticeable increases in visitors from France, Italy, and Spain. Valued in local dinars, the sector saw a 37 percent increase, but in dollar terms receipts declined to about 11 percent.[46] The growth of tourism was assisted by an unprecedented one-million-dollar international marketing campaign financed by the Jordanian government and the national airline with the assistance of the private sector.[47] In 1989 the number of tourist visitors to Petra shot up to about 96,000 (from a level of 12,000 in 1986).[48] In the same year, Jordan gained what would be the greatest marketing vehicle for attracting American tourists with the release of Steven Spielberg's *Indiana Jones and the Last Crusade,* which prominently featured the spectacular sight, as one emerges from a long narrow canyon, of Petra's brightly colored monumental carved stone facade, popularly known as al Khazneh (the Treasury).[49]

This expansion was not to last. On August 2, 1990, Iraqi tanks rolled into Kuwait. As the United States assembled its Gulf War coalition, Jordan's efforts to rebuild its tourism economy and promote economic cooperation with other Arab states were shattered. After a failed Arab League summit, Egypt quickly lined up at the center of the Bush administration's Arab coalition against Iraq. Jordan, in contrast, sought to stake out an impossible middle position constrained by its shared interests with Iraq, popular pro-Iraqi mobilization within Jordan's liberalizing public sphere, and the king's desire to maintain the unity of his people and the stability of his throne.[50] As a result, Jordan paid a heavy economic price during the war and in its immediate aftermath. Jordan's trade was impeded by the U.S.-led inspection blockade of its only port at Aqaba, which was required to enforce the UN-sanctioned embargo of Iraq.

Due to Jordan's stance during the war, aid from the Gulf states was cut, while U.S. aid declined. Moreover, hundreds of thousands of long-term Palestinian residents and migrant workers in the Arab Gulf states, most with Jordanian passports, were expelled, cutting off a major source of remittances. Tourism across the region, set to recover from the effects of the Palestinian *intifada* launched in late 1987, underwent a major crisis. Jordan experienced a 24 percent decline in the number of visitors.[51] As one index of the effect on the tourism economy, income from visitors to Petra was cut by about two-thirds from JD 96,000 in 1989 to JD 32,700 in 1991. The Jordanian government claimed that the Gulf War led to a loss of $230 million in revenues.[52] Just as the end of the Cold War was leading to new political and economic openings and opportunities in Europe, the Middle East seemed to be as politically fragmented as ever, with Jordan now more isolated than it had been for many decades. Jordan's effort to launch its tourism sector was again destroyed by regional geopolitical forces outside its control.

Israel and the Political Geography of Tourism Space in the Egyptian Sinai

Before exploring the role of tourism in the context of the 1994 peace treaty between Jordan and Israel, we need to examine the politics of tourism in the case of the 1979 treaty between Egypt and Israel that resulted in the Israeli return of Egyptian territory captured in the 1967 war. Israeli-Egyptian relations in the 1970s and early 1980s, in terms of both patterns of tourism development and peace negotiations, were shaped by rival nationalist versions of a realist-territorial geopolitical imaginary. While Egypt sought to regain territorial control over the Sinai, Israeli policy was shaped by an interest in retaining access and influence, if not sovereignty, over Egyptian spaces that had been incorporated into Israeli tourism during the period of its occupation.

Israeli territorial expansion during the 1967 war produced the opposite of Jordan's experience. Israel was able to extend its tourism economy into Arab territories, remaking those spaces to serve nationalist purposes. Israel annexed Arab East Jerusalem, including the Old City, and institutionalized its occupation over the rest of the West Bank, the biblical Judaea and Samaria. Israelis gained control over the Temple Mount and the Western Wall in East

Jerusalem, making them easily accessible to Israelis and Jews for the first time since 1948. On the occupied Golan Heights, captured from Syria, Israelis built the country's first ski resort, which became a popular destination for domestic tourism. With a new confidence and sense of regional military superiority, Israelis began touring the Arab lands that their army now occupied, and Jews from around the world were attracted to Israel as a travel destination. These flows made the country feel less isolated and provided a vehicle for gaining international economic and political support. As Richter observes, tourism in Israel has been "encouraged as a boost to domestic morale. The existence of tourism affirms the nation's legitimacy and a faith in its internal security."[53] Accordingly, Israel's international tourism market remained primarily Jewish into the 1970s, while in the late 1960s the nation saw a vast increase in the number of tourists opting to immigrate, with the rate reaching 10 percent of all visitors.[54] As the Israeli tourism industry now controlled the "Holy Land tourism" market, it increasingly attracted Christian pilgrims to expand its international tourism sector.[55] In contrast to Jordan, Israel had extensive new tourism development possibilities and committed itself to comprehensive promotion policies, making 1967–72 a "takeoff period" for the sector.[56] With the help of international investors, Israel transformed the southern port city of Eilat into a major winter-sun destination for European tourists, and the city soon experienced explosive Mediterranean-style growth.[57]

Farther south, Israeli control over the Egyptian Sinai Peninsula led to the opening of this territory to tourism development. In just two years after the 1967 war, Mount Sinai had become "one of the major stops on the itinerary of tourists visiting Israel."[58] Israel did away with Egyptian controls over travel and development in previously remote regions of the southern Sinai. French and Israeli investors, working with Club Med's Gilbert Trigano, were preparing a tourist camp down the coast from Israel's overdeveloped Eilat, at Nuwaiba, where accommodations would consist of Bedouin tents. The Israeli government facilitated tourism by building a road along the coast and connecting the area to its domestic air transportation system. The region was also incorporated into Israel's nature tourism sector by the Society for the Protection of Nature (SPN), which organized tours, led by young Israelis doing their military service, for Israeli and foreign tourists. During the years of the Israeli occupation, the territory of the Sinai became integrated into the Israeli tourism imaginary. As Smadar Lavie notes, for Israelis the SPN sought "to preserve (or recreate?) the pastoral idyll of a pristine Holy Land in the midst of 20th century military occupation."[59] Unlike the densely populated and politically mobilized West Bank, the Sinai was mostly populated by poor, rural Bedouins whom Israel could work around while constructing their tourism and transportation facilities on undeveloped land. The Israelis often viewed their efforts as providing economic opportunities for this marginalized community. And while Sinai locations, such as St. Catherine's monastery, attracted non-Israeli tourists, the region came to function as a national frontier region for a generation of young Israelis owing to "its magical landscapes and its hospitable inhabitants."[60] Chaim Noy and Erik Cohen observe: "Its primordial landscapes, imbued with mythical significance in the national memory, had been a popular destination for trekkers and backpackers. Its spectacular beaches served as places of escape for many youths."[61]

This Israeli attachment to the Sinai as a tourism space continued as Egypt and Israel entered into negotiations over troop disengagement, signed the Camp David accords, and later completed a peace treaty. With the help of the Carter administration, in the late 1970s the two sides were able to craft an agreement that served their "hard" economic and security interests related to land, security, oil resources, and the disposition of Jewish settlements. Egypt gained substantial economic and military aid from the United States, and Israel was assured of both oil flows and the demilitarization of the territory that would return to Egyptian sovereignty. While few had expectations for intense economic interaction and cooperation, many thought that the one sector that might "yield something tangible" was tourism. Two Israeli journalists noted, "It must be assumed that just as tens of thousands of Israelis will pour into travel offices when travel to Egypt becomes possible, similar numbers of Egyptians—though less than the Israelis of course—will flock enthusiastically to visit us. In such cases the temptation is great and can be immediately satisfied."[62] Some Americans would later even tout the benefits of "cooperative marketing of Israel-Egypt tours."[63] Such views, however, failed to recognize the realist-territorial geopolitical imaginary shaping the behavior of the two states. Tourism-related issues would remain in dispute for another decade and emerge as the terrain on which the future of the Israeli-Egyptian relationship continued to be negotiated and contested.

During the peace negotiations, Egypt's primary goal was to regain all its territory, though Sadat also sought a framework for addressing the "Palestinian problem" to limit criticism of his actions from his domestic opposition and other Arab states. Israel meanwhile sought to achieve full normalization of relations with Egypt, that is, to develop not only diplomatic ties but also economic and cultural relations. Israeli policy makers reasoned that these ties would institutionalize Sadat's strategic choice to break with Arab hostility toward Israel and constrain Egypt from aligning with Arab states against Israel again. Moreover, Israelis viewed normalization as a means to reduce the country's political and economic isolation from the Arab world. In seeking full normalization of relations with Egypt, Israel argued that Israelis should have the same access to Sinai resorts as they had enjoyed while they were under Israeli control. In the negotiations over how to operationalize the technical aspects of the peace treaty, Israelis demanded that "tourists who entered Egypt though Sinai . . . be granted visas 'on the spot.'"[64] Not only would this concession allow international tourists who visit Israel and Eilat to enter the Sinai with little added hassle, it would also allow Israelis to maintain their physical and psychological (if not political) connection to its tourism spaces.

Israel wanted to bind Egypt to Israel with cross-border flows of trade and tourism to break Israel's isolation from the Arab world. While commerce might take time to develop, Israeli officials saw tourism flows as an indicator of the Egyptian government's commitment to a robust form of normalization. A year after signing the treaty that opened the border between Egypt and Israel, Israeli politicians began complaining that "there is almost no Egyptian tourism to Israel and we don't feel it's being encouraged."[65] Some even threatened "to refuse to give back the remaining one-third of the Sinai peninsula that Israel occupies unless Egypt cooperates more to promote commerce and tourism."[66] At the same time, the Egyptian government under Husni Mubarak, who succeeded Anwar Sadat after his assassination by Islamist extremists, was seeking to prevent Egypt's isolation from the Arab world and appease domestic critics of the peace treaty with Israel. Most Egyptians did not appear ready for full normalization, and opposition parties used the issue to challenge Mubarak's consolidation of power. Popular opposition grew after Israel bombed an unfinished nuclear reactor in Iraq and invaded Lebanon. Mubarak's government became more resistant to normalization and even recalled its ambassador from Israel after the 1982 massacres at two Palestinian refugee camps in Beirut by right-wing Lebanese Phalangists with indirect Israeli assistance.

With their relations still defined by a realist-territorial geopolitical imaginary, the implementation of the Israeli-Egyptian peace treaty resulted in an intense territorial dispute. As the final Israeli evacuation of the Sinai approached, Israeli officials refused to agree to evacuate the seven-hundred-meter strip of Taba, located adjacent to the Israeli port of Eilat on the Gulf of Aqaba. They announced that their claim to the territory was based on recently unearthed maps made by a 1906 British military expedition that placed Taba within the territory of the Ottoman province in Palestine.[67]

While many on the Israeli right opposed giving land back to Egypt, it is unlikely that the dispute would have surfaced if Taba had not been ripe for tourism development. In 1977, before a peace deal with Egypt was expected, Eli Paposhadu, an Eilat hotel developer of Egyptian Jewish decent, had decided to built a luxury hotel on the small tract of beachfront property. He has since recalled, "When we built the hotel, we knew it wasn't on Israeli territory. But who cared?"[68] Paposhadu obtained land and set out to build the most luxurious resort in the Eilat area. About 70 percent of the hotel's $20 million price tag was underwritten by the Israeli ministry of tourism.[69] Construction halted temporarily as Egypt and Israel began work on a peace treaty, but with the help of a military official and the director of the army's cartography unit, Paposhadu was able to convince Israel's prime minister Menachem Begin, leader of the right-wing Likud bloc, to allow construction to proceed as Israel prepared to contest the border demarcation.[70] In late 1982, the ten-floor five-star hotel, managed by the U.S.-based Sonesta hotel chain, opened its doors, attracting Europeans on winter-sun packages, Israeli vacationers, and high-profile visits from politicians from the Israeli Right who opposed conceding the territory to Egypt. In 1984, Paposhadu was able to expand the resort to include a pier for yachts, as well as facilities for scuba diving and tennis, two restaurants, and a nightclub.[71] During the diplomatic dispute, which played out after Israel evacuated the rest of the Sinai (including other tourism facilities) in 1982, "Israelis flocked . . . to Taba, the last bit of 'occupied' Egyptian territory. It became a twilight of sorts."[72]

As Taba's future remained unclear, Israel continued to practice sovereignty over the territory. The applicability of Israeli law was demonstrated when authorities confiscated the slot machines Rafi Nelson provocatively installed at his bohemian beach village adjacent to the Sonesta.[73] Meanwhile, Egyptian authorities protested Israeli tourism development practices and tried unsuccessfully to organize a boycott of Taba. Many Israelis, however, considered Taba to have Eilat's nicest public beach and its most posh hotel. In the late 1980s, during the "'last battle' over Taba . . . occupancy at the [Sonesta] hotel was 96%—a kind of Israeli act of national pride, even if it was done with bikinis and wine."[74]

Without a settlement, Israeli-Egyptian relations in the early 1980s quickly came to be viewed as a "cold peace."[75] While tens of thousands of Israelis, many of them Jews of Egyptian origin, came to Egypt in the first years of the border opening, only a couple thousand Egyptians crossed in the other direction. Of the nearly one hundred thousand visitors to Egypt who crossed over the new borders from Israel between 1980 and 1984, most were Western tourists or Palestinians from Gaza and the West Bank. Only 16 percent were Israeli passport holders (of which an indeterminate number were Palestinian Israelis).[76] Most crossing in the other direction were Western tourists and Arab passport holders visiting the occupied Gaza Strip and West Bank, with only 2 percent of the traffic consisting of Egyptian visitors to Israel.[77] Israel complained that the Egyptian government created too many obstacles for its citizens to travel to Israel.[78] Many who did go or who hosted Israeli colleagues in Egypt faced "blacklisting" by opposition members within their professional associations. More generally, Egyptians resisted all forms of interaction and communication with Israelis. Although Egypt opened an air link to Israel, rather than adding Tel Aviv to the route map of its national carrier, Egyptian authorities created a "fictitious company called Nefertiti. Its lone plane is all-white, unblemished by any identification."[79] The flights were listed by flight number and time of departure but with no mention of destination or airline. Israel was thus denied any markers of normalization.

In this context, the Taba dispute became the focus for growing Egyptian-Israeli distrust and nationalist posturing on both sides.

Egypt insisted on submitting the case to binding arbitration. Israel refused. Many members of the right-wing Likud bloc resisted giving up what they considered an extension of the resort of Eilat and an integral part of the national territory.[80] Israel's 1984 election, however, resulted in a "national unity government" in which Likud and Labor party leaders took turns as prime minister. As Israel dragged out the negotiations for several years, it was able to get Egypt to commit to steps to improve bilateral relations. Egypt returned its ambassador to Tel Aviv and improved cross-border trade and tourism cooperation. With these minor normalization concessions, in January 1986, as Labor leader Shimon Peres took his turn as prime minister, Israel finally agreed to binding arbitration.

Almost three years later, after inspecting all claims and maps, an international arbitration panel ruled that Taba was part of Egypt.[81] Egypt paid compensation for the hotel, which remained under the same management (though now directed through Hilton's Cairo-based operations). Egyptians expressed nationalist pride upon regaining control over the territory. The location and history of the resort, however, dampened its tourist appeal for most Egyptians. Israelis were granted special access to Taba without the need for cumbersome visa procedures, while Egyptian visitors needed special approval from the Egyptian government to cross into Eilat, where the Taba hotel's utilities still originated. In the years after Egypt regained sovereignty over the territory, Taba became neither a fully Egyptian tourist space nor, as some Israelis on the left had hoped, a location for advancing bilateral cooperation and regional peace.[82] Instead Taba became a curious liminal space where Egyptians and other Arabs could vacation if they wished, but most tourists continued to come from the Israeli side and could pay for goods and services in Israeli currency. For many Israelis and Egyptians, Taba remained an extension of Israeli national tourism space rather than an Egyptian destination. As Egypt began to develop the south Sinai for tourism, Israeli tourists continued to visit the region, since Egypt had agreed to Israel's request that visitors crossing to southern Sinai would not need to apply for an Egyptian visa. But in the Sinai, Egypt and Israel never developed robust societal ties. In many ways, this was not a shared space but one that carried on as a space for Israeli travel, tourism, and exploration on Arab territory under Egyptian sovereignty. An Israeli anthropologist, Dan Rabinowitz, who spent many years in the Sinai while it was under Israeli control, wrote: "It is important to understand that even for those Israelis who did not go to Sinai—and most Israelis have never been there—the very existence of a calm Arab space as the direct continuation of Israel was both significant and reassuring."[83]

The continuing identification of the Taba as a space for Israeli tourism was part of the reason that the Taba Hotel was attacked in October 2004. While the attack was also directed at the Egyptian government, most of the victims were Israelis. Referring to the terrorist attack, Rabinowitz notes that "in one fell swoop it severs Sinai from the space of stability in which it existed until now and attaches it to the world space that has been exposed to global terrorism since the collapse of the twin towers."[84]

The Sinai case illustrates, first, how peaceful relations and the creation of cross-border tourism flows do not in themselves promote behavior that transcends the realist-territorial geopolitical imaginary. Even after signing their peace treaty, Egypt and Israel both used the Taba dispute to maximize their territorial resources and control over cross-border flows. Second, an examination of the geopolitics of tourism across the Sinai also demonstrates how sovereign borders and boundaries depicted on international maps do not always mark the limits of "national" territorial spaces. Nor, for that matter, do models of interdependence always explain the political implications of flows across those boundaries. The power of territory is defined not simply by its geographic location or national control but also by how visitors experience the territory through tourist consumption. The Egyptian-Israeli peace process did open a mutual border to tourist visits, but the bulk of these flows moved in one direction. Meanwhile, in the Sinai, the territory crossed by Israeli tourists was not in their minds the Egypt of Cairo or Luxor but a space that had already been inscribed with meaning from previous visits and processes of tourism development while under Israeli control. Jordan's peace treaty, in contrast, developed in a different context and gave rise to different understandings about tourism spaces and expectations about tourism's benefits and how, some hoped, it would transform regional geopolitics.

Imagining the New Middle East

It was not long after the transfer of Taba to Egyptian control that the geopolitical environment for tourism development in Jordan was transformed by global, regional, and national developments.

This process would lead to the emergence in the 1990s of a new geopolitical imaginary that reframed the tourism development process within Jordan as Israel and Jordan negotiated a peace treaty, promoted bilateral economic cooperation, and opened their border to tourism flows.

In the wake of the Gulf War of 1990–91, the United States used its broad regional influence to bring Israel together with several Arab states at a peace conference in Spain. After the introductory session, held in Madrid in October 1991, the peace talks broke up into a series of bilateral and multilateral negotiations. The bilateral negotiations between Israel and Palestinian representatives from the West Bank and Gaza made little progress. Meanwhile, in early 1992, a series of multilateral working groups to address regional security issues and economic cooperation was launched with the help of the international community. The multilaterals provided an important opportunity for Jordan. At the time, as Jordan's peace negotiators later wrote, "Some analysts thought that, with the economic hardships it was facing and the damage to its international reputation, Jordan was doomed, and it was only a matter of time before it would fall apart."[85] The talks allowed Jordan a means to engage Israel and begin to work out common understandings. Coming after the strain of the Gulf War, Jordan's embrace of the American-led initiative helped to repair its relations with the United States and play a supportive role in the realization of American regional policy goals. Moreover, the framework suited Jordan's geopolitical interest in working toward a less-fragmented region. Jordan's Crown Prince Hassan had even suggested a plan for regional economic cooperation before the Madrid conference.[86] And in 1992 at a conference in the United States, one of Jordan's leading peace negotiators, Dr. Jawad Anani, outlined plans for regional cooperation in water, infrastructure, and finance.[87]

The Peace Process and the Making of the New Middle East

The multilateral talks began only making progress in 1992 with the election of a Labor Party–led government in Israel. Shimon Peres, who served as foreign minister, was enthusiastic about the Regional Economic Development Working Group (REDWG), led by the European Union. In early 1993 Peres began speaking about his vision of how economic cooperation could transform the Middle

East.[88] In May 1993 he gave an interview to the *Jerusalem Report* describing the work of the multilateral talks as leading to a "New Middle East."[89] Peres suggested that once the regional negotiations on technical issues such as collective security, economic cooperation, and water resources led to new understandings of the parties' needs, interests, and worldviews, the political leaders would find it easier to address the "hard" territorial issues. The maps that mark sovereign boundaries, Peres noted, "can only reflect a situation; if we want to change the maps, we must first change the situation."[90]

In late August 1993 Peres revealed that Israel and the PLO had been conducting secret back-channel negotiations in Norway. By September these resulted in a public announcement of mutual recognition and the "Declaration of Principles" that outlined what would come to be called the Oslo peace process. With the resulting Oslo Accords, a new fundamental reality was created, leading to the formation of a Palestinian territorial entity in Gaza and the West Bank city of Jericho. The moment seemed to represent a breakthrough marking the beginning of the end of the Arab-Israeli conflict. Although the Oslo Accords were negotiated outside the framework of the ongoing bilateral and multilateral talks, they unleashed the possibility for a redrawing of the regional geopolitical map. Politicians, political analysts, and think-tank policy papers began to reimagine the political economy of the Middle East through the lens of a "New Middle East" based on regional economic cooperation. This vision was most emphatically articulated by Peres, who in December 1993 published his book *The New Middle East* simultaneously in English and Hebrew.[91] In this widely discussed text, Peres laid out a far-reaching plan for the future of regional integration and economic cooperation across the Middle East. In line with emerging discourses about globalization and neoliberal economic policies, Peres argued that "today, markets are becoming almost more important than politics."[92] He outlined how the states of the Middle East all had common strategic, economic, and environmental interests that could best be served by increased cooperation and interaction. These mutual gains could be realized, he argued, by building a more open regional transportation and communication infrastructure and joint projects in sectors such as energy, water, and tourism. Such forms of economic cooperation, he suggested, would lead to a remapping of Middle Eastern political identities. A

1994 report from his office announced, "Rapprochement between Israel and the Arab states creates a process that turns economics into the moving force that shapes the regional relations instead of national interests that were dominant in the past."[93]

The New Middle East represented Israel's view of what the full normalization of relations between Israel and the Arab states would look like. Although many considered Peres too idealistic in his portrayal of its feasibility, few Israelis on the center-left rejected the goals of his vision. Even when viewed from a "realist" perspective, the New Middle East would clearly provide Israel with the largest relative gains.[94] The New Middle East helped generate a wider basis of support for the peace process, as it not only mapped out a vision for the end of the Arab-Israeli conflict but described how regional peace and normalization would allow Israel access to long-denied business and investment opportunities across the expanding global economy. In other words, Israel would become a "normal" state and no longer suffer from the stigma of being in an unstable region bordered by hostile states. As such, the Israeli business community mobilized to become a major supporter of the peace process.[95]

After the Oslo breakthrough, the New Middle East quickly became the framework through which the United States viewed its regional interests and formulated its policies for pursuing them. As an Israeli-driven model, it offered for the first time a framework that could simultaneously advance American interests toward both Israel and the Arab world. While the George H. W. Bush administration had initiated the multilateral talks, the New Middle East concept followed the Clinton administration's global policies vis-à-vis free trade, economic liberalization, and globalization in the post–Cold War era. In the early 1990s, the United States was not ready to commit to additional "payoffs" of the magnitude it offered Egypt and Israel after the Camp David Accords. Instead U.S. policy focused on promoting free-market liberalization and private-sector-led development in Arab economies. American officials were also excited about the role that American firms and capital could play in transforming the region. Working closely with Israel and Jordan, American officials and businessmen took charge of the peace process by supporting various regional conferences, working groups, and multilateral institutions to promote and implement the New Middle East vision.

The Essential Role of Tourism

Clearly, the vision of the New Middle East would not fully or immediately displace the realist-territorial geopolitical imaginary. But one reason the New Middle East emerged as a powerful interpretative framework was that all parties could easily imagine the feasibility and immediate material gains from tourism development and regional tourism cooperation. Promoting regional tourism was widely viewed in the international community as the critical first arena in which linkages would be formed, economic cooperation would begin, and results would appear that would help make the process self-sustaining. The image of tourism as the leading edge of the New Middle East helped establish enthusiasm within the multilateral peace negotiations and propelled the drafting of plans for regional cooperation.

Tourism officials led the way in thinking about regional cooperation. As early as December 1993, only three months after the announcement of the breakthrough on the Palestinian-Israeli track, information was leaked that the Israeli Ministry of Tourism was already designing a plan for economic cooperation with the Palestinians and Jordanians to develop tourism around the northern end of the Dead Sea. As Mordechai Benari, the ministry's director of international relations, noted, at the time "there was an uproar in Israel, 'how could the Ministry of Tourism involve itself in such a political initiative?'"[96] Under the realist geopolitical imaginary, tourism development followed geopolitics rather than helping to map its transformation. With the emergence of the New Middle East vision, tourism officials played an important role in outlining the challenges and opportunities presented by possible future geopolitical transformations. In early 1994, just as high-level Jordanian-Israeli negotiations were getting under way, Benari explained to an international gathering of tourism specialists:

> If there are open borders to Jordan and tomorrow every Israeli can go to Petra, 450,000 Israelis will get up Friday morning and take their cars and head for Petra and create the biggest travel snarl in all the history of the Middle East! This is not wild imagination. Many thousands of people from Amman will want to go to Tel Aviv which is a much shorter ride to see the sea and to show the sea to their kids. Or they will come to the zoos in Israel and all the zoos will be packed with Jordanian children. This is a reality that can happen.[97]

In Peres's vision, tourism would play a central role in stitching the economies of the Middle East together. "Tourism," he wrote, is "one of the most important resources of the sun-soaked Middle East."[98] Even before there were any agreements on regional co-operation, he called for the building of an expansive tourism and recreation infrastructure along a "Red Sea to Dead Sea canal," joint tourism projects, and a major airport along the "Gulf of Eilat" serving Israel, Jordan, Egypt, and even Saudi Arabia. Claiming that "violence" had been the main barrier to tourism development in the region, he stretched his enthusiasm for tourism to suggest that a "flourishing and stable tourist industry is also good for stability—equal in importance to an international police force."[99] He also offered that "today, more than ever, the measure of a country's strength is not how many troops it has but how many tourists."[100] The geopolitical imaginary of the New Middle East was well captured by an Israeli journalist when he explained to the Syrian foreign minister, in the first-ever interview of a Syrian official on Israeli television, "The question that many Israelis ask themselves [is]: when will a guy like me be able to take his wife to visit [the ancient ruins at] Palmyra?"[101]

Peres and others also made a more immediately persuasive claim regarding the role of tourism in the New Middle East. He confidently stated that tourism "is an important industry, which can, *in a relatively short time,* generate profits and create employment opportunities."[102] He concluded that "were it not for the violence, tourism could become an *immediate* source of income, supporting millions of families in the region."[103] In such a context, a British journalist could report, "Islamic militancy will be killed off by the new economic boom that tourism will help bring to the region."[104]

Most observers who might have been skeptical of the other elements of Peres's vision, especially those in the Arab world, often agreed with his assessment about the prospects for tourism development, giving the New Middle East the one issue on which it gained immediate, widespread support. A 1994 report by the Washington Institute for Near East Policy, a pro-Israeli think tank, concluded: "Tourism . . . holds the prospect of demonstrating the material rewards of Arab-Israeli peace. Many of those rewards *will come automatically,* as a more peaceful environment encourages more visitors and stimulates private sector investment in tourism facilities."[105]

This view became manifest in the large contributions of American, European, and Japanese aid to support tourism development planning and antiquities preservation that were being mobilized at the time. A 1993 USAID tourism strategy report also concludes: "Tourism development has the potential to broaden Jordan's export base and provide an increase in foreign exchange earnings, without a huge outlay of expenditures, at least in the short run. This, in turn, can stimulate other sectors of the economy by creating linkages in areas such as agriculture and manufacturing."[106]

The Jordanian economist Riad Al Khouri would concur that "as a result of the prospects for peace . . . the Jordanian and Middle Eastern tourism markets are now recognized as having great potential for growth. Tourism . . . could provide a major stimulus to the Jordan economy and is now seen by many as a sector where quick and useful co-operation among Jordan and its neighbors seems to be possible."[107] In this context, the prospects for tourism development gave the New Middle East credibility in Jordan, as tourism was the one sector where Jordanians could expect to generate income for broad sections of the economy.[108] Moreover, the idea of regional cooperation in the sector and cross-border tourism flows provided powerful images for advocates of the New Middle East in depicting Jordan's role in a seemingly less-fragmented region. As this vision of Jordan's future came to appear realizable, more Jordanians were willing to make the most of the opportunities afforded by peace and embrace or at least acquiesce to aspects of the New Middle East.

Negotiating a Blueprint for the New Middle East

While other Arab states, including Egypt, remained skeptical of the New Middle East and the normalization of relations with Israel, Jordan viewed them as an important opportunity. On September 14, 1993, one day after the signing of the Israel-PLO declaration on the White House lawn, Jordan and Israel signed their own agreement, based on a previously negotiated agenda, mapping out a path to a peace treaty. Two weeks later, Jordan's ambassador to the United States, echoing some of Peres's hopes, noted in a speech to the American Jewish Committee, "I think this new phase is putting us on the threshold of a new era, and hopefully a new Middle East that is more in line with the realities of the last decade of the 20th century."[109]

Shimon Peres pushed his vision by proposing a conference of several thousand business leaders to be held in Jerusalem and Amman, during which participants would shuttle back and forth between the two cities. Dennis Ross, who took the lead in the American effort to promote both peace and economic cooperation between Jordan and Israel, wrote: "The purpose would be to capture the international imagination and demonstrate that the Middle East was open for business."[110] However, Jordan was not immediately ready for such a bold gesture.

King Hussein was seeking a peace treaty with Israel to maximize Jordan's future strategic interests in a changing geopolitical environment. Such a treaty would secure increased U.S. military support for Jordan while giving it a place in the emerging regional order dominated by the United States and its eastern Mediterranean allies, Israel and Turkey. Jordan also sought economic resources to maintain what Laurie Brand refers to as "budget security, understood in terms of reproducing the conditions necessary for the ruling coalition to continue to pay the bills, preempt the development of opposition, or cultivate sufficient domestic support to make coercion against such groups possible."[111] Hussein suggested that because of Jordan's dire economic situation, moving toward peace was a "no choice" affair.[112] The king and his negotiators understood that a peace treaty with Israel would help President Clinton secure from Congress military aid and the dismissal of Jordan's $700 million debt.[113] American officials often suggested that bold moves toward peace and normalization would make an impact on Congress, where support for Israel was particularly high. Ross told the Jordanians that he wanted "something dramatic."[114]

By the spring of 1994, Israeli and Jordanian negotiators were making progress on a range of issues. In early July, Hussein agreed to host a meeting of a new U.S.-led trilateral committee for Israeli-Jordanian economic cooperation. Ross reports the meetings were making "headway on very practical issues: tourism, Jordan Rift Valley Development, a transnational theme park in the Dead Sea, civil aviation, and the development of 'the Camp David road' that would connect Egypt, Israel, and Jordan."[115] On July 25, 1994, Hussein and Israeli prime minister Yitzhak Rabin met in Washington and issued the Washington Declaration ending the state of war between their two states.

Throughout the process, American officials encouraged Jordanians to view their interests though the geopolitical imaginary of the New Middle East and to commit to a program of economic liberalization and growth led by the private sector. In a New Middle East, they suggested, Jordan would gain the investment and market opportunities to drive national economic development. Normalized relations and cooperation would generate mutual economic benefits that would solidify closer relations by forging shared material and strategic interests between the governments and their respective private sectors.[116] As Jordan and Israel were about to sign a document ending their state of war, U.S. secretary of state Warren Christopher even claimed, "This is a situation where the economics of it may be driving the politics of it."[117]

On October 26, 1994, Jordan and Israel staged an elaborate treaty signing ceremony at the newly opened Wadi Araba crossing point. Robert Satloff observed, "Today, Israel and Jordan are at peace, having negotiated a remarkably creative treaty that not only ends 46 years of war but sketches a blueprint for a warm web of political, economic, and human relationships."[118] Building on several rounds of regional multilateral negotiations, the treaty reads as a road map to the New Middle East. Article 7, "Economic Relations," states: "Viewing economic development and prosperity as pillars of peace, security and harmonious relations between states, peoples, and individual beings, the Parties . . . affirm their mutual desire to promote economic co-operation between them, as well as within the framework of wider regional economic co-operation."[119] In addition to ending Jordan's participation in the Arab economic boycott of Israel, the treaty recognizes "that the principle of free and unimpeded flow of goods and services should guide their relations" and states that the parties will conclude an agreement on economic cooperation in no more than six months.[120]

The Political Logic of the New Middle East in Jordan

The vision of the New Middle East was not only central to Jordan's external relations but also critical to defining the domestic political logic of the peace treaty. It became the chosen means for Jordan to forge a postrentier political economy. "As Prince Hassan often explained," Lynch notes, "a Middle East Market could allow Jordan to break its dependence upon foreign aid and turn its particular combination of human capital, close ties to Israel, and poor natural endowments to its long term economic advantage."[121] The treaty was expected to establish the foundation for a new postrentier economic development strategy that would provide material benefits to wide segments of the Jordanian population. Economic development, the regime hoped, could provide the needed glue to forge a stronger allegiance between diverse elements of society while mitigating dissent. After the peace treaty with Israel, the king even announced that economic development and prosperity were now "the bedrock of stability and genuine security."[122]

Economic issues were particularly important for domestic stability and regime legitimacy because by the early 1990s, GNP per capita dropped below its 1980 level, and nearly 30 percent of the population was living below the poverty line.[123] As Lynch argues, at the time of the treaty Jordan had a relatively open public sphere, and backers of the peace treaty were required to engage in public debate to make the case that peace with Israel would have wide-ranging economic benefits. He suggests that the economic rewards of peace should be viewed as "a public sphere justification strategy" and part of an effort to redefine Jordan's national interests and identity.[124] State officials and other backers of the treaty used the New Middle East vision, with its map for how peace would benefit Jordan, to contest alternative societal geopolitical imaginaries that viewed the normalization of relations with Israel as a threat to Jordan's identity and interests. For the regime, promoting economic benefits was critical to containing the mobilization of political opposition. Trade and Industry Minister Ali Abu Raghrib "put the government's position quite bluntly, 'the success of the peace treaty . . . hinges totally on the success of [economic] development efforts.'"[125]

Soon after the treaty was signed, Prime Minister Majali boldly promised that "economic opportunities generated by the peace treaty would 'kill the specter of unemployment'" in Jordan.[126] Prince Hassan often ambitiously spoke of "bringing Jordan into the global economy and out of the IMF [debtors] club" by attracting global financing.[127] King Hussein himself assured Jordanians that "the economies of their region were indeed capable of rapid, widely shared sustainable growth. . . . Within five years, he declared, if matters proceeded as Jordan hoped, the kingdom would be economically independent and the people would have the opportunities to live the life they deserved."[128]

The expectations of economic dividends likely made the difference in mobilizing popular support for, and dampening opposition to, the regime's decision to rapidly sign such an extensive treaty agreement. George Hawatema, the editor of the English-language *Jordan Times,* estimates that 20 percent of the population, consisting mostly of Islamists, rejected the very idea of a treaty with Israel, while 20 percent, representing the core of the regime's support base, solidly backed the peace treaty. Meanwhile, he suggests the remaining 60 percent of the population were "giving the treaty a chance to provide its dividends."[129] A survey conducted by Allison Astorino-Courtois reported that "information regarding the *economic* benefits of a peace accord is associated with the highest mean support for peace."[130] Moreover, in 1994 Jordan's Center for Strategic Studies found that 82 percent of Jordanians thought the peace process would improve the country's economic situation, of which half expected these benefits in the short term.[131]

The tourism sector, in particular, was envisioned as being able in the short term to provide the national economy with tangible benefits. While not highly publicized at the time, it was understood in some quarters that many of the material rewards from the treaty would not come quickly, and even debt relief and aid from the United States and other countries might take years to materialize. Delivering a speech written by Prince Hassan to the Middle East Policy Council in Washington, Dr. Anani acknowledged that indeed, according to a World Bank study, Jordan's national income and state revenues would probably drop in the first years after a peace deal.[132] Dr. Anani thus suggested that Jordan would first have to invest heavily "in roads and infrastructure and hotels and restaurants" before the gains could be realized.[133] His remarks, though, also demonstrate that many officials believed Jordan could depend on the tourism sector to get through the difficult transitional phase: "So, what we're doing, we're doing like sometimes shopkeepers [do], looking for things which can generate cash, like encouraging tourism, you know. There is ready money there."[134] By linking the peace process so closely with the expansion of tourism in the official public discourse, Jordanian officials represented the treaty as a chance to promote economic development.

The king's policy of pursuing a rapid peace treaty with Israel nevertheless risked fostering domestic political opposition and the mobilization of geopolitical imaginaries generally incompatible with the New Middle East and the interests of the monarchy. Many Jordanians continued to reject peace and the idea of normalization, or at least viewed it as premature until Palestinian rights and sovereignty were fully realized. In the early 1990s, a liberalized media and the strong presence of Islamists and Arab nationalists in parliament allowed opportunities for voicing popular opposition to Jordan's increasingly enthusiastic participation in the U.S.-led peace process and indirect negotiations with Israel in multilateral talks.[135] In time, however, the space for political opposition and public debate declined. As other observers of Jordanian politics have noted, as progress toward peace with Israel advanced, Jordan's moment of political liberalization began to end.[136] Such moves began in August 1993, a few weeks before the announcement of the Oslo breakthrough, when the king decided to alter the national election law. Largely as a result of carefully crafted changes, the November 1993 election led to a shrinking of the representation of the Islamist and left/nationalist opposition forces in parliament. This change would allow for the easy 55-to-23 ratification of the peace treaty in the chamber of deputies. However, in May 1994 members of the opposition organized the Committee for Resisting Submission and Normalization (CRSN) to challenge Jordanian moves to normalize economic, political, and cultural relations with Israel, the very processes central to the notion of a New Middle East. Opposition to normalization also developed within the business community and professional unions, which often refused to interact with Israeli colleagues. The "antinormalization" movement, with its alternative geopolitical imaginary promoting political reterritorialization, would come to represent one of the most important vehicles for social mobilization against the regime and its policies. By the late 1990s, the regime enacted other laws to limit the scope for popular demonstrations, political organization, and free speech in the press—eventually closing up the Jordanian public sphere.[137] In the meantime, the government sought to battle the rise of antinormalization sentiment, particularly strong in the Palestinian-Jordanian community and among Islamists connecting the peace treaty to economic development. The regime also sought to build a new social base that relied on "business, political, and military elites with a common interest in opening Jordan to greater economic opportunities, from foreign investment to the revitalization of tourism and trade."[138] As the *Economist* observed in 1995,

"It is, in effect, a race: will the economic benefits of peace come in time to dampen political discontent?"[139]

Tourism and Itineraries of the New Middle East in Jordan

While many analysts of the Arab-Israeli conflict emphasize strategic and security issues as the main drivers of state behavior, Jordan's official embrace of the New Middle East cannot be understood without exploring the role of tourism development. Tourism was essential to the regime's effort to "sell the peace" and show that it could rapidly generate broad-based economic benefits. More generally, as tourism came to be viewed as Jordan's new engine for economic growth, the development of the nation's tourism sector, the creation of new tourism facilities, the promotion of transnational economic cooperation, and its marketing as a tourism destination all became critical for the incorporation of Jordan into the global economy. Moreover, Jordanian officials also viewed tourism development as a means to realize the New Middle East's vision of unleashing the private sector, but within a context that the state could centrally manage and direct. Government officials would guide development planning and marketing, while national resources such as coastal land and heritage sites could provide new sources of state revenue and authority. Thus tourism development would increase the state's bureaucratic powers, allowing it to control and direct the economic benefits of the sector.

Tourism Planning and the Making of the New Middle East

With few other options, the prospect for a boost in national income initiated by expansive tourism development was the linchpin in the peace treaty's viability for the regime. The arguments for realizing the economic gains of peace through tourism development were expressed in a nationally televised speech on November 23, 1993, by King Hussein. Hussein noted his pride in Jordan's national treasures, including its archaeological sites and historical buildings. He then announced that the government would support the development of tourism facilities so that they could receive tourists and that "this should increase economic returns in a manner that would support the balance of payments, replenish the treasury's hard currency reserves, augment the economic growth rate and expand the gross national product." He made particular reference to the private sector, which "would have a major role to play in tourist development" and would be encouraged "through incentive expanding investment, streamlined procedures and tourist development legislation."[140]

As the peace process advanced and multilateral negotiations were making progress, American, Israeli, and Jordanian government officials conducted both private and public campaigns to tout the economic logic of peace and promote private sector investment in tourism. At the opening session of the U.S.-Israel-Jordan Trilateral Economic Committee held at the Dead Sea on July 20, 1994, U.S. secretary of state Christopher echoed this vision: "Perhaps no sector offers more immediate promise than tourism. . . . Cooperative efforts to facilitate travel between the two countries could quickly result in a significant boost in tourism. And that would generate much needed jobs and revenue, attracting foreign investment."[141]

The end of the official state of war, established with the Washington Declaration on July 25, paved the way for the opening of border crossings. American Middle East envoy Dennis Ross recounts traveling north from Aqaba, where a crossing point was to be opened: "Suddenly I was moved by the most mundane of road signs: there in Arabic and English, was a new sign giving both the direction and distance to Eilat, a town that had never been acknowledged before in Jordan. . . . The world had changed in Jordan. I marveled at the sign. . . . I knew my dream of drawing Aqaba and Eilat together . . . had moved from dream to reality."[142]

Even before the two sides worked out arrangements for their own citizens to cross back and forth, Israelis with second passports began venturing across to be the first to explore the monuments and cultures of Jordan. While some felt unease, it is telling that a Jordanian guiding one of these tours reassured his Israeli visitors that "most people here are poor, and they believe King Hussein when he tells them the peace with Israel will make them richer. So you have nothing to fear."[143] In the following months, these travelers were joined by tens of thousands of Israeli visitors along with a flood of North American and European tourists and international journalists to witness the realization of the New Middle East. Banners even appeared in Amman urging the public to learn Hebrew, and hotels and restaurants were considering the creation of kosher kitchens. An Israeli journalist reported that in Jordan, "state-owned TV and radio, and the independent but loyal press, have been working round-the-clock promoting the coming peace . . . selling the tangible benefits that peace with Israel will bring. The media overflow with items about the expected increase in tourism—billed as 'Jordan's oil.'"[144] Expectations were building about the seemingly limitless possibilities of tourism development. As a Bank of Jordan representative suggested, "The agreement will increase tourism to Jordan by 100 percent yearly. . . . We need to open new hotels, restaurants, and travel agencies to deal with the expected influx of tourists."[145] The anticipated tourism explosion even made some fearful of an impending ecological disaster. Uri Avner of the Israeli Antiquities Authorities warned, "The only thing to do is to get to Petra before the Israelis get there . . . before it becomes covered all over with graffiti."[146] Due to a previous request by Jordan's Queen Noor, UNESCO sent a mission to study the potential threats to Petra.[147]

Meanwhile the peace process was being stage-managed with many public events designed to generate regional and international interest in tourism and tourism development in Jordan. Following the Washington Declaration, the tourism ministers of Israel and Jordan held a pair of meetings on opposite sides of the Dead Sea. During the first one, on the Israeli side, the Jordanian tourism minister Muhammad Al Adwan briefed Israeli travel agents about tourism in Jordan and agreed with his Israeli counterpart to market joint tourism packages in the United States. In addition, he announced a plan for twenty new investment projects, as he predicted a prosperous tourism industry in the coming years: "Tourism is a peace industry, [and] flourishes always within a peaceful environment that is based on stability and security. And we believe that all parties in the region . . . will benefit greatly once peace is achieved."[148]

In an October 1994 speech at Georgetown University, just before President Clinton was to fly to the signing of the peace treaty, Secretary of State Christopher spoke about the "warm peace" being forged between Jordan and Israel and about how "the two courageous leaders are determined that their border will become a gateway rather than a barrier. Already, there are ads in Israeli papers for tours of Jordan's great historical sites in Petra and Jerash." He noted that with the help of the U.S.-Israel-Jordan economic commission, projects of regional economic cooperation "will build bonds of human contact and common interest. They will cement an enduring peace."[149] Christopher spoke of how governments "must reduce economic barriers and help build infrastructure that joins the Middle East by road, air, fax, and microchip," while "through investment, trade, and joint ventures, private commerce can build ties that will transform peace between governments into peace between people."[150]

The signing of the treaty itself was a grand event with international dignitaries, congratulatory speeches, military bands from both sides, and the releasing of doves. The event took place along the newly agreed on Israeli-Jordanian border in the Wadi Araba (or Arava in Hebrew) desert just north of Aqaba and Eilat. Bringing development to this poor rural region was a major concern for Jordanian officials, and they thought that "the desert-like terrain would trigger the interests of leaders to support integrated development of the Jordan Rift Valley."[151] At the ceremony, President Clinton "spoke of transforming the arid lands of Wadi Araba into a Valley of Peace."[152] Pursuant to Article 17 of the Treaty on Tourism, the two sides established a joint commission to promote regional tourism development, and the Jordanian government pledged to realize a massive tourism infrastructure plan and began drawing up tax incentives for foreign and local investors in the sector.[153]

While the Clinton administration used Jordan's bold moves toward normalization to lobby Congress and U.S. allies for aid and debt relief, USAID was working to realize the economic cooperation and development envisioned by the New Middle East. The promotion of tourism development was at the center of these early efforts. As early as September 1993, the USAID contractor Chemonics International had prepared a technical feasibility study for a new tourism marketing strategy. It noted that "opening the borders to the West . . . could dramatically change the dynamics of tourism in the region."[154] The study outlined a multi-million-dollar program to revamp and expand the organizational structure of the sector and to develop tourism planning and marketing policies and capacities. In September 1994 USAID entered into an agreement with Jordan's Ministry of Planning to launch a $7 million project to develop Jordanian cultural and natural resources to generate foreign exchange from tourism.[155]

The official effort to publicly promote tourism investment gained its greatest international exposure at the U.S.-sponsored Middle East and North Africa (MENA) summits. The MENA summits represented American efforts to mobilize business elites and international investment for regional economic transformation. In his memoirs, Christopher gives Peres credit for originating the idea of the MENA summits.[156] At the first conference, held in Casablanca, Morocco, in 1994, Christopher announced that "an ambitious master plan for the development of the Jordan Rift Valley has been completed. Joint efforts to promote tourism in the Red Sea ports of Aqaba and Eilat are already attracting millions of dollars of investment in hotels, infrastructure, and tourist facilities."[157] Meanwhile real estate developers based in Israel were designing projects and gathering multinational sources of investment. In a sign of the times, the CEO of Koor Industries, one of Israel's leading conglomerates, established a joint-venture "Salaam 2000" with Palestinian, Spanish, and Moroccan investors.[158] Tourism was expected to be a leading interest of investors seeking to exploit the "peace bonanza." Christopher announced that the United States would help create a regional tourist board, stressing that "tourism is one of the clearest and quickest ways to generate hard currency reserves. The Middle East and North Africa abound with incredible archaeological and religious sites. Millions of tourists will flock to visit as package tours crossing previously closed borders."[159] After announcing, "The Middle East is open for business," he ended his speech by saying (in a nod to Humphrey Bogart's famous closing line in *Casablanca*), "The conference could be the beginning of a beautiful friendship."[160]

Following up their meetings at Casablanca and working under the auspices of the REDWG, government officials, representatives from international tourism organizations, and members of the private sector worked to draft the charter of the Middle East–Mediterranean Travel and Tourism Association (MEMTTA).[161] As an organization, MEMTTA sought to bring together public and private representatives from the Middle East, the United States, and elsewhere "in a common effort to make possible the movement of people across borders to visit on business and pleasure" and realize the "region's large travel potential." The charter, which would be signed at the following MENA summit held in Amman, states as one of its principles that its members "desire to demonstrate through economic cooperation the tangible benefits of a comprehensive peace in the Middle East" and "recognize that travel and tourism will play an important role in deepening cooperation and mutual understanding in the region."[162] The MEMTTA, headed by Cord Hansen-Strum, an American diplomat turned tourism promoter, sought to develop and market the region as a single destination.

At the second MENA summit, held in Jordan in 1995, Christopher announced, "Today, in Amman, it is time to play it again, Sam."[163] With political and business leaders from sixty-three countries expected to attend, the run-up to the summit generated great excitement and intense activity. Municipal workers labored to clean up Amman's streets, "banners proclaiming Jordan's economic promise hung over Amman's major thoroughfares," and "a detailed street map of Amman, the first of its kind prepared in Jordan, was printed by the Greater Amman Municipality in English and Arabic," complete with new street names honoring Transjordanian royal and nationalist figures.[164] The Jordanian parliament quickly drafted new investment codes and tax breaks.[165] Rami Khouri, a Jordanian journalist, laid out the stakes:

> This meeting is totally about politics, nationhood, survival, credibility, and even legitimacy; because in our world today the leading (maybe the only remaining) ideology is business, and the confidence and cash-flows of the global business community have become the most important sources of political validation and even legitimacy for many countries in the developing world.[166]

Jordanian officials viewed the quick mobilization of tourism development as critical to launching Jordan's economic recovery by making the country an attractive destination for international capital while eroding Jordan's image as a fragile state in a conflict-prone region. At the summit, both Jordan and Israel showcased their grand plans for tourism-related developments with long lists of investment opportunities for private capital. Many of their tourism-related ideas, such as building a binational park along the border, had been discussed at the REDWG talks and the meetings of the U.S.-Israel-Jordan Trilateral Economic Committee.[167] Jordan's plans focused on massive projects along the Dead Sea and Gulf of Aqaba.[168] Three weeks before the Amman summit, the Aqaba Regional Authority and an American investor signed a deal for a $132 million theme park and resort that "should kick-start the process" of transforming Aqaba with "Disney-style theme parks, golf courses, and resort hotels."[169] Of the twenty-seven high-priority projects announced by the Jordanian government, amounting to $3.5 billion of investment, the two private-sector tourism projects in Aqaba and the Dead Sea alone amounted to $1 billion.[170] The government's tourism infrastructure plan confidently spelled out the state's visions on a massive scale and explained that "the 6.3 percent annual growth in hotel rooms over the past 10 years is predicted to increase dramatically, along with the average occupancy rate of 65 percent and the current average daily room rate of $86."[171] Even more spectacularly, the Jordan Valley Authority's Dead Sea Master Plan envisioned building about 10,000 bed units in hotels and apartments by the year 2000 and another 20,000 or so over the following decade.[172] The plan committed the state to building all the needed infrastructure works in the area. In addition to presenting grand tourism development plans for the sleepy industrial port city of Aqaba, the tourism development projects offered by Jordan at the Amman and later MENA summits did not focus on archaeological sites like Petra but listed other projects up and down the Rift Valley.[173] These projects included a desert tourism center in the Wadi Araba, projects in the Northern Jordan Valley, and a plan for a multifunctional John the Baptist baptism pool and conference center along the river Jordan just north of the Dead Sea. While sites like Petra were sure to attract private local investment, these government-backed projects were located along Jordan's borders with Israel, where Israeli-Jordanian economic cooperation was to help build a regional tourism economy. Additionally, these planned projects were also set in the country's poorer areas, which had been rocked by riots in the wake of the implementation of economic austerity measures and thus were desperately in need of economic development and job creation.

Beginning in 1993 with the Oslo Accords but picking up steam in 1994 and 1995, Israeli investors took the lead in mapping out plans to realize the New Middle East through cross-border investment in projects designed to exploit the changing geography of capitalist development. In 1994 an Israeli-led group of investors imagined "creating an artificial lake in the Arava, in which they would plant an artificial island that would hold a 'City of Peace.' This city would be settled by people of various nationalities who would preserve their respective ethnic lifestyles."[174] The Peace City was to cost $1 billion and be surrounded by ten thousand hotel rooms around the lake. Various plans for a Disney World–style "Holy Land" amusement park, a Las Vegas–style Sun City, and lowest-place-on-earth Dead Sea park flooded the Israeli and international media. These ideas were supported by plans generated by the Israeli Foreign Ministry, depicting what a few years earlier would have been unthinkable. Israeli maps suggested that there could be up to nine "internodal" crossing points between Jordan and Israel or the West Bank.[175] These would expand the scope for desert tourism and, with the help of new superhighways, facilitate flows between Israeli, Palestinian, Egyptian, and Jordanian tourism sites that could function as "international nodes." The Israeli plans envisioned a reweaving of the tourism economies of Egypt and the Levant based on their shared multireligious cultural heritage. Rather than simply "national" tourism, Israel and the rest of the region could market itself as a destination for diverse transnational itineraries defined by the ancient spice route from Gaza through the Negev to Petra, the route of the annual Muslim hajj from Egypt across Israel on its way to Mecca, or Christian pilgrimage routes that follow the travels of Jesus, weaving back and forth through Israel, the Palestinian authority, Jordan, Lebanon, and Syria. Less ambitiously, Jordanian plans outlined the development of tourism sites along its side of the border. Noting that "similar facilities are successfully operated in Israel," Jordan's plans suggested that its sites would seek to attract visitors from Eilat/Aqaba and that "the long term aim would be to establish collaborate links with similar centers in Israel to promote cross border activities."[176]

Images from space looking down on the earth are often used to evoke notions of common humanity not separated by political boundaries and borders. With the signing of the peace treaty, a new geopolitical imaginary took shape. As Rebecca Stein reports: "In the Near East Travel's East Jerusalem office, a satellite photograph of the Middle East is framed under glass. . . . National borders are unmarked, The Holy Land—so the map is labeled—appears as a single, seamless territory."[177] Meanwhile tour operators began marketing transnational and regional itineraries. As tourists began crossing the newly open border between Israel and Jordan, air travelers to and from Jordan began experiencing the new reality of geopolitical space when Royal Jordanian Airlines was able to fly directly through Israeli airspace. Within minutes, travelers flying out of Amman airport were now able to see Jerusalem and then

Tel Aviv and Haifa.[178] More practically, saving eighteen minutes of flying time decreased the airfare on routes to Europe and the United States.[179] By 1996, Royal Jordanian established a subsidiary, Royal Wings, and began flying regularly along the thirty-five-minute route between Tel Aviv and Amman.[180] Aqaba and then other regional routes across the Levant were added to the Royal Wings flight map. In a telling sign of the contrasting relationships that Egypt and Jordan established with Israel, Air Sinai used all-white, generally unmarked, aircraft on its flights to and from Israel, while the Royal Wings flights sported a royal crown, an obvious Hashemite logo. Israel and Jordan did not limit their cooperation to airspace. The Jordanian-Israeli bilateral tourism commission sought to develop a joint "Peace Airport" at Aqaba. Working from a Jordanian idea, they developed plans to build a major airport centered on Jordan's existing Aqaba airport runway, which unlike Eilat's commercial strip can land large-capacity aircraft. The landing strip would be serviced by terminals on both sides of the border.[181] In the view of many Israeli and Jordanian officials, the Peace Airport could serve as the hub for an ambitious tourism development and economic cooperation project, the building of a "Red Sea Riviera."[182] This tourist development would stretch from Egypt's Sharm al Sheikh to Jordan's shore in the Gulf of Aqaba. Planners envisioned the extension of the Peace Promenade being built in Eilat to extend across the border to Aqaba and the development of a marina to serve the region. Tourism promoters hoped the land crossing would involve only quick passport checks, while the establishment of maritime crossings would facilitate boating and "windsurfing across borders."[183] As part of this vision, in the course of multilateral talks, Egypt, Israel, and Jordan had begun cooperating on creating a nature reserve in the waters of the gulf to protect it from environmental damage. Their efforts were assisted by the development of transnational NGOs, such as EcoPeace: Friends of Earth Middle East.[184] Thus, in contrast to the post-treaty dispute over Taba, Israel's treaty with Jordan seemed to be leading to the realization of Peres's New Middle East vision, driven by a deterritorialized geopolitical imagination and fueled by international capital, that would leave the Israeli-Jordanian border across the Wadi Araba and the river Jordan as well as the Gulf of Aqaba/Eilat dotted with deluxe hotels, amusement parks, rural tourist sites, and conference centers and connected by high-speed superhighways, man-made canals, and waterfront promenades.

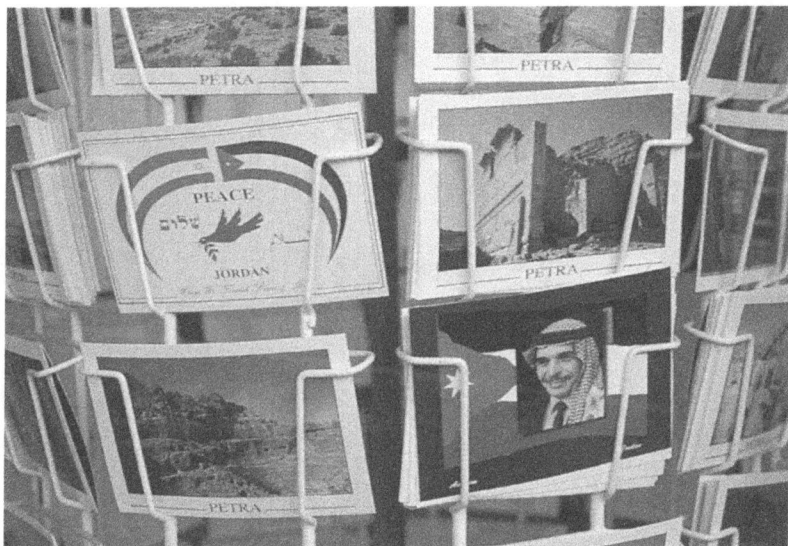

Figure 12. Postcards of the New Middle East for sale at Petra, April 1996. Photograph by Richard T. Nowitz.

Experiencing the New Middle East: The Beginnings of a Tourism Development Boom

The opening of the Wadi Araba border crossing in 1994 allowed tourists and package tours to easily travel from Israel to Jordan and back, leading to a vast increase in visits to Petra, which exploded as a tourist destination. Reporters from Israel and around the world came to Jordan to write stories about the Israeli-Jordanian peace process and the antiquities of Jordan, while politicians and tourism officials made special tours to focus media attention on Jordan and its sites. Tour operators, airlines, tourism ministries, and the MEMTTA launched marketing campaigns to promote regional Middle East tourism and travel to Jordan. As a result, between 1993 and 1995, European and American arrivals grew by 75 percent from 204,000 to 359,000.[185] The number of Israeli tourists ballooned from officially zero in 1993 to about 10,000 in November and December 1994 to over 100,000 in 1995. The number of bed nights spent by package tourists shot up from about 440,000 in 1993 to 1,141,000 in 1995, with Israelis making up almost 30 percent.

Table 5. Growth of package tourism to Jordan, 1993–96

Year	U.S. bed nights	change	Europeans bed nights	change	Arabs bed nights	change	Israelis bed nights	change	Total[a] bed nights	change
1993	17,934		380,696		8,003				439,762	
1994	31,253	74%	515,727	35%	11,848	48%	16,888		626,013	42%
1995	69,372	122%	646,731	25%	15,145	28%	329,780	1853%	1,140,830	82%
1996	78,773	14%	672,560	4%	16,891	12%	244,625	–26%	1,091,026	–4%

Source: Ministry of Tourism and Antiquities.

[a] Total includes tourists from all sources.

A major focus of these tourist flows was the stunning rock-carved city of Petra. As Jordanian and international archaeologists worked to discover, uncover, and preserve the ruins and monuments of the park, increased international marketing efforts and exposure in the world media further augmented the place-myth of Petra. In July 1994 the *New York Times* reported that during his visit to Jordan just before the signing of the Washington Declaration, Secretary of State Warren Christopher made a "whirlwind tour . . . of the Nabatean ruins at Petra where Steven Spielberg filmed the last scenes of *Indiana Jones and the Last Crusade* . . . largely aimed at encouraging American tourism."[186] As predicted, driven by curiosity and the almost mythic aura that the long-forbidden city of Petra had acquired for them, Israeli visitors rushed in.[187] American Express founded the World Monuments Watch with an image of Petra as its main logo, and the company's travel division put a picture of Petra's al Khazneh (the Treasury) on the cover of its "Israel, Jordan, Egypt and Turkey" *Vacations* guide, representing the rise of Jordan as a major regional destination long in the shadow of better known and developed regional destinations such as Cairo, Jerusalem, and Istanbul. Total visitors to Petra rose from below 41,000 during the 1991 Gulf War ebb to 200,000 in 1994 and jumped to 330,000 in 1995 and to 414,000 in 1996. In 1995 almost 20 percent of visitors to Petra traveled on Israeli passports.[188]

The dramatic increase of tourism visitors in 1994 and 1995 led to previously unheard of levels of overbooking at hotels, and all other aspects of the industry, such as bus lines and rental car agencies, quickly faced acute shortages. In 1995 a British tour operator reported that "the demand for Jordan is incredible and there are great problems booking space. It has become a seller's market, and the hoteliers can dictate their own terms. Prices have gone up 30 to 40 percent," and Jordan's hotels were expected to push rates up above 40 percent in the following year.[189] The occupancy rate of

Year	Visitors
1993	138,559
1994	200,505
1995	337,221
1996	414,448

Figure 13. Tourist visits to Petra Archaeological Park, 1993–96. *Source:* Department of Antiquities, Jordan.

hotels classified as five-star deluxe went from an average of 42 percent in 1993 to 66 percent over the course of 1995. Occupancy rates for all Amman hotels jumped from 54 percent in 1993 to 74 percent in 1995.[190] Well-established hotels like the Inter-Continental in Amman often experienced occupancy rates of over 90 percent.

Although Jordanian officials had reservations about many aspects of Israeli schemes for tourism cooperation, they were busy with their own efforts toward tourism development and economic growth in Jordan. An Israeli journalist reported at the time that "some of the circle of advisors who surround King Hussein think that priority should be given to developing the infrastructure to attract more tourists, so that within two or three years, tourism revenues will naturally filter through to all strata of society."[191] The key limiting factor, they thought at the time, was the volume of investment. As noted earlier, various officials at the Ministry of Planning and other agencies had outlined numerous costly projects they wanted to see funded by international investors and development agencies as well as local entrepreneurs.

In this context, investment was spurred on not only by marginal shifts in tax burdens or detailed market surveys but more critically by growing confidence in the future of the tourism market projected by the New Middle East vision. Many businesspeople in the private sector who chose to invest in tourism were influenced to some degree by meetings with state officials, including with Prince Hassan, where they were directly encouraged to invest for the sake of the national welfare. The broader public campaign sought international as well as domestic investment. Others were influenced indirectly by local and international reports of such meetings and press conferences concerning the likely economic consequences of the peace treaty. At a time when the economy was weak and there appeared to be few other opportunities, news stories about the Jordanian economy in both the local and international press singled out tourism.

Soon newspapers were reporting the number of hotels in the works, the names of international companies interested in investing in Jordan, and the publication of new editions of guidebooks for Jordan, including ones in Hebrew. In 1995 the local affiliate of Arthur Andersen published a series of studies titled "Business and Investment in Jordan." Its tourism report noted, "The outlook for generating profits, especially for the first class hotels, is very promising. . . . Jordan suffers from marked shortages of hotels and other tourism-related facilities *which makes unlimited possibilities for investment.*"[192]

The economic potential of tourism seemed to hold out opportunities for almost anyone regardless of skill, profession, or even capital endowment while avoiding the question of the limits or distribution of these gains. The leaders of the wealthy merchant families, who had close ties to the royal family, and other prominent businessmen were actively involved in the economic discussions surrounding the peace process. Many began lining up capital, feasibility studies, and rights to lease land. At the same time, the tribes of Wadi Musa (the town at the entrance to Petra), the former workers in the Gulf now driving cabs in the wealthy sections of Western Amman, and the souvenir hawkers in the poorer areas of Amman's downtown all envisioned new opportunities for gaining income. The rural regions in the south and along the river Jordan in the north, which had been hurt badly by the economic austerity measures, expected to benefit from new tourism-related development projects. Palestinian-Jordanians, from the assimilated bourgeois elites to the middle-class businessmen and shop owners who were most often opposed to the peace process, also expected to reap the dividends of peace. Unlike other forms of private-sector development, the benefits of tourism could potentially be spread widely down the class ladder and regionally across the whole imagined national community of Jordan. As more and more Jordanians began to open tourism-related businesses, others rushed to build their facilities and beat their competitors to the profits. Jordanian investments in tourism were soon spurred by growing confidence in the future of the market.

Redesigning Jordan's Tourism Economy: Tourism Planning and the "Big Push"

While the Israeli plans tended to project a vision of interconnected regional tourism dominated by Israeli investment and management, Jordanian tourism plans focused on the state management of Jordanian national space and economic resources. In plans on display at the MENA summits from 1994 to 1997, Jordan's Ministry of Planning (MOP) presented a series of tourism-related projects that the state was ready to support with tax breaks, new legal codes, marketing efforts, and costly infrastructure projects. The goal of these plans was to attract investment to launch tourism as the engine of national economic development. In *Jordan: A Winning Business Destination,* the MOP's tourism sector plan explains: "One major goal is to make tourism a major source of foreign exchange earnings for the country, and bring about a steady increase of investment and employment opportunities to support the national economy. In turn, stimulation of other sectors will create linkages in areas such as manufacturing and agriculture."[193]

Virtually the same language appeared in private-sector reports.[194] While opening the door to private-sector investment, tourism development was backed by extensive government promotion and planning. As noted earlier, before the peace process, the tourism economy existed in a low-equilibrium trap. As a newswire report explained in 1995, "For the government, the problem is how to sensibly kick-start a long-stagnant tourism industry."[195] Abdullah al-Khatib, Jordan's minister of tourism, explained that "tourism is an economic activity that, in order to develop, requires a steady flow of business. . . . I mean, you can't open a hotel if you don't have clients."[196] As a response to the challenge of the low-income-equilibrium trap, the development economist Paul Rosenstein-Rodan formulated the idea of the "big push."[197] In the big-push model, state planners seek to promote large-scale increases in supply—capturing economies of scale with modern production techniques and technologies—simultaneously with increases in demand generated by the workers hired in the newly established factories. The strategy of development is referred to as "balanced growth" because planners seek to simultaneously expand supply and demand to establish a new equilibrium at a higher level. Following the logic of the big push, an escape from a low-equilibrium trap in the tourism sector would require a large influx of foreign tourists simultaneously with large-scale investment in tourism development. Thus the prospect of a tourism boom in the wake of the peace treaty radically changed the dynamics of tourism development. The expected boom offered Jordan a means to escape from the trap and created a rationale for the implementation of extensive tourism plans by the government and the mobilization of capital for tourism development from the Jordanian private sector.

With the peace process, Jordan entered into a phase of extensive tourism development planning. Even as the dreams of joint Israeli-Jordanian megaprojects failed to initialize and then evaporated with Rabin's assassination in 1995, the move to the right in Israel, and the domestic opposition in Jordan to "normalization," the idea that Jordan needed to promote a state-led big push in tourism development remained. State agencies had always envisioned their own national development plans alongside the binational ventures, arguing that the national plans "neither depend critically on the rest of the binational development program nor pre-empt it."[198]

Jordan, however, was a country ill prepared for comprehensive centralized tourism development planning. Its bureaucracy was burdened by many of the same ills that are said to infect bureaucracies in developing countries, such as lack of competence, corruption, nepotism, overcentralization, overlapping jurisdictions, and excessive paperwork.[199] These surely hampered and distorted the promotion of tourism development in Jordan. Most fundamentally, though, the problem for tourism planning was its reliance on the notion that the New Middle East would lead to a big push in demand for the tourism sector.

The balanced-growth model powerfully represented much of the thinking about, and the expectations for, tourism development in the context of the New Middle East. The central motivation for adopting this approach was the need to generate positive external economies that could (seemingly) distribute income and job opportunities broadly across society and thus help "sell" the peace. This model of tourism development also reflected the private sector's interest in short-term, risk-averse investment opportunities. Moreover, this approach accorded with state interests in expanding regulatory powers, gaining revenues, and promoting national development. Even as the expansion of multinational corporations and the "more fluid circulation and value of money" have made national economies more elusive to define, measure, and represent as objects of state policy, tourism stands out as an economic sector where national objects—be they tourist sites, maps, air carriers, or development plans—are prominent identifiable features that states retain considerable power to manipulate.[200] Balanced-growth planning models could seemingly measure and represent the tourism economy as well as unambiguously depict how it should be developed. At the same time, the private sector and state planners could easily envision how to produce tourism commodities (in contrast to the challenges of creating other globally competitive goods and services). In most other sectors, such a top-down, centrally coordinated mode of development would quickly be viewed as economically inefficient or politically unfeasible. But since state agencies controlled much of the geographic and cultural resources of tourism, as well as the channels of tourist flows, they seemed well positioned to guide the promotion and regulation of the sector. The landscape of tourism—its representability and readability— suggested to policy makers that centralized states had the capacity to promote national tourism development.

A study in 1996 by the Japan International Cooperation Agency (JICA), which formulated the most extensive national tourism development plan for Jordan, follows the balanced-growth approach. From December 1994 to January 1996, a team of Japanese experts came to Jordan to draw up a National Tourism Development Plan in cooperation with Jordan's Ministry of Tourism and Antiquities. The result was a massive four-volume study setting out parameters for the promotion of tourism in Jordan as well as detailing a number of specific infrastructure and tourism site projects. It maps out a new tourism economy in Jordan based on expanded tourism hubs and the fashioning of tourism spaces across the country that were expected to create locational rents and positive external economies. The study is framed by an assessment of projected total national tourism demand and existing tourism supply. It begins by clearly recognizing "the importance of tourism as the prime mover of the Jordanian economy (tourism is the oil of Jordan.)"[201] In estimating the future of tourism demand, the study draws up three scenarios that estimate growth rates between 5 percent and 7 percent for the next five years. While not extrapolating from the 1994–95 era, the JICA study relies on the assumption that Jordan is now immune to the volatility previously caused by geopolitical conflict and regional political instability.

The big-push expectation is particularly evident in the Jordan Valley Authority's Dead Sea Master Plan (revised in 1996), which envisioned building about 10,000 bed units by the year 2000 and then another 20,000 or so over the following decade, with the plan committing the state to building all the needed infrastructure works in the area. The scale of the project was so enormous that it attracted concern about its environmental and ecological impact.[202] More to the point, the JVA plan calculates feasibility tables and the cost and revenues of the project using maximalist projections about future tourism flows in the context of the New Middle East:

> This set of potentialities places the development planning approach in the position of [a] "supply strategy"; in other words, the essential parameters [for planning tourism development growth] stem rather from the Study Area bearing capacity, within, naturally, "a sustainable development concept," than from any potential market appraisal![203]

In the plan, this statement is printed in boldface. This study, prepared by a French consultant, presents extensive research, analyzing numerous market segments and reporting on, for example, the incidence of certain skin diseases in the European population for which a stay at the Dead Sea would be a suitable treatment. Nevertheless the study suggests that the goal of the JVA tourism development policy should be to expand investment in the Dead Sea region, seemingly without limit, so as to absorb as great a share of the expected inflow of tourism to Jordan as possible. The feasibility of the project was calculated based on the maximum possible expansion of tourism supply with little concern about tourism demand. As in the balanced-growth models, the plan attempts to function as a replacement for, or at least an informed representation of, market information for the direction of the private sector, which would function as the source of capital for tourism development in the region.

Mapping and Remapping the New Middle East

The various plans drafted in the context of the tourism boom between 1994 and 1996 mapped out the redesign of Jordan's natural and built landscape. Amman's city center was to be repaved with tourist sidewalks and signage, and Wadi Musa, the rural village outside Petra, was to become a Euro-Mediterranean resort for the jet set. There were rival schemes, with some planners seeking to coat the shores of the Dead Sea and Gulf of Aqaba with dense tourism and resort developments to rival those in Israel, while others promoted eco-friendly visions that that blended well with the Jordanian natural environment and vernacular architecture.[204] In any case, all these grand visions to commodify the geography and culture of Jordan as a tourism product were enabled by the rise of the notion of the New Middle East in Jordan around 1994 in the context of "selling the peace."

This remapping of the Middle East represented a sharp contrast to the nature of Egyptian-Israeli relations in the wake of their peace treaty signed fifteen years before. At the time, while Israel was pushing for expanded normalization, neither side had embraced a geopolitical imaginary such as the New Middle East. Clearly, the post–Gulf War geopolitical environment, with the United States as a rising regional hegemon and the launching of the Oslo peace process, helped the much weaker Jordan adopt an attitude toward normalization that Egypt declined. Jordan's embrace of the New Middle East, however, cannot fully be understood through the lens of realist geopolitics, as internal threats and budget security have always constrained Jordanian foreign policy. During the Gulf War, popular mobilization supported a "neutralist," if not pro-Iraqi, stance, while the concerns for budget security as well as Jordan's traditional alliances pushed in the other direction. The New Middle East offered a model for realigning Jordanian strategic interests while forging a postrentier economy that could both provide budget security and garner domestic support by broadly increasing the standard of living for ordinary Jordanians. The promotion of tourism was an essential element of the effort to build a postrentier economy and the only means that could rapidly allow Jordanians to reap the dividends of peace. Thus not only did tourism help enable the New Middle East vision; it was also critical to the Jordanian government's implementation by helping to sustain enough popular support, just long enough to complete the geopolitical alignment while Jordan maintained and open public sphere and permitted limited political dissent.

The narrative of the New Middle East and the tourism boom, however, is only one side of the story. The tourism boom did not last, and after the breakdown of the Israeli-Palestinian peace process and the 1996 election of a right-wing government in Israel, Jordanian-Israeli cooperation and the vision of the New Middle East withered. Moreover, throughout the development and selling of the New Middle East vision, an alternative geopolitical imaginary was being articulated across Jordan. As I discuss in the next chapter, a powerful discourse of political reterritorialization developed in reaction to cross-border flows that heightened local awareness of cross-border differences and potential threats to local and national territorial identities and political and economic interests. At the center of this development were contrary understandings of the New Middle East shaped by various participants in these new interactions. The multilateral promotion of open border flows was supposed to make the Jordanian-Israeli peace treaty something more than simply an alliance between states with common geopolitical interests. Instead of a warm peace, however, it led to a view of Israel as no longer a military-security threat but a source of deterritorialized threats that could seemingly pervade all aspects of Jordanian life.

4. The Territorial Politics of Tourism in Jordan

The New Middle East offered a vision for transforming the political economy of tourism in Jordan. With the conclusion of the peace treaty with Israel in 1994 and initiation of bilateral economic cooperation, a regional tourism boom was expected to jump-start the sector. Tourism development plans outlined how the increasing flows of tourists and capital would promote economic reterritorialization, where joining global networks would generate economic benefits for Jordanians. In this way, Jordan would finally overcome its geopolitical confinement and rentier economy by becoming integrated into the global economy, allowing it to "catch up" with the globalizing trends transforming other regions. Even for many Jordanians skeptical of the New Middle East vision, the initial experience of busloads of Israeli and other tourists arriving in Petra and Amman seemed to represent a new geopolitical reality and imminent economic transformation.

While the breakdown of the Israeli-Palestinian peace process in the late 1990s halted the emergence of the New Middle East and created tensions in Israeli-Jordanian relations, tourism development patterns and the expansion of transnational flows across Jordan did not follow the intended New Middle East script. Rather, the result eroded domestic support for peace with Israel and the accompanying imagined geopolitical and economic transformations. The architects of the New Middle East and tourism planners had envisioned the transformation of Jordanian territory into a smooth space for flows of tourists and investment capital. Such visions of limited political deterritorialization unleashing the market-led forces of globalization failed to anticipate the territorial effects and political conflicts provoked by the remapping of Jordanian territory. As the promotion of the New Middle East moved from press conferences and tourism plans to the implementation of development policies and tourist flows, the New Middle East vision was shattered by territorial politics and alternative geopolitical imaginaries.

In contrast to Tunisian patterns of centralized state building and tourism development, in Jordan the state's administrative control over territorial tourism assets, tourism firms, and tourism development organizations was divided between rival state institutions and private actors. Fragmented territorial control impeded tourism development along the Jordan Rift Valley, which was to function as the seam zone for the New Middle East. When the short-lived tourism boom hit Jordan's premier tourist destination, Petra, these flows resulted in a wave of rapid rent seeking by rival public and private interests. State efforts to extend centralized control over the development process were confronted by private entrepreneurs and local indigenous communities already able to assert local territorial control over resources. Moreover, fearing the social, cultural, and environmental impact of tourism development, local and transnational civil society organizations began to mobilize to challenge state plans.

The patterns of tourism development that emerged in Jordan exposed the limits of the market-based neoliberal vision promoted by American and Israeli advocates of the New Middle East. Many Jordanian officials, politicians, and businesspeople resisted American plans for market-led reforms, economic cooperation with Israel, and the opening of the economy to unrestricted foreign investment. In the tourism sector, entrepreneurs who responded to the expected big push of the tourism boom found the rents they sought soon exhausted. The few successful efforts to promote economic reterritorialization have been realized by private-sector firms with the capital, skills, and political influence to develop luxury "enclave" tourism spaces and circuits.

The burgeoning transnational flows and schemes for regional cooperation initiated by the New Middle East also gave birth to an unexpected ideological dynamic in Jordan. As the peace dividends failed to materialize, a powerful discourse of political re-territorialization developed in reaction to cross-border tourism flows. The failures of regional tourism fostered geopolitical imaginations that viewed these flows as deterritorialized threats and propelled the "antinormalization" movement in Jordan, further challenging Israeli-Jordanian cooperation. With the collapse of the Israeli-Palestinian peace process, this process led to the eclipse of the New Middle East as a viable geopolitical vision for Jordan and the region.

The Consequences of Fragmented Territorial Control

In the early 1990s, the multinational architects of the New Middle East drew maps depicting how tourist circuits and investment flows would propel a regional tourism economy no longer fragmented by militarized frontiers and security concerns. Their bird's-eye view that envisioned political and economic deterritorialization was blind to territorial issues that would splinter the New Middle East's regional tourism economy as well as national tourism development plans in Jordan. Regardless of any hesitation that some Jordanian officials had about the plans for regional cooperation, the rapid integration of Jordan into a regional tourism economy linked to Israel was soon hampered by the fragmentation of authority over the development process. While a small team of Jordanian negotiators, seeking to advance the national strategic and economic interests of the kingdom, had helped craft plans for regional economic cooperation, the implementation of these plans would require coordination between diverse elements of the Jordanian bureaucracy and private sector involved with tourism development. These actors were not organized to pursue a common objective, nor did they all operate with the same geopolitical imaginary that animated the authors of the peace treaty.

The Ministry of Tourism and Antiquities (MOTA), formed in 1988, claimed authority over tourism development, but its direct authority was limited to the regulation of hotels and restaurants. Overseas tourism marketing was organized by the state-owned flag carrier, Royal Jordanian Airlines. The MOTA oversaw the Department of Antiquities (DOA) and exerted control over archaeological sites even though the interests of archaeologists (concern with historical knowledge and heritage preservation) often clashed with MOTA's primary interests in expanding revenues from tourism. At the same time, the MOTA had limited planning authority and little control over tourism development on private land near tourism sites. The string of rest houses located near tourist sites and the state-owned hotels in Amman and Petra were owned not by a tourism authority but by the Social Security Corporation and the Jordan Investment Corporation. Furthermore, national economic planning was directed by the Ministry of Planning.

The government's vision for tourism development was detailed in plans drawn up by the Ministry of Planning and presented at the MENA summits. These plans focused on the Jordan Rift Valley, which runs from Lake Tiberias (the Sea of Galilee) in the north to the Gulf of Aqaba and includes the Jordan Valley, the Dead Sea, and the Wadi Araba desert. Within this zone lie the two major regions targeted for tourism development, Aqaba and the Dead Sea, over which the MOTA had only consulting authority. Aqaba and its surrounding region were under the authority of the highly autonomous Aqaba Regional Authority (ARA) established in 1984, while the Dead Sea area was governed by the powerful Jordan Valley Authority (JVA), which had operated under the authority of the Ministry of Water and Irrigation since the late 1980s. Both regional organizations were established for functions other than tourism development. The ARA's central task has been the development of shipping and port facilities, as Aqaba is Jordan's only port and the main conduit for goods and raw materials to and from Jordan and Iraq. The JVA was established in the late 1970s to build irrigation works and promote agricultural and social development in northwest Jordan.[1]

In both zones the rival objectives and interests of the numerous government organizations, each with partial territorial control, prevented and delayed tourism development efforts. The autonomous regional development agencies generally seek to promote "local" interests such as job creation and economic opportunities for the region's inhabitants. At the same time, central state agencies, such as the Prime Ministry and the Ministry of Finance, are often concerned with extending centralized control over these regions to protect state-owned property and extract revenues. Moreover, with the reinstitution of competitive elections and the liberalization of political debate, central government institutions became more accountable to elected deputies, including those from the opposition.

The town of Aqaba played a critical role in the New Middle East vision for regional tourism development. Located near the site of the peace treaty signing ceremony, Aqaba was to become a gateway between Israel and the Arab world. With the opening of the border, Aqaba was expected to develop close ties with the Israeli resort town of Eilat, and together the cities were to share Aqaba's airstrip by building a "Peace Airport." In addition to becoming a major beachfront tourist resort, Aqaba was also expected to serve as a base for visitors to Jordan's well-known but ecologically fragile destinations of Petra, Wadi Rum, and small archaeological ruins across the Jordan Valley. These ambitious plans were immediately stalled owing to conflict between the autonomous ARA, the central government, and prospective investors. In 1993, in the midst of excitement about the formation of the New Middle East, a group of Jordanian investors created an elaborate master plan to develop the state-owned coastal region south of Aqaba. After a deal was signed with the ARA, the council of ministers in Amman "not only unanimously voted it down, but retroactively canceled all decisions taken by the ARA for the previous ten years."[2] This fiasco dealt a blow to investor confidence in the ARA. After 1994 the government raised the price of its parcels while private land values skyrocketed, further dissuading outside tourism investors.[3] Moreover, the geography of the coastline squeezed the potential for tourism development, as shipping and industrial facilities are located too close to the beachfront areas where most tourism developers wished to build. By the year 2000, the region was converted into a free trade zone, the Aqaba Special Economic Zone (ASEZ), designed to grant incentives for Jordanian and international investment in tourism and other sectors. Meanwhile the idea of the Aqaba-Eilat Peace Airport was scrapped because of "ongoing differences over security, sovereignty, and environmental issues as well as the bleak political climate and the creation of the Aqaba Special Economic zone in the same area [which] rendered the project unfeasible."[4]

The other major region expected to witness a massive wave of tourist flows and investment after the 1994 peace treaty was that controlled by the JVA. Because this region is located along Jordan's border with Israel and the occupied West Bank, land ownership, use, and redistribution have been particularly politicized. After the treaty signing with Israel, the Jordanian government legalized the sale and transfer of land to foreign nationals to encourage international investment in the region. The Prime Ministry, however, restricted the kind of land deals the JVA could offer to developers. In contrast to the ARA, the JVA enthusiastically promoted tourism development, as it did not impinge on the authority's other interest, agricultural development, and was expected to create badly needed jobs and demand for local goods and services. In fact, the JVA created a separate office called the Directorate for Tourism Development (DTD), run by an American-educated financial expert, to promote tourism. The DTD director explained that the JVA was interested in selling plots of land at "promotional prices . . . to get development rolling and use it to attract investors. Capital flows without borders and will invest where the conditions are best. If Jordan waits or makes it too hard they will lose the opportunity."[5] However, the Prime Ministry did not allow the DTD to sell the land, instead offering thirty-year leases with one renewal and a rent review every decade. At the end of the sixty years, the ownership of the hotels would revert to the state.[6] The prices and terms were unacceptable to the consortia of Jordanian and international developers poised to build four luxury resort hotels to compete against the Israeli monopoly on Dead Sea tourism. These projects were delayed several times until a lease agreement could be settled on. It was not until 1999 that the first of the four planned hotels was completed and the JVA floated tenders for leases on more plots along the shore.

By 2000 Aqaba and the Dead Sea had developed tourism facilities and emerged as important elements of the Jordanian tourism economy, but by then enthusiasm for developing these territories as part of an integrated regional tourism economy had waned. More critically, by the late 1990s the hopes of millions of Jordanians for the dividends of peace with Israel had long since evaporated. While Jordan would experience a tourism boom in the wake of peace, it would occur in other parts of the country and not follow the maps envisioned by the architects of the New Middle East.

Marketing Neoliberalism in the New Middle East

Secretary of State Warren Christopher summed up the American vision for the transformation of Jordan at the 1994 MENA summit in Casablanca when he announced that the Middle East was "open for business." He expected the American business leaders and investors brought in as part of the U.S. delegation at the MENA gatherings to help lead the transformation to build the New Middle East. In the realm of tourism, the Middle East–Mediterranean Travel and Tourism Association (MEMTTA) was to function as a transnational private-sector-led network of professionals to market regional tourism. In 1996 the assistant secretary of state for Near East affairs, Robert Pelletreau, spoke before the American division of the organization, led by an executive from American Express, urging its members to work "to make the Middle East more attractive to tourists, Americans in particular."[7] He noted that the tourism industry "is a linchpin for economic development because it reaches beyond travel and tourism to stimulate the development of infrastructure from construction to transportation and telecommunications." By the time of the 1996 MENA summit held in Cairo, the other multilateral efforts to promote regional economic cooperation had stalled, and the MEMTTA was "touted by some as the most tangible result of the Middle East peace process and a bright spot of the recent Cairo conference."[8] At the 1997 summit in Doha, Qatar, the new secretary of state Madeleine Albright commended the MEMTTA in a written statement "for the role you have played in laying the foundation for economic growth through increased cooperation in this key sector. You are helping to build prosperity. . . . Peace in the Middle East will be durable only when the people [of] the region share in its dividends. We in the U.S. Government are working hard to develop the critical economic dimensions of the peace process in order to help create these dividends."[9] While the MEMTTA had earlier that year won an award from the Peace through Tourism foundation, it continued to function better as a concept than a marketing tool. The prospect of tourism development had helped in the selling of the peace treaty, but it was unclear if tourism could help to sustain the peace, economic cooperation, and mutual understanding.

One aspect of the New Middle East's failure in the tourism sector was the unexpected termination of USAID tourism projects in Jordan, including the effort to develop Jordan's tourism marketing capability. USAID had a long history of tourism-related projects in Jordan, and in the days before the signing of the Israeli-Jordanian peace treaty, the U.S. government entered into an agreement with Jordan's Ministry of Planning to develop Jordan's cultural and environmental resources for tourism. A central element of these

USAID-funded programs was the planned $14 million effort to build Jordan's marketing capacity by forming the Jordan Tourism Board (JTB). The idea dated back to the late 1980s and represented the American preference for neoliberal economic policies. The JTB was to be a public-private partnership to market Jordan as a destination in which the private sector was the "dominant voice."[10] While partially funded by the government, it would be staffed by private-sector professionals—including an expatriate tourism expert—and privately managed independently of the government and the MOTA.[11]

The challenges of establishing the JTB highlighted the complex dynamics of relations between the state and private sector and the blurred boundaries between the two. As they began their negotiations with the Jordanian government, the Amman-based USAID staff debated among themselves the best formulation of the JTB. Some wanted greater Jordanian government involvement to give the JTB semiofficial status and more leverage and clout with the local private sector. As USAID representatives got involved in the negotiations, however, they came to feel that the JTB needed to be in the hands of the private sector, as the state did not seem capable of running the board as envisioned.[12] Most local hotel owners and other private-sector actors, for their part, wanted the JTB to be a private organization. Many did not want to pay JTB dues if it was state-run and could not challenge the authority of the MOTA or other government agencies. The Jordanian authorities, however, refused to support the JTB as a fully private entity and insisted on full control of the funds, fearing that it might otherwise become a slush fund for private firms.

Meanwhile USAID also alienated some the local private sector whose interests it was ostensibly promoting. Business leaders in the tourism sector might have been the group of Jordanian professionals most likely to be supportive of the peace treaty and hopeful about the economic opportunities it could create. But according to one Jordanian tourism professional, USAID "put up the money and had their own ideas, they wanted to impose their own agenda," and as a result, their efforts "lost direction."[13] While the Americans said they wanted an organization led by the private sector, they often did not seem to fully trust it to fulfill their vision for the JTB. At the same time, the Jordanian government did not accept USAID insistence on substantial private-sector autonomy over the JTB. By many accounts, both the Jordanian authorities and the USAID officials backed themselves into corners as personalities clashed and mistrust grew. In August 1996 it appeared that the JTB was ready to take off with a revised set of Articles of Association but then collapsed when they were rejected by the government.[14] The new USAID director in Jordan set a deadline for the JTB to be certified as a private organization. The MOTA, however, refused. On September 19, 1996, USAID abruptly terminated all their other tourism development efforts.[15] USAID funds originally allotted for the JTB were redirected into water projects, including one desperately needed in Wadi Musa. Other funds were channeled to the American Center for Oriental Research (ACOR). A year after declaring "strategic object 1: increased foreign exchange from culture and nature visitors," USAID deleted all mention of tourism from its annual congressional presentation.[16] The support for tourism planning in Jordan would then shift to other organizations, such as the World Bank and Japan's development assistance organization, JICA.

Jordan's Ministry of Tourism eventually established the JTB on its own terms.[17] The MOTA took over the JTB, appointing its director and placing the minister of tourism at the head of the board, which consisted of representatives from both the government and the private sector. For a few years, without the funding, strong private-sector leadership, and skilled staff of the USAID plan, the JTB's capabilities were limited. It printed maps and brochures, developed new marketing slogans, and represented Jordan at tourism trade fairs. As noted hereafter, the JTB later expanded its capabilities, function, and budget, and USAID eventually again supported its activities and helped Jordan project a new tourist image in the international media.[18] By that time, however, the postpeace tourism boom had come and gone.

The Commodification of Petra: Rent Seeking in Wadi Musa

Although a rapid expansion of the tourist infrastructure between Jordan and Israel with the treaty failed to materialize, waves of tourists poured into Jordan. They passed straight through to Jordan's most famous tourist site, Petra. Images from Petra, such as the facade of al Khazneh, became icons in the local and international media, representing Jordan both as a nation and as a tourist destination. A trip to Petra became de rigueur for visiting dignitaries. In the once-sleepy village of Wadi Musa, located outside the gate of the Petra Archaeological Park, a central boulevard was renamed Peace Way and soon dotted with hastily established restaurants and hotels. This rural town in southern Jordan quickly became the pivot point for the shifting regional geopolitical order. If tourism development was to generate peace dividends and bolster popular support for the peace treaty in Jordan, it would have to showcase its potential in Wadi Musa and then spread from there. In December 1994 the *Jerusalem Post* reported that the resort towns of southern Jordan were "clearly undergoing an economic boom."[19] Spotting a vendor sporting a hat that read "Blessed are the peace makers," an Israeli journalist reported, "In Wadi Musa negotiations are well under way for a glatt kosher restaurant and hotel. The whole village depends on tourism and whole families try to make the Israelis feel welcome. . . . It seems most people are learning Hebrew."[20] The New Middle East had arrived in Petra.

Refashioning Tourism Spaces

The expectation of a tourism boom drove local entrepreneurs across Jordan to rush to invest in the tourism sector. Jordanian planners and their consultants hoped to encourage visitors to stay longer and visit more of Jordan's many historical sites and nature landscapes. These flows would increase locational rents and generate external economies for firms in the tourism sector as well as create backward and forward linkages throughout the national economy. But as we saw in the case of Aqaba and the Dead Sea, the promotion of economic reterritorialization in a context of fragmented territorial control can generate local conflicts over the reterritorialization process and its benefits. Not only was the New Middle East vision for tourism development challenged by fragmented territorial control at the regional level, but government efforts to refashion Jordanian tourism spaces to promote economic reterritorialization confronted diverse actors seeking to extract rents, assert their own territorial rights, or challenge tourism development plans for their expected negative effects on the local population or environment.

Tourism development in Jordan was assisted by funding and technical assistance from an increasing number of foreign govern-

ments and international organizations. Most of these plans sought
to convert Jordanian locales into spaces for tourist consumption
by improving how they generated and commodified experiences of
place. The integration of Jordan into the networks of the global
tourism economy hinged not only on marketing Jordan as a safe
and intriguing destination for Western travelers but also on developing Jordan's ability to promote economic reterritorialization by
refashioning tourism spaces. The development of services and improved attractions within existing tourism spaces would create opportunities for private firms while drawing more tourists. One of
the earliest planning efforts in Jordan was introduced by USAID.
As one of the directors explained, "The project goals were to increase foreign exchange earnings through tourism, upgrade the archaeological sites for tourism, and maximize the value of Jordan's
cultural heritage through preservation and improved site management."[21] The USAID project focused on primary sites (such as
Petra and Amman) with the best ability to draw increased foreign
currency but also included plans for the development of secondary sites. Rather than outlining a long-range national strategy like
the JICA plan would, USAID was concerned with quickly preparing the sector to help realize the dividends of peace and thus offered blueprints that could be used immediately to build structures,
landscape environments, and create visitor programs. The plans for
developing tourism spaces called for the conservation of archaeological ruins, improvement of park management capacities, and the
design of interpretive themes that could be coordinated with international tourism marketing campaigns and programs of private-
sector tour operators.[22] A report prepared for USAID noted that
"the government of Jordan should establish tourist zones throughout the country to guide development to appropriate locations."[23]
These were to be "areas where development of hotels is mixed with
restaurants, outdoor cafes, tourist shops, recreational opportunities (horse- and camel-riding stables), small-scale parks, and open
areas where scenic vistas can be enjoyed." By "localizing tourist activity," these zones would "conserve and concentrate government
investment in water supply and distribution, wastewater collection
and distribution, road construction, and so forth." At the same
time, they were to be "developed with a high level of concern for
the physical and visual environment, sensitivity to the potential for
tourism activities to intrude on nearby settlements, and the need to

preserve sight lines to scenic vistas. Developers should be encouraged or required if necessary, to build in architectural styles that are harmonious with the site and indigenous architecture."

Territorial Rent Seeking

While tourist zones in Tunisia were often built in open spaces separated from existing settlements, the nature of archaeological and heritage tourism in Jordan required that tourism projects be set amid indigenous communities that had long resided and owned property near tourist sites. The presence of these residents and would-be entrepreneurs led to conflicts between state agencies and outside private-sector developers who sought to displace them from around archaeological ruins and other tourist sites to make the space amenable to the tourist gaze and ready for commercialization.[24] The expectation of tourism expansion only heightened these conflicts, in which local NGOs and transnational activists often promoted the interests of indigenous communities and challenged development plans promoted by the government, private-sector firms, and international development and donor agencies. Across Jordan, rival interests struggled to shape patterns of tourism development, site interpretation, and environmental preservation.[25] Nowhere were these conflicts more fierce and the stakes higher than in Petra and neighboring Wadi Musa.

The high-volume flows of tourists and investment capital into space where territorial control was highly fragmented prevented tourism development in Petra and Wadi Musa from following plans such as those outlined in the USAID blueprints. Instead the tourism boom led to a period of rapid rent seeking by rival private interests that failed to generate sustainable tourism economies. Moreover, the efforts of state institutions to extend centralized control, where different private-sector actors and local communities already asserted territorial control, generally faced significant resistance, challenge, or delay.

The one space the state controlled directly was the Petra Archaeological Park; the MOTA collected entrance fees at the park's front gate. As tourist visits to Petra expanded with the peace process, one of the first policy changes the MOTA implemented was to extract more rent by dramatically increasing the fee. Before 1993, when the fee was set at JD 1, the government barely made JD

100,000 per year. In 1993, when the Oslo peace process began, the price for a one-day ticket was raised to JD 5, allowing the MOTA to collect about half a million dinars. In 1994 revenues climbed to one million dinars. Toward the end of the year, as the peace treaty was about be signed, the MOTA again raised the price of a one-day admission ticket from JD 5 to JD 20. With the higher fee and increased tourist flows, state revenues increased 500 percent in one year to over six million dinars in 1995. This income was not controlled by local authorities in Petra or even the MOTA but went straight into the coffers of the Ministry of Finance. It alone amounted to nearly .5 percent of the total domestic government revenue from all sources that year.

In contrast, outside the park, in the town of Wadi Musa, land is mostly privately held by various local families and tribes. Land-ownership patterns across Jordan are the product of a British-conceived program begun in the late 1920s that allowed nomadic and settled tribes, as well as others, to secure property rights. State building and national identity formation in the fragile emirate were advanced through this arrangement, which helped Emir Abdullah establish control over the territory he was given to rule under the British mandate. The program of land registration encouraged agricultural production by villagers and the settlement of formerly nomadic, often warring tribes. In the process, the program "helped define for ordinary Jordanians the spatial dimensions of their property, their villages, and their new country."[26] The program ensured the livelihood of small-scale cultivators while establishing state recognition of the power of tribal leaders and wealthy merchant families. Social groups in Jordan came to link their identities and wealth to specific territories, thereby protecting their tribal organization and identity while granting the new state widespread loyalty.

As confirmed by travelers' accounts, in Wadi Musa members of the Layathna tribe—long before they were given legal title—had controlled most of the land from the Petra gate north to the village of Beida and east to Elji.[27] This control cemented the political power of the local tribe, dating back to the late 1860s, and ensured local access to rents and economic opportunities ever since. Although the Bedul Bedouin tribe lived inside Petra, the settled Layathna have been able to control much of the tourist-related rent extraction in the region.[28] As the Layathna came to staff the local rest house and set up stands to sell postcards and trinkets, they gained a "near monopoly of the tourist trade in Petra."[29] When hotel construction expanded in the 1990s, the Layathna further extracted rents by building their own hotels and exerting control over the construction supplies needed for the large hotels.[30] This power has also been manifest in the presence of the Layathna within the local political and authority structures from the police force to the archaeological officials.[31]

In the 1990s, however, the expansion of tourist flows and the central state's increased reliance on developing tourism as an engine of economic growth soon clashed with the interests of the local population and various local and transnational NGOs. Signs of the divergence between the contradictory interests of various state actors also emerged. In 1992 Jordan's Queen Noor expressed concern about how the rise of tourism flows might threaten the integrity of the archaeological ruins inside Petra and requested that UNESCO write a report about the condition of the World Heritage site outlining a master plan for the development of the region. Drawing on the expert knowledge of Jordanian as well as international archaeologists and anthropologists, the report was released in 1994 just as tourism development in the region was expanding rapidly. While supportive of the concept of cultural tourism, the report also expressed concern that hotel development "has not been well controlled" and was a "detriment of the site," especially "in areas where their visual impact and effect on the landscape would be negative, or in environmentally important areas."[32]

The government was torn between a short-term need for hard currency and rapid economic growth and a long-term interest in ensuring that Petra remained a sustainable source of income. While private developers and MOTA officials generally pushed to allow the expansion of hotel building, other forces sought to regulate tourism development. The Petra National Trust (PNT), a Jordanian NGO supported by members of the royal family such as Queen Noor as well as by various archaeologists, promoted the recommendations of the UNESCO report. Government interest in tourism development, however, was too high, and "political pressure, applied by influential businessmen, land owners and deputies" led to the overruling of the PNT's recommendations.[33] Moreover, in Wadi Musa, local officials in charge of building permits were themselves "too close to the people and part of the community."[34]

The number of hotels built in Wadi Musa was also a product of land tenure patterns. Over the years, the land had been subdivided between tribes and clans and their descendants. By the 1990s, numerous families held property around the town, which they sought to use to build a hotel or other tourist enterprise. Many families had income available to invest because of family members working abroad, typically in the Gulf states. Others found easy access to credit from Jordanian banks. They viewed gaining income from tourism as their right, and in the early 1990s the prospects never seemed better. Local officials found that once they allowed some families to build a hotel, for the sake of fairness and balance, they could not say no to other families who also wished to build.[35] By the time the government stopped issuing permits, the transformation of the built environment around Wadi Musa was well under way.

As a result, throughout the boom when tourist flows generated rents for landholders across Wadi Musa, the state had little control over these developments. At the time of the 1994 peace treaty, Jordanian officials would "admit the sudden onslaught of peace caught them flat-footed. Never a high priority, tourism suddenly has burst from back-burner to front as the government scrambles to reap the rewards of 'non-belligerency' with Israel."[36] The rapid influx of tourism set the hotel developers spinning and made developers out of just about anyone in Wadi Musa. "Just weeks, maybe even days," after the peace agreement, local residents started building hotels while existing ones started to expand their capacity.[37] In downtown Wadi Musa, a string of small hotels sprang up. Some residents converted their existing apartments into makeshift hotels; others who were building private houses quickly tried to remodel them into hotels.

Even with the rush of hotel building, throughout 1995 a shortage of hotel space kept occupancy rates high and encouraged more building. At peak times many hotels were overbooked. Some tourists resorted to "asking if they can sleep in the lobby."[38] With such high demand, hotels pushed rates up by 30 percent to 40 percent.[39] Meanwhile Jordanian authorities raised the value-added tax from 7 percent to 10 percent to reap a share of windfall.

Tourism ministry officials and other state officials were interested in increasing Petra's capacity for high-paying tourists and luxury packaged tourism to attract the largest possible amounts of hard currency and local spending. Most of the hotels built by Wadi Musa residents were small and operated by locals with limited management experience. The MOTA encouraged experienced and well-connected players in the Jordanian tourism sector to build hotels in Petra and directed them to the unfinished Taybeh road leading south from Wadi Musa, which offered spectacular views of the hills around Petra. Soon big developers from Amman were buying up expensive plots of land and rushing to complete their larger four- and five-star hotel complexes. In 1995 MOTA reported that there were already 175 bed spaces in the area, with another 1,904 in hotels and expansions under construction.[40] At the request of Queen Noor, however, a semiofficial review committee made up of leading Jordanian architects was asked to review the designs of the larger hotels being built on the road overlooking the Petra valley. According to some reports, in contrast to the concerns of archaeologists and environmentalists working in the area, "the government was apparently not concerned about the damage development had done to the environment and historical sites as much as it was concerned with architecture."[41] The commission was interested in limiting the color, material, and height of the buildings to prevent them from damaging the integrity of the visual landscape. One of the committee members described the effort as "semi-effective," while one of the hotel developers complained that the commission delayed his hotel building and added costs by requiring him to redo the building's color.[42] Between the delays in building the Taybeh road, the requirements of the design committee, and the difficulty of securing the needed materials and water for the projects, the hotels opened just as the tourism boom was fading and soon to collapse. By the time they were operational, they could not expect a steady flow of large group tours for which they had been built.

In just two years after the peace treaty, the hotel capacity of Wadi Musa had quadrupled to over two thousand rooms. According to MOTA records, between 1990 and 1996, the number of classified hotels (between one to five stars) expanded from two with 244 beds to twelve with 1,920 beds, while the number of unclassified hotels expanded from three with 66 beds to eighteen with 815 beds. Total hotel construction costs were estimated in the neighborhood of $70 million to $80 million.[43] By 1998, although the official government statistics show 23 classified hotels and 18 nonclassified, others counted at least 64 in Wadi Musa.[44]

One stark indicator of the increased territorial commodification provoked by increased tourism flows is the rise of land values. While most of the smaller hotels were built by Wadi Musa's landowning families on their own plots, the developers of the larger luxury hotels had to negotiate land deals with the local owners. Before land in Wadi Musa was valued for its tourism potential, a dunam of land (equal to 1,000 square meters) could go for about JD 700.[45] By the time the first hotel developers were buying plots, prices were still a reasonable JD 2,000 to JD 10,000 per dunam.[46] After the peace treaty and the flood of tourists in 1994, prices shot up to around JD 35,000 per dunam.[47] At the extreme high end was the Mövenpick, a luxury hotel set on the strip near the entrance of Petra, which is reported to have paid JD 140,000 per dunam. In 1996, asking prices for land along the Taybeh road were as high as JD 100,000, and near the main approach to Petra, they reached a reported JD 230,000 per dunam.[48]

The increased land values made some locals very wealthy, and the increased employment generally added to local income, as represented in increased house building, larger family sizes, and new mosque construction.[49] Tourism development, however, proceeded across Wadi Musa at an uncontrollable speed and without planning or regulation. Building in Wadi Musa was characterized by haphazard and ill-designed construction and was replete with "visual horrors."[50] It also generated a landscape that lacked the development and integration of diverse tourism-related businesses and services. For example, opportunities were lost as there was "little effort to develop and advertise activities or excursions for visitors who may wish to prolong their stay," such as long-distance nature hikes or "opportunities to experience or learn about Bedouin or nomadic lifestyles."[51] This pattern jeopardized the ability of tourism to be an engine of sustainable growth and provide the conditions needed to promote economic reterritorialization. The result was a landscape that one guidebook declared "must also stand alone as about the most expensive tourist trap in the world."[52]

Expanding State Control

To bring some order to the process, in 1995 the Ministry of Tourism sought to expand state authority and capacity over tourism development in Petra by forming the Petra Regional Planning Council (PRPC). While the PRPC's director explained that "the government wanted a 'decentralized' authority to control development, protect the heritage site, and promote tourism,"[53] the council can also be understood as a tool for projecting central state control into a region located far from the capital and subject to competing local interests. The council was given control over an 850-square-kilometer region that includes the 264 square kilometers of the government-owned Petra Archaeological Park and a wide belt of territory, mostly privately held, circling Wadi Musa. The establishment of the new authority required the disbanding of the local municipalities of Wadi Musa, Taybeh, and Rajef as the council superseded their powers and took over their functions such that it gained "absolute power pertaining to building permits, usage of land, implementation of regulatory plans, and infrastructure" within its defined territory.[54]

While the responsibilities of the council include planning, infrastructure, tourism, protection of the environment, and the social well-being of the population, its primary task is "to maximize the potential of Petra, which is the basic economic resource of the area."[55] It was only after its establishment that a ban on hotel building permits was put into place. By 1997 new hotel construction was also limited by the rise in land prices and the contraction of tourist flows. In early 1996 the Ministry of Tourism commissioned Dar Al Handasah, a leading engineering and consulting firm, to study the conditions and immediate needs for public action in the area of tourism development in Petra. The report, the *Petra Priority Action Plan Study,* was completed in October 1996.[56] The Petra Priority Action Plan set out to create an attractive and appropriate natural and urban environment while encouraging the growth and management of sustainable tourism. The implementation of the plan included a freeze on hotel building and created, for the first time, a zoning-based land-use scheme for the region.

Its plan for refashioning the tourism space outside the archaeological park centered on creating a "tourist park zone" near the Petra entrance gate "with additional hotels, shops, markets, restaurants, recreational and visitors center, with expanded parking and transport facilities."[57] In contrast to the dispersed, haphazard geography of existing tourist services across Wadi Musa, the Petra Plan, following the vision outlined in the earlier USAID blueprints, sought to build a central tourism enclave with close visual and physical connections to the archaeological park.[58]

The effort to develop the zone has been hindered and compromised by competing interests, visions, and fragmented territorial control over this space. For example, the plan called for leaving the sloping hill across from the Petra entrance gate and above the proposed tourist zone undeveloped so that it would not visually distract from the natural environment of the park. To do so, however, would prevent the owners of these plots from gaining income from them. The Petra Plan warned that the PRPC "must identify ways and means to minimize loss to the land values as a result of the present zoning."[59] As the head of the PRPC planning department explained:

> [The] problem with planning in Petra and Wadi Musa is that land is mostly privately held. Since the 1940s it has been registered. It is divided into small plots and spread into the region owned by various families. If you want to, for example, zone two percent commercial, where do you put it? If you put it in one place then that set of people benefit, so you are forced to try to spread it around.[60]

As a result, "rational planning" in Petra was frustrated. Moreover, the planning chief complained, "people try to violate the zoning" rules.[61]

Following the USAID/Chemonics tourism strategy, the Petra Plan called for collecting all the vendors strewn around the entrance and inside the park and restricting them to a central *souq*, or marketplace. The *souq* would be located in the tourist zone near the entrance of Petra together with a cluster of outlets providing information and commercial services for tourists. This plan, however, provoked social conflict and local resistance. The *souq* and the tourist zone would be outside the Petra gate entrance and thus within what was understood as Layathna tribal area. Although the land was government owned, the Layathna still claim it within their tribal space, meaning that only Layathna should be able to work there. The Bedul, who have traditionally lived and worked inside Petra itself, resisted the plan, as it was intended to displace the unregulated Bedul vendors who have traditionally operated inside the park. In the same fashion that the government had relocated the settlements of the Bedul who once lived in the park, it eventually also moved most of the Bedul vendors, but not without resistance from the tribe and its supporters among the archaeological teams and NGOs that work with the community inside Petra.[62]

Another major tension for the PRPC is that tourism development must struggle to coexist with antiquities conservation and preservation. The discovery, preservation, and management of the archaeological ruins in Petra rely heavily on external technical expertise and financial support. Much of the skill and funding for this work are driven by concerns about history and heritage preservation, not tourism per se. Many archaeologists are frustrated by the paradox that mass tourism threatens ruins and other artifacts of cultural heritage, although the income that tourism generates often provides a rationale for governments and other agencies to fund their archaeological work.[63] This situation often pits various Jordanian government agencies with rival goals (such as the MOTA and the DOA) against each other as well as against the agencies of foreign states, the interests of civil society groups, and transnational epistemic communities. While foreign archaeologists work with their professional colleagues in the DOA, the Jordanian archaeologists at DOA must report to the MOTA officials, who are usually more concerned with pleasing foreign tourists and tour operators than following the professional norms of heritage preservation. The MOTA has at times even been known to override the concerns of its own DOA in its drive to expand tourism development. The MOTA, however, must also rely on foreign archaeological teams with external financing to uncover archaeological remains, prepare them for visitors, and manage other aspects of site development.

"The Dream of Tourism"

While Petra is only one of Jordan's tourist attractions and Wadi Musa accounts for less than 7 percent of the hotel capacity in the country, with the 1994 peace treaty, it became a showcase for the economic dividends of peace. But by the time planners took charge of refashioning the rural village into what one PRPC director envisioned as a "Euro-Mediterranean city," the volume of visitors had peaked. By the late 1990s, the New Middle East evaporated in the wake of renewed regional conflict and the failure of the 1994 treaty to provide Jordan with economic benefits after the initial boom. Combining a drop in tourism with an expansion of capacity, occupancy rates declined from 62 percent in 1994 to 31 percent in 1997. In 1998, when occupancy rates across Jordan increased slightly, many hotels around Petra recorded rates as low as 11 percent for the year.[64] During the quieter months, many of them were left standing empty or closed. According to one manager, hotels at Petra were able to maintain a healthy average daily rate for half board of $60 in 1994, but by 1997, when about half of the hotel capacity of Wadi Musa was located in four- and five-star hotels, most hotels could only maintain a rate of about $30.[65]

A few years after the peace treaty, many hotel owners had difficulty paying off their loans. While fighting accusations that they had misled hotel developers, the Jordanian government instructed banks to allow the hotel owners to reschedule their loans.[66] Consider the example of the owner of the Petra Inn that boasts on its large billboard "The Dream of Tourism." The hotel was built by members of the Tawaissi clan, who owned land in the lower area of Wadi Musa near the Petra entrance gate.[67] With the signing of the peace treaty, they thought a hotel "would be a good idea," and without any market data, feasibility study, or training in the hospitality industry, they were able to acquire sufficient bank loans to build a modest thirty-room hotel. The owner-manager had sold his architecture and construction office to help pay for the building, but two years later, with the leveling off of tourism flows and increased competition from other establishments, he was earning about a quarter of the income he used to. He complained that with a hotel he found himself tied down with little interesting work to do. He hoped someone would buy the hotel from him, land and all, so that he could set up a different sort of business.

In 1997, when the secretary general of the MOTA visited Petra, he "slammed the levels of service offered at the country's largest tourist attraction [and said that] the low level of standards and lack of quality services harm the tourism industry. . . . He intends to recommend [that] the ministry monitor these places, [and] urge them to improve the quality of services."[68] By 1998 Wadi Musa, located in a stunningly beautiful and unique natural location, was burdened with a built environment replete with what might be called "the bland homogeneity" that David Harvey notes often "goes with pure commodification" and "erases monopoly advantages."[69] While private developers rushed to construct buildings, it was only afterward that the region's infrastructure had a chance to catch up: "A visitor to Petra might stay at a luxurious hotel but he'll be driving on badly maintained roads, walking on dirty streets, and struggling to find a public bathroom or payphone, clean or otherwise."[70] While "there is general agreement amongst the local

Figure 14. Hotels in lower Wadi Musa, Jordan. Photograph by Michelle Woodward.

population that in general the impact of tourism on the area has been positive," Matthew Teller, the author of the *Rough Guide to Jordan,* poignantly notes, "Plagued by disastrously bad management of resources and town planning of the most tragically short-sighted kind, Wadi Musa is filled with a tawdry and rather sad air of powerlessness, a small agricultural community resigned to a collective free-for-all scrabbling at the whirlwinds of cash drifting through its fingers."[71]

The Mutations of the Tourism Economy, 1994–2000

The experience of hotel development in Wadi Musa represented an intense microcosm of patterns of tourism development experienced across Jordan after the peace treaty. Efforts to exploit windfall rents from tourism were witnessed in other areas and across other subsectors. In the mid-1990s, Jordan saw an explosion of new tourist bus companies, rental car firms, and travel agencies. Hotel construction sites dotted Amman. Restaurants in Amman, Wadi Musa, and Aqaba prepared to cater to a new wave of tourists, with some printing menus in Hebrew. These efforts by local private entrepreneurs reflected a popular understanding of what was thought to be the ongoing expansion of the tourism economy since backers of the peace treaty had sold it as bringing dividends and pointed to tourism as the first sector that would experience these rewards.

The Jordanian tourism sector, however, was ill prepared for such an expansion. The surge of tourism demand in 1995 outstripped supply, leading to severe shortages and overbooking. Worse, this shock did not reflect future patterns of tourism demand, nor did it result in entrepreneurs holding on to excess profits to invest in expansion and upgrading. The growth spurt soon leveled. While overall tourism receipts in 1995 and 1996 for Jordan grew by over 12 percent per year, in 1997 they grew only 4 percent. Tourism patterns began to shift just as would-be tourism entrepreneurs were in overdrive expanding supply to capture rents from what they expected to be a continuing increased demand. For most Jordanians, the end of the much-hyped tourism boom exposed how fleeting the exercise in rent extraction had been. The general public, and hotel developers in particular, had greatly misjudged the future of the peace process and the prospects of the tourism economy in Jordan.

This boom-and-bust cycle of tourism flows came unexpectedly for those who had been following the New Middle East script. Many Jordanians would come to blame the fortunes of the tourism sector on the Israeli election of Benjamin Netanyahu of the right-wing Likud party in May 1996. While Netanyahu stalled the Israeli-Palestinian peace process and put a strain on the relations between Israel and Jordan, the fate of the Jordanian tourism sector, which experienced more of a mutation than a crash, was not only shaped by external political factors. The New Middle East vision had misrepresented the dynamics that govern tourism economies, contributed to inadequate state policies for tourism promotion, and led to misguided entrepreneurial strategies by much of the private sector. In particular, it led many Jordanians to seek to exploit short-term opportunities for rent capture by rapidly commodifying Jordanian geography and cultural heritage. Most firms in the sector were unable to build institutional mechanisms for monitoring and promoting demand for their products within the increasingly complex and competitive global tourism economy. By the time such institutions were being developed, the New Middle East had come and gone.

Unexpected Itineraries of the New Middle East

Much of the Israeli and international media coverage of the first wave of tourists crossing into Jordan from Israel radiated with images from the New Middle East script. The sight of Israelis shopping in Amman markets and walking into Petra was viewed as representing something akin to the fall of the Berlin Wall. It marked a radical shift in regional geopolitics and the integration of Jordan into the transnational flows that were driving late-twentieth-century globalization. Some early reports seemed to confirm expectations that tourism was going to bring the dividends of peace. They described excited Israeli travelers exclaiming, "It's fantastic . . . there is nothing like this in all the world," and cited pleased Jordanian tour operators who noted, "They are good explorers. . . . They ask to go to places specifically to shop."[72] By mid-1995, however, the local Jordanian press was presenting a much more mixed picture, and the still mostly celebratory reports in the international media became tinged with complaints, drawbacks, and signs of opposition.

The mixed blessing of the tourism boom becomes clear as these flows and the new, often unexpected, itineraries of the New Middle East are more closely scrutinized in relation to the immature Jordanian tourism sector. A large element of the surge consisted of overland day trippers and short-term visitors from Israel, up to nine hundred a day, who might have paid visa and entry fees to the Jordanian government but spent relatively little on the sorts of goods and services provided by private Jordanian firms in the tourism sector. The other major element of the surge was an explosion in the number of package tour arrivals. Between 1994 and 1995, they more than doubled and increased from 16 percent to 28 percent of total arrivals.[73] The Jordanian tourism infrastructure, including bus transportation, multilingual guides, and hotel accommodation, lacked the capacity and skills for dealing with either aspect of the market. Together these trends challenged both the government and the underdeveloped tourism sector.

The first wave of Israeli tourists, while it led to overbooking in hotels, "resulted in wild competition among Jordanian tour companies, which have slashed their profit margins in an effort to attract Israeli tourists."[74] In 1996 the Jordanian tourism minister, Dr. Saleh Irsheidat, remarked, "Israeli tourists form 10 percent of our visitors. Last year, we received 100,000 Israeli tourists, most of them came for a one-day visit and go back without having the opportunities to spend nights or stay in Petra or Aqaba. We are not happy about this. We have received many complaints from areas where we have tourist sites."[75] The influx caused other problems when the Jordanian government increased fees and put a quota on the number of Israeli entrances, leading to confusion and conflict between Israeli and Jordanian tour companies that had sought to coordinate these visits. This experience encouraged Israeli firms to program only day and short-term visits to Jordan as add-ons to tour packages for international visitors to Israel who spent most of their nights in Israel even while visiting sites in Jordan during the day (as well as in the Palestinian West Bank).

Moreover, when Israelis did spend a night or two, they often disrupted the market for other travelers, leading to overbooking, higher prices, and inadequate service. The experienced firms within the Jordanian tourism sector catered to long-haul cultural, religious, and heritage tourists, including both independent travelers and small package groups who mostly came from Europe and traveled in the spring.[76] Israelis, however, represented almost 29 percent of package tourists in 1995, the year when package tourism's share of total arrivals peaked at over 28 percent. Some Jordanians working in the tourism sector even complained that "people here don't want Israeli tourists. . . . They bring their own food and water, take up hotel space, and crowd out the big spenders from Europe."[77] The territorial and cultural proximity of Jordan also resulted in Israeli tourists who were less interested than Jordan's European and American visitors in spending money on souvenirs and other products. For these Israeli tourists, Jordan might be a "former enemy," but it also represented a culture too similar to the one found within Israel, Jerusalem, and the Palestinian territories. Souvenir shop owners often grumbled that Israeli tourists did not buy much from them because the items for sale did not differ significantly from those easily available in Arab East Jerusalem. When they did buy, the Israelis seemed to haggle much more than the higher-spending European visitors.[78] Unlike the upscale, long-haul tourists who formed the bulk of the market targeted by the Jordanian tourism sector, short-term Israeli tourists were more likely to be, on average, budget conscious. The Israeli share of total tourism and package tourism would drop sharply in the next few years. By 1998, package tourists accounted for only 20 percent, and non-Arab Israeli tourists became scarce.

In the end, the highly touted influx of Israeli tourists resulted in a disruptive "shock" rather than a "big push" to kick-start the Jordanian tourism sector. This effect was most clearly reflected in the experience of Jordanian firms that boldly sought to cater to visitors seeking a kosher meal. After receiving several requests, in December 1994 Amman's Inter-Continental Hotel began serving kosher meals and was looking into the idea of installing a kosher kitchen. Meanwhile a Jordanian tour firm was planning to build a chain of kosher restaurants near major tourist sites in Jordan.[79] In June 1995, following the wave of Israeli tourists in the spring, the Istanbul Restaurant, owned by a Palestinian Jordanian, worked with an Haifa-based Israeli company, SAZ International, to establish a kosher restaurant located across the street from the temporary Israeli embassy at the Forte Grand Hotel in Amman. Maintaining its Levantine cuisine but serving chicken and lamb slaughtered under the supervision of an Israeli rabbi who crossed into Jordan for the purpose, the restaurant replaced the cutlery and plates, installed a mezuzah in the doorway, and posted a sign, in English, noting the kosher offerings. The project seemed to have the blessing of Israel's new ambassador to Jordan, who described the economics of the establishment as "quite sound," estimating that "even if only 10 percent [of the 100,000 Israelis who visited Jordan in 1995] insist on kosher food it's a lot of customers."[80] The kitchen and staff were prepared to serve hundreds of meals a day, but the business quickly proved a failure. The busloads of tourists promised by the Israeli partner never materialized, and the restaurant's owner felt he could not afford to pay a monthly fee to secure a kosher certificate. Moreover, after its conversion, the Istanbul Restaurant lost most of its Arab clientele, who, even on bad days, had previously kept the establishment profitable. A month after opening, only a handful of diners were being served each day. A supply of kosher fare remained packed in the freezer. By the early fall, the restaurant was going bankrupt. The two partners were not on speaking terms, threatening lawsuits. Its Jordanian owner announced: "Enough is enough. . . . I am turning it into a nightclub with dancers, bar girls and Saudi patrons. It's time I start making some money instead of being taken for a ride."[81]

While much of the public debate in Jordan about tourism focused on the impact of Israeli tourists, this represented only one of the unexpected itineraries of the New Middle East. The integration of Jordan into the global tourism economy was accomplished by making the territory more porous through its borders with Israel. This openness, however, resulted in more flows but less economic reterritorialization. As a small country with two new direct crossing points with Israel (in addition to the bridge between Jordan and the West Bank), most of Jordan's tourist sites, including Petra in the south, Jerash in the center, and Um Qays in the north, became accessible from Israel via day trips. As borders were being erased from tourism maps, many Western tourists were experiencing "regional tourism" by visiting Jordan as an adjunct day trip from Israel. In 1996, 47 percent of the 90,000 tourists entering Jordan across the Wadi Araba crossing were day visitors.[82] The Israeli tourism sector was able to market Petra as part of packages that might include a week touring Israel and only a day, or at most a night, in Petra. Israeli firms were now able to replicate in Jordan strategies they had developed for marketing and packaging tourism to Arab East Jerusalem and the Palestinian West Bank. From the point of view of a Western tourist traveling on a tour organized by an Israeli firm, the New Middle East was being realized through the seamless extension of the infrastructure of the Israeli tourism industry. As Jordanian minister of tourism Dr. Irsheidat noted, "We are fully aware the Israelis are promoting Jordan through their programs."[83]

While the proponents of the New Middle East suggested that the short distances and shared cultural heritage of the region of the Holy Land and the Levant would serve as a basis for increased cooperation and mutual gains, these same factors allowed travelers to forgo more intimate interaction with Arab society. Petra saw more visitors in this era, but Jordanian hotels, tour operators, and airlines were often bypassed. Overall the average length of stay for package tours decreased from about 5 nights in the 1989–94 period to 3.7 nights in the 1995–97 period.[84] In fact, generally only tourists with a deep interest in Jordanian history and culture considered additional overnight stays outside one in Wadi Musa or Amman. Such tourists traditionally represented a major market for Jordanian hotels and tour companies. Many of the American and Israeli travelers who made up the wave of postpeace tourism had a limited understanding and appreciation of Jordanian, Arab, and Islamic culture. During 1991 and 1992, before the Oslo agreement, American visitors stayed an average of about 4 nights, while between 1993 and 1997, following the agreement, Americans averaged fewer than 2.5 nights per visit.[85]

Dr. Irsheidat suggested that Jordanian firms should replicate the strategies of Israeli firms in the other direction: "We can give these tourists more incentives to visit Jordan four or five days, and get two days free in Jerusalem or in Eilat, and counterattack. This is what we have to do."[86] Jordan, however, had limited marketing capabilities at the time. Moreover, Dr. Irsheidat noted, the Israelis were "delaying people, and not only Jordanians. Even Western people who are crossing the bridge have to stay on the Israeli side between one and two hours. On our side, within ten minutes they are passing the crossing point."[87] The efforts of Jordanian firms to develop new strategies to exploit the possibilities for regional tourism in the New Middle East remained constrained by Israeli security concerns and Israeli fears that Jordanians traveling to Israel would overstay their visas while looking for opportunities for employment lacking in Jordan.[88]

The Exhaustion of Rents

Tourism development in the wake of the peace process resulted in the unsustainable overcommodification of the tourism landscape. Creating tourist products such as hotel rooms, handicrafts, and cultural experiences proved easier for local entrepreneurs than attempting to coordinate and ensure demand for such products, which remained unfeasible. These effects were, in part, generated by the promotion of a strategy of national tourism development— beginning with the negotiation of the peace deal and represented in tourism development plans—where firms were encouraged to imagine potentially unlimited markets for tourism products and to invest considerably to meet those markets. The state, in the process of selling the peace deal, became a critical source of market information for these firms. In granting licenses for hotel development and announcing infrastructure projects, the state was directly presenting the private sector with signals about the future market for tourism. Meanwhile government agencies and their consultants were producing tourism figures, projections, and plans that touted tourism as the new oil for the national economy. Driven by unwarranted optimism and the political imperative of overpromoting tourism development to advertise the expected economic rewards of peace, state agencies and plans lacked an accurate vision of what the tourism economy would look like from the vantage point of individual private firms.

As in Petra, similar stories of rent seeking can be told about firms in various subsectors of the national tourism economy. In 1995, after the monopoly held by the state-owned bus company JETT was eliminated, 270 addition buses went into service with the establishment of two new bus companies. By 1997, however, the tour bus operators began facing ruinous oversupply and announced large losses. The three companies formed a cartel to keep a floor on prices, and increased competition was limited by government-imposed capital and volume requirements. Travel agents soon complained about price increases and decreased service in the midst of a difficult season. This cartel system, for which travel agents blamed both the bus companies and the bus law, seemed to allow JETT to maintain monopoly prices and has since become a subject of antitrust legislation in parliament.

Travel agents faced a similar boom-and-bust cycle. In 1991 there were only 228 registered travel agents in Jordan. Their number grew to 326 in 1994 and 390 in 1996. Many had to shut their doors only a few years after opening, while the ones who remained suffered from stiff competition. Unlike bus companies and hotels, travel agents do not have assets to sell or borrow against when they get in trouble, leading some agents to stiff their clients as they go bankrupt. The government responded by imposing capital requirements to limit the number of travel agents, and in 1997 the number of agents shrank back down to 267.[89]

The stakes in the hotel sector remained far higher. Between 1994 and 1998, the total number of classified hotels rose from 129 to 211, with the bed capacity of four- and five-star hotels expanding from 4,577 to 7,594.[90] While the hotel market in Wadi Musa was particularly volatile, at the national level, hotel occupancy rates across Jordan declined from 46 percent in 1995 to 38 percent in 1997. Meanwhile in Amman a massive hotel-building boom continued across the city. In 1998, eighty-two hotels were under construction across Jordan.[91] By March 1999, Amman sported six five-star and four four-star hotels, with a total of almost 2,800 rooms. Another twenty-four three-star hotels held about 1,700 rooms.[92] Tourism industry officials estimated that the $700 million being invested in the hotel sector would bring online another 26,000 hotel beds, with the bulk of these in Amman.[93] At the same time, room occupancy rates in Amman were the lowest among Middle Eastern countries.[94] As shown in Table 6, the vast increase in hotel capacity along with sluggish tourism demand led to a decline in occupancy rates and yields per room.

As one Jordanian economist put it, "Hotels, tourist buses, and travel agencies are real and sad examples of how parts of the economy went on an investment binge in 1995, only to come down to earth with a thud a year later and then start to wallow in a depression which continues."[95] At the macro level, the tourism economy did not appear to collapse. Between 1996 and 1999, tourism receipts grew at an average rate of 5.2 percent per year (in nominal terms) and represented over 10.5 percent of GNP. In the run-up to the year 2000, tourism promoters predicted that the millennium would bring a new explosion of tourists eager to visit Jordan and the Holy Land. A visit by the pope was planned to coincide with the opening of the newly discovered John the Baptist site along the Jordan River ("Bethany beyond the Jordan"). In 2000, however, tourist receipts fell by 9 percent, followed by a drop of 3 percent in 2001. The contribution of tourism receipts to GNP dropped to below 8.5 percent.[96] Even before 2000, some banks were forced to freeze the assets of hotels in Petra when the number of visitors dropped more than 50 percent. In 2001 the hotel sector had estimated losses of about US$280 mil-

Table 6. Performance of Amman hotels in the 1990s

Year	Room occupancy rate	Average daily room rate US$	Revenues per available room US$
1993	54%	76	41
1994	61%	67	41
1995	74%	75	55
1996	71%	83	59
1997	61%	83	50
1998	56%	81	46
1999	56%	71	40

Source: HVS International

lion.[97] These declines of the Jordanian tourism economy were generally blamed on the collapse of the Palestinian-Israeli peace process and the outbreak of the second *intifada,* showing how a regional approach to tourism made Jordan even more vulnerable to events outside its control.

These numbers do not reflect the changing value of the tourism product and the economic costs of tourism development that took place following the peace treaty. The overdevelopment of similar products and the high fluctuations in tourism inflows have led to destructive competition, downward price spirals, and wasted resources, not to mention dashed hopes. For many in the hotel sector, the overcapacity of supply and the desperate quest for revenues have made paying back loans impossible while eroding efforts to improve the quality of products and services. One result has been the prevention of the development of robust linkages to the small and informal businesses associated with tourism as was often promised and predicted during the peace process.

Forging Enclaves

The picture presented so far depicts the environment that most tourism-related business came to face in the years following the outbreak of peace. It does not, however, represent the experience of all firms in the sector. The most successful tourism firms in Jordan have been not the many seeking to capture windfall rents with hasty investments but the few that have been able to promote forms of economic reterritorialization by shaping their own tourism spaces within territory under their control. These firms have worked to create their own networks within the local tourism economy; through vertical and horizontal integration, these firms have been able to exploit the rents and externalities generated by flows within particular tourism spaces. In Tunisia, government agencies controlled tourism spaces and built the infrastructure needed for private firms to develop such strategies. In contrast, the Jordanian government, as we saw in the case of Petra and parts of the Jordan Rift Valley, was impeded by fragmented territorial control and authority over the sector. Moreover, using their access to the global marketing and distribution capacity of transnational corporations, these firms have been able to connect directly with the networks of the global tourism economy.

Before the explosion of rent-seeking behavior in the wake of the peace treaty, some Jordanian tourism developers were working to provide new and unique experiences of place. One leading example is the themed restaurant complex of Kan Zaman built by Jordan Tourism Investments (JTI). Kan Zaman was created by remodeling Al-Yadoudeh, the mountaintop homestead of the Abu Jaber family south of Amman.[98] Working with the family, Munir Nassar, one of Jordan's most experienced travel agents, developed a restaurant and various craft and spice shops set within vernacular Transjordanian architecture. The private venture was able to create and commodify a unique experience of place that also represented elements of history not previously marketed as part of Jordan's tourist image. Although the project was originally targeted to international businessmen and tourists, the themed restaurant also proved particularly popular among the Jordanian middle class, which helped to sustain its business when tourist flows were low.

JTI elaborated the idea of a rural-village-themed environment by building the Taybet Zaman resort near Petra. The self-styled "authentic nineteenth-century tourist village" of Taybet Zaman sought to create a new form of tourist development in Jordan. This resort was established within the disused stone-built structures of an old village, its architecture a remnant of the nineteenth-century vernacular style.[99] Rather than leasing or buying the land, Nassar and JTI created a profit-sharing agreement with the property owners while also providing some jobs to the villagers, who now mostly lived up the hill from the old village. JTI rebuilt the stone houses and turned the complex into a five-star resort complete with leisure and entertainment facilities. The complex contains a small museum and a series of workshops that produce local handicrafts for sale. The structure of the village follows the territorial logic of the integrated tourism complex. It limits the cultural and environmental impact of tourism by containing most tourist activity, besides visits to Petra, within its walls. At the same time, by providing facilities and commercial outlets, it creates and captures the benefits of locational economies characteristic of economic reterritorialization.

While JTI sought to create a set of privately owned tourist complexes that commodify Jordanian heritage, the Zara Tourism Investments companies founded by the late Khalil Talhouni constructed a network of luxury tourist facilities across the country. Zara, like other firms, entered the tourism business as a result of the peace process and expectations of increased economic liberalization in Jordan.[100] Zara's first tourist assets were established by buying up government shares in existing hotels, such as the Amman Inter-Continental, when they were being privatized in the early 1990s. Zara was then able to build some of the most luxurious and well-designed five-star hotels in the country because of its access to capital, which included the resources of Jordan's financial and banking community, other private Arab investors, and funds from the World Bank's private investment arm, the International Finance Corporation (IFC). In contrast to many other developers, Zara relied on experienced Jordanian and international professionals with expertise in the hospitality industry to develop detailed and sophisticated feasibility studies and hotel building plans. In many ways, Zara has operated in the opposite manner of much of the tourism sector in Jordan. As one hotel developer noted, "Khalil Talhouni is an entrepreneur with his own style. One method for a developer is to do market research to find an existing demand, and then go out and meet it. But Talhouni believes that you can go about it another way. That you can build a destination that did not exist before, and thus there was no demand for it, because it did not exist. You thus create your own market. To do this you build really nice hotels, places where people will want to stay."[101]

Zara set out with a new vision for what the tourist experience of Jordan could be. They sought to craft luxury hotels that would define a visitor's experience of the country, often drawing on the talent of some of Jordan's most creative architects and designers. In each location, Zara sought to take advantage of unique natural and cultural features such as Petra and the Dead Sea. Rather than following the modernist international style used by many hotels to create a familiar environment for visitors, Zara hired architects, designers, and landscapers to define a distinct atmosphere within each of their hotels. They specifically sought to create an experience in contrast to the large-scale mass tourism developments that dominated the Israeli tourism sector, as well as the bland style of most of the older high-end hotels in Jordan. After developing a base with the Inter-Continental in downtown Amman, Zara built a "boutique" hotel resort in a prime location near the main entry gate to the Petra Archaeological Park. Mövenpick was chosen to manage the hotel based on their proven ability to maintain profitable, high-quality resorts in other isolated locations in the Middle East.[102] In contrast to other hotels in Wadi Musa, Zara's Mövenpick Resort Petra was designed to create its own experience of place within the hotel rather than capture rents from the tourism boom or rely on Petra itself to define the experience of visitors to the hotel. Zara's Petra hotel was designed in a style evocative of Arab and Islamic architecture (though resembling a style associated with Damascus more than southern Jordan) and included a high-quality restaurant, shops, and an ice cream and coffee stand that would be used by other tourists to Petra. Unlike most other hotels in Petra at the time, Zara's Mövenpick could draw on the distribution and marketing network of its management company to find the pools of potential visitors. In slack times, these channels could be used to efficiently mobilize demand by knowing which travel agents and individual tourists to offer discounts to.[103]

Zara also created their own positive externalities and exploited them through backward and forward linkages. For example, they built a series of luxury hotels throughout the country with the idea that if they attracted high-end tourists to the Jordan market, they could then capture that business in different parts of the country. As this market was being developed, Zara was able to capture opportunities in the tourism economy through the expanding volume of their own operations. They created their own hotel supply company, engineering consulting firm, a Dead Seas product company, and a travel agency. With these firms, Zara could provide high-quality services to their own hotels and their clients, and with the skills and economies of scale these firms gained from doing Zara projects, they could then outperform other firms and provide goods and service to other hotel developers and tourists.

This strategy could only be attempted by a developer with tremendous financial resources, and Zara's ability to gain financing for expanding its network of hotels has been a mark of its success. By 2003, Zara-owned hotel rooms represented about 35 percent of the total number of five-star rooms available in Jordan.[104] Each Zara-owned hotel is managed by a leading international hotel firm, such as Mövenpick and Hyatt, under a carefully negotiated management contract that creates incentives for the hotel chain to draw on its own marketing networks and ties to tour operators to ensure occupancy. Zara's success is also represented by the fact that while the tourism sector was suffering a crisis after the Israeli reinvasion of the West Bank and the U.S. war in Iraq, between January and

March 2004, Zara's Grand Hyatt Amman maintained an occupancy rate of 68 percent, and its Mövenpick Resort Petra had one of 40 percent.[105]

With the failure of state-sponsored efforts to develop tourism spaces and launch extensive international marketing campaigns, and with information and transaction costs so high, economic reterritorialization that produces sustainable rents and externalities has occurred mostly in enclave spaces around niche markets such as the luxury sector. Instead of generating opportunities for independent entrepreneurs, these linkages are formed through vertical and horizontal integration within complexes across networks of tourism firms owned by the same set of investors. This pattern of development limits the scope of the economic benefits gained from tourism and shuts out those who lack the capital and skills to conduct such strategies. This result is the reverse of what the peace process was supposed to produce. Instead of providing an engine of national economic growth that raises the standard of living throughout the population, this process has led to the development of tourism enclaves governed by a narrow set of elite firms. Politically, this group is dominated by the Transjordanian business elites, while the Palestinian Jordanians who own many of the medium-size hotels and other tourist businesses must struggle in a volatile economy. Though this form of luxury enclave tourism is often derided as offering commercialized and socially insulated forms of cultural experiences, characterized by staged authenticity, these firms do not operate only by capturing windfall rents. Rather, they are able to create spaces that generate locational rents and positive externalities because they have the skills, capital, and access to market information, which other firms lack.

The Decline of the New Middle East

Just a few years after the triumphant signing of the peace treaty at the Wadi Araba crossing point and a public campaign by the treaty's supporters to sell the peace, most Jordanians came to realize that the economic benefits would prove meager. Jordanian policy makers cannot be blamed for the decline of the Israeli-Palestinian peace process or the Israeli actions against Palestinians that so infuriated Jordanians and helped erode interest in the normalization of relations with Israel. Nevertheless, lack of peace dividends soured support for the treaty and put the regime on the defensive. From the start, the treaty had opponents among Jordan's Islamist, Arab nationalist, and leftist opposition parties. To make matters worse, in 1996 Israel's new prime minister, the right-wing Netanyahu, opposed the ongoing Israeli-Palestinian Oslo peace process, which strained relations with Jordan. In the face of these challenges, the supporters of the peace treaty were hard pressed to show its positive benefits. Worse, after the hyped expectations of the mid-1990s, economic conditions deteriorated. At the time of the fourth anniversary of the peace treaty, the *Jordan Times* reported, "rightly or wrongly many Jordanians now blame the deepening economic recession and the decline in their living standards on the Peace treaty with Israel [which has become] the favorite punching bag for the opposition."[106] As one former peace negotiator declared, "The model of peace to which we aspired would achieve improved living conditions, mainly through increased trade with our neighbors. This hasn't happened, and this is why the anti-peace camp is now having a heyday."[107]

The state of the Jordanian tourism sector, with hotels going bankrupt and travel agents closing down their operations, stood as a visible marker of the failure of peace to revitalize the economy with foreign investment or to jump-start the tourism sector. The images of internationally financed megatourism projects along the Jordan Valley creating jobs and national wealth were soon distant memories that many in the tourism sector were weary of even recalling. Moreover, as a political movement mounted to oppose the normalization of relations with Israel, Israeli tourists, who seemed to flood Jordan in the first year after the peace treaty, came to function as a publicly debated symbol of the failures and dashed hopes of the peace. These visitors, many came to feel, seemed to have left nothing positive in their wake. Jordanian impressions of these flows helped give rise to a critical discourse that viewed such manifestations of normalization as posing a threat not only to Jordan's economy but also to its society, culture, and national heritage.

The Difficult Transition to a Postrentier Economy

While an economic turnaround could not have been expected so quickly, a year after the 1995 MENA summit in Amman, Jordanians came to recognize how bumpy the path toward economic transfor-

mation was going to be. Instead of an economic boom and massive American aid, Jordanians were suffering economic austerity
measures. To maintain access to IMF credit, Jordan was following an economic program in line with the so-called Washington
Consensus, which required maintaining a tight budget. To do so,
the government of Prime Minister Kabariti sought to decrease consumer subsides on bread and increase utility rates. Wary owing to
the reaction to the first wave of austerity measures enacted six years
before, Kabariti's government crafted a program that included cash
transfers to public-sector workers and the poor to compensate for
the rise in prices.[108] The government sold the austerity program as
an effort to eliminate waste and forge a more efficient social welfare system. Nevertheless, riots, sometimes violent, broke out in
Karak and spread to other towns in southern Jordan.

Unlike the late 1980s, in 1996 Jordan was not at the end of
its financial rope. Following policies to restructure the economy,
Jordan's macroeconomic situation even showed signs of improvement over the past year, with increased foreign reserves and a drop
in the official unemployment rate from 15 percent to 13 percent.[109]
A closer look, however, reveals a different story. The small drop
in unemployment was due to the Arab Gulf states reopening their
labor markets to Jordanians and a government effort to restrict
foreign labor in the country.[110] Moreover, between 1993 and
1996, the standard of living declined 13 percent, resulting in one
out of every four Jordanian families living in poverty.[111] Southern
and rural Jordan had long been a stronghold of regime support
due to patronage in the form of civil service employment, military
recruitment, and the maintenance of political ties with tribal leaders. This support base, however, was now finding that the current transformation to a postrentier economy was only increasing the challenges they faced. To the degree that the peace treaty
and new economic policies were leading to more investment and
economic development, these effects were mostly only evident in
urban areas or in sectors, such as tourism, mining, and port trade,
all controlled by the state, urban business interests, or the larger
merchant families. Increasingly, Jordanians came to view the
new era of economic development as one that "benefited the few
and excluded the many."[112] To make matters worse, it seemed to
many Jordanians that government policies were no longer geared
to serving the public but sought to please Western interests and

Israel, from which the government expected aid, investment, and security.

Most businesses and employees in the private sector failed to see increased economic opportunities in the wake of the peace treaty. As noted earlier, in sectors such as tourism, the new opportunities could mostly be exploited only by business elites who were willing and able to pursue investment and market opportunities in Israel and Western economies. Across most of the rest of the private sector, dominated by businessmen (mostly of Palestinian origin) operating small and medium-size firms, the most sought-after benefit from the peace treaty was increased access to the West Bank Palestinian economy, where business owners saw a ready and accessible market half the size of the Jordanian economy. Those seeking these opportunities, however, complained that Israel continued to restrict Jordanian access to the Palestinian economy by limiting the import of products that might compete against Israeli firms and imposing burdensome procedures for transporting goods into the West Bank.[113] Instead Israeli officials promoted the notion of American-sponsored Qualified Industrial Zones (QIZ) in Jordan where factories with a minimum percentage of Israeli capital and inputs could take advantage of lower-cost Jordanian labor and export, duty free, to the U.S. market. Some businessmen were so frustrated that they charged government officials with having known that the benefits of peace would be limited and promoted them as "a mere ploy to gain support for the treaty."[114]

In September 1999, Jordan's minister of planning Rima Khalaf-Hunaidi gave a speech to the Washington Institute for Near East Policy, presenting a frank overview of her changing understanding of the performance of Jordan's economy following the peace treaty. She began by noting that "in 1994 . . . economists anticipated an unparalleled expansion in economic activity . . . expected to lead to a sizable increase in per capita income and *a significant improvement in the standards of living of the average Jordanian.*"[115] Following that introduction, she launched into a blunt assessment of the current situation: "Since 1996, the standard of living in Jordan progressively deteriorated, as real growth rates dropped from an average of 10% during the period 1992–1994, to 5.6% in 1995, and then to a mere 1.5% during the period 1996–1998." As an advocate of peace and regional economic cooperation, one of Jordan's most experienced planners sadly noted that progress on the Aqaba

Peace Airport was halted, the MENA Regional Bank never saw the light of day, the REDWG multilateral talks were dormant, and the MENA summits were by then a thing of the past.

The failure of regional economic cooperation especially hurt the Jordanian regime because it undercut its rationale for embracing peace and normalization.[116] The regime had argued that Jordan was helping to lead a transformation of the Arab order that would include the formation of an independent Palestinian state, the end of the Arab-Israeli conflict, and regional prosperity. With the decline of the regional framework, the Jordanian regime was forced to defend the treaty exclusively in terms of Jordan's own national interests. Many in Jordan read this to mean the interests of the Hashemite monarchy and its closest allies rather than the interests of its heterogeneous population.

The Changing Discourse about Tourism

At the U.S.-backed MENA regional economic summits in 1996 and 1997, Jordan went through the motions of recycling its collection of investment opportunities in the tourism sector. By then, however, enthusiasm in Jordan for regional economic cooperation had waned. In the following year, planning for future MENA summits was abandoned, and with that, the American initiative for the private-sector-led economic transformation of the region died. In 1999, Shimon Peres visited Jordan as minister for regional development in the new Labor-led government of Ehud Barak. Seeking to resurrect his New Middle East vision, he carried in tow a group of American and Canadian investors and presented Jordanian officials with Israel's latest version of its billion-dollar schemes for joint tourism development projects. Upon receiving the delegation's ideas, the Jordanian prime minister politely noted his government's willingness to establish a logistics committee to consider the plan. More bluntly, one Jordanian official complained to an Israeli reporter:

> Were you to give me 10 dinars for every Israeli plan that's been presented to us, we wouldn't need any more investments in Jordan. When the peace agreement was finalized, you would have needed trucks to convey proposals concerning five-year plans, budgets, development ideas and, more than anything else, promises. Hotels at the Dead Sea, factories, a joint airport at Aqaba, free trade with

Israel and the Palestinian Authority, Jordanian workers employed in Israel, the establishment of manufacturing plants in Jordan and what have you. They pounded on the drums, banging out the so-called fruits of peace.[117]

The fate of the tourism sector was emblematic of the changes in the Jordanian economy in the years since the peace treaty. By the late 1990s, the series of large luxury-hotel projects that had begun while enthusiasm for tourism expansion was still high reached completion. With few other options, officials continued to support the notion of tourism as the engine for economic development. In 1999 Prime Minister Adur-Ra'uf Rawabdeh declared that "tourism will constitute the *main* revenue for the national economy in coming years and the government is determined to develop and modernise the tourism industry."[118] Meanwhile, on a visit to Jordan, the director of the World Bank's Middle East Department "described tourism as 'the thrust' to create jobs and more jobs."[119] More broadly across Jordanian society, with too many hotel owners in debt, tourism development no longer seemed to represent a means for generating broad-based benefits or opportunities for new entrepreneurs. The successful hotels and tourism businesses were those owned by the large business interests, merchant families, or wealthy Arab investors who could have their establishment managed by big-name global firms such as Hyatt, Marriott, and Four Seasons. As one foreign reporter noted, "Tourism and foreign trade are expanding fast, and the Amman skyline is being transformed by real estate investment. But there is a widespread perception (among the middle class as well as the poor) that the economic benefits accrue only to a minority."[120]

At the same time, many Jordanians came to view their economy's openness to cross-border tourism and investment flows from Israel as an economic liability, if not a threat to the nation. During the early post-treaty era, stories about the influx of foreign tourists represented tangible, highly viable markers of the coming benefits of peace. This narrative, however, was soon challenged by the rise of a popular discourse highly critical of the Israeli visitors. Locals, intellectuals, critics, and even other travelers have been complaining about tourists since the rise of modern tourism in the nineteenth century.[121] And foreign tourists who are rude, disruptive, or ignorant of local norms of behavior and dress are typically denigrated privately in Jordanian conversations. In the Jordanian context, however, a specifically anti-Israeli tourist discourse emerged. What was particular in this discourse was that the expectation of reaping peace dividends through tourism development led Jordanians to have a certain definition for what they viewed as "correct" tourist behavior. In both private and public conversations, regardless of their attitude toward the peace treaty with Israel, Jordanians routinely denigrated Israeli tourists for bringing their own food and water, not buying souvenirs, and not sleeping in Jordanian hotels. Reports of such behavior dominated Jordanians' impressions of their Israeli visitors, and "many Jordanians regarded this as no less than an Israeli plot and an attempt to damage the Jordanian economy."[122] Jordanians in the tourist sector also complained to newspapers and directly to government officials. Many in the sector went from welcoming the Israeli tourists to viewing them as disruptive to the tourism economy and crowding out higher-spending tourists from Europe. "The low-spending propensity of many Israeli tourists," suggested one report, "has meant an opportunity to create a constituency that would have had vested interests in advocating greater interaction with Israel has been lost."[123]

This discourse can be read in a manner similar to the way the anthropologist Rebecca Stein reads popular Israeli discourses about their own tourists traveling to Arab states such as Jordan.[124] Stein notes that "in Israeli newspapers, stories about tourism were simultaneously stories about the nation-state, [and] about the meaning and boundaries of [national] identity, citizenship, and culture" in the wake of the peace treaty.[125] She describes how "tales of the Jewish Israeli leisure traveler, traversing borders into neighboring states heretofore off-limits, were deployed to narrate the effects of regional reconfiguration. Through the image of the traveling tourist body, crossing borders made porous by 'peace,' the press illustrated Israel's new diplomatic and economic place within the Middle East."[126] Jordan was the most important terrain for these stories that, according to Stein, were recounted as narratives of "first contact" with the Arab world. Meanwhile Jordanians told an opposing set of stories about these Israeli travelers. Stein notes: "As Caren Kaplan has suggested, the traveling subject as trope of global flows tends to obscure the historical conditions of travel for differently situated communities and the discrepant relations of power that attend them."[127] In her essay, Stein sets out to unmask these conditions that are suppressed, ignored, or elided in popular Israeli accounts.

In contrast, Jordanian discourses about Israeli tourists reflected popular understandings of the historical conditions of travel and the discrepant relations of power between guest and host societies. They emphasized Jordanian concerns about the challenges that the normalization of economic relations with Israel might pose while resonating with their own long-standing narratives about what most Jordanians, especially those of Palestinian origin, viewed as the exploitative nature of Zionism and Israel's relations with its Arab neighbors. The Israelis in these stories were not simply another version of the "ugly tourist." They were burdened with Jordanian disappointments and growing anxieties about the peace treaty and normalization. To add to the ubiquitous complaints about their frugal spending habits, Jordanian newspapers and gossip became filled with stories such as the one about Israeli guests who swiped not only towels but curtains, paintings, and even the bathroom faucet from an Amman hotel. Another story accused Israelis of taking advantage of Jordanians' unfamiliarity with Israeli currency by exchanging worthless out-of-circulation shekels into Jordanian dinars. More troublesome stories told of Israeli tourists hammering chips from the colorful Petra rock faces to take home as souvenirs, and some accused Israelis of damaging or stealing Jordanian antiquities and rare wildflowers. One of the most provocative allegations was that a group of Israeli tourists had scrawled graffiti in Hebrew at Aaron's tomb in Petra, damaging the existing Arabic inscriptions. Several of these incidents appear to be true, and Israeli, Jordanian, and even American officials vowed to investigate.[128]

These stories came to displace the positive narratives about "peace through tourism" that had animated the geopolitical imaginary of the New Middle East. Even as telephone lines and air links were being established between Jordan and Israel and officials on a joint tourism commission continued to coordinate, societal reactions to Israeli tourists were hampering steps toward realizing the New Middle East vision. Tourism firms that had generally been enthusiastic about benefiting from Israeli tourism often felt the impact of these societal attitudes. For example, the company running the Kan Zaman complex near Amman was pressured by its Jordanian patrons into removing mugs in its gift shop sporting Israeli and Jordanian flags and the slogan "Peace 1995."[129] The Jordanian minister for the economy was even moved to complain in front of the Israeli media during a visit to Bethlehem that "the behavior of some of the Israeli tourists in Jordan is liable to endanger the peace process and strengthen those in my country who oppose peace."[130] The Jordanian government sought in vain to counter these sentiments. The few tourism firms that continued to benefit from Jewish Israeli tourists did not publicize the fact. Meanwhile, across parts of the tourism sector, rather than welcoming Israeli investment, accusations circulated about which hotels had Israeli investment or catered to Israeli tour groups.

The Rise of the Antinormalization Movement

With the erosion of the post-peace-treaty tourism economy and growing disparagement of the impact of Israeli tourism flows, political forces opposed to the peace process and normalization were able to exploit the shifting terms of public discourse and popular opinion. Polls by the University of Jordan's Centre for Strategic Studies had found that in 1994 about 80 percent of the population supported peace with Israel, with a similar number expecting the peace to bring economic benefits in the short term.[131] Much of this support was soft, contingent on the realization of peace dividends and a negotiated end to the other aspects of the Arab-Israeli conflict. As Russell Lucas notes, "If the economic rewards of peace had been greater, perhaps the Jordanian public would have more warmly greeted normalization with Israel."[132] By 1997 the share of Jordanians who supported the peace treaty had dropped to 50 percent, and 80 percent considered Israel an enemy.[133] By 2001, 73 percent of Jordanians wanted to curtail economic relations with Israel.[134] This shift in public opinion created an opening for a growing coalition of opposition forces to coalesce into the antinormalization movement. Meanwhile, as Mustafa Hamarneh remarked, the "pro-peace camp in Jordan went underground."[135] The antinormalization movement has not been able to mount enough pressure to shift Jordanian policy and is unlikely to force the regime to abrogate the peace treaty and rob the monarchy of its strategic gains and alliances. Nevertheless popular opposition to normalization has come to define the Jordanian societal response to the treaty. It has helped shift the relationship of Jordan and Israel, defined as a warm peace marking the rise of the New Middle

East in 1994, to a much colder peace at all levels except at the top, characterized by minimal interaction between the two societies. Jordanian-Israeli relations are a conflicted hybrid, consisting of a strategic relationship between states while most of Jordanian society actively or passively opposes such ties.

Opposition to the king's early moves toward peace was launched by the so-called Committee for Resisting Submission and Normalization (CRSN), which organized demonstrations and rallies. Upon the signing of the Washington Declaration in 1994, the CRSN called for a day of mourning. In 1995, as parliament was considering the repeal of laws that prohibited economic ties to Israel, the CRSN sought to hold an antinormalization conference. Meanwhile many Jordanian businessmen were refusing to attend the MENA summit in Amman because it included Israeli involvement.[136] In the following year, when a private Jordanian businessman sought to hold a trade fair for Israeli products, members of the Amman Chamber of Commerce, Amman Chamber of Industry, and the Jordanian Businessmen Association opposed the idea.[137] As the antinormalization movement grew, it gained the support of the professional associations and attracted major political figures such as former prime minister Ahmed Obeidat. The professional associations, generally led by a small group of politicized leaders aligned with the opposition parties, played a critical role in leading societal opposition to normalization. Since membership in these associations is generally required for professionals to legally work in their field, the political activists within the associations began blacklisting members who engaged in what they denounced as "normalization activities." Not only were advocates of normal relations targeted, such as those who traveled to Israel and met with Israeli colleagues, but even attending an international conference that Israelis took part in might get one in trouble and require a public disavowal of normalization. The dentists' association barred its members from treating visiting Israelis except in an emergency.[138] The press association sought to boycott a government-owned newspaper that accepted ads for airline flights to Tel Aviv. The trade union council banned all interactions with the Radisson SAS hotel in Amman after it agreed to host an event put on by the Israeli embassy. The boycott was lifted only after the hotel manager sent a letter to the head of the council apologizing for holding the event and noting that the hotel had done so only for financial gain rather than as a political statement. The hotel also pledged to join with other international hotels in Amman in refusing to host "normalization" events such as the Israeli national day ceremony.[139]

The antinormalization movement articulated a discourse of political reterritorialization that resonated with many Jordanians as they sought to redefine Jordan's interests and identity. The vision of mutual absolute gains resulting from normalization and economic cooperation was replaced by one that understood normalization as leading to vastly unequal relative gains.[140] Such a discourse was viewed in geopolitical terms as Israel's quest for regional domination. The Egyptian economist Mahmoud Abdel-Fadil, for example, writes: "'Peace' for Israel is the resumption of its war against the Arabs on economic, financial, technological and cultural fronts. In the shadow of a new Middle East and the inequitable distribution of the dividends of peace, Israel could well become the focal point [of economic activity] while Arab countries will become the periphery."[141]

Within this regional Arabist critique of the New Middle East, Jordan was viewed as "increasingly becoming a market place and political space for Israel which is emerging as a 'regional imperialist,' connected to the 'international capitalist center.'"[142] While the Israeli private sector was never able to wield this sort of economic influence in Jordan, the tourism sector was one of the few examples where Israeli firms did intrude into Jordanian economic space. The Jordanian Islamist Ishaq Farhan described the goals of the antinormalization movement as preventing the integration of Israel into the regional economy and resisting Israel's efforts to forge a new Middle East order in which "Jordan would serve as a bridgehead for Israeli economic, political and military hegemony over the entire region."[143] Calling for the treaty to be abrogated, a leftist MP declared, "We will be swallowed up by the Israeli economy. I think our industry is going to be ruined by this open market that they're preaching."[144] These discourses presented normalization as not just an economic and political challenge but also a threat to Jordan's Arab-Islamic heritage and identity. These forces even resisted efforts to define Jordan as part of the "Middle East," as this label was thought to obscure the nation's organic connection to the Arab and Muslim world.

With the rise of this discourse, the experience of the tourism sector, especially the image of Israeli tourists visiting Jordan, was mobilized to evoke a sense of threat. While Israeli newspapers were recounting stories of "first contact" and the international media was celebrating Israeli tourism to Jordan as a symbol of the New Middle East, "a newspaper sympathetic to the Islamic opposition published a picture of the first Israeli arrivals under the headline 'The Entry of the Conquerors.'"[145] Islamists would also accuse the Ministry of Tourism of "failing to establish [real] tourism and [suggest] that what is taking place is sinfulness and debauchery resulting from the growing number of nightclubs and Jordan's sudden openness."[146]

Territory, Violence, and Spaces of Insecurity

While Jordanian discourses about Israeli tourists, and the anti-normalization movement more generally, often drew on fictions equivalent to Israeli narratives of "first contact," they did nonetheless express a heightened awareness of the geopolitical conditions and imbalances of power that enable cross-border travel for some communities but not for others. In their understandings of territory and spaces of insecurity, these discourses reflect a geopolitical imaginary at odds with that of the New Middle East vision.

From the point of view of the Jordanian regime, the signing of a peace treaty with Israel helped ensure territorial security by establishing a close strategic relationship with the United States and a new strategic understanding with Israel. The treaty also helped provide budget security for the regime by increasing access to aid and credit from the United States and other sources. But the embrace of peace and the normalization of relations with Israel were also predicated on a vision of cross-border economic cooperation and transnational flows transforming the Jordanian economy and integrating it into the global economy. The treaty and this integration required that Jordan liberalize its laws concerning property. After some delay owing to obstruction by opposition lawmakers, in 1995 Jordan abolished its 1973 Law for Preventing the Sale of Immovable Property to the Enemy, which defined the sale of land in Jordan (or the West Bank) to Israelis as constituting a crime against state security punishable by death.[147] However, just as Jordan was adjusting its legal statutes regarding trade and property rights to gain membership in the World Trade Organization, many Jordanians came to fear the "threat" of Israeli investment, in particular that Israelis were buying up land. This fear became embedded in societal discourses of insecurity that challenged the geopolitical imaginary promoted by the regime. For example, as the government drafted laws to encourage foreign investment and allow non-Jordanians to buy property, deputies in the lower house of parliament began to complain that the liberalization of the rules would allow Israelis to buy land in an area that was once a security zone. Some farmers in the Jordan Valley feared Israelis would use the land to develop mechanized farms to grow produce for the Israeli market or possibly drive them out of business in the Jordanian market. They successfully pressured lawmakers to respond to their concerns, which many members of the burgeoning antinormalization movement also shared. Eventually, after much heated debate, the parliament rewrote the JVA Development Law to restrict ownership to Jordanian nationals approved by the prime minister's office.[148]

In many ways, these fears and protests echo the discourse of antiglobalization activists, but they should also be viewed as shaped by anti-Zionist narratives about the threat posed by Jews buying Arab land in Palestine, resonating with the Palestinian loss of a homeland in 1948. This connection helped exaggerate fears and mobilize concerns about not only economic domination but, in the view of some, territorial encroachment by Israel.

Together with the lack of peace dividends, the societal fears of Israeli control over Jordanian land erode two of the core arguments that Jordanian supporters of the peace treaty had used to defend it. These included, as Jawad Anani explained to a caller during an appearance on a TV talk show: "First, Jordan has recovered every inch of territory that was controlled or occupied by Israel. . . . Second, Israel's borders with Jordan have been defined for the first time . . . and will put an end to the aspirations by Israeli extremists to expand eastward at Jordan's expense."[149] At the same time, many Transjordanian nationalists celebrated the notion of the kingdom's renouncing claims to the Palestinian West Bank and clearly defining its borders. These nationalists, who represented some the strongest supporters of the monarchy, saw the treaty as helping to define its own territorial identity as one rooted exclusively in the East Bank and thus classifying those Jordanians of Palestinian origin as "guests" of the kingdom.

While advancing such arguments in the public defense of the

treaty, during the negotiations over the treaty itself, King Hussein and his negotiators took a highly pragmatic approach to the protection of Jordanian sovereign territory. Their attitude violated the norms of those opposing normalization. Anani also noted during his talk show appearance that according to the treaty, "Israeli farmers are permitted to continue their activities on two farms under Jordanian sovereignty and Jordanian law." In contrast to the territorial disputes that plagued the Egyptian-Israeli peace in the 1980s (such as the one over Taba discussed in chapter 3), Hussein chose not to make an issue of Jordanian territory on which Israeli farmers had encroached since the 1967 war. While claiming Jordanian sovereignty over this area in the peace treaty, Hussein agreed to allow Israeli farmers to lease the land and continue their operations ostensibly under Jordanian law but effectively maintaining the status quo. At the same time that Hussein could claim to his own population that Jordan had regained sovereignty "over every inch of its territory," he could please Israelis by allowing their continued use of the land. Moreover, even before plans for a joint peace center got off the ground,[150] the Israelis declared part of the Jordanian territory they retained control over at Naharayim the "Island of Peace" and have since organized trips for Israeli youths to the spot as a way for them to "experience the meaning of peace." An Israeli tourism scholar notes that the "Island" includes the remains of a bridge over which before 1948 the Damascus-to-Haifa train traveled. "It is a remnant of the age of no boundaries in this area. The visitor can think of it as a real example of a 'bridge between nations.'"[151] He notes that now opening the gates to this "neutral space that is a symbol of peace and co-operation . . . can symbolize the opening of hearts . . . and a better future shared by the neighboring states."[152] Naharayim, however, remains an odd sort of tourism space, especially when compared to Taba. Jordan agreed to a settlement that Egypt rejected even though it had an undisputed claim to the territory. In effect, Naharayim (or Baqura in Arabic) is a Jordanian "Taba" that remains on the Israeli side of the border. As an Israeli peace theme park, it represents a section of sovereign Jordanian territory under Israeli control that Israelis can visit to experience a safe journey to the territory of a former enemy. Within the antinormalization movement, this "special regime" of territory under Jordanian sovereignty but private Israeli ownership was regarded as a "highly negative precedent."[153]

For all the fears that many Jordanians maintained about Israelis gaining control over Jordanian land, the only new encroachment that Israel has made into Arab territory since the beginning of the Madrid peace process has been to build settlements, create roadblocks and barriers, and confiscate land in Arab East Jerusalem and the Palestinian West Bank. Regardless of the new strategic relationship between Jordan and Israel, these events still directly affected and concerned most Jordanians, especially Palestinian refugees in Jordan and Palestinian Jordanians who maintain ties to the West Bank and Gaza. The Jordanian regime, together with many Jordanians, especially Transjordanian nationalists, fears that such Israeli policies might result in another influx of West Bank Palestinians and prevent the relocation of the Palestinian refugees in Jordan, creating a politically untenable social imbalance between Transjordanians and Palestinians. In other words, the peace process might have created a legal boundary between Israeli and Jordanian territory, but it did not replace the geopolitical imagination of Jordanians who have connections to the other side of the river Jordan.

With these continuing societal ties between Palestinians on both sides of the river Jordan, politics in Jordan remained highly sensitive to developments on the Palestinian-Israeli front that detracted from the peace process. One of Israel's most provocative actions was Prime Minister Netanyahu's opening in late 1996 of a tourist tunnel under the Haram al-Sharif, or Temple Mount, in East Jerusalem, to which King Hussein had secured from Israel a special status as guardian of the Islamic holy places.[154] Such actions provoked Jordanians of all backgrounds, heightening the intensity of Jordanian societal discourses of insecurity regarding Israel. They also unnerved King Hussein, who viewed them as a violation of the trust he sought to build between the leaderships of the two states.

The depth of Jordanian anger at Israel and the power of antinormalization sentiments were most starkly revealed in early 1997 when a Jordanian army sergeant, Ahmaed Al-Dawamisah, stood at the Jordanian military post above the Island of Peace and opened fire on a group of forty Israeli schoolgirls on a class trip. Dawamisah, by some reports mentally unstable, killed seven of the children and injured many others. King Hussein rushed to personally express his condolences to the girls' families and impressed many Israelis with his compassion. Many Jordanians, however, viewed the king's actions as excessive, publicly wondering if an Israeli leader would have done the same thing if the victims and perpetrators were reversed.[155] By many accounts, Jordanians from all walks of life seemed to celebrate Dawamisah's actions, declaring the man a hero. Many of the kingdom's lawyers and professional organizations, including the bar association itself, even vied to represent the soldier at his trial in front of a military court.[156] Dawamisah was eventually sentenced to life in prison, but the incident (and the Jordanian reaction) marked a milestone in the decline of Jordanian support for normalization. Israelis might have gained appreciation of the king's commitment to peaceful relations, but his condolences did nothing to make Jordanian territory and tourism spaces feel any more secure for potential Israeli tourists.

The unfortunate popular reaction to Dawamisah's murder of the Israeli schoolgirls does not so much reflect fears of Israeli tourists on "Jordanian" territory but rather speaks to the anger at Israeli policies toward the Palestinians and the Jordanian regime's continuing embrace of normalization even as the Israeli-Palestinian peace process began to collapse. Many Jordanians and Palestinians who once supported the peace process understood its demise as a product of the failure of the Oslo framework to construct an Israeli-Palestinian security community to protect the territorial security of both Palestinians and Israelis. While the New Middle East vision referred to the demilitarization of borders, economic cooperation, and a regional trading zone woven together by cross-border flows of capital, peoples, and goods, Palestinians in the West Bank and Gaza came to experience the Oslo process as leading to increased territorial confinement and the further fragmentation of their emerging national community. As Israel granted the Palestinians authority over Gaza and patches of the West Bank, new checkpoints and a system of passes and closures came to restrict their mobility.[157]

This experience of restrictions and territorial fragmentation contravened the expectations of most Palestinians, including the Palestinian citizens of Israel (referred to as "Israeli Arabs" in official Israeli discourse), that the peace treaty would increase their mobility and allow them to expand cross-border social and economic connections in and out of Israel as well as across the river Jordan. As an Israeli journalist optimistically observed in early 1995, "For the Palestinians, it's now possible to reweave the fabric that had come unraveled."[158] Of the tens of thousands of Jordanians traveling across the new border crossing with Israel in the years after the peace treaty, the vast majority, some say 90 percent, were of Palestinian origin. While most were meeting with family members or looking for work or new business opportunities, unlike most Jewish Israelis traveling the other direction for leisure tourism, they all had some sort of tangible territorial connection to the land they visited, a connection they sought to further develop. These travelers were generally not welcomed by the Israeli government, and the Israeli media often portrayed them as criminal infiltrators or an underclass mob.[159] Like the Israelis visiting Jordan, these Arabs did not follow the New Middle East script and meet Israeli expectations. As Stein notes, "The Israeli press and private sector eagerly anticipated 'the wealthy of Amman' and the Gulf States, 'tempted by Eilat's nightclubs and the availability of alcohol,' destined for Tel Aviv's malls and tourist complexes."[160]

The Palestinians who struggled against Israeli obstacles to their mobility to exploit the new possibilities for increased access between Jordan and Israel/Palestine also had to face the antinormalization movement in Jordan. For example, in 1999 Amman's international theater festival came under attack for hosting Palestinians from East Jerusalem whom they viewed as "Israelis." The antinormalization committee of the professional associations condemned these cross-border flows and sought to expel their members who traveled to Israel, even if it was to meet Palestinian colleagues and family members, and members who had earned degrees from Israeli universities.[161] Within the geopolitical imaginary of the antinormalization, as Danishai Kornbluth notes, "the dual identity of Israeli Arabs was most puzzling."[162] Just as Palestinian citizens of Israel became more bold in their efforts to gain equal rights as Israeli citizens while publicly embracing their communal Palestinian Arab identity, Arab nationalists and Islamists often viewed dealings with this community as equivalent to recognizing the legitimacy of the Israeli state.[163]

While Palestinian Jordanians, like other Arabs, might have feared that Israel sought economic hegemony over the Arab Levant through the New Middle East, many others hoped that the more porous borders would create economic and social opportunities for them. These opportunities, however, proved limited. The Oslo process, with its creation of fragmented Palestinian spaces of autonomy, resulted in the social, economic, and political isolation of the Palestinians and expanded their feelings of insecurity. With the rise of suicide bombings launched by the militant Hamas movement targeting Israeli civilians, Israelis too were made to feel insecure, leading to the election of Netanyahu, who, according to Avi Shlaim, "declared war on the peace process."[164] The counterposing of these two dynamics is well captured by the appearance of side-by-side news stories published in the *Washington Post* on January 25, 1995. One is titled "Israeli Tourists Pour into Jordan" and quotes an Israeli tourist in Jordan exclaiming, "It's like a dream. It is so special to walk into enemy territory and feel he is no longer the enemy." The story next to it, however, reports that in the hours after a suicide bomb that killed nineteen Israelis, an Israeli soldier suggested, "We should put them all in a cage and leave them there and make it so they can't get out."

In Jordan, fear and distrust of Israel only increased. In September 1997 critics of normalization were given powerful ammunition when Israeli Mossad agents visited Amman to try to assassinate a militant Hamas leader by injecting poison into his ear. The agents botched the operation and were caught by Jordanian authorities. King Hussein was infuriated, viewing this action as a blatant violation of the peace treaty. He forced the Israeli agents to give the Hamas leader the antidote and allowed the agents' return to Israel only once their government agreed to release a large number of Palestinians held prisoner, including Sheikh Yassin, the spiritual leader of Hamas. To make matters worse, the agents infiltrated Jordan by posing as Canadian tourists, adding a degree of credibility to Jordanian fears that more open borders increased Jordanian insecurity. In forcing the release of the Palestinian Islamists, King Hussein might have hoped that he could gain some credit with Jordan's more moderate Islamist movement and begin to divide the antinormalization movement.[165] At the same time, Hussein feared the opposition would use such events to mobilize popular support against the treaty and the regime.

By 1997, with the lack of peace dividends, Netanyahu in power in Israel, and the mobilization of the antinormalization movement, it became clear that the regime had lost the battle for public opinion and failed in its effort to forge a New Middle East. Moreover, the antinormalization movement began to pose a political threat by defining a basis on which the political opposition to the regime could unify and mobilize against government policies against. In response, the regime began to reverse its steps toward political liberalization by banning demonstrations, enacting press restrictions, jailing leaders, and adjusting election rules to favor pro-regime parties.[166] According to Laurie Brand, the king even sacked Prime Minister Kabariti for his criticism of Netanyahu and opposition to the royal visit to the homes of the victims of the Naharayim incident.[167] The regime tried to shut down the domestic public sphere after failing to retain support for its redefinition of Jordanian interests and identity.[168] As noted in chapter 2, Tunisia suffers a "paradox of openness" in which increasing economic openness and the superficial state commitment to upholding a facade of democracy have allowed for an increasingly repressive authoritarian regime. In Jordan the paradox of liberalization is that the monarchy's commitment to the peace process and its ties with the United States led to overwhelming societal opposition, which prompted the regime to reverse its commitment to political liberalization.

While opposition politicians and the professional associations battled the regime to find means to voice their antinormalization sentiments in the face of increasing repression, the most extreme opponents have exploited the vulnerabilities created by the state's embrace of normalization by targeting Israelis who travel across the border. During the initial wave of Israeli tourist flows from late 1994 to mid-1996 there appeared to be several efforts to plan attacks but no reported violence against Israeli visitors. The regime blamed the first schemes they discovered on Iranian and Syrian agents who, according to a government official, were "trying to hit at our model of peace with Israel."[169] In response to these threats, in 1996 the Israeli foreign ministry began issuing travel advisories to citizens traveling to Jordan, asking them not to emphasize their nationality or leave their passports with hotel clerks.[170] Israeli tourists, however, remained conspicuous because of their protection by Jordanian police cars and plainclothes security agents. In the wake of Netanyahu's election, a series of alleged plots against Israeli-frequented tourist sites surfaced. In October 1996, around the second anniversary of the peace treaty, three Jordanians were arrested and charged with digging up land mines near the Israeli border and transporting them to the crusader fortress at Ajlun, in northern Jordan. The father of one of the plotters tried to explain, "They are not members of any political group. . . . Perhaps they believed that peace with Israel would improve their lives, but two years after the peace treaty all they face is more poverty and un-employment."[171] While no excuse for violence, such a sentiment does reflect the popular disappointment in Jordan at the time. The following year, in one of the few reported cases of violence, an Israeli tourist was stabbed by a Jordanian college student from Irbid while visiting Um Qays at the northwest tip of Jordan over-looking Israel and the occupied Golan Heights.[172] In 1998 another three Jordanians were arrested for plotting to attack Israeli tourist buses in Jordan.[173] A year after the 1998 U.S. embassy bombings in Africa, Jordanian and American authorities acquired intelligence about what they said were militants affiliated with al-Qaeda plan-ning attacks on American and Israeli interests in the country. By December, authorities had arrested several dozen Jordanians, who were charged, and most later convicted, of planning New Year's attacks on Western and Israeli tourists and tourist sites in Jordan, including the recently opened baptismal archaeological site along the river Jordan. In December 2000, Jordanian authorities arrested a young Jordanian whom they charged with planning to carry out a suicide attack against a five-star hotel in Amman. At the same time, Jordan withdrew its ambassador from Israel to protest the ex-cessive force used to suppress Palestinian demonstrators after Ariel Sharon's provocative tour of the Haram al-Sharif/Temple Mount with an armed entourage. By the end of 2000, as the Al Aqsa *inti-fada* led to violent clashes between Palestinian militants and Israeli authorities, Jewish Israeli tourism to Jordan had become a rarity. Israel began to warn its (Jewish) citizens about the dangers of trav-eling to Arab countries, including Jordan.[174] The director general of Israel's agriculture ministry called for a boycott of goods from Jordan and the Palestinians territories, noting, "In view of the lat-est confrontations, we can't import agricultural products from those who instigate violence."[175] In August 2001, after an Israeli businessman traveling in Jordan was shot dead and Israeli embassy personnel were attacked, the Israeli ambassador to Jordan, who five years before had encouraged Israelis to come to Jordan, found himself warning Israelis not to visit.[176] As the violence in Israel/Palestine increased, later leading to an Israeli reinvasion of territo-ries evacuated as part of the Oslo process, the Israeli, Palestinian, and Jordanian tourism economies went into free fall.

Locations that relied on long-haul leisure travelers, such as Petra, were especially hard hit. In the years after the peace treaty, Petra saw thousands of visitors a day, of whom about five hundred on average were Israelis, and many hotels in Wadi Musa maintained an occupancy rate of about 60 percent. For a time, in some hotels, one out of every five guests might be an Israeli. In the wake of the Palestinian *intifada* beginning in 2000, tourism plummeted with hotel occupancy rates dropping from 38 percent in 2000 to below 15 percent for the next several years. Between 2000 and 2002, the average number of tourists visiting Petra each day dropped from 1,330 to 440, with an average of 372 spending the night in the area (Wadi Musa's seven five-star hotels alone have a capacity of 880 beds). By 2002, the four- and five-star hotels were selling rooms at a fraction of their average rates of a few years before and closing down for parts of the year, while others were forced to shut down for good. As one restaurant manager told an American reporter, "Nobody believes in peace anymore. . . . Everyone has changed. They hate the Israeli people."[177] This era marked the decline of one aspect of normalization and the death of New Middle East visions of economic cooperation and cross-border tourism flows.[178]

The End of the New Middle East

In 1999, as King Hussein entered the last stages of a terminal disease, he switched the line of succession, replacing his brother Prince Hassan, Jordan's leading advocate of the New Middle East vision, with his eldest son, Abdullah. By the end of the 1990s, Jordan's strategic environment was changing. Popular opposition to the U.S.-enforced UN sanctions on Iraq led to protests and demonstrations against the Jordanian regime, which Jordanians viewed as growing ever closer and more dependent on the United States. Most of the population also sympathized vocally with their Palestinian cousins and neighbors, and anger increased toward the administration of George W. Bush for its strong backing of Israel's new right-wing government led by Ariel Sharon. While his "plucky" father was famous for survival instincts that required constantly adjusting to new threats and opportunities, the young, American-educated King Abdullah II, often said to be more comfortable in English than Arabic, seemed to embody Jordan's new unilateral dependence on the United States. A former soldier who had led counterterrorism operations in the kingdom, Abdullah II was the first Arab leader to embrace the Bush administration's post–9/11 "war on terror." Meanwhile he constantly balked at any moves toward political liberalization. In this new, challenging context, Jordan's leadership decided to promote a policy of "Jordan First."[179] Politically, the policy sought to disconnect the fate of Jordan from the ongoing Palestinian-Israeli conflict and the conflict in Iraq and to encourage citizens to prioritize the interest of Hashemite Jordan over other affiliations based on Palestinian, Arab, or Islamic identity. In terms of tourism development and economic globalization, Jordan redirected its efforts away from economic (inter)dependence and cooperation with Israel and sought to use a new flow of U.S. aid to revamp the tourism industry.[180] At the same time that Israel was seeking to focus on ideologically committed tourists, such as American evangelical Christians,[181] Jordan was delinking itself from the New Middle East and rebranding itself as a tourist destination that it hoped could disassociate itself from its unstable neighbors and its strategic partner on the other side of the river Jordan.[182]

5. The View from Dubai: Post-9/11 Geographies of Travel

In the late 1990s, while the tourism industries in Jordan and Israel were adjusting to the decline of the New Middle East, across other parts of the region, the sector was developing rapidly. Egypt recovered from the wave of Islamist attacks against visiting tourists and was building a new line of integrated tourism complexes along the Red Sea. As in Tunisia and Jordan, neoliberal economic policies expanded private-sector tourism development while fostering the rise of a business class with close ties to the regime.[1] In Syria, where state control over the economy remained heavy-handed, limited liberalization sought to encourage local and foreign private investment in the tourism sector.[2] Meanwhile the reconstruction of downtown Beirut helped lead a revival of Lebanon's tourism sector, and the Arab states of the Gulf were developing tourism industries to diversify their oil-based economies. Successfully exploiting its position as a regional trade and transportation hub, the emirate of Dubai was fast becoming a major tourist resort destination by building gleaming luxury hotels and shopping malls. Overall, between 1995 and 2000, the Arab Middle East's share of global tourist arrivals climbed from 2.5 percent to 3.5 percent.[3]

On the morning of September 11, 2001, the future of this expansion seemed in jeopardy. In the midst of the airplane hijackings, American airspace was abruptly shut down. Across the globe, many feared they were witnessing the violent beginnings of a "clash of civilizations" between the West and the Arab/Islamic world, the region where the hijackers originated. By mid-October, when the U.S.–led war in Afghanistan was launched to root out the base of Osama Bin Laden's transnational al-Qaeda network, worldwide travel reservations had declined by 20 percent to 30 percent. In early 2002, George W. Bush's "global war on terror" began shifting its focus toward the Middle East. Tour operators complained, "Talk of the 'axis of evil' is causing potential travelers to rethink travel to the Middle East and North Africa region."[4] Of the tourists who did travel, more were "choosing destinations that are closer to home, perceived as 'safer,' rather than long haul destinations."[5] Due also in part to "fears of a backlash against western visitors," travel agents across Jordan, Egypt, Turkey, and North Africa reported cancellations reaching 60 percent to 70 percent.[6] A "crisis of confidence" in travel to the region developed as the U.S. government issued travel advisories and American tour operators began to cut their programming of the region.[7] Many European agencies followed suit as international airlines, already in financial trouble, were forced to slash their flights to the region. The last four months of 2001 saw a worldwide drop of 11 percent in tourist arrivals, with the Middle East suffering the largest regional decline of 30 percent. Over the course of 2001, when global tourism arrivals suffered their first annual decline since 1982, tourism receipts across the Arab Middle East declined 5.2 percent following an annual growth rate of 6.8 percent for the previous five years.[8]

To make matters worse, in the following years, a wave of bombings targeted tourists and hotels across Muslim countries from Indonesia to Morocco. These included the bombing in April 2002 at a synagogue in Jerba, Tunisia, that killed more than a dozen visiting Europeans and five Tunisians. And in November 2005, Iraqi suicide bombers struck three luxury hotels in central Amman, killing sixty people and injuring many more. Tourists and the tourism industry have often been targets of political violence because they are easily identifiable "soft targets" and such attacks are likely to garner wide international media converge. Moreover, in highly tourism-dependent economies, such attacks offer a means to strike at a vital source of national income. As Heba Aziz noted about the wave of attacks by Islamist militants in Egypt during the early 1990s, "Tourists are used as a tool to attack the government and to knock down one of the main pillars of the Egyptian economy."[9]

Figure 15. In response to the bombing of three hotels in Amman on November 9, 2005, Jordanians march in front of the Zara-owned Grand Hyatt, one of the hotels hit. Ammar Awad/Reuters/Landov.

Additionally, others have suggested, "Sometimes, terrorism is explicitly oriented against tourism itself, . . . considered as a movement of 'alien' visitors representing a form of neo-colonialism or a threat to well-established societal norms, traditions, value systems and religious convictions."[10] The perpetrators of the Amman hotel bombings specifically noted that the hotels were targeted because they provided not only "a secure garden for evil Jewish tourists and other westerners to practice their prostitution" but also were the "preferred location" for American and Israeli intelligence forces and meetings with officials of the new U.S.-backed Iraqi government.[11]

The post–9/11 attacks appeared to many observers as the beginning of a new global war that threatened international tourism, conducted by loosely linked cells of transnational terrorist networks motivated by similar radical Islamist ideologies that sought to rid the Middle East of Western influences. Media analysts and travel experts began to speak about "tourism in a time of terror," noting that the sector was "caught directly in the forefront of these new conflicts."[12] The editors of the *Economist* even feared that "the bombers exposed the fragility of the liberal world order" by converting the economic strength of open borders, air transport networks, and information technologies into security weaknesses.[13] And the international relations theorist Robert O. Keohane announced that "the agents of globalization are not simply the high-tech creators of the internet or multinational corporations, but also small bands of fanatics, traveling on jet aircraft and inspired by fundamentalist religion."[14] Along with others, they worried that the fate of globalization might hang in the balance.

But as Ala Al-Hamarneh and Christian Steiner have written, "the predicted wide-ranging collapse of the tourism industry in the Arab countries after the attacks did not take place."[15] In 2002, as global tourism arrivals grew a weak 2.7 percent, arrivals across the Arab Middle East shot back up, with 16.7 percent growth, the highest rate of all regions of the world.[16] Dubai formed the epicenter of the rebound. Like other destinations, Dubai was hit by 9/11. In late 2001, hotel occupancy levels fell as low as 20 percent as beaches remained deserted. With this downturn, hotels were laying off staff and shutting down whole floors to save costs.[17] By the first quarter of 2002, however, visitor numbers and revenues were back up. Dubai has since emerged as one of the fastest-growing tourism destinations in the world. Lebanon barely recorded a post–9/11 decline, showing double-digit growth in both arrivals and receipts for 2001 and 2002. Egypt also saw a remarkable turnaround, from a 14.8 percent decline in arrivals to a 12.6 percent increase.

Table 7. International tourist arrivals, 2000–2005 (in thousands)

	2000	2001	2002	2003	2004	2005
Egypt	5,116	4,357	4,906	5,746	7,795	8,244
Jordan	1,580	1,478	1,622	2,353	2,853	2,987
Lebanon	742	837	956	1,016	1,278	1,140
Dubai	3,420	3,627	4,756	4,980	5,420	6,160
Subtotal	10,116	9,462	11,284	13,079	16,068	17,391
change		−6.5%	19.3%	15.9%	22.9%	8.2%
World	687,000	686,700	707,000	694,600	765,400	806,800
change		−0.0%	3.0%	−1.8%	10.2%	5.4%
Subtotal share	1.5%	1.4%	1.6%	1.9%	2.1%	2.2%

Source: World Tourism Organization

Table 8. International tourism receipts, 2000–2005 (thousands of nominal $US)

	2000	2001	2002	2003	2004	2005
Egypt	4,345	3,800	4,345	4,584	6,125	6,851
Jordan	722	700	786	1,111	1,330	1,441
UAE	1,012	1,064	1,328	1,438	1,593	2,233
Subtotal	6,079	5,564	6,459	7,133	9,048	10,525
change		5.14%	24.81%	8.28%	10.78%	40.18%
World	481,600	469,900	488,200	534,600	634,700	682,700
change		−2.43%	3.89%	9.50%	18.72%	7.56%
Subtotal share	1.26%	1.18%	1.32%	1.33%	1.43%	1.54%

Source: World Tourism Organization

Perhaps most remarkable was the short-lived impact of the U.S. invasion of Iraq in 2003. While the run-up to the war sent jitters through tourist destinations such as Jordan and Lebanon, tourism flows to Egypt continued to grow steadily. In the second quarter of 2003, arrivals across the Arab Middle East declined 15 percent. But in the following quarter, tourism arrivals rebounded: Egypt saw almost 24 percent growth, Lebanon 16 percent, the United Arab Emirates (UAE) 9.4 percent, and Tunisia 9 percent. When the World Tourism Organization released its 2003 report, the numbers came as a surprise to many. The *New York Times* noted, "After the triple shocks of Sept. 11, the war in Iraq and the SARS outbreak, the patterns of tourism around the world shifted last year. . . . The biggest loser was the United States. And one of the few winners, unusually, was the Middle East."[18] Tables 7 and 8 illustrate this "big bounce back" for selected Arab countries.[19] In 2004 the Arab Middle East saw 35 million visitors, a record number, representing nearly a tripling since 1994. The travel and tourism industry across the Arab Middle East was estimated to have generated over $100 billion in economic activity in 2004 and was predicted to continue growing at 4 percent a year in real terms.[20] Tourism economies also found that they had become more insulated from the violence of terrorist attacks. For example, in the wake of the 1997 massacre at Luxor, Egyptian tourism was in shambles, with revenues dropping 50 percent, but following the July 2005 bombings that killed up to ninety people at Egypt's swanky Sharm el Shaykh resort on the Red Sea, tourism receipts saw only a short-term 30 percent decline. In the third quarter of 2005, arrivals surpassed 2004 levels, and in the fourth quarter, Egypt posted a rise in receipts compared to the same quarter the year before.[21] Reflecting the reaction of many, one regional business news outlet referred to "the Middle East tourism paradox," noting, "Turn on the television and the scenes of violence in the Middle East tell one story. Yet tourism is also booming in the region."[22]

These trends suggest more than a paradox. They provide a vivid illustration of Jonathan Culler's comment that "there are few clearer indicators of shifting lines of force within the economic order than changes in the flow of tourists."[23] Since 2001 the Middle East has emerged as a leading international destination for tourism and investment, with the cities of the Arab Gulf becoming important nodes in regional and global tourism networks. In this final chapter, I explore the territorial factors underlying patterns of tourism flows and tourism investment and suggest how they might provide a guide for reading the emerging forces that are reshaping the economic and geopolitical order of the region and its position within the global system. Dubai's rise as a node within global economic and tourist networks is not simply a product of its being a space open to transnational flows. Rather, it has been guided domestically by a regime of territorial control and externally by the emirate's geopolitical position. Dubai is only the most vivid example of urban and coastal spaces across the region being remade by new partnerships between the government and the private sector. These have "defragmented" regimes of territorial control and privatized planning processes to more easily refashion spaces as concentrated enclaves of high-income commercial, leisure, and business activity. By promoting economic and cultural reterritorialization, these processes have securely integrated the Arab world into the global tourism economy. These trends also suggest that as actors within the region gain greater agency within the global tourism economy, they will continue to promote tourism development as an engine of economic growth and vehicle for globalization and transnational integration.

These structures of tourism development do not exhaust the full range of possible patterns of change. I conclude by considering alternative modes of tourism development and emergent itineraries and styles of travel, such as Islamic tourism, and the travelogue of Egyptian playwright Ali Salem of his drive through Israel at the height of hopes for the New Middle East. While presenting a critique of the deterritorialization logic of the New Middle East and most "peace through tourism" schemes, these itineraries suggest alternative geopolitical imaginaries for the Middle East and show how international tourism can be a vehicle to connect territories and their populations.

Tracing the Rise of Regional Tourism Networks

The most notable feature of the post–9/11 rebound is the expansion of intraregional flows of Arab tourists and tourism investment and their integration into the organized tourism economy. An increasing volume of petrodollars circulating within the region is supporting Arab tourist and investment flows, which are being facilitated by shifting business strategies and tourism development policies that predate 2001. As a result, regional transnational networks have emerged to cater to these Arab, as well as global, travel flows. Within each territory, new forms of tourism development and more intensive commodification of experiences of place have created more diverse tourism economies. The economic potential of tourism has also led more countries to develop their own tourism industries, leading to a wider range of regional destinations.

While still limited, the centrality of the Arab Middle East within the networks of the global tourism economy is increasing as the number of regional nodes and the density of connections between them and those outside the region expand.[24] And though forms of political and economic integration across the geopolitically fragmented Middle East remain weak, the increasingly dense landscape of locations promoting economic reterritorialization, combined with the rise of regional transnational networks within the tourism sector, has sustained the emergence of a process of economic reterritorialization at the regional scale.

As in Tunisia and Jordan, states and private firms in other parts of the Arab world have promoted global integration and economic reterritorialization by constructing enclave spaces for tourism development within their territories. In such cases, the developers have little control over the transnational flows and other actors in networks of the global tourism economy, such as tour operators. What is different about recent trends is that because of expanded regional flows of Arab tourists and capital, new patterns of consumption and entrepreneurial strategies, and better marketing, many Arab states and firms have increased their ability to influence the size and pattern of these transnational flows. As a result, they can now promote economic reterritorialization not only by controlling local tourism spaces but also by influencing networks at the global, but more so the regional, level.

Defining an Intraregional Tourism Economy

In the year following the 9/11 attacks, the number of Arab visitors to the United States dropped by 50 percent, and Arab travel to Europe was cut by 35 percent.[25] In addition to being subject to more security checks and bureaucratic hassles, many Arabs visiting North America and Europe felt stigmatized by the negative cultural reactions and increasing "Islamophobia." By the summer of 2002, many travelers from the Arab Gulf who decided to forgo travel to Europe or the United States headed for destinations in other Arab states, such as Lebanon, Egypt, Syria, and Jordan. These destinations were accessible by land, making them affordable destinations for large families. Moreover, owing to the decline of visitors from Europe and North America, governments and tourism firms proved more welcoming to Arab tourists. While these itineraries were not new, the shift in the volume of these flows reflected geopolitical and cultural forces developed in the immediate aftermath of 9/11.

The shift in regional itineraries was soon supplemented by a vast increase in regional oil wealth and the increased tendency for Arabs and Arab capital to circulate within the Arab region. In 2003 the growing world demand for oil and limits on production during an era of heightened political turmoil in the Middle East lifted prices to a level 50 percent higher in real terms than during the 1990s.[26] With little sign that oil prices would decline soon, the increased wealth sustained high levels of travel spending in the Arab world. For example, each year citizens of Saudi Arabia spend about $6.7 billion, or about 5 percent of the kingdom's GDP, on travel overseas. Emiratis spend almost $5 billion, or an average of $1,700 per person, which is about $500 more than the average European spends on international travel.[27]

The redirection of Arab travel patterns, combined with increased leisure spending, marks a decisive shift in the structure of tourism economies in the Arab Middle East, which are increasingly being influenced by regional actors. Between 2001 and 2004, the share of tourist arrivals from within the region expanded from 22.4 percent to 40.8 percent. This shift helps explain the rise in Middle East and North Africa tourism revenues, which grew at a rate of over 15 percent in 2003, up from a rate of about 9 percent during the 1990s.

Evolving Tourism Development Policies

Within most Arab states, policy makers and business owners had long failed to view Arab visitors as part of the tourism sector. These visitors tend not to stay in the hotels, use the buses and tour guides, or visit the tourist spaces that have been developed for international visitors.[28] Instead they travel as extended families, stay in rented apartments, and visit restaurants, amusement parks, and cafés owned and managed by a different set of entrepreneurs. Many of these visitors are attracted to the shopping malls and cultural or musical events patronized by the well-off segments of the local population, rather than the shops and museums that cater to Western tourists. They often travel around national and religious holidays and during the summer months (the low season for international travel to inland destinations like Jordan). In addition to the annual hajj pilgrimage to Mecca, increasing numbers of Arabs and Iranians travel across the region for religious visits to Islamic shrines and other holy places. Another subsegment of the Arab tourism market consists of adult male travelers who patronize the nightclubs and bars of Beirut, Cairo, Dubai, and other Arab cities.

In previous decades, tourism officials did not seek to promote an industry that catered to these markets. It was only in 1998, when tourist traffic from Western states was depressed due to a crisis over the UN weapons inspections in Iraq, that the Jordan Tourist Board (JTB) fully engaged the Gulf market with a promotional campaign and a concerted effort to ensure that the country had plenty of short-term apartment rentals available. In the first seven months of 1998 compared to 1997, Jordan saw a 15 percent drop in European and U.S. arrivals but a 36 percent increase in arrivals from Arab Gulf states, which accounted for 67 percent of Jordan's tourism revenues.[29] In 2001, as the outbreak of the second Palestinian *intifada* again reduced Western tourism to the region, the JTB began promoting Jordan as a "family destination." Together with local travel agents, the board created "lucrative family packages" and even guided tours of Jordan's undervisited archaeological sites targeted at the Gulf market, where the JTB opened offices.

These experiences primed tourism officials in Jordan to view the Arab market as a critical segment to develop, even if these efforts did not do much to help out the hotels in Petra. While the income from the Gulf visitors helped offset the loss of Western visitors, Jordanian officials, such as Jordan's minister of tourism Taleb Rifai, realized that to further develop this sector, the country would "need to do more to cater to the demand of Arab tourists which usually opt for parks [and] recreational centers."[30] In addition, Jordanian tourism officials even sought "to promote Jordan to the Islamic market, particularly pilgrims from Iran."[31] In Syria, where private investment in the tourism sector geared for international visitors lagged behind other regional destinations, the development of leisure and religious tourism from Arab states and Iran has been more successful. Between 1990 and 1997, Syria's tourism promotion efforts led to only a 19 percent rise in Western visitors but an 82 percent increase in Arab tourism.[32]

In the post–9/11 era, the diversification across intraregional Arab, domestic Arab, and well-seasoned international tourism markets helped insulate tourism economies in many destinations from regional violence and the "neighborhood effect," in which destinations across the Middle East suffer because of an incident in one location.[33] Following 2001, the redirected flows of Arab travelers helped to sustain tourism receipts in economies that suffered declines in tourists from elsewhere. In 2001 Jordan saw a 25 percent increase in visitors from the Arab world together with a 20 percent decline from other sources. In 2002 Jordan's largest Arab markets registered gains (plus 14 percent in Saudi visitors and plus 35 percent in those from Kuwait) and saw declines in two of its largest European markets (minus 23 percent from Germany, minus 31 percent from France).[34] In 2002 Egypt saw a 22.5 percent increase in bed nights from Middle East visitors.[35] Lebanon's tourist economy was sustained through post–9/11 crises by the fact that it had rebuilt its tourism economy on traffic from the Gulf, the Lebanese diaspora, and other Arab countries. The Saudi share of visitors nearly doubled between 1995 and 2000, from 7.7 percent to 15.1 percent. In 2001 Lebanon saw a 19 percent increase in Saudi visitors and, in 2002, an increase of 23.6 percent.[36]

Facilitating Regional Cross-Border Flows

While Arab regimes have long maintained restrictive border-crossing procedures, many of these states have more recently come to support policies that facilitate cross-border travel, especially for tourists. In some cases, states have responded to the changing experience of European travelers who can vacation in southern European destinations without ever having to show a passport. As part of its post–9/11 recovery strategy, Egypt began to allow Italian and German tourists to visit with only personal identity cards and considered extending the policy to all fifteen signers of the Schengen accord on free movement between European states.[37] Meanwhile the importance of the Arab market led Egypt, along with Jordan, Syria, and Lebanon, to encourage travelers from the Gulf by eliminating the requirement that citizens of Gulf Cooperation Council (GCC) states obtain visas. The GCC, which includes all Gulf states except Iraq and Iran, has been seeking to develop a common visa. Due to their interest in developing tourism, Oman, long a closed society, and Qatar also liberalized their visa procedures. Saudi Arabia has sought to expand religious-based tourism by granting *umra* visas in an effort to attract off-season pilgrims who stay longer than the standard hajj visitors. In 2005 Jordan's King Abdullah II responded to a major liability noted in the country's recently released *National Tourism Strategy* and ordered procedural and bureaucratic reform that would facilitate travel and customs procedures at airports and border crossings, especially for tourists and visiting investors.[38]

Many of the trends toward official policies to facilitate cross-border tourist traffic predate 9/11, as they were encouraged by the growing recognition in the 1990s of the importance of inter-Arab tourism flows. These issues were addressed at the March 2001 Arab League summit, held in Amman, Jordan. The summit's final communiqué acknowledges "the relatively growing importance of the tourism sector on the Arab level and the competition this sector is facing on the international level." It therefore calls on states to "spur inter-Arab tourist activities" by supporting investments, promoting transportation services, and facilitating entry.[39] This statement was followed by the establishment of the Arab Tourism Council, which, at its June 2001 meeting, addressed efforts to boost inter-Arab tourism.[40] After 2001, the Arab states and their private sectors have expanded coordination on tourism issues through meetings, workshops, and, since 2002, the annual convention of the Arab World Travel and Tourism Exchange (AWTTE).[41]

While the Arab states collectively will likely develop only limited regionwide forms of cooperation and regulatory reform, individual Arab states have made more progress expanding regional tourism cooperation through bilateral agreements. Before 9/11 Syria eliminated the need for its own citizens to apply for exit visas and eased its entry restrictions for visitors from Iraq. Following the U.S. invasion of Iraq, this liberalization allowed an expanded number of visits from Iraq, and Syria has worked to encourage tourist travel from its strategic ally Iran, consisting mostly of Shi'i pilgrims visiting important religious sites. Meanwhile Jordan and Egypt engaged in more robust forms of cooperation. Since 2001, officials have discussed measures to remove the financial and administrative obstacles impeding the flow of passengers and goods between their countries. This agenda includes "unifying transportation and transit fees" and even "reinstating the use of the Triptych, a regional transport document to facilitate cross-border travel among Arab states."[42] One tangible result of Jordanian-Egyptian cooperation was the opening in 2003 of a maritime tourism route between

Aqaba and Sharm el Shaykh. At its inauguration, its developers claimed, "The line will surely enhance tourism in both countries," which has developed as middle- and upper-class Jordanians increasingly vacationed over short holidays in Red Sea locations.

Widening the Diversity of Tourism Segments and Range of Destinations

Intraregional flows form only one factor driving economic reterritorialization on the regional scale. The geography of tourism in the Arab Middle East is also being reshaped by the expanding diversity of tourism within destinations as well as the spread of tourism development to areas that had previously seen few leisure visitors. The region has increased its share of global flows and become more fully integrated into global tourism networks by focusing development efforts on increasingly segmented and specialized tourism markets. As tourism markets become larger and more diverse, the Arab Middle East has also attracted greater interest by more firms in the global tourism industry. International hotel management and airline companies have sought to increase their presence across the region, which is now seen as one of the fastest-growing markets with the most potential. Moreover, the diversification also helps reshape the external image of Arab destinations. Much of the neighborhood effect in the past was a product of a negative external image and stereotypes about the region. In contrast to Western images of the Arab Middle East in the 1980s, since 2000 increased marketing efforts and more coverage in the travel sections of print and electronic media have generated new images of the region. These include the revival of cosmopolitan nightlife in Beirut, beach resorts in Egypt, boutique hotels in Tunisia, ecotourism in Jordan, and international sporting events in Dubai.

Jordan's *National Tourism Strategy, 2004–2010,* developed with American aid and technical support, represents an effort to better address the complexity of global tourism markets by identifying the diverse niche segments to which Jordan should adapt its tourism development and marketing efforts.[43] These include growing markets beyond cultural heritage (archaeology) tourism such as religion-oriented tourism, adventure travel, and low-impact ecotourism and nature-based tourism. Jordan has since shifted its marketing efforts to present an external image of the country that no longer consists mostly of images of Petra, Bedouins, and King Hussein. Instead the JTB has sought to rebrand Jordan with an emphasis on its verdant nature parks, underwater sea life, impressive mountainscapes, and seaside vacation options. Some of the segments target particular markets, such as Arab gulf visitors or Christian pilgrims from Europe and America, while others have cross-market appeal. The promotion of medical (or health and wellness) tourism seeks to draw Europeans to Dead Sea spas as well as patients from neighboring states seeking affordable surgical procedures at health clinics in Amman. Jordan has also sought to enter new international markets by attracting cruise ships to Aqaba, hosting international sporting events and meetings, and encouraging filmmakers to follow in the footsteps of David Lean and Steven Spielberg.

Arab states have also begun to acknowledge that historical monuments associated with their national or Islamic past can be developed to provide unique tourism experiences appealing to domestic, regional Arab, and international visitors. In Egypt, the Aga Khan Trust for Culture is one of the foundations that have helped to restore, renovate, and preserve Cairo's Islamic monuments. More ostentatiously, the vast wealth of the Arab Gulf states is being translated into the realms of culture and education. Adu Dhabi is drawing on the architectural talents of Zaha Hadid and Frank Gehry to build a multi-billion-dollar cultural district, complete with its own Guggenheim museum.[44] And with a focus on Islamic arts and history, the building of the National Museum and National Library in Doha is part of an effort to "make Qatar a premier cultural and architectural destination."[45]

The multiplication of experiences of place within the region's leading tourist destinations has been matched by an increasing range of Arab states seeking to expand their tourism industries. Income from oil and gas, a ready market of regional travelers, and the rising profile of Dubai have prompted other Gulf states to develop their own tourism industries. Bahrain's tourism sector developed in the wake of the opening of the causeway to Saudi Arabia, which has facilitated the travel of visitors from other Gulf states, including many expatriates, drawn to the more liberal social atmosphere in Bahrain. Bahrain has sought to promote family-oriented tourism and luxury leisure tourism on its Hawar Island resort, which supports water-based sports and boating activities. Oman, slower to enter the international tourism economy, has liberalized its visa policies, upgraded its airport, and developed a master plan and marketing strategy. In contrast to most Gulf states, Oman is focusing on nature- and culture-based tourism, usually organized through small group tours. Saudi Arabia's efforts have been more cautious, but recognizing the need for job creation and the potential to redirect Saudi leisure consumption inward, it has commissioned a tourism master plan. While the kingdom has plans for creating coastal resort complexes geared to Saudi and other Gulf visitors, it is currently allowing a limited number of small highly controlled group tours from Western markets, focusing on diving, nature tourism, and visits to its cultural heritage sites.[46]

More recently, the new Iraqi government is hoping to draw religious pilgrims to its Shia holy cities, while entrepreneurs in Iraqi Kurdistan have ambitions for attracting tourism to the most stable region of the country. Someday the successful development of a tourism sector in Iraq might assist in the country's reconstruction and recovery from civil war. Meanwhile, after the lifting of economic sanctions and an air travel ban, Libya has sought to promote tourism as a means to gain income and present a new external image for the county. Commenting on Libya's announcement of its plans to build a massive nature reserve and ecotourism park, George Joffe explains, "They want to show the world that Libya has turned a corner—that they can fit into the modern world."[47]

Expanding Circuits of Petrodollar Flows and Business Networks

While petrodollars have long sustained hotel building across the Arab world, since 2001 Arab investment and holdings have shifted away from North American assets and increasingly taken advantage of the expanding opportunities within the region. Increased regional access to capital has come in the wake of a post–9/11 reallocation of assets when many Arab oil exporters withdrew from numerous U.S. investments and sought to diversify by investing regionally, where they have found new economic opportunities in the tourism as well as the energy, telecom, and real estate sectors.

These opportunities arose after more Arab states, as we saw in the cases of Tunisia and Jordan, enacted neoliberal economic reforms and policies to attract foreign investment as part of a broader effort to promote global economic integration. Firms in Egypt and Kuwait, for example, now have easier access to other regional markets. These investment flows have helped finance a new wave of ambitious luxury tourism projects across the region. Most of the new developments in Jordan, Tunisia, and Lebanon, not to mention across the Gulf, have been driven by excess petrodollars in search of investment opportunities. At the same time, the rise in petrodollars has also helped sustain regional business and infrastructure development and expanded flows of business tourism.

The oil wealth and increased concentration of economic growth in the Gulf and other Arab capitals have led to a new wave of regional Arab firms in tourism-related businesses such as hotel management, real estate development, restaurant chains, shopping malls, and airlines. Often drawing on expert expatriate management, these firms have been able to exploit local knowledge and connections not only within the country of their home base but also in other regional Arab states. Moreover, one implication of most investment in the tourism sector coming from local and regional sources is that incidents of political violence do not cut off investment flows. Local investors tend to be less risk averse than international investors and international management companies owing in large part to their more fluid and "detailed local knowledge of markets and political risk."[48]

One of the notable examples in the tourism sector is Rotana Hotels, which has grown to become a leading regional hotel management firm. Based in Abu Dhabi, the company grew from two properties in 1993 with plans for a total of fifty-three by 2010, with properties in all major Middle Eastern cities. Like Zara's operations within Jordan, Rotana has developed a set of firms in related sectors such as spa facilities, travel agencies, health clubs, and business conference services. The emergence of firms such as Rotana gives hotel developers the option of having their properties managed by a regionally owned firm with specialized knowledge of the Middle East market. The success of firms like this has been followed by the founding of new ones, including Golden Yasmine in Tunisia, Red Sea Hotels and Tropicana in Egypt, and Metropolitan in the UAE.[49]

Other Arab firms are reaching beyond the Middle East market to develop a standing within the global travel industry. With the oil boom of the 1970s, Gulf-based airlines found themselves purchasing excess aircraft from declining American airlines. The recent expansion of air travel to and through the region, which is predicted to experience faster growth than in Asia, has provided an opportunity for airlines such as Emirates in Dubai and Qatar Airways based in Doha to find niches within the global long-haul market. With a limited local market at home, Qatar Airways has targeted global luxury travelers. It brands itself a "five-star airline" and has built a luxury transfer terminal for first-class passengers crossing from Europe to Asia or from these regions to other parts of the Middle East. A more recent venture at the other end of the scale is Air Arabia, a low-cost airline based in the emirate of Sharjah. The firm can draw on not only a new generation of younger Arab travelers but also the region's population of expatriate and migrant workers. The region's evolving position within the networks of the global tourism economy is best represented by Emirates airline, which has gained strong brand recognition in Europe. Emirates' broad business strategy seeks to exploit more than Dubai's booming tourism sector and flows of business travelers. As the airline's CEO explains, "The Middle East enjoys a geocentric location that is a key advantage in facilitating and optimizing global air traffic flows east–west or north–south."[50] It operates as a critical east–west transfer point for flows between the North America and Europe to and from parts of the Middle East and Central and South Asia. It also increasingly provides links to and from parts of Africa.[51] While the global geography of international air travel is only one map of global economic networks, the strategies of firms like Emirates suggest the new itineraries being pursued by more and more states and firms in the region.

The Making of Dubai as a Global Node

At the center of these new patterns of development is the rise of Dubai as a hub for regional tourism and a node within global tourism networks. With its extraordinary and continuing growth, by 2005 Dubai alone represented over 8 percent of all tourism receipts collected across the Arab Middle East. Dubai's ostentatious success has allowed it to emerge as a leading world tourism destination with a recognizable brand image. While unique in many ways, this success has influenced developments across the region and helps project outside the region a new, alternate tourist image for the Arab world. As a model, Dubai will likely remain an important factor in shaping early-twenty-first-century tourism patterns in the region, if not other parts of the world as well.

From Entrepôt to Tourist Resort

While the hypermodernist skyscrapers and ambitious architectural wonders appear as shiny, almost faddist creations of the present, the success of Dubai's tourism sector has been decades in the making. Unlike its regional neighbors, the semiautonomous emirate of Dubai has limited oil reserves. Even before its independence from Britain as a constituent of the UAE in 1971, the hereditary monarchs who ruled the emirate realized the need to develop other sectors. To do so, Dubai followed policies similar to those implemented when it was still counted among the many strategically located ports governed as British protectorates in the naval network that sustained British sea power. While Dubai in the first half of the twentieth century served as a maritime hub, attracting merchants and traders from across the Gulf and Indian Ocean, in the second half it emerged as what Jeremy Jones calls "the Airport State," which "derives its existence and livelihood from establishing itself as a hub" through which global flows of people, capital, and goods pass.[52]

Dubai sought to promote commerce and development by becoming a nexus in regional transit-trade flows. In 1960 Dubai opened an international airport suitable for commercial airlines and immediately instituted an "open skies" policy that allowed any airline to use it with no need for bilaterally negotiated landing rights.[53] As regional airline traffic picked up in the late 1970s after the first oil boom, Dubai's airport received far more transit passengers than arrivals or departures.[54] The positive externalities these flows generated were exploited by the establishment of extensive high-quality duty-free shops and helped in the successful expansion of Emirates airline. When Dubai discovered oil in 1966, the income was used to build the man-made harbor of Jebal Ali port. In 1985 Dubai launched the Jebal Ali free zone, where local and foreign businesses can operate outside Dubai's own customs and legal regimes. Jebal Ali and heavy investment in transportation infrastructure helped Dubai become a center for cargo operations, a commercial trade entrepôt, and a competitive location for warehousing and manufacturing. These ventures were largely funded by the second regional oil boom of the early 1980s, which flooded the region with petrodollars. Dubai benefited as a location for investment, for firms that lived off the boom of government and other oil-related spending, and for a range of service sectors (from banking to tourism) that catered to those firms and their employees. Centrally located in the oil-rich Gulf, Dubai emerged first as a critical regional nexus for shipping, trade, and air transportation flows and later developed as a manufacturing, finance, and communications hub.

Like the other business centers and capitals that sprang up across the Gulf with the oil boom, Dubai developed a luxury hotel sector based on demand from business travelers. As was the case for other newly independent, modernizing states, luxury hotels—with their architectural sophistication and international management teams—were often built as prestige projects to mark the state's wealth and growing importance. Dubai's first international brand hotel, an Inter-Continental, was built in 1975.[55] At the time, several of the emirates and other cities around the Gulf found themselves competing for a limited number of business visitors, and Gulf states expressed little interest in building facilities for leisure tourism.[56] In Dubai, by contrast, state authorities built a tourism industry that would become a major pillar of their service-oriented economy. Between 1980 and 1990, Dubai doubled its number of tourist arrivals. As oil incomes declined in the late 1980s, the need to diversify its economy into other fields such as communications and real estate became more pressing, and Dubai met the challenge by expanding the tourism sector.

Dubai soon stood out from other destinations by forging ahead with plans to expand its clientele beyond business travelers. As a result, between 1990 and 2000, tourist arrivals expanded nearly fivefold while annual tourism receipts grew from $170 million to over $700 million.[57] Over the same period, the number of hotels expanded from 70 to over 260, and by 2000 Dubai possessed over 30,000 hotel rooms, amounting to more than one-quarter of all the hotel rooms in Egypt.[58] In 2001, with 3.6 million visitors, tourism represented 12 percent of GDP.[59] The tourism sector was able to benefit from the city's status as a commercial and aviation hub that connected Europe and the Far East. One of its early successes was developing shopping tourism. For Dubai, shopping was not considered simply one activity that tourists engage in. Rather, developers and marketing firms crafted shopping tourism into a themed niche market. Arabs from other states as well as regional expatriates and local Emiratis were drawn to Dubai for its high-end boutiques and opulent shopping malls. With the rise of East Asian economies and the fall of the Soviet Union, Dubai began to draw a new class of conspicuous consumers and neophyte capitalists from Asia to Eastern Europe. Its image as a shopping hub has been promoted with an annual shopping festival that includes monthlong discounts and events such as fireworks displays, art exhibits, and raffles for luxury automobiles. In the process, Dubai has been able to carefully build its upmarket tourism model, seeking, as a senior tourism official stated, "to give people what they want, but only attract who we want."[60]

Dubai soon began marketing itself to holidaymakers from Europe and Asia by building beachfront hotels and entertainment complexes. Tourism projects were developed by both local and international firms, drawing largely on funds from state-owned real estate companies and private companies owned by members of the royal families of Dubai or the other emirates and states of the Gulf. As such, the regime had little concern about the possible political effects of private-sector development. The state itself, as Dubai's Emir Sheikh Mohammad al-Maktoum is fond of noting, is run like a large, diverse private corporation relying on a highly talented, largely expatriate management elite.[61] By fostering diversified economic growth, it has attracted a large range of foreign investors and upper-middle-class expatriates who enjoy a comfortable, high-consumption lifestyle. In total, noncitizens account for over 80 percent of Dubai's population. While this number includes many low-paid manual laborers and workers in the service sector, it also ensures the constant presence of middle- and upper-class expatriates whose consumption patterns overlap with those of tourists.

Post–9/11 Development

In the aftermath of 9/11 there were plenty of reasons to think that Dubai's high-octane tourism economy would suffer a deflation, if not come crashing down. The disruption, however, was brief. Dubai's tourism economy quickly bounced back. In 2002 Dubai was ranked as the fastest-growing tourist destination in the world with an over 30 percent rise in visitors following four straight years of double-digit growth. Throughout 2003, the year of the U.S. invasion of Iraq, the city's hotels maintained an average occupancy rate of over 72 percent, and in the following year they averaged a rate of

81 percent.[62] Meanwhile Dubai saw little letup in investments in hotel construction, expanding its bed capacity from about 30,000 in 2000 to 41,500 by the end of 2006. Plans for a string of projects are set to more than double existing bed capacity by 2016.[63]

Global Image

The experience of Dubai represents the most stunning example of the so-called Middle East tourism paradox. Policy makers and investors in Dubai responded to growing regional turmoil by announcing an unrestrained blitz of headline-making projects. These projects have been part of a grand effort supported by Emir al-Maktoum to forge and maintain a unique brand image for the emirate. Dubai's external image is closely associated with its efforts to expand the tourism sector, in which many of its grandest projects are built by "state-owned" (that is, owned by the royal family) real estate and tourism firms. Since its opening in 1999, the beautifully designed hyperluxury Burj al Arab Hotel, shaped like a billowing sail, has become a defining icon for the city. The hotel markets itself as the tallest and only "seven-star" hotel in the world, and it functions as the Eiffel Tower does for Paris and the Statue of Liberty for New York City. The iconic, if not also

Figure 16. Dubai's iconic image, the Burj al Arab Hotel. Charles Crowell/ World Picture Network.

cinematic, nature of the Burj al Arab image was no accident. Its designers began with the objective of fashioning a symbol, the "ultimate landmark for Dubai and indeed the city."[64]

Set offshore on its own exclusive island, the building is framed on all sides by the sea and sky, emphasizing its easy-to-recognize silhouette. Facing the sea, as if representing Dubai on the leading edge of progress, the structure's shape is meant to evoke the sails of both the traditional dhow that long sailed the Arabian Gulf as well as "the profile of a J-Class Racing Yacht [which is] itself a symbol of opulence and technology" more commonly sighted along the coasts of Europe or North America.[65] As an exclusive, isolated luxury hotel, the Burj al Arab is a microcosm of Dubai's image of itself reproduced endlessly on publicity materials and official documents. Dubai might be the only major city in the world whose defining image is a single hotel. Its only competitor would be Las Vegas, and the comparison is not lost on many. Like other shiny new cities sprouting gleaming skyscrapers from the sands of the Arabian Peninsula, Dubai evokes images of a seemingly incongruous post-industrial petro-hypermodernity. Its golf course greens, marinas, and beaches mimic Las Vegas's conceit in forging a lush outdoor playground in a seemingly barren, waterless region. A touch of Las Vegas's reputation for being a sin city is all the more striking when located on the border of Saudi Arabia. At the same time, while Las Vegas is driven by middlebrow showiness and fueled by gambling, Dubai has been able to maintain a focus on the high-end market segment. Unlike the divide between the hotels and clubs of the Las Vegas strip and the city's residential spaces, in Dubai it is possible to claim that for much of the population, excluding its massive low-wage workforce, "there is little difference between holiday accommodation and housing."[66]

Diverse Markets

Dubai's unique global image has helped support a continuing flow of long-haul visitors in the post–9/11 era, accounting for nearly two-thirds of visitor arrivals. The United Kingdom, under whose protection Dubai began its development as a modern city-state, remains the emirate's largest inbound market, but it does not suffer from overdependence on a single source or type of tourist. The diversity of its tourism markets, in terms of the geographic spread of its source markets as well as the plethora of high-end leisure and business tourism markets it caters to, allows Dubai to retain a steady growth of international visitors regardless of global economic and political conditions. Geographically, Dubai's core high-spending long-haul market includes visitors from the United Kingdom, Germany, South Africa, Russia, India, and Japan, who come to Dubai for its "clean beaches, top class hotels, fine dining and variety in shopping."[67] Dubai's image and attractiveness in the United Kingdom, Far East, and many other markets is supported by Dubai's success in becoming a sponsor and a location for various European and international tours of leading golf, horse racing, tennis, and auto racing events. Since 1993 Dubai has expanded its cruise tourism sector from one visit that year to twenty-six during 2003.

At the same time, Dubai also has a steady market of intra-regional travelers who are repeat visitors year after year, often making multiple visits to Dubai each year.[68] These visitors have a diverse range of profiles, including extended Arab families on vacation, who come for shopping and family-oriented activities, as well as weekend ventures by young Arab male travelers "attracted to Dubai for the 'freedom, fun, and entertainment' it offers."[69] Regional Arab travelers are supplemented by the large non-Arab high-income expatriate community living in the Gulf states, as well as the friends and family of Dubai's own majority expatriate population. With a large element of its expatriate professionals coming from South Asia, such visits help account for the nearly 9 percent of international tourist nights at hotels.[70] Dubai has also long had a strong market in meetings, incentives, conferences, and exhibitions (MICE), which attracts Arab and expatriate visitors for regional conferences, as well as long-haul visitors for international meetings such as those of the World Bank and IMF in 2003. Another element of Dubai's diverse range of markets includes a sizable and growing number of visits from Iran. Economic ties between Dubai and Iran were built by businessmen who left Iran during waves of state taxation and repression under the shah. These ties have expanded as a new generation of Iran-based merchants seeks external business connections via Dubai, escaping both their own regime's tight control as well as the U.S.-backed effort to isolate Iran economically.[71] Iran's market share of hotel nights expanded from 2 percent to 4.7 percent between 1995 and 2002 as the number of tourist arrivals over this period grew at an average annual rate of over 30 percent.[72]

An Ever-Expanding "Cosmopolitan Oasis"

Protected by this diversification and connection to multiple markets, Dubai's unique image has been critical to its ability to survive and grow as a tourist destination in the post–9/11 era. While the emirate is well established as a regional business hub and entrepôt, Dubai's tourism economy and external image have come to rely on a relentless effort to develop a stream of spectacular headline-grabbing tourism-related projects. A critical element of Dubai's success as a tourist destination, especially in the post–9/11 environment, is built by using such megaprojects to help create and maintain a diverse range of market segments. Always catering to the family-oriented market with its shopping malls and entertainment complexes, Dubai has also been at work on a nearly $10 billion Dubailand theme park with Disney-style rides as well as retail outlets and sports and culture venues. The megapark, twice the size of Disney World, is really a collection of five different parks, with themes ranging from sports to ecotourism, with a "downtown" urban-themed space with shops, restaurants, movie theaters, and hotels at its center.[73] The more than forty different planned developments, often drawing on the work of leading designers in the field, include projects such as Aviation World, Motor Racing World, Arabian Theme Park, Pharaohs Theme Park, Snow World, and Restless Planet, a dinosaur theme park that will anchor its Retail and Entertainment World.[74] In 2008 the opening of the ten-million-square-foot Dubai Mall will make it the world's largest, coinciding with the completion of the Burj Dubai, planned to be the world's tallest building. Not only does Dubai aim for superlatives; it also has established a reputation for daring, imaginative projects such as an underwater hotel, a mall with an indoor ski slope, and the development of man-made islands off its coast. One motivation for the construction of these islands was the desire to create more beachfront property, for which Dubai confidently assumes there will be a market. Island creation projects such as the Palm, with its seventeen palm fronds encircled by a twelve-kilometer-long protective barrier reef, create for Dubai long stretches of exclusive beachfront property where land values generally soar. More visually stunning is the World, a series of small, privately owned man-made islands that form a global map when viewed from the sky, on Google Earth, or seen plastered on billboards along the highways of Amman, Beirut, and elsewhere. Such a project epitomizes how Dubai creates spaces of privatized luxury for the global elite while projecting to the world the image of Dubai as a global city. Even a visiting Israeli journalist notes, "Those . . . who get to Dubai will discover a cosmopolitan oasis in the middle of the desert. . . . Although Dubai is in no way a microcosm of the large Arab world, it is an interesting example of what can be achieved."[75]

A Smooth, Open Space or a Jagged, Enclosed Place

In an era when media commentators, policy makers, and many scholars commonly refer to the Arab world as a territorial exception to globalization where modernity has yet to take root, Dubai is often (mis)read as the exception that proves their rule. Dubai is referred to as "a compelling example of an Arab city embracing modernity."[76] In these discourses, Dubai has come to represent a new, alternative model for successful globalization in the Middle East based on economic liberalization, "dynamic free trade zones," and "sound economic management."[77] Noting the skepticism with which many across the Middle East approach the concept of economic globalization, Anoushiravan Ehteshami writes that Emir al-Maktoum offers "unreserved support for the process of globalization."[78] In his speech to the 2004 World Economic Forum held in Jordan, he called on others to "embrace the opportunities offered by globalization," explaining that among "the key factors of success . . . were . . . economic freedom and openness to the world."[79] The spectacle of Dubai's economic success is made all the more alluring by the seeming contradictions it embodies, located in a region increasingly torn apart by war and geopolitical struggles between great and would-be-great powers.

Thomas Friedman exemplifies this view of Dubai when he refers to it as one of the few places within the Middle East region that has let go of traditional territorial attachments and now exists within the plane of the "flat world" smoothed by the global flows of capital, technology, information, and human capital. In such a reading, Dubai represents "a bridge of decency that leads away from the failing civilization [of the Arab world] to a much more optimistic, open and self-confident society." Friedman's decontextualized understanding praises "Dubaians" for "building a future based on butter not guns, private property not caprice, services more than oil, and globally competitive companies, not terror networks." In short, he concludes, "You could not have a better friend and more of a symbol of globalization and openness."[80]

As Ahmed Kanna observes, in celebrations of Dubai as a space of economic liberalism, "political economy has become invisible. Globalization has made all that is solid, such as national borders and the constraints they impose, melt into air."[81] Beginning at Dubai's airport (DXB), Kanna contrasts the fluid movements of capital and citizens from affluent nations with the constricted spaces of the largely invisible wage laboring population predominately from South and Southeast Asia. Rather than a flat world, Kanna suggests that Dubai functions with the "jagged edges of a more archaic order, carved into the grid of nationality."[82] He also describes how the seemingly utopian cosmopolitan spaces that make up Dubai— including the airport, shopping malls, hotels, and residential and office complexes—are closed, interior spaces.[83] This jagged view of Dubai hints at the often overlooked territorial dynamics and geopolitics that undergird its rise as a space of transnational flows and a node within global networks.

The Territorial Partitions of Globalization in Dubai

As others have noted, Dubai's development as a nexus for transnational flows of capital, people, and goods has been, in part, a product of regional geopolitics.[84] Since the first oil boom of the early 1970s, as geopolitical conflicts, civil wars, and authoritarian-statist regimes of economic governance have dominated much of the region, Dubai has been poised to benefit from the expansion of legal and illicit flows of capital and trade. In the 1970s and 1980s, the civil war in Lebanon led to Beirut's decline as a regional hub for finance and business headquarters. Coinciding with a rise in regional oil wealth, Dubai was able to attract banking operations, financial expertise, and capital flows. In the 1980s, the Iranian revolution and the Iran-Iraq war pushed more commercial and financial businesses from Iran and Iraq, as well as from Kuwait and Bahrain, to Dubai. Moreover, the city has long benefited from the

British and American military presence in the Gulf, which helps Dubai maintain its territorial security and escape the ravages of regional conflict. This external backing, combined with close ties to the local merchant class, contributes to political order and stability. Thus the economic success of the emirate and its ability to maintain policies that attract capital flows and tourists have been supported by its geopolitical relationships and stand in contrast to the dynamics that led to the fall of Lebanon as a regional economic node.

While well situated geopolitically, Dubai's position as an entrepôt has been exploited and enhanced with development policies that target the particular needs of various sectors of the transnational economy, including, but not limited to, the tourism sector. Rather than a single open space within Friedman's globe-spanning flat plane, Dubai is a collection of rigidly controlled, specialized spaces. Its success in these efforts has been guided domestically by a regime of total territorial control that allows the state to segregate spaces of economic deterritorialization, where state policies and business contracts manage the transnational flows of unskilled workers, from spaces of economic reterritorialization, where private capital and tourists benefit from specialized locational benefits and well-crafted experiences of place. The partitioning of these spaces allows Dubai to maintain engagement with both dynamics of territorial competition simultaneously.

Dubai's model of globalization contrasts to that of Tunisia in the 1970s, when the early *infitah* policies led to an erosion of territorial control and social dislocation. Rather than producing similarly politically destabilizing effects, in Dubai such dislocation is experienced mostly by migrant workers who have no political rights or claims on the state. Even for private firms who compete in sectors dominated by economic deterritorialization (such as light manufacturing), these tend to be foreign-owned enterprises employing expatriate labor and risking their own capital within the offshore production zone of Jebal Ali, which operates outside Dubai's customs regime, employment laws, and company ownership regulations.[85]

At the same time, Dubai has established spaces that promote economic reterritorialization. Mike Davis describes Dubai as "a huge circuit board which the elite of transnational engineering firms and retail development are invited to plug in high-tech clusters, entertainment zones," and even "artificial islands."[86] Each sector has been given a set of special legal rules and characteristics designed to allow it to develop connections to global networks and flows within a particular niche. Dubai provides the infrastructure, services, and tax breaks needed to efficiently generate positive external economies for the firms that establish themselves within each zone. Within each cluster, the locational benefits are intensified by the agglomeration of firms within the cluster, the locational branding and identity that the theming offers, and homogeneity within each cluster. This limits the dispersion of locational benefits that would be caused by proximity to unrelated businesses that might generate negative externalities (such as Jordan's challenge of promoting tourism in Aqaba, where port facilities intrude on potential tourism spaces). The segments are constructed in confined, partitioned locations where processes of economic reterritorialization can be promoted but also contained under a regime of territorial control. Dubai has mastered the strategy of creating specialized zones such as the Jebal Ali port, as well as newer ones like Media City and Internet City, to segment the forms of openness the territory allows. For example, to encourage media firms to relocate to Dubai, media censorship needed to be relaxed in Media City but was not in the rest of the emirate.[87] The spatial segregation and interiority of both residential and leisure spaces also allow the coexistence of Dubai's tourism industry, where prostitution can be tolerated, with a socially conservative indigenous population. At the same time, the presence of other firms within each cluster, as well as those in other clusters, limits transaction costs and generates positive external economies.

Total Territorial Control

The construction of these tightly controlled spaces is made possible by a master plan designed by the British in 1960 that gives state authorities "strong central control over urban development" and almost total control over land rights and allocations.[88] Michael Pacione describes the resulting regime of development as "a hybrid model between state control and economic liberalism in which urban development is determined largely by the planning vision of the ruling family within an environment of market capitalism that seeks to attract foreign investment and reduce restrictions to free enterprise."[89] As a result, the city plan is itself "a spatial expression of economic strategy and a mechanism for ensuring the provision of the required infrastructure and services."[90]

While Dubai's land regime has similar origins as in Jordan, following customs of property in the Arab-Islamic world, Dubai's rulers never had to make the same bargains with indigenous tribes and the merchant families as in Jordan to consolidate state power. Nor was land in Dubai settled in patterns that led to a fragmented structure of ownership and use. Dubai's current land regime dates back to 1960, when the population was small and settlements limited to a few clusters. Land that had been settled for a lengthy period before that date was considered the property of its inhabitants, while all remaining territory, the vast majority of the emirate, was claimed by the ruling family, giving the al-Maktoums and the state complete control over urban planning. Within this regime, the ruler "may sell the land, lease it, put it to special uses over a set period, or allocate it to the municipality for public utilities."[91] Moreover, if land is granted without charge, "the ruler reserves the right to reclaim it at a future date."[92] Even those with property rights have only limited autonomy over the range of uses they may make of it. In this form of capitalism, the private sector is given rights to ownership of capital and to profits, but the state retains the prerogative over the disposition of territory. The more successful the private sector is, the greater the value of locational benefits that the state retains control over. Moreover, like other authoritarian regimes, Dubai's rulers are able to create dependent social classes. But in contrast to socialist-statist regimes that did so through unsustainable, budget-draining consumer subsidies and public-sector enterprises, Dubai is able to do so by using the disposition of land to create housing for its citizens and by supporting, while controlling, private-sector development. At the same time, while the management of public affairs and governance of the economy are broadly viewed as efficient and effective by the local and foreign private sector, the state is never required to grant any means for political participation or popular accountability. The fusing of the state and private sector, together with the segmentation of space according to their specialized rules, limits conflicts over the disposition of territorial resources and territorial control over the processes of economic reterritorialization.

While this regime of total territorial control operates in other sectors, it is particularly effective in the tourism sector. Land and its location are a critical resource for most aspects of tourism development, especially for hotel building and the development of shopping malls and entertainment parks. Under the guidance of state planning, tourism development is fostered by granting land to private interests, though more often to state- and family-owned real estate firms, for such purposes. As noted earlier, when beachfront property grew scare in Dubai, state-owned property development companies began creating artificial islands. Eventually, to help promote the real estate market in this sector, Dubai established some of the most liberal land regulations in the region, even allowing, in the case of the recent Palm Island tourism and real estate development project, foreigners to buy 100 percent ownership of property while granting them an unlimited residency visa.[93]

Dubai has also benefited from trends in the global tourism market that have sustained demand for artificial and simulated experiences of places. Rather than building an industry on natural environments or locations and monuments of historical significance, with ready financing Dubai has nearly endless potential to generate economic reterritorialization by creating interior spaces in resort hotels, theme parks, and shopping malls. In Dubai, "nature tourism" takes the form of a theme park attraction, while downhill ski slopes provide a "winter snow" experience embedded within a massive indoor shopping mall. Even many of the emirate's outdoor attractions are constructed, such as its skyscraper skyline and artificial islands.

While Dubai seeks to brand itself as a unique destination, the forms of its tourism development project follow global trends. Even historic cities in the United States and United Kingdom (many of which suffered deindustrialization in the 1970s) have created urban "tourist bubbles," often centered on the "festival shopping mall," as part of programs to revitalize economic development in their downtown areas and project new images of progress, safety, and entertainment.[94] The logic of segmentation, creating a space of economic reterritorialization centered on entertainment and shopping within a landscape that suffered the dislocations of economic deterritorialization, is similar. This mode of development, centrally planned and managed by public-private partnerships with limited accountability, also works to displace negative images of the "troubled" parts of their cities while creating a tourist enclave where "a non-democratic, directive, and authoritarian regulation is attempted and generally achieved."[95] Across the Middle East, the structure of enclave tourism, found in beach resorts as well as urban shopping malls, serves to physically insulate tourists, granting them a feeling of greater security while limiting the negative social and cultural impacts of tourism development.

The Local Political Geographies That Sustain Global Flows

Other cities across the Middle East are not likely to rival Dubai's relative centrality within global and regional tourism networks, but its economic success has increasingly influenced processes of tourism development across the region. As a professor at Emirates University suggests, "Dubai has become a trendsetter of sorts. All Arab cities today emulate Dubai one way or another."[96] Attempts to imitate Dubai are not simply a response to fashion and the economy of images. These patterns reflect increasing territorial competition driven by increased flows of petrodollars fueling investment, consumerism, and leisure travel. They must also be understood as products of local territorial struggles and regimes of territorial control.

As specific localities become valuable commodities or spaces that generate locational economies owing to increasing flows of tourists and capital, the competition over control of these spaces and access to the economic benefits they generate intensifies. As we saw in Petra, where territorial control is fragmented, efforts to refashion places into tourism spaces that generate economic re-territorialization may result in ruinous competitive rent seeking or conflicts between the diverse agents involved in the process. These dynamics help explain a practice that has come to characterize tourism development patterns in the Middle East and elsewhere. In each case, political authorities, backed by interests in the private sector, have been able to promote their territory's incorporation into transnational networks to the degree that they can assert territorial control over the spaces of development and promote forms of tourism development characterized by economic reterritorialization. By constructing and asserting territorial control over locations to be converted into tourism spaces, which often requires "defragmenting" existing forms of territorial control through expropriation, private firms and state institutions are able to drive the reterritorialization process and control the generation of rents and external economies. This in turn draws more tourists, tourist spending, and investment capital. Dubai is only the most vivid example of recent trends in patterns of tourism development. Urban and coastal spaces across the region are being remade by new partnerships between the government and the private sector that have defragmented regimes of territorial control and privatized planning processes to more easily refashion spaces as concentrated enclaves of high-income commercial, leisure, and business activity.

Before Dubai captured the international media spotlight, the reconstruction of postwar Beirut was the focus of discussions about the rise of global nodes "strongly connected with the global exchange of flows of people, money, goods, and information" within the Arab Middle East.[97] In the 1990s, the Saudi-Lebanese businessman Rafik Hariri sought to reestablish Beirut as a regional, if not global, hub by converting the downtown area, turned to rubble during decades of civil and regional war, into a modern-looking central business district to serve as the heart of the city's new real estate, finance, and tourism-oriented urban economy. After becoming prime minister, Hariri assigned the task of designing and reconstructing the area to a new organization, Solidere (Société Libanaise de Développement et Réconstruction).[98] What made the project possible was its initial defragmenting of territorial control by expropriating the property rights of over one hundred diverse owners, tenants, and leaseholders in exchange for shares in the company.[99] This strategy converted the rights of former residents and property owners over specific plots into stock in an organization that effectively operated as a private firm under the direction of Hariri, who was simultaneously prime minister and the leading shareholder in the company. Solidere and its backers argued that without such an approach, the "extreme fragmentation and entanglement of property rights" would have created legal and political obstacles inhibiting the reconstruction effort, which was critical to rebuilding the national economy.[100]

More recently, a similar logic has driven the Abdali Urban Regeneration Project, which is converting eighty hectares into a "smart urban center" to serve "as a new downtown for Amman."[101] The project is one of three being undertaken in Jordan by the quasi-public entity Mawared (the Arabic name for the National Resources Investment and Development Company), which is now

Jordan's largest real estate developer and ranks among Jordan's top five land owners. Working with the private real estate developer Saudi Oger, Mawared's Abdali project is a sign of the "privatization of planning" in Jordan, in which development is centrally managed by a politically autonomous entity granted territorial control to realize its project. The mangers of the Abdali project have this territorial control owing to King Abdullah II's decision to relocate buildings that house military and security apparatus out of the central city, thus clearing the space to form "the largest contiguous, single owned, vacant plot in central Amman."[102] Urban development patterns in Amman had been spreading the city further westward, giving the capital a diffused, horizontal commercial landscape,[103] whereas the new project seeks to create a central hub that will include high-rise office complexes, luxury apartments, medical facilities, a "vibrant retail and entertainment hub," a new private American university, and a cultural quarter connected to a library and other government buildings.[104] Businesses will be drawn to this new "heart of the city" for its "world class infrastructure and integrated business environment in one single package in a central location."[105] The project seeks to create a space separated from the existing landscape and the city's "run-down downtown" that will collect together new hubs for business, residential, commercial, and entertainment activities in the city.[106] As the Jordanian architect and scholar Rami Daher comments, the project will increase the "spatial polarization . . . between this new 'elitist urban island' and the rest of the city," and worse, he notes that it "represents a symbolic replacement of the existing historic downtown . . . and its current civil/urban symbols (such as the Husseini Mosque)."[107] In addition to a number of leading regional developers, such as the Dubai-based EMAAR, other investors include major banks, investment companies, and Rotana Hotels, situating Amman within the regional circuits of capital flows and business links. The project is also beginning to serve as a base for business, government agencies, and international organizations operating in Iraq.

In the cases of redevelopment in Beirut and Amman, a new entity is not only granted territorial control for planning but also disconnected from most avenues of political accountability, replicating the politics of Dubai. The territorial logic of these projects is similar to those of "free zones" in Dubai and elsewhere. The creation of the Aqaba Special Economic Zone (ASEZ) is a public effort to form a space of economic reterritorialization for tourism, trade, and other activities within Jordan's only port city by exempting the territory from government regulation, duties, and taxes. Even before the rise of Dubai as a global node, Iran developed islands in the Gulf to operate as commercial hubs. In the 1990s, visa and tax regulation were liberalized on Kish Island in an effort to promote it as an alternative tourism and shopping haven in the Persian Gulf, even while it was already serving as a transfer point for trade and smuggling flows between mainland Iran and Dubai.[108] These examples illustrate how states increasingly seek to define their integration into global networks and negotiate their interactions with globalization by asserting control over local spaces and territory.

Looking for Cosmopolitanism at the Ibn Battuta Mall

A tour of Dubai's skyscraper-lined highways, massive shopping malls, and themed entertainment parks leaves many observers with the impression that Dubai is an artificial city with no history or culture, where imported enclave spaces of modernity intrude into, cover over, or push to the margins the remnants of an authentic identity and indigenous population. A closer look into these spaces, however, reveals the possibility of "a city whose decentered multiplicity informs and accommodates everything it touches," suggesting that, in fact, "Dubai is a global city of the post-national future."[109]

Where in previous chapters I explored tourism development as a transnational process that connects and often reshapes the relations between Arab and non-Arab peoples, firms, and states, I have surveyed here how tourism contributes to increasing connectivity across the Arab region. Tourism promotion in Dubai, however, does not generally serve to connect its citizens, firms, and politics to those of other territories but rather operates mostly at scales both wider and more narrow. Within the widest sphere, Dubai serves as a transit hub for regional and globe-spanning travel flows that only briefly set foot on its territory. Within smaller zones, as noted earlier, tourism-related development projects define enclave spaces—such as airports, shopping mall, hotels, and entertainment parks—which allow a selected group of people from diverse national origins to interact in spaces that express their cosmopolitan or hybrid-national identities. With a large, mobile expatriate community, within the spaces they co-inhabit, Dubai often blurs distinctions between tourists (guests) and residents (hosts) while defining a highly pluralistic, cosmopolitan community in which the minority of Emirati citizens form a crucial, but not dominant, presence.

Drawing on the work of Saskia Sassen, Jones suggests that Dubai represents a new sort of space created by globalization where there is an "uncoupling of a person's sense of identity from a particular territorial location."[110] But rather than viewing Dubai's cosmopolitan culture as a product of placelessness and cultural deterritorialization, unmoored from a territorial source of identity, it is useful to consider how the architecture of its urban form sustains a mosaic of connected cultures attached to multiple locations.

Faisal Devji argues that since Dubai is "one of the few societies not founded upon nationality," it represents a unique, pluralistic cultural form where, for example, many of its mosques are "built to imitate those from other Muslim lands" and one hears "the call to prayer broadcast amidst the glass and marble of upmarket European shops, with American fast-food outlets set alongside prayer rooms." In fact, he concludes, "I'm inclined to think the emirate's only distinctive religious environment is the shopping-mall."[111]

There may be no better reflection of this understanding of Dubai's cosmopolitan character than the Ibn Battuta Mall. Its creator, the Dubai-owned real estate and development company Nakheel, refers to the mall as "the most unique entertainment and shopping destination not only to Dubai, but to the world as well."[112] The mall's distinctive architectural design is "based around the travels of renowned 14th century explorer, Ibn Battuta, a man from Tangiers, Morocco who traveled over 75,000 miles during his lifetime." The mall is made up of six zones, each with a different commercial function and architectural theme representing regions visited by Ibn Battuta during his adventures. From west to east, they include Andalusia, Tunisia, Egypt, Persia, India, and China. In each section, Nakheel has built a Las Vegas–style themed building inspired by a different fourteenth-century style, "allowing visitors an invaluable glimpse into the past." The Egypt Court, for example, "mirrors 14th century Cairo, the largest city in the Middle East during medieval times. The minor court and exterior is themed with hieroglyphic friezes, representative of ancient Egypt."

According to its developers, the Ibn Battuta Mall seeks to "reflect the unique combination of the various heritages and cosmopolitan lifestyle that is the very essence of Dubai." In this space, the diverse nationalities of its patrons—including Arabs from across the region and Dubai residents from Iran and South Asia—can find expressions of their various origins. And unlike Disney World and Las Vegas, these representations do not exoticize "foreign" cultures via stereotypical icons but rather present them within a common cultural space defined by the travels of an educated Muslim for whom "it seemed only natural . . . [to] leave his home in order to increase his understanding of the world that surrounded him."

As the Arab world's most famous traveler, the character of Ibn Battuta surely serves the objectives of Nakheel and Dubai's image makers well. The mall's diverse clientele is also likely to value and appreciate the cultural and historical resonances of the mall's theme. Writing about the hybrid Arabic-English used in the transliteration and translation of corporate signage at another Dubai mall, Kanna notes that "a certain minimal level of Western cosmopolitanism is required to interpret the shop signs in the mall."[113] Based on his ethnographic research, Kanna concludes that many residents and citizens identify with such (postnational) hybridity, which blurs together aspects of their identities, backgrounds, and affiliations. The Ibn Battuta Mall expands the scope of this hybridity by incorporating imagery from diverse societies, including non-Muslim majority societies in both the developing and less-developed worlds.

By reflecting aspects of the cultural identity of many of Dubai's residents and visitors, the mall defines a commercial space useful for drawing shoppers. Like other aspects of globalization in Dubai, however, the production of this space relies on an insidious form of spatial segmentation. It creates a space with which a certain class of residents and visitors can identify with and feel safe in, in much the manner that gated residential compounds define "communities" by partitioning themselves off to exclude others. In the case of Dubai's malls, not only do they fail to serve the needs of Dubai's less affluent classes, such as South Asian migrant workers, their management often restricts such communities from access to these spaces.

More broadly, while the societies of his era surely possessed more extreme forms of exclusion and segmentation, Ibn Battuta must be understood as providing a model of cosmopolitanism far richer than the one represented by the themed-consumerism of his namesake mall. The example of the historical Ibn Battuta provides an expression of the deeply embedded Islamic practice of seeking knowledge and spiritual enlightenment through travel. Beginning his journey with performance of the hajj, Ibn Battuta ended up traveling as far as China before heading back to North Africa. Ibn Battuta's travelogue (know as a *rihla*) gives us a rich depiction of the social world of the fourteenth century in which Islam, in all its diverse forms, gave rise to a "cosmopolitan social and cultural system that spanned the hemisphere."[114] Literate Muslims like Ibn Battuta formed a cultural elite whose traveling between urban centers within the frontiers of the Islamic world helped maintain "an integrated, growing, self-replenishing network of cultural communication."[115] Ibn Battuta traveled in an era when the vast, ethnically diverse Islamic world was politically fragmented but nevertheless sustained a highly cosmopolitan civilization integrated by flows of travel, trade, and communication. Across this space, a traveler from its far western edge could travel to its easternmost frontier, lands not even populated by Muslim majorities, and find hospitality as well as enough respect for his legal knowledge to gain employment as a judge. As Roxanne Euben argues, notions of cosmopolitanism do not only have exclusively "Western" origins. Highlighting the Islamic ethos of travel, she suggests that the Arab-Islamic world "offers a particularly rich countergenealogy of cosmopolitanism."[116]

The Possibilities for Islamic Tourism

One of the contemporary vehicles for exploring the cosmopolitan possibilities suggested by Ibn Battuta is the effort to promote "Islamic tourism." Unlike the consumerism on display in Dubai, which might represent a shared culture between narrow segments of diverse societies, the rise of Islamic tourism suggests the emergence of new motivations and modes of travel that may help chart dense networks of connections between peoples and places across the Islamic world. More critically, it offers a basis for tourism development in which travel and experiences of place spill out from enclave spaces to form new configurations of tourism economies and tourism networks. These can penetrate deep within societies across multiple class levels and into rural and socially conservative communities alienated from many forms of cosmopolitan consumerism and dominant Western styles of travel and leisure tourism.

The notion of Islamic tourism builds from existing practices of religious pilgrimage, including the hajj to Mecca and visits to holy cities, important mosques, and places of religious learning, as well as the tombs of historical figures from early Islam. The hajj is a unifying spiritual duty for all the world's Muslims, a major economic phenomenon for Saudi Arabia, and it represents one of the largest annual organized transnational movements of people from all parts of the globe.[117] As the home to the Shi'i holy cities of Najaf and Karbala, Muslim pilgrims have historically constituted an important feature of Iraq's tourist industry, supporting the building of numerous hotels and other facilities in these cities. After the fall of Baghdad in 2003, while U.S. secretary of defense Rumsfeld was praising the tourist potential of ancient Babylon, the Iranian foreign minister Kamal Kharrazi "predicted confidently" that with the opening of the Iraqi border to Iranian pilgrims, "Iraq would be assured of at least 100,000 tourists every month and they would spend at least $500m annually."[118] As the first region outside the Arabian peninsula that Islam spread through, Jordan contains many important historic sites and tombs from early Islamic history and now promotes an Islamic component of its "religious and spiritual" tourism sector to supplement its historical emphasis on Christian sites.[119]

While these forms of tourism closely follow traditions and practices of religious pilgrims, the term "Islamic tourism" is increasingly being used to refer to other forms of religiously inspired travel that blend into the category of leisure tourism. In the same way that Western tourism developed from forms of religious pilgrimage and voyages of education and enlightenment (as in the European Grand Tour), emerging forms of Islamic tourism can be viewed as an expression of the globalization and pluralization of international tourism.

One articulation of these possibilities is found in the pages of a bimonthly magazine published in London, *Islamic Tourism*. Its publisher, Abdel-Sahib Al-Shakry, views tourism as a means to build bridges across the Islamic world to serve cultural and spiritual purposes as well as vehicles for political and economic development.[120] Al-Shakry is driven by an ethos found in Ibn Battuta as well as a commitment to forge people-to-people ties across the Islamic *umma* (the community of the faithful). Such a project, he writes, seeks "not to replace existing tourism activity in our areas but [to open] up new and exciting opportunities for growth, as well as marketing a new type of commodity for which we are convinced there is an urgent need."[121] As Al-Hamarneh and Steiner note, "Part of the vision includes reorienting tourist destinations towards less consumption and 'western-culture loaded' sites and towards more Islamic historical religious and cultural sites. . . . A special place in this concept is held by the new 'touristic' interpretations of pilgrimage and efforts to merge religious and leisure tourism in joint programs."[122] Such efforts are being promoted by a diverse set of actors that include government officials, religious authorities, devout entrepreneurs, and a range of Islamic-oriented nongovernmental organizations. Islamic tourism can provide a basis for new forms of religiously inspired leisure and entertainment in which tourism practices and leisure-oriented enterprises develop from within the cultural and economic fabric of Middle Eastern societies.

Mona Harb offers the example of Al Saha Traditional Village, a leisure complex built within the marginalized Shia-dominated al Dahiya (southern suburbs) of Beirut and managed by the Islamic philanthropic foundation al-Mabarrat.[123] The complex is designed to resemble a "traditional village" and includes seven restaurants, cafés, shops, a wedding hall, a motel, a children's playground, and a library that specializes in Arabic poetry. Its development follows a logic similar to the economic reterritorialization in integrated tourism complexes, theme parks, and the Taybet Zaman village near Petra (discussed in chapter 4). The complex's designer notes that al Dahiya does not possess tourism assets, such as a shore or mountains, so he thought "of creating a project turned inwards." The Islamic theme that defines the architecture and educational mission of the village is one that can "mobilize a mosaic of different publics" including Lebanese, other Arabs, and foreigners. Harb explains that the success of the tourist village is in part a product of being located within a dense urban area with a large middle-class population and filling the need for "pious entertainment" (i.e., it does not serve alcohol). The complex also provides a location for visiting Arab tourists to spend their leisure time and money while contributing to an Islamic charity. Moreover, the complex also attracts foreign (non-Muslim) tourists by offering a unique cultural experience within what is often viewed as a forbidding "Hezbollah stronghold." Rather than seeking to define an "authentic" Shia religious experience, the village explicitly projects a hybrid cultural identity that incorporates Lebanese and broader Arab aspects. It draws on the nostalgic novels of a well-known Lebanese author who wrote mostly about Christian mountain villages, and through its poetry readings and other events, it also embraces broader Arab and Islamic cultural themes. While Al Saha (meaning open space) serves as a means to generate income for a Shia foundation, it also functions as a public space for daily users, draws some visitors who do not follow norms of modest dress (in Harb's words, who "dress provocatively"), and is used by other associations as a place to hold public talks and fund-raising events. Encouraged by its success, the developer has plans to open a branch in Qatar. The project holds lessons for Dubai, as it demonstrates how tourism-related developments can take the form of "enclaves" that draw on no local territorial features but still produce a meaningful experience of place that resonates with the local community and avoids partitioning itself off from the surrounding cultural and economic context.

Al Saha Traditional Village is only one example within the growing trend of religious consumerism witnessed across the Arab world and beyond. These efforts adopt many existing conventions, practices, and forms of international tourism while redefining them to serve new purposes in different contexts. Such developments mark a sharp divergence from the structure of the first organized tourism economies in nineteenth-century Egypt developed by Thomas Cook & Son, when native Egyptians had little agency as either tourism developers or travelers themselves.[124] In Al-Shakry's view, the drive for Islamic tourism must be part of an effort to promote tolerance and pluralism within Islam. By reconstructing mausoleums of imams, the prophet's companions, and saints who are revered by the different sects of Islam, he suggests, ties between communities can be fostered as they work together to provide economic opportunities to the local inhabitants near holy sites.[125] In short, Islamic tourism provides a means to promote economic reterritorialization by creating sites that generate locational rents and positive externalities (on the supply side) while fostering the expansion of travel flows across the Islamic world (the demand side). Within such tourism economies, public agencies, religious authorities, charitable associations, and local private firms would have effective tools to regulate both supply and demand, making them less dependent on external networks and flows.

The discourse of Islamic tourism suggests one aspect of a broad set of possible cultural, economic, and spatial logics for tourism development. Driven by developers seeking to maximize their own returns in an often volatile market, most tourism-related development projects—such as those in Dubai, Hammamet, Amman, Sharm al Shaykh, and elsewhere—have increasingly resulted in self-contained enclaves in the form of coastal resort complexes, all-inclusive package tours, or urban hotel complexes providing a range of onsite services. These forms of tourism development have even been merging with exclusive housing and vacation villas built within gated communities. Notwithstanding efforts such as the Ibn Battuta Mall or the Médina Mediterranea near Hammamet, Tunisia, such enclave tourism projects have generally produced tourism experiences that are devoid of a strong sense of local places and cultures or connections with the local community, often making their experiences interchangeable with tourism to other destinations. In fact, these tourism enclaves are designed to limit social and economic interaction between tourists and host societies. Within and near such developments, local shops, restaurants, and other businesses will often cater to the "tourist market," seeking to capture rents while producing goods and services of little value to the local community and generating limited forward and backward linkages between the tourism sector and other parts of the economy. For tourism spending to have a larger positive impact on local economic development (as opposed to mainly generating hard currency for the government and national economy), there needs to be greater overlap between tourism and nontourism activities, for example, where tourists and local middle-class residents enjoy the same set of restaurants and cultural facilities. Al Saha Village and other expressions of Islamic tourism development provide examples of how tourism economies can be constructed to produce these benefits.

Islamic tourism is just one of the many resources the Middle East can draw on to define alternative narratives and referents in efforts to produce hybrid experiences of place that use local features to craft compelling tourism experiences for a diverse range of potential visitors inside as well as beyond the Middle East. State authorities have many cultural, natural, and historic resources for developing such forms of tourism. Like the creation of national parks in the United States, the development of nature reserves, while designed to help preserve natural ecosystems and biodiversity, creates new ways to experience the natural environment and support ecotourism and nature-based tourism. A Jordanian NGO, the Royal Society for the Conservation of Nature (RSCN), has pioneered the creation and management of nature reserves that generate incomes for local communities while helping the country redefine its tourist image.[126] Long recognized but slow to develop, Arab cities across the region have rich architectural forms that can provide unique tourism experiences appealing to domestic, regional, and international visitors. A critical method for developing alternative tourism possibilities is to explore the rich cultural traditions and material culture found in Arab urban landscapes and their communities.[127] The development of urban tourism could provide a vehicle for defining experiences of place that draw on aspects of Arab culture shared between cities as well as on experiences that express the diversity of regional, national, and ethnic cultural production. Arab cities are too often presented to Western tourists as dead "ruins," with a focus on historic buildings, or as showcases for government and nationalist monuments and displays that recount an official nationalist narrative and glorify the nation-state, its ruler, and his power. With a focus on contemporary urban culture, alternative programs could help present the region as one possessing a modern culture driven by cosmopolitan artists, musicians, and filmmakers who draw on aspects of traditional Arab culture as well as regional and international influences. In particular, the development of museums, monuments, films, and guidebooks focusing on aspects of cultural heritage that resonate within Arab populations (rather than depict the political power and legitimacy of the state) can also help integrate the international tourism sector with domestic and regional Arab tourism.[128] Such programs would have the potential of translating the ongoing process of economic reterritorialization at the regional scale into one that also promotes a heterogeneous sphere of cultural reterritorialization.

Excavating Territorial Identities

One limit of these emerging itineraries of travel, however, is that while they support cultures of travel that promote flows not confined by the boundaries of enclave tourism spaces, they still remain limited by existing geocultural and geopolitical imaginaries and bounded territories of cultural and political spaces.[129] Even Ibn Battuta's cosmopolitanism was ultimately territorially limited by the boundaries of Dar al-Islam and culturally and socially limited to the Arabic-speaking elite of his day.[130] While travelers, as opposed to tourists, are sometimes defined as those who wish to wander off the beaten track,[131] the process of converting the itineraries of such journeys into organized tourism flows often results in packaged forms of cultural engagement that present cultural difference as a symbolic commodity that can be readily consumed within existing, popular geocultural and geopolitical imaginaries.

During the rise of the New Middle East in the mid-1990s, Israeli tourists and the international media reporting on their travels to Jordan sought to frame these encounters in Jordan as experiences of "first contact" with its land and peoples.[132] These narratives of Israeli tourism to the cultural space of Jordan suggested that Israeli society and Jordanian society had no modern-era connections between them. Framing these encounters as "first contact" served as a bridge between the shifting geopolitical imaginaries in Israel and Jordan. The two national spaces, with political relations long defined in terms of realist-territorial imaginaries, were now beginning to become connected to the New Middle East defined by cross-border economic flows and cooperation.

At the same time, these travel narratives and the Israeli public discourse about tourism in the New Middle East erased and pushed to the margins the numerous existing connections between the peoples of Israel and Jordan. To recognize these subaltern connections would have cut against the new kinds of political and economic ties that the Israeli and Jordanian governments, with U.S. backing, sought to forge. The most prominent of these subsovereign or nonstate linkages is that of the Palestinian Arabs, whose community was fragmented by the shifting political and military boundaries and partitions between Israel and Jordan. In different ways, this community is viewed as a threat to the legitimacy of the official identity and historical narrative of each state. As a result, in Israel, cross-border flows of Palestinian Jordanians that did not fit the accepted models of leisure tourism were often viewed as a threat to Israel's security, national identity, and economic well-being. In Jordan, the failure of the peace process to generate economic prosperity and address the Palestinian question prompted Jordanians to challenge the government's embrace of the

New Middle East narrative and to view flows of Israeli tourists as an economic and cultural threat.

The stories of "first contact" and the fears of antinormalization advocates stand in contrast to the travelogue written by the Egyptian playwright Ali Salem describing his drive through Israel at the height of American, Israeli, and Jordanian enthusiasm for the New Middle East.[133] Salem set off by car in April 1994 to remind both his Egyptian readers and the Israelis whom he met that the two peoples were neighbors and shared a common border. Salem was an unabashed advocate of the New Middle East. In his humorous style, he was able to poke fun at his Egyptian critics who opposed normalization while providing one of the most sincere efforts to experience and express the values of the New Middle East.[134] Read alongside both Peres's speeches and the reporting about Israeli tourists to Jordan, Ali Salem's text presents a far more powerful and complex vision for a New Middle East and the nature of cross-border flows that could connect territories across the old fault lines that marked the region's geopolitical fragmentation. His vision is built on a recognition of the existing, but often overlooked, connections between people in Israel and the Arab states. Throughout his journey, Salem ridicules the irrational fears of many of his compatriots that the New Middle East would lead to an Israeli cultural invasion that would threaten Egyptian national culture. More critically, by viewing Egyptian and Israeli societies as overlapping cultures with interwoven histories and interconnected presents, he suggests an alternative cross-border travel itinerary composed of hybrid cultural experiences. When he stops at a gas station, checks into a hotel, or lands in a hospital, we often find Salem speaking Arabic to Palestinians and Israeli Jews of Arab origin. He reminds his readers that Israel is, in part, an Arab nation. Like some of the *mizrahi,* or "Arab Jews," and Palestinians of both Israel and the West Bank whom he meets, Salem sees Israel itself as a country composed of conflicted parts, its people and their identities not fully represented by the dominant narrative of a European-oriented Zionist imaginary. While this portrayal seeks to open up ways for Egyptians and other Arabs to find points of identification with Israel, Salem also traces the connections in the other direction. He writes that "the strongest bridges of peace between Egypt and Israel are the Egyptian Jews."[135] While the crossing of such bridges will trigger suspicions and difficult memories of displacement, Salem prefers a route along a palimpsest of territorial memories to one of civil but cold encounters between peoples who have nothing in common beyond strategic and economic interests. Salem even suggests that Arab societies, by first marginalizing and then forcing their Jewish populations to flee, have lost something of themselves, which ties to Israel might someday help to heal. In the end, Salem even wishes that Jewish and Egyptian narratives of displacement and oppression could be reinterpreted in ways that suggest a shared history between Egyptian Arabs and Jews suffering under authoritarian rulers.[136]

One motivation of promoters of Islamic tourism is to show the cultural connections that exist between peoples of the Middle East of different nations and sects. Rather than promoting the vision of a single deterritorialized Islamic identity, tourism composed of visits to historic places, tombs, and sites of religious learning recognizes territorial distinctions while simultaneously highlighting the historical and contemporary connections between these places. Similar travel itineraries could be planned between North Africa, Spain, and France—visiting people and places associated with Andalusia, northern Africa's Jewish population, and Arabs now living in Europe—to trace the interconnectedness of these territories.

Shimon Peres wrote that the Middle East should build bridges to facilitate the circulation of trade, capital, and Western tourists. He suggested that Arabs should become less concerned about defending their Arab identity and instead be driven by the imperative of economic growth. But many Arabs viewed such a program as a threat to their identity, as it suggests that Arabs should disconnect from territorial attachments to become integrated into the transnational flows of the global economy. Salem, in contrast, calls for Arabs and Jews to face up to and embrace the existing, often problematic connections and interdependencies that cross political borderlines.

While Palestinians from Israel and Jordan began to explore and forge connections after the 1994 peace treaty, neither Peres's New Middle East nor the antinormalization movement in Jordan recognized or facilitated these connections between communities across the Israeli-Arab frontier. Such recognitions would require a redefinition of the geopolitical imaginaries that animate nationalist politics in Israel and Jordan. Salem's text can only suggest a journey toward such a redefinition, but it could become the basis for travel itineraries and tourism development. Such itineraries could be developed along with emerging forms and networks of Islamic and Arab tourism. As cross-border connections and flows are encouraged, territorial connections must also be recognized and local communities given autonomy to help define tourism development efforts and promote their own forms of cultural reterritorialization.

The realization of these various forms of cross-cultural tourism may enable the development of new geopolitical and geocultural imaginaries by challenging the mobilization of discourses of political reterritorialization while forging heterogeneous configurations of both cultural and economic reterritorialization. These connections between peoples and territories can be forged rhizomatically. As William E. Connolly reminds us, "A *rhizome* is a form of plant life stabilized by a dense network of connections close to the ground. . . . Grasses are rhizomatic."[137] Rather than displacing territorial attachments, such connections pluralize them by disrupting their sealed borders and territorial definitions and recognizing multiple, alternative relationships between territory and identity, such as postnational, transnational, and diasporic identities.[138] Rather than seeking to promote what some define as a deterritorialized identity, meaning without territorial attachment, these processes can promote a cosmopolitanism defined, as Bruce Robbins suggests, in terms of a "density of overlapping allegiances rather than the abstract emptiness of non-allegiance."[139]

Tourism, Territory, and Beyond

In the spring of 2006, the complex nature of the connections between the United States and the emirate of Dubai emerged at the center of the controversy that broke out over the Dubai Ports World (DPW) deal to take over the management contracts of several American port terminals. In supporting the deal, the Bush administration argued that Dubai (as a member of the UAE) was an ally in the so-called War on Terror and provides the region with a compelling model for globalization. The administration, however, faced an unanticipated torrent of criticism from the left and right, leading to an unusual configuration of battle lines. In the end, the Bush administration was unsuccessful in its efforts to defuse populist opposition. Gaining support for this business transaction in 2006 proved more difficult than launching the invasion of Iraq in

2003. Oddly, the administration found itself battling elements of the post–9/11 geopolitical imagination that it had helped to promote in the run-up to the war. It could not prevent Dubai from being associated with the deterritorialized threats posed by nonstate terrorist networks and being viewed less as an Arab model for globalization than as a nexus for money laundering and trade in dangerous contraband goods.

The debate within the United States about the Dubai-owned firm reveals less about the process of globalization in Dubai than about how nativist American discourses of political reterritorialization and perceptions of globalization in the Arab world are shaping the politics of globalization in post–9/11 America. More generally, it also illustrates the value of the analytical framework presented in this book, which views globalization in terms of both deterritorialization and reterritorialization and recognizes the importance of geopolitical imaginaries. The DPW controversy and the ongoing debates about immigration in the United States and Europe are examples of phenomena that cannot be understood fully without analyzing them with the tools used here to explore the international political economy of tourism in the Arab world.

In the Arab world as well as the United States, the process of becoming increasingly enmeshed in the networks of the international economy has led to conflicts between those who fear that integration will lead to social dislocation, political dependence, and vulnerability to uncontrollable flows and those who are capable of taking advantage of the new opportunities offered by integration and thus urge their societies to adapt to the changing global environment rather than close themselves off from it. In every case, actors will support aspects of deterritorialization when they can influence (and benefit from) the networks involved while resisting other forms of deterritorialization that they fear they cannot contain in segmented spaces and insulate themselves from its effects. States and societal actors generally resist aspects of globalization over which they have little influence, especially when they are viewed as posing challenges to the territorial foundations of their security and identity. Both state and nonstate actors often seek to promote forms of political reterritorialization to protect their territory from forms of deterritorialization that erode their local control while simultaneously promoting forms of economic reterritorialization that enhance their influence over global networks and their local effects.

The resulting nature of political, economic, and cultural patterns across each territory is less a product of a generalized resistance to globalization, or states failing to promote economic liberalization, than the result of specific struggles between state, societal, and international forces over the control of transnational flows and national territories. While the maps of these flows and territories are always complex, the political struggles that take place over them are generally driven by geopolitical imaginaries that simplify and abstract their features.

International tourism is only one aspect of how globalization is transforming patterns of economic development, state building, and geopolitics throughout the world. By using tourism as a lens through which to explore the ways globalization generates deterritorialization and reterritorialization, I have sought to enrich the analysis of globalization in comparative and international political economy. This framework also helps explain why globalization should be viewed not as a linear process leading inevitably toward increased deterritorialization but as an uneven, dynamic, and politically contingent process continually reshaping the economic and political landscape of localities across the globe.

Acknowledgments

The process of completing this book was aptly described by Buffy the Vampire Slayer when she explained to a foe, "We can do this the hard way, or . . . actually, there's just the hard way." Along this path, which ends here in Beirut, I was assisted by many fellow travelers and kind strangers. My journeys of fieldwork were aided by researchers and professionals who shared their knowledge and insights about tourism in Tunisia, Jordan, and Dubai. I would particularly like to thank Ridha Boukra, Laurie Brand, Jafar Tukan, Ammar Khammash, Habis Samawi, Rami Daher, Rami Khouri, Megan Perry, and Najib Hourani. Over the years I benefited from thoughtful comments on my tourism writings from Nazli Choucri, Malik Mufti, and Michael Clancy. Generous and helpful readings of the manuscript were provided by Jeannie Sowers, Arang Keshavarzian, Ahmed Kanna, Yasser Elsheshtawy, and Robert Vitalis. Pieter Martin and the staff of the University of Minnesota Press smoothly converted the manuscript into a book. Nicole Hughes helped prepare the index.

The completion of this project would not have been possible without generous financial support (in the form of travel and research grants and subsidized housing) provided by Albert and Lily Hazbun; American Center for Oriental Research (Amman, Jordan); American Institute for Maghribi Studies; Konrad Adenauer Foundation; World Economic Forum; American University of Beirut;

Rita Hazboun; Berta and the late Joe Hazbun; Tabitha and Bosco Wilson's editing retreat; John and Betty Woodward's mountain writing workshop; and a residency fellowship from the Arborway Center for the Study of Art, Culture, and Food under the direction of Anthony Apesos and Natasha Seaman, who were aided by visiting fellows Dawn Opstad and Matthew Hull. The writing of the text in the manner of my choosing and with continuing enthusiasm for the topic was enabled by the creative intellectual environment sustained by my colleagues in the Department of Political Science at the Johns Hopkins University, including Siba Grovogui, William E. Connolly, and Jane Bennett.

If this project can be thought to have an origin, it must be traced back to the itineraries of displacement, travel, and leisure tourism experienced by my parents and those on which they later guided my sisters and me throughout Europe, the Arab world, and beyond. The final journey, with its many unexpected but interesting challenges, was not undertaken alone. For a decade Michelle Woodward has been the steadfast slayer of my demons (those real, imagined, produced by the tortured grammars of my mind), as well as my travel and adventure partner across several continents. She provided several of the images for this book and untangled its prose. In the final scene, set in our Hamra flat, her computer became the project's martyr. Through it all, her intrepid, inquisitive spirit and gracious, humanist vision never failed to offer me ways to better see and understand the people and places encountered along the way as well as appreciate the enchantments that seem to follow us around like rabbits.

Notes

Introduction

1. Tourism receipts exclude international transportation costs. For tourism data, see World Tourism Organization (UNWTO), *Tourism Highlights 2006,* and the organization's online statistical database, http://www .world-tourism.org.

2. Culler, "The Semiotics of Tourism," 167.

3. One noteworthy exception is a brief but insightful survey by Robert Vitalis. It addresses the political, economic, and cultural issues surrounding the incorporation of the Middle East and North Africa into the global tourism economy and anticipates many of the issues I discuss in this book. See Vitalis, "Middle East on the Edge," 2–7. See also M. Gray, "Development Strategies"; Gray, "Economic Reform"; and Gray, "Political Economy of Tourism."

4. Eric Schmitt, "Rumsfeld Says More G.I.'s Would Not Help U.S. in Iraq," *New York Times,* September 11, 2003.

5. Said, "The Arab Right Wing," 5.

6. For a study of the rise of tourism as a modern economic enterprise that develops concepts from actor-network theory, see Hazbun, "The East as an Exhibit."

7. See Organization for European Economic Cooperation, *Tourism and European Recovery;* and Endy, *Cold War Holidays.*

8. "A New Itinerary," *Economist,* May 17, 2008, 85.

9. The best comprehensive review of the field remains Crick, "Representations of International Tourism." For a more recent survey in economics,

see Sinclair, "Tourism and Economic Development." For one in geography, see Ioannides, "Strengthening the Ties." On the neglect of tourism by the field of political science, see Richter, "Tourism Politics"; and Matthews and Richter, "Political Science and Tourism."

10. Martin, "Leverage of Economic Theories," 39.

11. Waters, "The American Tourist," 110.

12. Economist Intelligence Unit, "Role of Tourism," 53; Sinclair and Bote Gómez, "Tourism."

13. Waters, "The American Tourist," 109 (italics mine).

14. For a brief overview of the industry, see Porter and Sheppard, "Tourism and Development," 540–52.

15. Lanfant, "Introduction," 27–29. See also the essays collected in a section titled "Tourism as an Export Industry," published in the USAID journal *Development Digest 5*, no. 2 (July 1967): 49–88.

16. Diamond, "Tourism's Role"; Smith, *Hosts and Guests;* de Kadt, *Tourism.*

17. Matthews, *International Tourism;* Lanfant, "Introduction"; Britton, "Political Economy." But see also Dunning and McQueen, "Multinational Corporations"; and United Nations, *Transnational Corporations.*

18. Turner and Ash, *The Golden Hordes;* Louis Turner, "International Division of Leisure"; Britton, "Political Economy."

19. Britton, "Tourism, Capital, and Place"; Harrison, "Tourism, Capitalism, and Development"; Mowforth and Munt, *Tourism and Sustainability.*

20. Pleumarom, "Political Economy of Tourism"; Pattullo, *Last Resorts;* Nicholson-Lord, "The Politics of Travel."

21. Brohman, "New Directions"; Clancy, "Tourism and Development"; Clancy, *Exporting Paradise;* Sharpley and Telfer, *Tourism and Development.*

22. For a similar critique, see Steiner, "Tourism," 162–66.

23. Clancy, "Commodity Chains."

24. See Strange, *Retreat of the State,* 99.

25. Endy, *Cold War Holidays,* 38–39.

26. Huntington, *The Clash of Civilizations.*

27. Said, *Orientalism,* 54, 88–89. See also Gregory, *The Colonial Present,* 17.

28. Lijphart, "Tourist Traffic."

29. Endy, *Cold War Holidays.*

30. Stock, "Political and Social Contributions"; Matthews and Richter, "Political Science and Tourism," 127.

31. Davidson and Montville, "Foreign Policy According to Freud."

32. D'Amore, "Tourism," 24.

33. Krasner, *Structural Conflict.*

34. Richter, "Tourism Politics," 325.

35. Richter and Waugh, "Terrorism and Tourism."

36. Smith, *Hosts and Guests;* Gregory, "Colonial Nostalgia."

37. Pizam, "Does Tourism Promote Peace."

38. Barber, *Jihad vs. McWorld.*

39. Appadurai, *Modernity at Large;* Rosenau, *Along the Domestic-Foreign Frontier;* Rosenau, *Distance Proximities.*

40. Rosenau, *Along the Domestic-Foreign Frontier,* 110.

41. Rosenau, *Distance Proximities,* 11–16.

42. Held et al., *Global Transformations;* Scholte, *Globalization.*

43. See, for example, Blyth, *Great Transformations;* Keck and Sikkink, *Activists beyond Borders;* Keohane, *Power and Governance;* and Wendt, *Social Theory.*

44. Short, *Global Dimensions.*

45. See Berger and Dore, *National Diversity;* Keller and Pauly, "Globalization at Bay"; Weiss, "Globalization"; and Gilpin, *Global Political Economy.*

46. See Newman, "Geopolitics Renaissant."

47. Agnew, *Hegemony,* 33.

48. Jeffrey Henderson et al., "Global Production Networks," 446.

49. Ó Tuathail, *Critical Geopolitics,* 1.

50. Ibid., 230 (italics mine). The terms "deterritorialization" and "reterritorialization" were developed in the work of Gilles Deleuze and Félix Guattari. I thank William E. Connolly for leading me to an appreciation of their work. Gearóid Ó Tuathail and Timothy Luke explain: "Using both Freud and Marx they develop an understanding of capitalism and state power as forces which simultaneously seek to produce rigid identities and assert fixed geographies, yet tend in their very operation to undermine traditional identities, social relations, and the very geographical codes set down in practice." Ó Tuathail and Luke, "Present at the (Dis)Integration," 395. In reference to their own uses of these terms, they note, "We use Deleuze and Guattari's terminology, as they encourage their readers to do, for our own purposes and our own end" (395). It is in the same spirit that I have fashioned my own understanding of these terms.

51. Ó Tuathail, *Critical Geopolitics,* 230.

52. This presentation draws from a more extensive treatment in Hazbun, "Globalization." See also Krugman, *Development,* 49–52; Storper, "Territories"; and A. Scott, *Regions and the World Economy.*

53. As Harvey notes, "Rent is the theoretical concept through which political economy (of whatever stripe) traditionally confronts the problem of spatial organization and the value to users of naturally occurring or humanly created differentials in fertility." Harvey, *The Urban Experience,* 90. Technically, economists understand rents to be incomes gained

by holders of scarce property rights in excess of what would otherwise be earned (under perfect market conditions) without the addition or improvement of existing factors of production. In contrast, an economic externality "is any occurrence or activity that lies outside the range of control of the individual firm, but that then has definite effects on the firm's internal production function." A. Scott, *Regions and the World Economy*, 81. As I use the terms, locational rents and locational external economies are related aspects of the same phenomenon where differentials in the fertility of territorial resources are products of the spatial organization of productive assets (rather than the distortion of market contexts). Locational rents are aspects of the marginal differential fertility that can be privatized and directly controlled by ownership, while locational external economies are the aspects that are public goods (or, when exhaustible, common-pool resources) that can be regulated by control over the infrastructure that sustains them. Locational external economies can be privatized, as when a single firm captures all the benefits, or be converted into club goods, when payment can be extracted for access to the economic benefits.

54. Saxenian, *Regional Advantage;* Storper, *The Regional World;* A. Scott, *Regions and the World Economy.*

55. Sassen, *The Global City.*

56. A. Scott, "The Cultural Economy"; Kotkin, *The New Geography.*

57. Hannigan, *Fantasy City;* Judd and Fainstein, *The Tourist City.*

58. The notion of "territorial control" can be viewed as a component of social control as understood by Joel Migdal. See his *Strong Societies and Weak States,* 22–23.

59. Harvey, *The Condition of Postmodernity,* 295.

60. Ibid.

61. Brand, *Jordan's Inter-Arab Relations;* Chaudhry, *The Price of Wealth;* Henry and Springborg, *Globalization;* Lynch, *Voices of the New Arab Public.*

62. See MacCannell, *The Tourist.*

63. For an elaboration of this framework, see Hazbun, "Globalization," 326–33.

64. On the notion of tourism spaces as mechanisms for rent creation, see Gray, "Contributions of Economics," 108–12; Britton, "Tourism, Capital, and Place," 455; and Harvey, "The Art of Rent."

65. See Lash and Urry, *Economies of Signs and Space,* 260, 261.

66. Urry, "The Tourist Gaze 'Revisited,'" 173. For an excellent study of the "invention" of New England tourism, see Brown, *Inventing New England.*

67. Judd, "Constructing the Tourist Bubble."

68. See Hazbun, "Globalization," 333–34; and Harvey, "The Art of Rent."

69. Rosenau, *Along the Domestic-Foreign Frontier;* 110, Rosenau, *Distance Proximities,* 15.

1. Fordism on the Beach

1. See Braudel, *Mediterranean.*

2. White, *Comparative Political Economy.*

3. Richards and Waterbury, *Political Economy of the Middle East,* 233.

4. Britton, "Political Economy of Tourism," 347.

5. Turner, "International Division of Leisure," 260.

6. See Mzabi, *La croissance urbanie accélérée;* Sethom, *L'Influence de tourisme;* Sethom, "L'Industrie et le tourisme"; Belhedi, *Societe, espace et developpement;* Sethom, *L'Industrie et le tourisme en Tunisie: Etude de géographie du développement.* See also Cazes, "Le tourisme international"; Signoles, *L'Espace Tunisien;* Miossec, "Le tourisme en Tunisie."

7. The notion of Fordism refers to the establishment of political, economic, and technological arrangements that help sustain the mass production of standardized goods by ensuring a stable supply of labor and demand for those goods. See Harvey, *The Condition of Postmodernity,* 124–40.

8. This language draws on the Marxist-inspired regulation school of political economy that explores how the development of regulatory institutions and practices can coordinate demand and supply across national economies to prevent crises produced by over- or underproduction. My approach follows the variant developed in Piore and Sabel, *The Second Industrial Divide.* For a regulation school view of Fordism and the international division of labor, see Lipietz, *Mirages and Miracles.* Efforts by Tunisian scholars to apply regulation theory include Dimassi, "La crise économique"; Zaiem, "Les forces sociales"; and Ben Hammouda, *Tunisie.*

9. On the politics of decolonization and state building in Tunisia, see Anderson, *State and Social Transformation;* and Hazbun, "Rethinking Anti-colonial Movements."

10. When the Tunisian dinar (TD) was established in December 1958, its value was pegged to the U.S. dollar at a rate of TD 0.42 = US$1. In 1964 the dinar was devalued to TD 0.525 = US$1, which lasted until the end of the gold standard and the devaluation of the U.S. dollar in 1971.

11. Vitalis, "Middle East," 7.

12. Bergaoui, "Des caravanserails," 128–29.

13. Furlough, "Une leçon des choses," 442.

14. See Bergaoui, *Tourisme et voyages en Tunisie,* 51.

15. Ibid., 52.

16. Ibid., 53.

17. Bergaoui, "Des caravanserails," 131.

18. Moudoud, *Modernization,* 152.

19. Group Huit, "Sociocultural Effects," 286.

20. John Ardagh, "Modernity Comes to the Madina," *Washington Post,* November 29, 1964.

21. Williams and Shaw, "Introduction," 4.

22. As Piore and Sabel suggest, "consumption patterns result from the interplay of culture and relative costs" where the consumers' "acceptance [of standardized goods] facilitated the extension of the market and the reduction of prices, through increasing economies of scale; and thus the growing gap between the price of mass-produced goods and that of customized goods further encouraged the clustering of demand around homogeneous products." *The Second Industrial Divide,* 190–91.

23. CNSTT, *L'Evolution du tourisme,* 10.

24. Bergaoui, *Tourisme et voyages en Tunisie,* 88.

25. Ibid.

26. Hamouda, "Quelques aspects economiques."

27. Burkart and Medlik, *Tourism,* 185.

28. Economist Intelligence Unit (EIU), "North Africa," 31.

29. TERPLAN, *How to Plan Tourism?*

30. ONTT, *Realisations du IVème plan,* 14; Sethom, L'Influence de tourisme, 26.

31. Sethom, *L'Industrie et le tourisme,* 158.

32. Bergaoui, *Tourisme et voyages en Tunisie,* 55.

33. Boukraa, *Hammamet,* 87.

34. Jedidi, "L'Expansion du tourise," 155.

35. Bellin, *Stalled Democracy,* 23.

36. N. Hopkins, "Tunisia," 387.

37. See Falise and Masson, "La politique de développement"; Kamelgarn, "Tunisie"; Dimassi and Zaiem, "L'Industrie"; Bellin, "Tunisian Industrialists"; Bellin, "Politics of Profit."

38. Sethom, *L'Influence de tourisme,* 31.

39. Ibid., 26.

40. These real-value figures were calculated from CNSTT, *L'Evolution du tourisme,* 11; ONTT, *Le tourisme Tunisien;* and economic and financial data from the World Bank.

41. Turner, "International Division of Leisure."

42. Fröbel, Heinrichs, and Kreye, *New International Division of Labour;* Lipietz, *Mirages and Miracles.*

43. Burkart and Medlik, *Tourism,* 186–87.

44. Sethom, *L'Influence de tourisme,* 111; Signoles, *L'Espace Tunisien,* 791.

45. Signoles, *L'Espace Tunisien*, 879.

46. William H. Jones, "Tunisia Tourism Target for New Type Aid Plan," *Los Angeles Times*, June 26, 1969.

47. Ibid.

48. Signoles, *L'Espace Tunisien*, 771, 879.

49. United Nations, *Transnational Corporations in International Tourism*.

50. Signoles, *L'Espace Tunisien*, 887.

51. Ibid.

52. Sethom, *L'Influence de tourisme*, 95.

53. Sethom, *L'Industrie et le tourisme*, 218–19.

54. Sethom, *L'Influence de tourisme*, 95–97; Signoles, *L'Espace Tunisien*, 887.

55. Boukraa, *Hammamet*.

56. Findlay, "Tunisia," 233–35; ONTT, *Le tourisme Tunisien*.

57. ONTT, *Le tourisme Tunisien*.

58. Ibid.

59. Poon, *Tourism, Technology, and Competitive Strategies*. The 1973–74 watershed is also generally viewed as the peak of mass production leading to new forms of flexible, post-Fordist as well as neo-Fordist production. See Piore and Sabel, *The Second Industrial Divide*; and Harvey, *The Condition of Postmodernity*.

60. ONTT, *Realisations du IVème plan*, 8.

61. Sethom, *L'Industrie et le tourisme*, 159.

62. Cazes, "Le tourisme international," 96.

63. Signoles, *L'Espace Tunisien*, 892.

64. CNSTT, *L'Evolution du tourisme*, 49, 51.

65. Simon Scott Plummer, "Prices Attractive for Tourist in Country Where Unemployment Is the Main Problem," *Times* (London), December 18, 1974.

66. Referring to the impact of the Arab-Israeli conflict on tourism in Tunisia, some officials also noted that "people still confuse Tunisia with the Middle East" and that the hostage crisis at the 1972 Munich Olympics "had an adverse impact on tourism to the Arab countries." See Joy Gerville-Reache, "Tunisia Wants More Tourists," *Christian Science Monitor*, March 5, 1974.

67. Sethom, *L'Industrie et le tourisme*, 159.

68. Sethom, *L'Influence de tourisme*, 25.

69. Plummer, "Prices Attractive for Tourist"; Mzabi, "Le tourisme en Tunisie," 225.

70. Cazes, "Le tourisme international," 122.

71. UN, *Transnational Corporations in International Tourism*; Cazes, "Le tourisme international," 122–23.

72. EIU, "North Africa," 31, 35.

73. Burkart and Medlik, *Tourism,* 189.

74. EIU, "Tunisia," 25.

75. Wall, *Rural Small Industry,* 74.

76. Löfgren, *On Holiday,* 191.

77. Ibid., 205.

78. Sethom, *L'Influence de tourisme,* 102.

79. ONTT, *Realisations du IVème plan,* 15; Tunisian Secretariat of State for Information, *Tunisia Moves Ahead,* 194.

80. Evans, "Foreign Capital," 315. See also Evans, *Dependent Development.*

81. Bellin, *Stalled Democracy,* 25.

82. Tunisian Secretariat of State for Information, *Tunisia Moves Ahead,* 196.

83. ONTT, *Organisation et fonctionnement.*

84. ONTT, *Realisations du IVème plan,* 21.

85. *L'Officiel du tourisme en Tunisie,* 255–60.

86. J. Scott, *Seeing like a State.*

87. See Buck-Morss, "Envisioning Capital."

88. Tunisian Secretariat of State for Information, *Tunisia Moves Ahead,* 196.

89. Joy Gerville-Reache, "Tunisia Wants More Tourists," *Christian Science Monitor,* March 5, 1974.

90. ONTT, *Realisations du IVème plan,* 31; Signoles, *L'Espace Tunisien,* 794.

91. Jedidi, "L'Expansion du tourise," 157. After 1973 the Tunisian dinar was subject to a managed float. It was valued at TD 0.777 = US$1 before it was devalued in 1986 to TD 0.86 = US$1.

92. ONTT, *Realisations du IVème plan,* 20.

93. Miossec, "La croissance du tourisme," 174.

94. Sethom, *L'Influence de tourisme,* 38.

95. ONTT, *Realisations du IVème plan,* 24–25.

96. EIU, "North Africa," 34.

97. Signoles, *L'Espace Tunisien,* 862.

98. Sethom, *L'Industrie et le tourisme,* 158.

99. Signoles, *L'Espace Tunisien,* 793; Jedidi, "L'Expansion du tourise," 157.

100. Signoles, *L'Espace Tunisien,* 793.

101. ONTT, *Realisations du IVème plan,* 26.

102. "Comment construit un hôtel," *Information Touristique,* March 1990, 34.

103. ONTT, *Realisations du IVème plan,* 28–30. See also Smaoui, "Tourism and Employment."

104. Sethom, *L'Influence de tourisme,* 148.

105. Tunisian Secretariat of State for Information, *Tunisia Moves Ahead,* 192.

106. Jedidi, "L'Expansion du tourise," 156.

107. EIU, "Tunisia," 38.

108. Scott, *Seeing like a State,* 58.

109. Ibid., 59.

110. M. Chadli Ayari, quoted in *La Presse de Tunisie,* December 19, 1972; cited in Signoles, *L'Espace Tunisien,* 797.

111. These figures are calculated from Group Huit, "Sociocultural Effects," 292; Smaoui, "Tourism and Employment," 106; Cazes, "Le tourisme international," 90; ONTT, *Le tourisme Tunisien;* and economic and financial data from the World Bank.

112. Smaoui, "Tourism and Employment," 109.

113. Group Huit, "Sociocultural Effects," 302.

114. Ibid., 298.

115. EIU, "North Africa," *International Tourism Quarterly,* no. 2 (1977): 31.

116. ONTT, *Le tourisme Tunisien.*

117. Signoles, *L'Espace Tunisien,* 889.

118. These real-value figures were calculated from ONTT, *Le tourisme Tunisien;* and economic and financial data from the World Bank.

119. Sampson, *Empires of the Sky,* 160.

120. Sethom, *L'Industrie et le tourisme,* 219.

121. Ibid., 220.

122. Ibid., 221–23.

123. Calculated from ONTT, *Le tourisme Tunisien;* and economic and financial data from the World Bank.

124. Group Huit, "Sociocultural Effects," 298.

125. Ibid., 299.

126. Ibid.

127. Ibid.

128. Jedidi, "L'Expansion du tourise," 168.

129. Pearce, *Tourist Development,* 270–76; Furlough and Wakeman, "La Grande Motte."

130. Cazes, "Le tourisme international," 144.

131. Sharp, "Port El Kantaoui," 94.

132. Cazes, "Le tourisme international," 144.

133. Sethom, *L'Industrie et le tourisme,* 323.

134. Huxley, "Development in Hamman Sousse," 144; Sethom, *L'Industrie et le tourisme,* 577.

135. *L'Officiel du tourisme en Tunisie,* 124.

136. Sharp, "Port El Kantaoui," 89.

137. Ibid., 95.

138. Ibid., 90.

139. Ibid., 89.

140. "Tourism Faces Major Changes: The Industry Must Move Up-Market to Continue to Attract Holiday Makers," *Financial Times,* March 16, 1984; Sethom, *L'Industrie et le tourisme,* 577.

141. Sharp, "Port El Kantaoui," 93.

142. Morris and Jacobs, *Tunisia: The Rough Guide,* 182.

143. James Holloway, "Popularity Grows for Garden Resort," *Courier-Mail* (Queensland, Australia), October 8, 1988.

144. "Tourism Faces Major Changes," *Financial Times,* March 16, 1984.

2. Images of Openness, Spaces of Control

1. Edwards, "Tunisia: Sea, Sand, Success."

2. Moore, "Tunisia and Bourguibisme"; Dimassi, "La crise économique."

3. See, for example, Friedman, *Lexus and the Olive Tree.*

4. World Bank, *World Tables* (1991), 584–87.

5. Grissa, "Tunisian State Enterprises," 112.

6. See Fröbel, Heinrichs, and Kreye, *New International Division of Labour.*

7. Hamil, *Mediterranean Textiles and Clothings,* 101–2.

8. Ibid.; Signoles, *L'Espace Tunisien.*

9. Hamil, "Multinational Activity," 103.

10. Ibid.

11. Ben Hammouda, *Tunisie;* Ben Hammouda, "Globalization et crise."

12. Hamil, *Mediterranean Textiles and Clothings,* 144; Ben Hammouda, *Tunisie,* 175.

13. Moudoud, "Les stratégies"; Mody and Wheeler, *Automation and World Competition,* 25–65.

14. Ben Hammouda, "Globalization et crise"; Signoles, *L'Espace Tunisien.*

15. Moudoud, *Modernization;* Signoles, *L'Espace Tunisien,* 900.

16. See Belhedi, *Societe, espace, et developpement.*

17. Findlay, "Tunisia," 229.

18. Seddon, "Riot and Rebellion," 125.

19. Vasile, "Re-turning Home"; Charmes, "Secteur non structuré"; Lobban, "Responding."

20. Francis Ghiles, "An Unofficial Safety Valve," *Financial Times,* July 27, 1990.

21. On the notion of social contracts as a basis for authoritarian state building, see Waterbury, "From Social Contracts."

22. Vasile, "Devotion as Distinction."

23. See Paul, "States of Emergency," 3–6.

24. See Seddon, "Winter of Discontent."

25. Seddon, "Riot and Rebellion," 124.

26. Ian Black, "Tunisian Hopes Could Lead to Trouble," *Guardian,* June 25, 1986.

27. Bedoui, "Analyse de la dynamique sociale."

28. Francis Ghiles, "Tourism Helps Fill Oil Gap," *Financial Times,* November 12, 1985.

29. Ministere de L'Economie Nationale, *VIème Plan,* 2.

30. Harik, "Privatization and Development," 216.

31. Perkins, *History of Modern Tunisia,* 171.

32. ONTT, *Le VIIème Plan,* 1–2.

33. Lash and Urry, *Economies of Signs and Space;* Piore and Sabel, *The Second Industrial Divide;* Harvey, *The Condition of Postmodernity.*

34. Jenner and Smith, *Tourism in the Mediterranean,* 10.

35. Poon, *Tourism, Technology, and Competitive Strategies,* 124–25.

36. Ibid., 64–65.

37. Lash and Urry, *Economies of Signs and Space,* 269–77.

38. John Harlow, "Tour Firms to Axe Million Cheap Holidays," *Daily Telegraph,* August 31, 1989; Michael Elliott, "Travel and Tourism Survey," *Economist,* March 23, 1991.

39. See Morgan, "Homogeneous Products."

40. Harlow, "Tour Firms to Axe"; Elliott, "Travel and Tourism Survey."

41. Ministere de L'Economie Nationale, *VIème Plan,* 1.

42. Francis Ghiles, "Tunisia: Decline of the Dinar Benefits Visitors from Europe," *Financial Times,* November 2, 1987.

43. ONTT, *Le VIIème Plan,* 9.

44. Susan Macdonald, "Tunisians Face Dilemma over Double Standards, Tourist Industry," *Times* (London), August 29, 1988.

45. Waltz, "Islamist Appeal in Tunisia," 668–69.

46. Abderrazak, "Aspect socio-cultural." See also Nouri Bouzid's film *Bezness* (1992), which boldly addresses issues of prostitution, homosexuality, and AIDS within the social milieu of Tunisia's tourism industry. See Menicucci, "Review of *Bezness.*"

47. See Nigel Disney, "Review of *Hyena's Sun,*" 22.

48. Boukraa, *Hammamet;* Sethom, *L'Influence de tourisme;* Sethom, *L'Industrie et le tourisme.*

49. Anderson, "Prospects for Liberalism," 133.

50. Esposito and Voll, *Makers of Contemporary Islam,* 106.

51. Rached Ghannoushi, "IntraView: With Tunisian Sheikh Rached Ghannoushi," February 10, 1998, http://web.archive.org/web/20011116142927/http://msanews.mynet.net/intra2.html.

52. Pranay B. Gupte, "Moslem Militants Worrying Tunisia," *New York Times,* November 11, 1981.

53. Henry Kamm, "Islamic Group Claims Role in Tunis Riot," *New York Times,* January 9, 1984. Note, however, that Ghannouchi's own view contrasts with the perspective of Gamma Islamiyya, the militant movement in Egypt responsible for the wave of attacks against tourists, and with that of some extremists at the edge of the Tunisian Islamist movement. For example, Ghannouchi notes that Islam does not call for a closed society or for imposing its ethical norms on others. He once stated in a column for the French newsweekly *Jeune Afrique* that if he were president, he would not forbid alcohol and ban topless beaches in places like the tourist resort of Hammamet. See Ghannoushi, "IntraView."

54. On the rise of the Islamist movement and activities in the 1980s, see Waltz, "Islamist Appeal in Tunisia"; N. Salem, "Tunisia"; Burgat and Dowell, *Islamic Movement in North Africa;* Shahin, *Political Assent;* Hamdi, *The Politicisation of Islam.*

55. "Tourism Faces Major Changes: The Industry Must Move Up-Market to Continue to Attract Holiday Makers," *Financial Times,* March 16, 1984.

56. Hamdi, *The Politicisation of Islam,* 52.

57. *Le Monde,* August 12, 1987.

58. Simon Ingram, "Tunisian Bomber Hanged," *Guardian,* October 9, 1987.

59. *Le Monde,* August 13, 1987; *Le Monde,* August 19, 1987.

60. Richard H. Curtiss, "Justice Minister Describes Tunisia's Battle against Islamist Takeover," *Washington Report on Middle East Affairs,* November–December 1996.

61. Hamdi, *The Politicisation of Islam,* 53.

62. Michael Collins Dunn, "Tunisia: Untold Story from the Arab World," *Los Angeles Times,* August 28, 1988.

63. ONTT, *Le VIIème Plan,* 14.

64. Unless otherwise noted, all tourism data related to Tunisia are gathered from Office National du Tourisme Tunisien (ONTT), *Le tourisme Tunisien en chiffres,* and from the ONTT Web site, http://www.tunisietourisme.com.tn/professionnels-e/stat.htm.

65. Murphy, *Economic and Political Change,* 106, 114–15.

66. Ministere du Tourisme et de L'Artisanat, *VIIIème Plan,* 11.

67. M. Hopkins, *Tunisia to 1993,* 72.

68. EIU, "Tunisia and Malta," *EIU Country Report,* no. 2 (1987): 26.

69. EIU, "Tunisia," *EIU Country Report,* no. 2 (1988): 17.

70. EIU, "Tunisia," *International Tourism Report* 4 (October 1988): 37.

71. Harik, "Privatization and Development," 217.

72. Mohamed Jegham, closing remarks at "Le Tourism Tunisien Face aux Défis de l'An 2000," a colloquium sponsored by Centre de Recheres

et d'Études Adminstratives and *Information Touristique,* May 19, 1989, Tunis, 46–47.

73. Ibid.

74. Hédi Mechri, "Les commentaires du rédacteur," *Réalités* (Tunis), July 7, 1989.

75. Hédi Mechri, "Tourisme Tunisien: Un choix irréverible," *Réalités* (Tunis), July 7, 1989.

76. World Tourism Organization (UNWTO), *Yearbook of Tourism Statistics.* Figure for tourism receipts is in nominal U.S. dollars.

77. Saihi, "La Tunisie," 7.

78. Ministere du Tourisme et de L'Artisanat, *VIIIème Plan,* 38.

79. Tunisian External Communication Agency, *Tunisia, 1992–1996,* 22.

80. Cited in Testas, "Contribution of EU Investment," 23.

81. Murphy, "Economic Reform," 142.

82. World Bank, *Tunisia's Global Integration,* xiii.

83. King, "Political Logic," 120.

84. Dillman, "Facing the Market," 204.

85. See Roula Khalaf, "Franchises: Long Wait for Fast Food," *Financial Times,* September 22, 1997; and U.S. Department of Commerce, *Doing Business in Tunisia.* Thomas Friedman seems to have missed this fact, suggesting that only "rogue states" such as Syria, Iran, and Iraq have so deprived themselves. See Friedman, *Lexus and the Olive Tree,* 195.

86. Henry, *Challenges of Global Capital.* On the government's control and monitoring of Internet use, see Human Rights Watch, *False Freedom.*

87. Denoeux, "La Tunisie de Ben Ali," 48; Zamiti, "Le fonds."

88. November 12 would later become the "National Day of Saharan Tourism."

89. See "Développement touristique régional: Le soleil brille pour tous," *Tourisme Info* (Tunis), no. 22 (November 16–30, 1998).

90. Ministere du Tourisme et de L'Artisanat, *VIIIème Plan,* 67.

91. Bleasdale and Tapsell, "Saharan Tourism," 29.

92. Tunisian National Tourism Office, "Tunisia: The Oases," pamphlet.

93. Ministere du Tourisme et de L'Artisanat, *VIIIème Plan,* 67.

94. Gant and Smith, "Tourism and National Development," 335.

95. Bleasdale and Tapsell, "Saharan Tourism," 31; Mohamed Aziz Tajina, "Le tourisme Saharien," 169–70.

96. Tajina, "Le tourisme Saharien," 148–51.

97. Bleasdale and Tapsell, "Saharan Tourism," 44.

98. Tajina, "Le tourisme Saharien," 173.

99. Gant and Smith, "Tourism and National Development," 335.

100. Bleasdale and Tapsell, "Saharan Tourism," 44–45.

101. "Sahara: Oasis et sable," *Tourisme Info* (Tunis), no. 23 (December 1–15, 1998).

102. Bleasdale and Tapsell, "Saharan Tourism," 37.

103. Anver Versi, "Destination Made in Heaven," *Middle East,* March 1999.

104. As cited in Versi, "Destination Made in Heaven."

105. See Claude Llena, "Tozeur, ravagée par le tourisme," *Le Monde Diplomatique,* July 2004. In contrast to the uncritical accounts typically found in outlets such as the *Middle East,* travel magazines or newspaper travel sections (not to mention the sponsored sections of the *International Herald Tribune*), Llena presents a devastating picture of the impact of tourism on the local society and environment. He notes, for example, that the tourism industry's demand for water has commercialized it, making access to the resource expensive for many local farmers.

106. See *Profession Tourisme* (Tunis), no. 53 (April 15, 1997).

107. See Guillemette Mansour, "Du cinéma au tourisme: 'Le Patient Anglais': Dans le sillage d'un grand film," *Profession Tourisme* (Tunis), no. 53 (April 15, 1997): 21–23.

108. This case study is presented in "Integrated: Tunisia," *Marketing,* September 10, 1998.

109. Many devoted fans travel as adventure archaeologists to "dig" up remnants of the "past." See the report of the first archaeological field survey of the shooting of *Star Wars* in Tunisia, David West Reynolds, "Return to Tatooine," *The Insider* (The Star Wars Fan Club magazine), no. 27 (December 1995), 68–74. See also Andrew Smith, "Archeologist Digs 'Star Wars,' Turns Up Trove for Fans," *Commercial Appeal* (Memphis, Tenn.), September 5, 1999.

110. Jon Levy, "Seen the Movie Now Visit Tunisia and Buy the Props," *Daily Telegraph,* July 24, 1999.

111. Cited in Mark Huband, "Industry Shifting Focus to Quality," *Financial Times,* September 22, 1997.

112. Lash and Urry, *Economies of Signs and Space,* 274; Poon, *Tourism, Technology, and Competitive Strategies.*

113. Torres, "Cancun's Tourism Development."

114. Mitchell, "Worlds Apart," 10.

115. Mahmoud Hosni, "Tourisme: Le nord-ouest devrait se prendre en charge," *La Presse de Tunisie,* June 16, 1997. See also Kagermeier, "Le développement"; and Kagermeier, "New Touristic Centres."

116. See "Le Palace-Gammarth: À la recherche du produit complete," *Profession Tourisme* (Tunis), no. 45 (December 15, 1996): 18; EIU, "Tunisia," *EIU Country Report,* 3rd quarter 1995, 21; EIU, "Tunisia," *EIU Country Report,* 1st quarter 1996; EIU, "Tunisia," *EIU Country Report,* January 2001, 29; EIU, "Tunisia," *EIU Country Report,* January 1, 2006.

117. Sophie Bessis, "Carthage's Long-Awaited Rescue," *UNESCO Courier,* September 1999.

118. Isabel Choat, "Tunisia: Charme Offensive," *Guardian,* June 19, 2004.

119. See "Grand recontre sur la commercialisation de produit tunisien en septembre," *La Presse de Tunisie,* June 7, 1997.

120. M'hamed Jaibi, "Hammamet-Sud, la marina: C'est parti!" *La Presse de Tunisie,* May 12, 1997; "Le nouveau joyau de Hammamet Sud," *Tourisme Info* (Tunis), no. 18 (September 1997): 23; and EIU, "Tunisia," *EIU Country Report,* 3rd quarter 1994, 18.

121. Adrian Mourby, "Artists and Millionaires Once Flocked to Hammamet," *Independent* (London), December 10, 2000.

122. See Mark Huband, "Industry Shifting Focus to Quality," *Financial Times,* September 22, 1997.

123. Raymond Matar, "Le Casino–Le Médina," *L'Eonomist Maghrébin* (Tunis), no. 366 (2004).

124. Ridha Lahmar, "La Médina de Yasmine-Hammamet," *Réalités* (Tunis), October 7, 1999.

125. "Cartes sur table avec M. Abdelwahab Ben Ayed, Président du Groupe POULINA," *Réalités* (Tunis), February 19, 2004.

126. Joel Stratte-McClure, "Protecting and Enhancing the Cultural Legacy," *International Herald Tribune,* November 25, 1999. See also Khalaf, "Franchises," *Financial Times,* September 22, 1997.

127. Association Sauvegarde de la Medina, *Projects et Realisation.*

128. World Bank, "Project Appraisal Document," 4.

129. Fawzia Zouari, "Cap sur la culture," *Jeune Afrique,* June 11, 2006.

130. Leslie Plommer, "Hannibal Revived as Tunisia's New Mascot," *Guardian,* April 11, 1997.

131. World Bank, "Project Appraisal Document," 22.

132. Nora Boustany, "Punic Partnership," *Washington Post,* January 28, 1998.

133. See Memmi, "Jews, Tunisians, and Frenchmen."

134. Michael Widlanski, "Tunis Invites Jews to Return," *Jerusalem Post,* August 25, 1993.

135. See Christopher Hitchens, "At the Desert's Edge," *Vanity Fair,* July 2007; Geyer, *Tunisia;* and Anver Versi, "Tunisia: Special Report, Celebrating 45 Dynamic Years," *New African,* March 2001.

136. Hitchens, "At the Desert's Edge." All the following unattributed quotes are drawn from this essay.

137. Calculated from IMF, *Tunisia: Recent Economic Developments;* ONTT, *Le tourisme Tunisien en chiffres;* World Bank, *World Tables.*

138. Denoeux, "La Tunisie," 34–35.

139. "Tunisia: Behind the Beaches," *Economist,* January 13, 1996.

140. See Chaabane, *Ben Ali.*

141. Cassarino, "EU-Tunisian Association Agreement," 65.

142. Ibid., 71.

143. Ibid., 69.

144. Bellin, *Stalled Democracy*.

145. "Tunisia: Under the Shadow," *Economist,* April 15, 2000, 41.

146. Susan Hack, "Desert Bloom," *Condé Nast Traveler,* January 2007, 230.

147. Hitchens, "At the Desert's Edge."

3. The Geopolitics of Tourism and the Making of the New Middle East

1. See Khalaf, *Civil and Uncivil Violence,* 196–203.

2. See Dana Adams Smith, "'If' Key Word to Mideast Tourist Rise," *New York Times,* February 22, 1970; "Jordan's Royal Airline Fighting Syrian Blockade," *New York Times,* December 26, 1971.

3. Smith, "'If' Key Word to Mideast Tourist Rise."

4. Blyth, *Great Transformations,* 37.

5. For efforts to modify neorealism to explain the behavior of Third World states, see S. David, "Explaining Third World Alignment"; and Ayoob, "Subaltern Realism."

6. Lynch, *State Interests;* Lynch, "Jordan's Identity and Interests."

7. Burckhardt, *Travels in Syria,* 418–34.

8. Brendon, *Thomas Cook,* 252–53.

9. Shoup, "Impact of Tourism," 280.

10. Brand, "In the Beginning," 158, 159.

11. Katz, "Holy Places."

12. Gendzier, *Notes from the Minefield,* 104; AeroTransport Data Bank, "Profile for Air Jordan" (2006), http://www.aerotransport.org/php/go.php?query=operator&luck=1&where=43952.

13. USAID, "Jordan 1993 Tourism Strategy," 1.

14. Kovach, *A Tourism Plan of Action for Jordan,* 22, 10.

15. Odeh, *Economic Development in Jordan,* appendix.

16. Ibid.

17. Hussein ibn Talal, *Uneasy Lies the Head,* 280.

18. Pascoe, *Airspaces,* 186–88. See also Khaled, *My People Shall Live.*

19. "Jordan's Royal Airline Fighting Syrian Blockade," *New York Times,* December 26, 1971, 46.

20. World Bank, *World Tables;* Brand, *Jordan's Inter-Arab Relations;* Central Bank of Jordan, *Yearly Statistical Series (1964–1993),* 28–31.

21. Day, *Troubles on the East Bank,* 102.

22. EIU, "Jordan," *International Tourism Report,* no. 3 (1987): 45.

23. Ibid., 46.

24. Ibid.

25. M. Gray, "Development Strategies."

26. Massad, *Colonial Effects,* 74. See also Layne, *Home and Homeland.*

27. Maffi, "De l'usage de l'histoire," 94.

28. B. Anderson, *Imagined Communities,* 164.

29. This problem is similar to the one addressed by postwar development economics in considering the challenge of "traditional" economies trying to escape from low-productivity, low-income-equilibrium traps. See Hirschman, "Rise and Decline"; and Sabel, "Learning by Monitoring."

30. Fahd Fanik, "Tourism to Jordan Takes a Beating," *Jordan Times,* July 8, 1984.

31. Ibid.

32. Pannell Kerr Forester, *Future Course of Tourism,* II-2.

33. Ibid., I-1.

34. Ibid., VII-1.

35. Satloff, *Troubles on the East Bank,* 20; Brand, *Jordan's Inter-Arab Relations,* 110–12.

36. World Bank, *World Tables;* Brand, *Jordan's Inter-Arab Relations;* Central Bank of Jordan, *Yearly Statistical Series (1964–1993),* 28–31.

37. Winckler, "Economic Factor," 163.

38. Brynen, "Economic Crisis," 88; Piro, *Political Economy,* 89. By 1989 the dinar would be pegged to the U.S. dollar at the rate of JD 1 = $1.85, having fallen from a rate of JD 1 = $2.65.

39. Satloff, "Jordan's Great Gamble," 138.

40. Brynen, "Politics of Monarchical Liberalism"; Mufti, "Elite Bargains."

41. Brand, "Economic and Political Liberalization"; Brynen, "Economic Crisis."

42. See Lucas, *Institutions.*

43. Brand, *Jordan's Inter-Arab Relations,* 291.

44. USAID, "Jordan 1993 Tourism Strategy," 7.

45. Lisa Fliegel, "In Search of a Jordanian Architectural Style," *New Middle East Magazine,* June–July 1994.

46. EIU, "Jordan," *International Tourism Report,* no. 3 (1992): 25.

47. M. Gray, "Development Strategies," 313.

48. Ibid., 314.

49. On the origin of this name, see Hammond, "Petra: Myth and Reality."

50. Brand, "Liberalization"; Harknett and VanDenBerg, "Alignment Theory"; Mufti, "Jordanian Foreign Policy," 23–31; Lynch, *State Interests,* 140–65.

51. M. Gray, "Development Strategies," 314.

52. Cited but contested in Clawson and Rosen, *Economic Consequences of Peace,* 28.

53. Richter, *Politics of Tourism,* 6.

54. Stock, "Political and Social Contributions," 34–35; Richter, *Politics of Tourism,* 6–7.

55. Hisham Awartani, "Palestinian-Israeli Economic Relations," 295.

56. Mansfeld, "Acquired Tourism Deficiency Syndrome," 162.

57. Ibid., 169.

58. "Notes from the Field of Travel," *New York Times,* December 7, 1969.

59. In her review of Dani Rabinowitz's *Ru'ah Sinai* (The Sinai Spirit), Lavie argues, "Rabinowitz betrays a peculiar tendency to confuse Bedouin culture with nature," folding representations of the local population and its culture into experiences of the material landscape. Lavie, "Sinai for the Coffee Table," 41.

60. Dan Rabinowitz, "A Formative Attack," *haaretz.com,* October 10, 2004. See also "A Disputed Slice of Sinai," *New York Times,* September 23, 1986.

61. Noy and Cohen, "Introduction," 10.

62. Dov Janhovski and Gideon Eiset, "Economic Consequences of Camp David," *Yediot Aharonot,* September 19, 1978; reprinted in *Journal of Palestine Studies* 8, no. 2 (Winter 1979): 156.

63. See Cord Hasen-Sturm's testimony to Congress in Richter, *Politics of Tourism,* 7.

64. "Israeli-Egyptian Talks Leave Some Tourism Related Issues Unsettled," *New York Times,* September 19, 1981.

65. Christopher W. Wren, "Distrust Mars Egyptian-Israeli Ties More than a Year after the Pact," *New York Times,* August 18, 1980.

66. Ibid.

67. Thomas L. Friedman, "Israel in Accord on Arbitration in Land Dispute," *New York Times,* January 13, 1986. See also Ding and Koenig, "Boundary Dispute"; and Kemp and Ben-Eliezer, "Dramatizing Sovereignty," 332–34.

68. Kemp and Ben-Eliezer, "Dramatizing Sovereignty," 321.

69. Lesch, "The Egyptian-Israel Accord," 99; Kemp and Ben-Eliezer, "Dramatizing Sovereignty," 321.

70. Kemp and Ben-Eliezer, "Dramatizing Sovereignty," 321–22.

71. Lesch, "The Egyptian-Israel Accord," 100.

72. Joel Brinkley, "A Sandy Corner of Egypt Sadly Misses Its Israelis," *New York Times,* February 28, 1990.

73. Dan Fisher, "Israel Test of Arab Position," *Los Angeles Times,* December 14, 1984.

74. Kemp and Ben-Eliezer; "Dramatizing Sovereignty," 340.

75. Beinin, "The Cold Peace," 3–5.

76. Meital, "Economic Relations," 288.

77. Ibid., 293.

78. Fineberg notes: "The Egyptian Government required that their citizens undergo a screening process before being allowed to go to Israel in an attempt to restrict the movement of elements wishing to attack Israeli interests. Tourism representatives in Egypt now, however, feel that the screening process tends to discourage Egyptians from going to Israel." Fineberg, "Regional Cooperation," 2. Egyptian officials also note that Israel does not possess tourist attractions that interest Egyptians, except for those that Egyptians consider under occupation, such as the holy sites in East Jerusalem. See Meital, "Economic Relations," 294.

79. David K. Shipler, "Egypt-Israel Tourism: Mostly One-Way," *New York Times,* March 15, 1981. The air service was later renamed Air Sinai.

80. Kemp and Ben-Eliezer, "Dramatizing Sovereignty," 326.

81. See Ding and Koenig, "Boundary Dispute."

82. Gideon Rafael, "Taba—Bridge or Barrier?" *Jerusalem Post,* January 27, 1989. The left-wing Israeli politician Shulamit Aloni advocated the joint development of Taba into a tourism-for-peace enclave that would eliminate the need to define specific national borderlines. See Kemp and Ben-Eliezer, "Dramatizing Sovereignty," 326.

83. Rabinowitz, "A Formative Attack."

84. Ibid.

85. Majali, Anani, and Haddadin, *Peacemaking,* 128–29.

86. Kaye, *Beyond the Handshake,* 53.

87. Anani, "Cooperation," 121–25.

88. Yadgar, "A Myth of Peace," 299.

89. Leslie Susser, "Peres's Grand Design," *Jerusalem Report,* May 6, 1993.

90. Ibid.

91. Peres, *The New Middle East.* See also Yadgar, "A Myth of Peace."

92. Peres, *The New Middle East,* 108.

93. As cited in Goldstone, *Making the World Safe for Tourism,* 155.

94. Nsour, "Arab-Israeli Economic Relations."

95. Shafir and Peled, "Peace and Profits"; Ben-Porat, "Business and Peace." For a reading of rival Israeli geopolitical imaginaries, see Newman, "Citizenship, Identity, and Location."

96. As cited in Twite and Baskin, *The Conversion of Dreams,* 23.

97. Ibid., 24.

98. Peres, *The New Middle East,* 149; see also 50–53.

99. Ibid., 74.

100. Peres, *Battling for Peace,* 199.

101. As cited in Drake, "Arab-Israeli Relations," 21.

102. Peres, *The New Middle East,* 74 (italics mine).

103. Ibid., 151 (italics mine).

104. Sarah Helm, "Profits Beckon in the Holy Land," *Independent* (London), July 17, 1994.

105. Clawson, "Tourism Cooperation" (italics mine).

106. USAID, "Jordan 1993 Tourism Strategy," 1.

107. Al Khouri, "Intra-regional Business Facilitation," 127.

108. Winckler and Gilbar, "Development of the Tourism Industry."

109. "Remarks of Fayez Tarawneh, Jordanian Ambassador to the U.S., at the American Jewish Committee's Ambassador's Forum," *Federal News Service*, November 2, 1993.

110. Ross, *The Missing Peace*, 167.

111. Brand, *Jordan's Inter-Arab Relations*, 26. See also pp. 295–97; as well as Zunes, "The Israeli-Jordanian Agreement"; and Ryan, "Jordan in the Middle East Peace Process."

112. Stephanie Genkin, "The Billing of Peace," *Jerusalem Report*, September 8, 1994.

113. Ibid.

114. Ross, *The Missing Peace*, 171.

115. Ibid., 169.

116. See, for example, the remarks of U.S. secretary of state Warren Christopher at the Royal Palace, Casablanca, October 30, 1994, "Building the Structures of Peace and Prosperity in the New Middle East." Christopher, *In the Stream of History*, 207–12.

117. See Elaine Sciolino, "The Mideast Accord: The Impact," *New York Times*, July 26, 1994.

118. Satloff, "The Path to Peace," 109.

119. As reprinted in Majali, Anani, and Haddadin, *Peacemaking*, 337.

120. Ibid.

121. Lynch, *State Interests*, 180.

122. *Jordan Times*, October 28, 1995; cited in Beal, "Consumerism," 204.

123. Winckler, "Economic Factor," 165, 168.

124. Lynch, *State Interests*, 179.

125. As quoted in Mark Power-Stevens, "Overt Tension as Jordan Faces Up to a New Era," *Middle East International*, July 21, 1995; cited in Astorino-Courtois, "Transforming International Agreements," 1043.

126. Speech to the Senate on November 9, 1994, cited in Astorino-Courtois, "Transforming International Agreements," 1043.

127. Cited in Isabel Kershner, "The Fruits of Stability," *Jerusalem Report*, November 2, 1995.

128. Susser, "Jordan," in *Middle East Contemporary Survey*, vol. 19, *1995*, 391.

129. Ibid., 390.

130. Astorino-Courtois, "Transforming International Agreements," 1043.

131. Lucas, *Institutions,* 94.

132. Hassan Bin Talal, "Jordan and the Peace Process," 39. See also World Bank, *Peace and the Jordanian Economy.*

133. Hassan Bin Talal, "Jordan and the Peace Process," 39.

134. Reported in the *Federal News Service,* September 26, 1994. This quote does not appear in the transcript reprinted in Hassan Bin Talal, "Jordan and the Peace Process."

135. Lucas, *Institutions,* 72.

136. Brand, "Effects"; Lynch, *State Interests;* Lucas, *Institutions.*

137. Lynch, *State Interests.*

138. Ryan, "Jordan in the Middle East Peace Process," 168.

139. "Jordan, Charging Ahead of His People," *Economist,* December 16, 1995.

140. *BBC Summary of World Broadcasts,* November 25, 1993.

141. Warren Christopher, "Address by Secretary of State Christopher at the Opening of the U.S.-Israel-Jordan Trilateral Economic Committee at the Dead Sea, July 20, 1994," http://www.mfa.gov.il/MFA/Foreign%20Relations/Israels%20Foreign%20Relations%20since%201947/1992-1994/207%20Addresses%20by%20Secretary%20of%20State%20Christopher-%20P.

142. Ross, *The Missing Peace,* 185.

143. Dan Perry, "First Israelis Find Two Jordans—One Welcoming, Other Foreboding," *Associated Press,* November 19, 1994.

144. Genkin, "The Billing of Peace."

145. Lamia Lahoud, "Jordan Business Community Welcomes Economic Ties with Israel," *Jerusalem Post,* July 31, 1994.

146. Helm, "Profits Beckon."

147. UNESCO/SECA, "Jordan: Petra National Park Management Plan."

148. Radio Jordan broadcast in English, August 17, 1994, transcribed in *BBC Summary of World Broadcasts,* August 19, 1994.

149. Christopher, *In the Stream of History,* 197.

150. Ibid., 200.

151. Majali, Anani, and Haddadin, *Peacemaking,* 305.

152. Ibid.

153. Winckler and Gilbar, "Development of the Tourism Industry," 191–93.

154. USAID, "Tourism Marketing Strategy," i.

155. Chemonics, "Jordan Sustainable Tourism." See also US/ICOMOS, "Management Analysis."

156. Christopher, *In the Stream of History,* 204.

157. Ibid., 209. For a list of projects, see "Projects of Peace," *Middle East Economic Digest,* November 25, 1994.

158. John Rossant et al., "The Peace Dividend for Israel and Jordan," *Business Week,* August 8, 1994.

159. Christopher, *In the Stream of History,* 212.

160. Ibid., 203.

161. See U.S. Department of State, "Fact Sheet."

162. Ibid.

163. Christopher, *In the Stream of History,* 500.

164. Beal, "Consumerism," 219.

165. See the Hashemite Kingdom of Jordan, *Tourism Infrastructure;* and Industrial Promotion Corporation, "Investment Promotion Law," law no. 16 for the year 1995, regulation no. 1 of 1996, and regulation no. 2 of 1996.

166. *Jordan Times,* October 1, 1995; cited in Beal, "Consumerism," 225.

167. U.S.-Israel-Jordan Trilateral Economic Committee, "Summary Report of the U.S.-Israel-Jordan Trilateral Economic Committee, July 20–21, 1994" (1994), http://www.mfa.gov.il/MFA/Foreign%20Relations/ Israels%20Foreign%20Relations%20since%201947/1992-1994/209%20 Summary%20Report%20of%20the%20US-Israel-Jordan%20Trilate.

168. Hashemite Kingdom of Jordan, *Jordan's Development Showcases.*

169. Pamela Dougherty, "Special Report: Amman Summit," *Middle East Economic Digest,* October 27, 1995, 9.

170. Ibid.; Hashemite Kingdom of Jordan, *Jordan's Development Showcases.*

171. Hashemite Kingdom of Jordan, *Tourism Infrastructure,* 3.

172. Hashemite Kingdom of Jordan, *Dead Sea Tourist Area.*

173. Hashemite Kingdom of Jordan, *Jordan: A Winning Business Destination.*

174. Moshe Kohn, "Concepts of Regionalism," *Jerusalem Post,* October 28, 1994.

175. Government of Israel, "Chapter 7: Tourism Development Options"; Ministry of Foreign Affairs Israel, "The Jordan Rift Valley—Tourism" (1997), http://www.mfa.gov.il/MFA/Peace%20Process/ Regional%20Projects/Jordan%20Rift%20Valley-%20Tourism.

176. Hashemite Kingdom of Jordan, *Jordan: A Winning Business Destination,* 21.

177. Stein, "Itineraries of Peace," 16.

178. In contrast, some thirty-five years before, it was only in the course of hijacking a TWA flight out of Rome that the PFLP member Leila Khaled gained a similar experience by directing the captain to fly a seven-minute tour of her "fatherland" before landing in Damascus. Khaled, *My People Shall Live,* 141–44.

179. M. Gray, "Development Strategies," 321.

180. EIU, "Jordan," *EIU Country Report,* 3rd quarter 1996, 17.

181. Gradus, "Is Eilat-Aqaba a Bi-national City?" 90.

182. Israel, "Chapter 7: Tourism Development Options," 8–11.

183. John Lancaster, "With Peace, Israel and Arabs Plan a Tourist Paradise on Sinai Coast," *Washington Post,* November 14, 1994; Israel, "Chapter 7: Tourism Development Options," 9.

184. EcoPeace, "The Gulf of Aqaba."

185. Tourism statistics were gathered from the Ministry of Tourism and Antiquities, Statistical Section. Figures have been rounded off.

186. See Sciolino, "The Mideast Accord: The Impact," *New York Times,* July 26, 1994.

187. See Stein, "First Contact." On the history of Israelis who illegally ventured across the border to visit Petra before the peace treaty, see Serge Schmemann, "Through the Gorge to Petra," *New York Times,* February 11, 1996; and Massad, *Colonial Effects,* 295.

188. MOTA/Dar Al-Handasah, *Petra Priority Action Plan Study: Phase One Report,* 4–7.

189. Oliver Bennett, "Travel: No Room at Petra's Inns," *Daily Telegraph,* July 15, 1995.

190. Seamus O'Loughlin and Gerard Greene, "Middle East Hotels—Trends and Opportunities," HVS International report, 2000 edition, http://www.hvs.com.

191. Ehud Ya'ari, "The Jordanians' Option," *Jerusalem Report,* February 9, 1995.

192. Hammudeh, "Tourism Industry," 94 (italics mine).

193. Hashemite Kingdom of Jordan, *Jordan: A Winning Business Destination,* 1.

194. See Hammudeh, "Tourism Industry," 89–90.

195. Canadian Press Newswire, "Jordan Copes with Tourism Boom," *Canadian Business and Current Affairs,* November 10, 1995.

196. Ibid.

197. Rosenstein-Rodan, "Problems of Industrialization"; Rosenstein-Rodan, "Theory of the 'Big Push.'" See also Meier, *Leading Issues in Economic Development,* 637–47.

198. Hashemite Kingdom of Jordan, *Aqaba: An Overview of Projects.*

199. On the state as obstacle to tourism development, see Kelly, "Jordan's Potential Tourism Development."

200. Mitchell, "Nationalism, Imperialism, Economism," 422.

201. MOTA/JICA, *Study on Tourism Development,* abstract page.

202. EcoPeace, "Dead Sea Challenges: Final Report" (East Jerusalem: EcoPeace, 1996); EcoPeace, "Final Report on Symposium on Promoting an Integrated Sustainable Regional Development Plan for the Dead Sea Basin (Amman, May 26–27, 1998)" (1998), http://www.foeme.org.

203. Jordan Valley Authority, *Tourism Development Project,* 22.

204. See Lisa Fliegel, "In Search of a Jordanian Architectural Style," *New Middle East Magazine,* June–July 1994.

4. The Territorial Politics of Tourism in Jordan

1. Khouri, *The Jordan Valley.*

2. MELAD, "Dark Skies over Sunny City," *Middle East Land and Development (MELAD) Newsletter,* June 1996.

3. MELAD, "Aqaba—Part One," *Middle East Land and Development (MELAD) Newsletter,* June 1996.

4. Kjorlien, "Peace Monitor," 117.

5. Yasser Tukan, head of Directorate for Tourism Development, Jordan Valley Authority, interview by author, Amman, Jordan, April 2, 1998.

6. EIU, "Jordan," *EIU Country Report,* 1st quarter 1996, 18. See also "Construction Special Report: Dead Sea, Peace Opens Up a Potential Paradise," *Middle East Economic Digest,* April 2, 1999, 2.

7. Robert Pelletreau, "Successful Peace Process Enhances Mideast Development: Pelletreau Remarks, MEMTTA Americas Division," March 31, 1996, http://www.usembassy-israel.org.il/publish/press/state/archive/june/sd4_6-4.htm.

8. Betsy Hiel, "Will MEMTTA Tap the Potential of Regional Tourism?" U.S.-Arab Tradeline, November 22, 1996, http://www.arabdatanet.com/news/docresults.asp?docid=368.

9. Madeleine Albright, "Letter Read at MEMTTA Press Conference, Doha, Qatar," http://telaviv.usembassy.gov/publish/peace/archives/1997/me1118a.html.

10. USAID, "Jordan 1993 Tourism Strategy," 9.

11. USAID, "Tourism Marketing Strategy," V-6.

12. Tim Miller, USAID official, interview by author, American Embassy, Amman, Jordan, March 25, 1998.

13. Interview with Jordanian travel agent, Amman, Jordan, February 14, 1998.

14. Munir Nassar, "JTB . . . Alive Again," *Jordan Tourism Chronicle* 1, no. 8 (August 1996); Munir Nassar, "JTB on the Brink?" *Jordan Tourism Chronicle* 1, no. 10 (October 1996).

15. Chemonics International, "Jordan Sustainable Tourism," I-2.

16. USAID, USAID Congressional Presentation: Jordan: FY 1998 (Washington, D.C.: Department of State, 1997). USAID director Brian Atwood would list this termination as an example of his "results oriented management system." See U.S. House of Representatives, Subcommittee Hearing, Foreign Operations, Export Financing, and Related Programs Appropriations for 1998, Wednesday, March 19, 1997.

17. See By-law no. (62) for the Year 1997 Governing the Jordan Tourism Board, adopted by the Council of Ministers, October 25, 1997.

18. The tensions between the government and the private sector, however, did not end. See Suha Ma'ayaeh, "Finance Ministry Decision Sparks Furor in Tourism Board," *Jordan Times,* July 12, 2001. For a follow-up, see Suha Ma'ayaeh, "JTB, Finance Ministry Resolve Dispute over Board's Finances," *Jordan Times,* July 25, 2001.

19. Liat Collins, "Those in the Hashemite Kingdom Call It 'Shalom,'" *Jerusalem Post,* December 2, 1994.

20. Ibid.

21. Chemonics International, "Jordan Sustainable Tourism."

22. US/ICOMOS, "Management Analysis."

23. USAID, "Jordan Tourism Development Project," ii. The following quotes are taken from this source. See also Chemonics, "Jordan Sustainable Tourism," B-7.

24. See Brand, "Displacement for Development."

25. On Wadi Rum, see Brand, "Development in Wadi Rum"; and Chatelard, "Conflicts of Interest." On Salt, see Daher, "Urban Regeneration." On Um Qays, see Brand, "Resettling."

26. Fischbach, *State, Society, and Land,* 207.

27. Kenneth W. Russell, "Ethnohistory," 22; UNESCO/SECA, *Jordan: Petra National Park Management Plan,* 74.

28. On the extraction of rents from early travelers, see Burckhardt, *Travels in Syria,* 418–34.

29. Shoup, "Impact of Tourism," 281.

30. MELAD, "Petra," *Middle East Land and Development (MELAD) Newsletter,* April 1996.

31. Shoup, "Impact of Tourism," 286.

32. UNESCO/SECA, *Jordan: Petra National Park Management Plan,* 117, 118.

33. Osama El-Sherif, "Flood of Visitors Threatens to Take Bloom off Jordan's Rose-Red City," *Star* (Amman), October 2, 1997.

34. Saad Rawajfeh, head of Planning Department, Petra Regional Planning Council, interview by author, Wadi Musa, Jordan, April 1, 1998.

35. Ibid.

36. Kevin Coughlin, "Peace Accord Opens New Era of Tourism," *Iowa Plain Dealer,* November 20, 1994.

37. Interview with travel agent, Petra Moon Travel, Wadi Musa, Jordan, March 20, 1998.

38. Interview with front office manager, Petra Forum Hotel, Wadi Musa, Jordan, March 31, 1998.

39. Oliver Bennett, "Travel: No Room at Petra's Inns," *Daily Telegraph,* July 15, 1995.

40. MOTA/Dar Al-Handasah, *Petra Priority Action Plan Study: Phase One Report*, 4–27.

41. MELAD, "Petra."

42. Jafar Tukan, architect, interview by author, Amman, Jordan, July 18, 1998; Nader Shalhoub, owner of Petra Plaza and Shepherd's Hotel, interview by author, Amman, Jordan, July 21, 1998.

43. MOTA/Dar Al-Handasah, *Petra Priority Action Plan Study: Phase One Report*, 4–27.

44. Brian Cope, "Letter to the Editor," *Jordan Times*, May 10, 1998, Teller, *Jordan*, 233.

45. After October 1995, the JD was pegged to the U.S. dollar at a rate of JD 1 = US$1.43.

46. MELAD, "Petra."

47. El-Sherif, "Flood of Visitors Threatens."

48. MELAD, "Petra." See also MOTA/Dar Al-Handasah, *Petra Priority Action Plan Study: Phase Two Report*, 2–8.

49. MOTA/Dar Al-Handasah, *Petra Priority Action Plan Study: Phase One Report*.

50. Simonis and Finlay, *Jordan and Syria*, 172.

51. MOTA/Dar Al-Handasah, *Petra Priority Action Plan Study: Phase One Report*, 4–28.

52. Simonis and Finlay, *Jordan and Syria*, 171.

53. Dr. Kamel O. Mahadin, director general of the Petra Regional Planning Council, interview by author, Wadi Musa, Jordan, April 1, 1998.

54. World Bank, Infrastructure Sector Group, Mashreq Department of Middle East and North Africa Region, "Project Appraisal Document on a Proposed Loan of US$32 Million to the Hashemite Kingdom of Jordan for a Second Tourism Development Project," report no. 16485-JO, July 11, 1997.

55. PRPC, "Petra Regional Planning Council" (Wadi Musa, Jordan: Petra Regional Planning Council, 1998).

56. MOTA/Dar Al-Handasah, *Petra Priority Action Plan Study: Phase One Report*; MOTA/Dar Al-Handasah, *Petra Priority Action Plan Study: Phase Two Report*; MOTA/Dar Al-Handasah, *Petra Priority Action Plan Study: Phase Three Report*.

57. MOTA/Dar Al-Handasah, *Petra Priority Action Plan Study: Phase Two Report*, 2–91.

58. Ibid., 2–145.

59. Ibid.

60. Rawajfeh interview.

61. Ibid.

62. The removal of the Bedul from the park was recommended in a 1968 plan drafted by the U.S. National Park Service. See U.S. National

Park Service, *Master Plan;* and Simms and Kooring, "Bedul Bedouin of Petra."

63. See Hadidi, "Conservation"; and Greene, "Tourism and Archaeology."

64. Travel and Tourism Intelligence, "Jordan," *Country Report,* no. 2 (1999): 63.

65. Usama E. Ma'ayeh, hotel manager, interview by author, Amman, Jordan, July 21, 1998.

66. Ibid.

67. Ziyad Tawaissi, hotel manager, interview by author, Wadi Musa, Jordan, April 1, 1998.

68. Info-Prod Research (Middle East), "Low Level of Standards in Petra," *Middle East News Items,* October 30, 1997.

69. Harvey, "The Art of Rent," 396.

70. MELAD, "System vs. Petra," *Middle East Land and Development (MELAD) Newsletter,* April 1996.

71. MOTA/Dar Al-Handasah, *Petra Priority Action Plan Study: Phase One Report,* 10–15; Teller, *Jordan,* 232.

72. Kirk Albrecht, "Shalom Means Tourism," *Middle East,* January 1995, 30.

73. Travel and Tourism Intelligence, "Jordan," 68.

74. Dan Izenberg, Haim Shapiro, and Jose Rosenfeld, "Bentsur: Reports Amman Unhappy Are Inaccurate," *Jerusalem Post,* December 28, 1994.

75. Interview with Tourism Minister Dr. Saleh Irsheidat, *Star* (Amman), August 8, 1996.

76. Wen Xinnian, "Jordanians Face Severe Tourism Pressure," *Xinhua News Agency,* April 27, 1995.

77. Martin Cohn, "An Unsettled Peace," *Toronto Star,* May 21, 1995.

78. Natasha Bukhari, "Jordanian Tourism Industry Has Not Reaped Dividends of Peace," *Deutsch Presse-Agentur,* April 9, 1995.

79. Associated Press, "Amman Hotel Serves Kosher Food," *Jerusalem Post,* December 16, 1994.

80. Barton Gellman, "Amman's Kosher Leftovers," *Washington Post,* July 3, 1995.

81. Youssef M. Ibrahim, "Amman Journal: Kosher in Jordan, an Idea Whose Time It Wasn't," *New York Times,* September 14, 1995.

82. Barham, "Tourism in Jordan," 132.

83. Interview with tourism minister Dr. Saleh Irsheidat, *Star.*

84. Barham, "Tourism in Jordan," 132.

85. Ibid., 142.

86. Interview with tourism minister Dr. Saleh Irsheidat, *Star.*

87. Ibid.

88. EIU, "Jordan," *EIU Country Report,* 4th quarter 1996.

89. EIU, "Jordan," *EIU Country Report,* 3rd quarter 1997, 18.

90. Travel and Tourism Intelligence, "Jordan," 61–62.

91. Ibid., 64–65.

92. Ibid., 62–63.

93. Tareq Ayyoub, "Amman Has the Lowest Hotel Occupancy Rate in Mideast, Study Shows," *Jordan Times,* May 20, 1999.

94. Ibid.

95. Riad al Khouri, "Bandwagon Economics Lead Nowhere," *Jordan Times,* July 23–24, 1998.

96. Export and Finance Bank, "Tourism Sector Report," 3.

97. Dalya Al-Dajani, "Tourism Sector Seeks Reprieve from Creditors," *Jordan Times,* February 15, 2002.

98. See Abujaber, *Pioneers over Jordan.*

99. Fakhoury, "Reuse of the Vernacular."

100. Yassin Talhouni and Dalia Amasheh, Zara Investment Holding Co., Ltd., interview by author, Amman, Jordan, June 8, 1998.

101. Melvyn L. Johns, architecture and project manager for Arabtech-Jardaneh, interview by author, Amman, February 15, 1998.

102. Talhouni and Amasheh interview.

103. Mousa Barrieh, sales and marketing manager, Mövenpick Resort, Petra, interview by author, Wadi Musa, Jordan, March 29, 1998.

104. Export and Finance Bank, "Tourism Sector Report," 14.

105. Ibid.

106. *Jordan Times,* November 23, 1998; cited in Asher Susser, "Jordan," in *Middle East Contemporary Survey,* vol. 22, *1998,* 380.

107. Amy Henderson, "Jordanian-Israeli Peace Treaty: Mixed Bag of Success, Failure," *Jordan Times,* November 30, 1999.

108. Ryan, *Jordan in Transition,* 53–57.

109. Susser, "Jordan," in *Middle East Contemporary Survey,* vol. 20, *1996,* 424.

110. Ibid.

111. Ibid.

112. Ibid., 423.

113. Carroll, *Business as Usual,* 66.

114. Ibid., 68.

115. Rima Khalaf-Hunaidi, "Peace in the Middle East and the Jordanian Economy," Washington Institute for Near East Affairs, September 30, 1999, http://www.washingtoninstitute.org/templateC07.php?CID=33.

116. Lynch, "Jordan's Identity and Interests," 51–53.

117. Zvi Bar'el, "Jordanians Want Bread, Not Fruits of Peace," *Ha'aretz,* December 22, 1999.

118. As reported by the *Jordan Times,* July 31, 1999 (italics mine).

119. As reported in Samir Ghawi, "MENA Recommends Attracting Private Investments and Boosting Exports," *Jordan Times,* September 12, 1999.

120. "A Monarchy in Trouble," *Guardian,* August 20, 1996.

121. See Boorstin, "From Traveler to Tourist"; and Buzard, *The Beaten Track.* But also note MacCannell, *The Tourist,* 10.

122. Scham and Lucas, "Normalization," 61.

123. EIU, "Jordan," *EIU Country Report,* 3rd quarter 1997, 18.

124. Stein, "First Contact."

125. Ibid., 518.

126. Ibid., 516.

127. Ibid., 519. See also Kaplan, *Questions of Travel.*

128. John Donnelly, "Israeli Tourists' Behavior May Rock Fragile Peace with Jordan," *Houston Chronicle,* March 18, 1995; Rana Sabbagh, "Jordan Reels under Tourist Hordes," *Globe and Mail* (Toronto), May 10, 1995; David Horovitz, "Israeli Vandals Shock Jordan Tourism Officials," *Irish Times* (Dublin), March 7, 1995. See also Khashan, "The Levant."

129. Nora Boustany, "Israeli Tourists Pour into Jordan," *Washington Post,* January 25, 1995.

130. Donnelly, "Israeli Tourists' Behavior."

131. Lucas, *Institutions,* 94.

132. Ibid., 96.

133. Ibid., 95. Kornbluth, "Jordan and the Anti-normalization Campaign," 105.

134. Kornbluth, "Jordan and the Anti-normalization Campaign," 105.

135. Alia Shukri Hamzeh, "Warm Peace with Israel Grows Cold," *Jordan Times,* October 26, 2004.

136. P. Moore, *Doing Business,* 172.

137. Raed Al Abed, "Israeli Fair Provokes Angry Response from Businessmen," *Star* (Amman), November 28, 1996.

138. Lucas, "Jordan," 92.

139. "Amman Hotel Not to Host Israeli National Day Ceremony This Year," *Al Arab Al Yawm,* April 13, 2000.

140. Nsour, "Arab-Israeli Economic Relations."

141. Ibid., 300.

142. As cited in Moussalli, "Globalization," 11.

143. As cited in Kornbluth, "Jordan and the Anti-normalization Campaign," 89.

144. Martin Cohn, "An Unsettled Peace," *Toronto Star,* May 21, 1995.

145. Joel Greenberg, "Israeli Tourists Get New View of Promised Land," *Jordan Times,* November 28, 1994.

146. See "Jordanian Tourism Minister on Israeli Tourists, Alcohol, Entry Visas," *Ad-Dustur,* September 9, 2000.

147. Human Rights Watch, "Justice Undermined: Balancing Security and Human Rights in the Palestinian Justice System" (2001), http://www.hrw.org/reports/2001/pa/isrpa1101.pdf.

148. Khalid Dalal, "New JVA Law Sufficient to Protect Area against Foreign Domination," *Jordan Times,* July 10, 2001.

149. Majali, Anani, and Haddadin, *Peacemaking,* 308.

150. One plan envisions flooding a lake to form a bird sanctuary for international visitors, fashioning the ruins of a power plant built by Zionist settlers before 1948 into a visitors' center, and converting the old homes of the plant workers into an eco-lodge. On these plans to develop the King Abdullah/Rotenberg Peace Park, see http://www.foeme.org/projects.php?ind=123; and http://www.yale.edu/opa/newsr/08-05-01-05.all.html.

151. Gelbman, "Border Tourism in Israel," 207.

152. Ibid., 208.

153. Kornbluth, "Jordan and the Anti-normalization Campaign," 86. King Abdullah I had created the precedent by first granting rights in 1927 to Pinchas Rotenburg, a Russian immigrant, to build a hydroelectric power station at the location for the Palestine Electric Company.

154. Lucas, *Institutions,* 88–89.

155. Ibid., 89.

156. Kornbluth, "Jordan and the Anti-normalization Campaign," 96.

157. For one reading, see Gregory, *The Colonial Present,* chapters 5 and 6.

158. Ehud Ya'ari, "The Jordanians' Option," *Jerusalem Report,* February 9, 1995.

159. Stein, "First Contact," 535–36. Stein notes: "The Israeli state's policy on incoming Arab and/or Muslim tourism was contradictory and perpetually shifting. The Israeli Ministry of Tourism declared Israel open to 'all Muslim and Arab travelers'; two months later, ministry spokespersons 'clarified' that Muslim tourism to Jerusalem would not be 'encouraged' at a time when the political status of the city was so fiercely contested" (534–35).

160. Ibid., 534–35. See also Savar Plotzker, "Hahalom evar kan" [The dream is already here], *Yediot Aharonot,* July 25, 1994; and Margo Lipschitz Sugarman, "Make Tours, Not War," *Jerusalem Report,* August 25, 1994, 34–36.

161. "Engineers Body Denies Membership to Graduates of Israeli Universities," *Al Arab Al Yawm,* August 1, 1999.

162. Kornbluth, "Jordan and the Anti-normalization Campaign," 100.

163. *Jordan Times,* September 25, 1999; cited in Kornbluth, "Jordan and the Anti-normalization Campaign," 100. Some Jordanian leftists, in

contrast, challenged this attitude to Palestinian citizens of Israel. On Palestinian citizens of Israel, see Rabinowitz and Abu-Baker, *Coffins on Our Shoulders*.

164. Shlaim, *The Iron Wall*, 568.

165. Lucas, *Institutions*.

166. Brand, "Effects of the Peace Process"; Lucas, *Institutions*.

167. Brand, "Liberalization," 62.

168. Lynch, "Jordan's Identity."

169. Reuters, "Jordan: We've Foiled Spate of Bombing Plots," *Jerusalem Post*, June 4, 1996.

170. "Jordan Confirms Arrests in Tourist Plot," *United Press International*, May 15, 1996.

171. Shyam Bhatia, "Jordanians 'Planned to Blow Up Tourist Site,'" *Guardian*, October 25, 1996.

172. David Rudge, "Israeli Tourist Stabbed in Jordan," *Jerusalem Post*, May 1, 1997.

173. "Three Men Sentenced for Plotting Attacks on Israeli Tourists," *Jordan Times*, May 13, 1999.

174. "Israel Warns Citizens against Travel to Jordan," *Star* (Amman), October 12, 2000.

175. Ibid.

176. Kornbluth, "Jordan and the Anti-normalization Campaign," 80.

177. Neil MacFarquhar, "A Fabled Place Forsaken, Contaminated by War," *New York Times*, May 1, 2002.

178. A few proponents of the New Middle East within the tourism sector remained, though efforts to promote cross-border visits between Israel and its Arab neighbors were dropped. In 2004 the Israel Hotel Managers' Association, with the help of the Peres Center, created Tourism4Peace "to promote Middle East tourism and peace through shared visits from abroad." Its 2007 meeting on the Jordanian shore of the Dead Sea, however, "ultimately reflected the fractured geography and politics of the region." See Nathan Burstein, "Tourism as a Boost to ME Peace," *Jerusalem Post*, June 30, 2007.

179. Greenwood, "Jordan."

180. See, for example, Matt McNulty and Chemonics International Inc., *Work Plan for the National Tourism Strategy Initiative, Design and Lead 2010 Strategy Process—Phase I*, Final Report (USAID, 2003). While this new strategy recycles many mantras from programs past— such as "tourism is the best immediate engine for growth for Jordan's economy" (1), "tourism is the 'oil' equivalent in Jordan's natural patrimony" (4), and "tourism is not concentrated in cities, but distributes its benefits widely" (5)—it also seeks to correct and overcome many of the problems and challenges that have been outlined here.

181. Molly Moore, "Israel Cultivates a New Breed of Tourist," *Washington Post*, December 11, 2003.

182. EIU, "Jordan," *EIU Country Report*, June 2001, 24; "Rebranding the Kingdom," *Middle East Economic Digest*, September 10, 2004.

5. The View from Dubai

1. M. Gray, "Economic Reform."

2. M. Gray, "Political Economy."

3. References to the "Arab Middle East" correspond to the World Tourism Organization's Middle East region, which includes the Arab states stretching from Egypt to the Gulf. Unless noted otherwise, tourism data are collected from World Tourism Organization (UNWTO), *Tourism Market Trends*; UNWTO, *Inbound Tourism*; and the tables at http://unwto.org/facts/menu.html.

4. UNWTO, *Inbound Tourism*, 21.

5. Ibid., 20.

6. EIU, "Tourism: Vacancy," *Business Middle East*, November 16–30, 2001, 2.

7. UNWTO, *Inbound Tourism*, 20.

8. Unless otherwise noted, tourism receipts data are measured in nominal U.S. dollars.

9. Aziz, "Understanding Attacks," 94.

10. Wahab, "Tourism and Terrorism," 176.

11. "Communiqué from 'Al-Qaida's Jihad Committee in Mesopotamia,'" November 10, 2005, http://www.globalterroralert.com/pdf/1105/zarqawi1105-2.pdf.

12. Peter E. Tarlow, "Taking a Realistic Look at Tourism in a Time of Terror," *USA Today Magazine*, March 2003, 52.

13. John Micklethwait and Adrian Wooldridge, "Globalism under Siege," *Wall Street Journal*, November 9, 2001.

14. Keohane, *Power and Governance*, 284.

15. Al-Hamarneh and Steiner, "Islamic Tourism," 18.

16. UNWTO, *Tourism Market Trends*, 24–25.

17. EIU, "Slowdown? What Slowdown?" *Business Middle East*, June 1–15, 2002, 5.

18. Alan Cowell, "Tourism Report Finds U.S. a Big Loser," *New York Times*, March 7, 2004.

19. Josh Martin, "The Big Bounce Back," *Middle East*, May 2005.

20. Rhona Wells, "Middle East Destinations," *Middle East*, April 2006.

21. EIU, "Egypt," *EIU Country Report*, February 2006.

22. Peter J. Cooper, "The Middle East Tourism Paradox," *AME Info*, May 5, 2004, http://www.ameinfo.com/39057.html. See also Abdul

Rahman Al-Rashed, "Tourists in Bin Laden's Land," *Asharq Al-Awsat,* August 9, 2006.

23. Culler, "The Semiotics of Tourism," 167.

24. On the notions of density and centrality in social network analysis, see Stanley, "Middle East City Networks."

25. P. Smucker, "As Arabs Skip Disney World, Gulf Resorts Thrive," *Christian Science Monitor,* July 17, 2002.

26. World Bank, *Middle East and North Africa Economic Developments,* 71.

27. "Arabs Spend US$12 Bil. on Vacations," *Chinapost.com.tw,* October 10, 2005.

28. For an ethnography exploring contrasting Western and Arab Gulf tourist experiences and cultures of travel in Egypt, see Wynn, *Pyramids and Nightclubs.*

29. "Thank Allah for the Gulfies," *Economist,* October 3, 1998; "Gulf Arabs Rescue Jordan's Tourism," *Jordan Times,* August 29, 1998.

30. Saad Hattar and Suha Ma'ayeh, "Arab Tourists Give Depressed Tourism Sector a Boost," *Jordan Times,* July 26, 2001.

31. Suha Ma'ayeh, "JTB Efforts to Promote Jordan despite Limited Funds and Regional Instability," *Jordan Times,* January 23, 2001.

32. "Thank Allah for the Gulfies," *Economist,* October 3, 1998.

33. In addition, local and regional Arab tourists are more likely to have a fine-grained understanding of the geography of violence (or, in the case of ideologically and religiously motivated travelers, to view their visit as an act of political defiance or expression of faith).

34. UNWTO, *Tourism Market Trends,* 67.

35. Ibid., 61, 67.

36. Ibid., 75.

37. EIU, "Egypt," *EIU Country Report,* May 2002, 31.

38. "King Orders Immediate Steps to Facilitate Travel, Customs Procedures," *Jordan Times,* May 13–14, 2005. See also Hashemite Kingdom of Jordan, *National Tourism Strategy, 2004–2010,* 14.

39. "Text of the Final Statement Issued by the Arab Summit in Amman on 28 March," *Al Rai* (Amman), March 29, 2001.

40. Suha Ma'ayeh, "Arab Ministers Address Challenges to Regional Tourism Industry," *Jordan Times,* June 5, 2001.

41. Al-Hamarneh, "New Tourism Trends," 54.

42. Saad G. Hattar, "Jordan, Egypt Hold Meeting to Facilitate Cross-Border Travel," *Jordan Times,* May 7, 2001.

43. Jordan, *National Tourism Strategy, 2004–2010,* 28–32.

44. Hassan Fattah, "Celebrity Architects Reveal a Daring Cultural Xanadu for the Arab World," *New York Times,* February 1, 2007.

45. Press kit, "From Cordoba to Samarkand Masterpieces from the

New Museum of Islamic Art in Doha, Qatar," Musée du Louvre exhibition, March 30–June 26, 2006.

46. Gwenn Okruhlik, "Image, Imagination, and Place"; EIU, "Saudi Arabia: Selective Welcome," *Business Middle East,* June 1–15, 2001, 9.

47. Elisabeth Rosenthal, "The Greening of the New, 'Civilized' Libya," *International Herald Tribune,* September 11, 2007.

48. Steiner, "Contributing to Vulnerability," 16.

49. Al-Hamarneh, "New Tourism Trends," 54.

50. Flanagan, "Long-Haul Hubs," 95.

51. See Marchal, "Dubai."

52. Jones, "Dubai," 181.

53. Sampler and Eigner, *Sand to Silicon,* 102–3.

54. Ibid., 187.

55. Ibid., 14–15.

56. Ritter, "Tourism in the United Arab Emirates," 175.

57. Sampler and Eigner, *Sand to Silicon,* 191; Joan Henderson, "Tourism in Dubai," 89.

58. Ibid.

59. Sampler and Eigner, *Sand to Silicon,* 17.

60. Laws, *Tourism Destination Management,* 188.

61. Davis, "Fear and Money," 61.

62. Joan Henderson, "Tourism in Dubai," 96.

63. "Dubai Maps Out Another 45,000 Rooms," *Travel Trade Gazette,* January 26, 2007.

64. Elsheshtawy, "Redrawing Boundaries," 187.

65. Ibid.

66. Katodrytis, "Metropolitan Dubai."

67. UNWTO, *Inbound Tourism,* 60–61.

68. Ibid., 62.

69. Ibid., 61.

70. UNWTO, *Tourism Market Trends,* 103.

71. On the dynamics of these "legal smuggling" flows, see Keshavarzian, *Bazaar and State,* 170–76.

72. UNWTO, *Tourism Market Trends,* 102–3.

73. Oryx Real Estate, "Proposal for Dubailand Development" (Dubai, UAE: Prepared by Ray Hogan, MAC Corporation LLC, 2004).

74. Tim Knipe, "In Dubai, the Situation Is Developing," *Amusement America,* November 2005.

75. Dan Gerstenfeld, "Beduin Business," *Jerusalem Post,* October 17, 2003.

76. William Wallis, "An American Style Emirate? Dubai Sees a Future Ally, Entrepôt, and Playground," *Financial Times,* March 8, 2006.

77. Hanouz and Yousef, "Assessing Competitiveness," 9.

78. Ehteshami, *Globalization and Geopolitics,* 36.

79. Ibid.

80. Thomas Friedman, "Dubai and Dunces," *New York Times,* March 15, 2006.

81. Kanna, "Dubai in a Jagged World," 23. See also Davis, "Fear and Money."

82. Kanna, "Dubai in a Jagged World," 23.

83. See Kanna, "State Philosophical," 67.

84. Kanna, "Dubai in a Jagged World," 23–24; Davis, "Fear and Money," 55–59.

85. Michael Pacione, "City Profile," 257; Sampler and Eigner, *Sand to Silicon,* 16–17.

86. Davis, "Fear and Money," 51.

87. Ibid.

88. Pacione, "City Profile," 260.

89. Ibid., 264.

90. Ibid.

91. Ibid., 260.

92. Ibid.

93. Elsheshtawy, "Redrawing Boundaries," 190.

94. See Judd, "Constructing the Tourist Bubble." On the case of Baltimore, see Harvey, "View from Federal Hill."

95. Judd, "Visitors," 24, 25.

96. Magdi Abdelhadi, "Capital of Arab Freedom," *Khaleej Times* (Dubai), June 30, 2006.

97. Huybrechts, "Beirut," 237.

98. On the controversy over its legal standing, see Lysandra Ohrstrom, "Solidere: 'Vigilantism under Color of Law,'" *Daily Star* (Beirut), August 6, 2007.

99. See Kassab, "On Two Conceptions"; and Daher, "Tourism."

100. Kassab, "On Two Conceptions," 50.

101. The Hashemite Kingdom of Jordan, "Al-Abdali Urban Regeneration Project," http://www.jordanecb.org/pdf/investment/majdev_abdali .pdf.

102. Ibid.

103. See Tukan, "Architecture and Society."

104. Jordan, "Al-Abdali."

105. "Abdali: The Future of Amman," *Executive Magazine* (Beirut), April 2007; Jordan, "Al-Abdali Urban Regeneration Project."

106. "Abdali: The Future of Amman," *Executive Magazine.*

107. Rami Daher, "Mideast Cities Compete for Global Inward Investment," *Star* (Amman), February 9, 2006. Some fear, however, that replication of certain patterns of development may produce re-deterritorialization

in which these spaces become generic by adopting similar architectural forms, chain retail outlets, and artificial attractions and forms of entertainment. See Summer, "Neoliberalization of Urban Space," 7. Note, however, that others are beginning to appreciate aspects of the new regional vernaculars, especially in the Gulf. See Koolhaas, Khoubrou, and Bouman, *Al Manakh.*

108. Hannah Allam, "Iranians Seek to Create a Tourist Haven on Persian Gulf Island," *Charlotte Observer,* September 11, 2006.

109. See Faisal Devji, "Dubai Cosmopolis," *Open Democracy,* April 19, 2007.

110. Jones, "Dubai," 203. See also Sassen, *Globalization and Its Discontents,* xxxii.

111. Devji, "Dubai Cosmopolis."

112. All unattributed quotes in this section are drawn from the Web site of the Ibn Battuta Mall, http://www.ibnbattutamall.com.

113. Kanna, "State Philosophical," 64.

114. Dunn, "International Migrations," 83. See also Euben, *Journeys to the Other Shore,* 63–89.

115. Dunn, *Adventures of Ibn Battuta,* 10.

116. Euben, *Journeys to the Other Shore,* 178.

117. See Bianchi, *Guests of God.*

118. Karen Dabrowska, "Can Baghdad Rise from the Ashes?" *Middle East,* March 2004.

119. See http://www.seejordan.org/experience_religious_islam.shtml.

120. Abdel-Sahib Al-Shakry, "How to Build Bridges of Communication between Islamic Nations in the 21st Century?" *Islamic Tourism,* no. 18 (July–August 2005).

121. As cited in al-Hamarneh and Steiner, "Islamic Tourism," 179.

122. Ibid., 180.

123. The material in this paragraph is drawn from Harb, "Pious Entertainment," 10–11. See also http://www.assahavillage.com.

124. See Hazbun, "The East as an Exhibit."

125. Al-Shakry, "How to Build Bridges."

126. Royal Society for the Conservation of Nature (RSCN), *Conservation of the Dana Wildlands;* RSCN, *Socio-economic Development;* and Hazbun, "Mapping the Landscape," 342–43. On other modes of tourism development within nature reserves, see Sowers, "Nature Reserves."

127. See World Bank, *Cultural Heritage and Development.*

128. In a similar vein, the Palestinian NGO the Alternative Tourism Group has sought to create tourist itineraries centered on Palestinian contemporary culture and political realities. See Alternative Tourism Group, *Palestine and Palestinians* (Beit sahour: Alternative Tourism Group, 2005).

129. Geocultural imaginaries are similar to geopolitical ones, but they

relate to how people understand spaces of cultures (such as their boundaries and connections to particular territories) and the impact of flows between spaces and possibilities for pluralism within them.

130. See Euben, *Journeys to the Other Shore,* 76.

131. See Buzard, *The Beaten Track.*

132. Stein, "First Contact."

133. Salem, *A Drive to Israel.*

134. Although Ali Salem's account of his trip became a best-seller in Egypt, he was not able to avoid expulsion from the writers' union by those opposed to normalization. See Salem, *A Drive to Israel,* 9–11.

135. Ibid., 118.

136. For a critical reading of this effort, see Daniel Levine, "Ali Salem's Exodus," unpublished manuscript, Johns Hopkins University, 2005.

137. Connolly, "Speed." See also Deleuze and Guattari, *A Thousand Plateaus.*

138. See also Rabinowitz, "Postnational Palestine/Israel?"; and Alcalay, *After Jews and Arabs.* On the role of violence in the making and the challenges of unmaking the nationalist geopolitical imaginaries that define state building and international relations in the Middle East and elsewhere, see Shapiro, *Violent Cartographies.*

139. As cited in Kaplan, *Questions of Travel,* 126.

Bibliography

Abderrazak, Ammar. "Aspect socio-cultural du tourism à Hammamet."
In *Medinas de Tunisie: Hammamet,* ed. Taoufik Bachrouch, 77–117.
Série Histoire no. 7. Tunis: Cahier du CERES, 1996.

Abujaber, Raouf Sa'd. *Pioneers over Jordan: The Frontier of Settlement
in Transjordan, 1985–1914.* 2nd ed. London: I. B. Tauris, 1989.

Agnew, John. *Hegemony: The New Shape of Global Power.* Philadelphia,
Pa.: Temple University Press, 2005.

Alcalay, Ammiel. *After Jews and Arabs: Remaking Levantine Culture.*
Minneapolis: University of Minnesota Press, 1993.

Al-Hamarneh, Ala. "New Tourism Trends in the Arab World." *Islamic
Tourism* 16 (March–April): 50–54.

Al-Hamarneh, Ala, and Christian Steiner. "Islamic Tourism: Rethinking
the Strategies of Tourism Development in the Arab World after September 11, 2001." *Comparative Studies of South Asia, Africa, and
the Middle East* 24, no. 1 (Spring 2004): 18–27.

Al Khouri, Riad. "Intra-regional Business Facilitation: The Case of
Jordan." In *Regional Economic Cooperation in the Mediterranean,*
ed. Olaf Köndgen, 123–32. Amman: Konrad Adenauer Foundation,
1997.

Anani, Jawad. "Cooperation in the Context of the Middle East Peace
Process." In *Arab-Israeli Search for Peace,* ed. Steven L. Spiegel. Boulder, Colo.: Lynne Rienner, 1992.

Anderson, Benedict. *Imagined Communities: Reflections on the Origin
and Spread of Nationalism.* Rev. ed. New York: Verso, 1991.

Anderson, Lisa. "Prospects for Liberalism in North Africa: Identities and Interests in Pre-industrial Welfare States." In *Islam, Democracy, and the State in North Africa,* ed. John P. Entelis, 127–40. Bloomington: Indiana University Press, 1997.

———. *The State and Social Transformation in Tunisia and Libya, 1830–1980.* Princeton, N.J.: Princeton University Press, 1986.

Appadurai, Arjun. *Modernity at Large: Cultural Dimensions of Globalization.* Minneapolis: University of Minnesota Press, 1996.

Association Sauvegarde de la Medina. *Projects et realisation 1980 . . . 1990: Pour la promotion de la Medina.* Tunis: Ville de Tunis, 1990.

Astorino-Courtois, Allison. "Transforming International Agreements into National Realities: Marketing Arab-Israeli Peace in Jordan." *Journal of Politics* 58, no. 4 (November 1996): 1035–54.

Awartani, Hisham. "Palestinian-Israeli Economic Relations." In *The Economics of Middle East Peace,* ed. Stanley Fischer, Dani Rodrik, and Elias Tuma. Cambridge, Mass.: MIT Press, 1993.

Ayoob, Mohammad. "Subaltern Realism: International Relations Theory Meets the Third World." In *International Relations Theory and the Third World,* ed. Stephanie Newman, 31–49. New York: St. Martin's Press, 1998.

Aziz, Heba. "Understanding Attacks on Tourists in Egypt." *Tourism Management* 16, no. 2 (1995): 91–95.

Barber, Benjamin R. *Jihad vs. McWorld: How Globalism and Tribalism Are Reshaping the World.* New York: Ballantine Books, 1997.

Barham, Nasim. "Tourism in Jordan: Development and Perspective." *Jordanies,* no. 5–6 (June–December 1999).

Beal, Elizabeth Anne. "Consumerism and the Culture of Consumption: Class, National Identity, and Gender among Jordanian Elites." Ph.D. diss., University of Chicago, 1998.

Bedoui, Abdeljelil. "Analyse de la dynamique sociale dans le contexte de l'application du plan d'adjustment structurel en Tunisie." *Mondes en Développement* 23, no. 89–90 (1995): 53–73.

Beinin, Joel. "The Cold Peace." *MERIP Reports,* no. 129 (January 1985): 3–10.

Belhedi, Amor. *Societe, espace, et developpement en Tunisie.* Publications de la Faculté des Sciences Humaines et Sociales-Études de Géographie, vol. 27. Tunis: Université de Tunis, 1992.

Bellin, Eva. "Contingent Democrats: Industrialists, Labor, and Democratization in Late-Developing Countries." *World Politics* 52, no. 2 (2000): 175–205.

———. "The Politics of Profit in Tunisia: Utility of the Rentier Paradigm?" *World Development* 22, no. 3 (March 1994): 427–30.

———. *Stalled Democracy: Capital, Labor, and the Paradox of State-Sponsored Development.* Ithaca, N.Y.: Cornell University Press, 2002.

———. "Tunisian Industrialists and the State." In *Tunisia: The Political Economy of Reform,* ed. I. William Zartman, 45–63. Boulder, Colo.: Lynne Rienner, 1991.

Ben Hammouda, Hakim. "Globalization et crise de l'industrie textile en Tunisie." Economic Research Forum for the Arab Countries, Iran, and Turkey (Cairo, Egypt) working paper 9815 (1998).

———. *Tunisie: Ajustment et difficulté de l'insertion internationale.* Paris: Éditions L'Harmattan, 1995.

Ben-Porat, Guy. "Business and Peace: The Rise and Fall of the New Middle East." *Encounters: Political Science in Translation* 1, no. 1 (March 2005): 40–52.

Ben Romdhane, Mahmoud. "L'accord de liber-échange entre la Tunisie et l'Union européenne: Un impératif, des espoirs, des inquiétudes." *Confluences Méditerranée,* no. 21 (Spring 1997): 49–64.

Bergaoui, Mohamed. "Des caravanserails aux stations integrees." *Les Cahiers de l'Orient,* no. 56 (2000): 127–34.

———. *Tourisme et voyages en Tunisie: Le temps des pionniers, 1956–1973.* Tunis: Mohamed Bergaoui, 2003.

Berger, Suzanne, and Ronald Dore, eds. *National Diversity and Global Capitalism.* Ithaca, N.Y.: Cornell University Press, 1996.

Berry-Chikhaoui, Isabelle. "Le logement social 'mis à niveau.'" *Maghreb Machrek,* no. 157 (July–September 1997): 47–57.

Bessis, Sophie. "Carthage's Long-Awaited Rescue." *UNESCO Courier,* September 1999.

Bianchi, Robert R. *Guests of God: Pilgrimage and Politics in the Islamic World.* New York: Oxford University Press, 2004.

Bleasdale, Sue, and Sue Tapsell. "Saharan Tourism: Arabian Nights or Tourist 'Daze'? The Social-cultural and Environmental Impacts of Tourism in Southern Tunisia." In *Tourism and Cultural Change,* ed. Mike Robinson, Nigel Evans, and Paul Callaghan, 25–48. Newcastle: Centre for Travel and Tourism, University of Northumbria, 1996.

Blyth, Mark. *Great Transformations: Economic Ideas and Institutional Change in the Twentieth Century.* Cambridge: Cambridge University Press, 2002.

Boorstin, Daniel J. "From Traveler to Tourist: The Lost Art of Travel." In *The Image: A Guide to Pseudo-events in America,* 77–117. New York: Atheneum, 1971.

Borowiec, Andrew. *Modern Tunisia: A Democratic Apprenticeship.* Westport, Conn.: Praeger, 1998.

Boukraa, Ridha. *Hammamet: Le paradis perdu, etude anthropologique et écologique de la métamorphose d'une communauté.* Aix en Provence: Centre des Études Touristique, 1993.

Brand, Laurie A. "Development in Wadi Rum? State Bureaucracy, External Funders, and Civil Society." *International Journal of Middle East Studies* 33, no. 4 (November 2001): 571–90.

———. "Displacement for Development? The Impact of Changing State-Society Relations." *World Development* 29, no. 6 (2001): 961–76.

———. "Economic and Political Liberalization in a Rentier Economy: The Case of the Hashemite Kingdom of Jordan." In *Privatization and Liberalization in the Middle East,* ed. Iliya Harik and Denis J. Sullivan, 210–32. Bloomington: Indiana University Press, 1992.

———. "The Effects of the Peace Process on Political Liberalization in Jordan." *Journal of Palestine Studies* 28, no. 2 (Winter 1999): 52–67.

———. "'In the Beginning Was the State . . .': The Quest for Civil Society in Jordan." In *Civil Society in the Middle East,* ed. A. R. Norton. Leiden: Brill, 1995.

———. *Jordan's Inter-Arab Relations: The Political Economy of Alliance Making.* New York: Columbia University Press, 1994.

———. "Liberalization and Changing Political Coalitions: The Bases of Jordan's 1990–1991 Gulf Crisis Policy." *Jerusalem Journal of International Relations* 13, no. 4 (1991): 1–46.

———. "Resettling, Reconstruction, and Restor(y)ing: Archaeology and Tourism in Umm Qays." *Middle East Report,* no. 216 (Fall 2000): 28–31.

Brendon, Piers. *Thomas Cook: 150 Years of Popular Tourism.* London: Secker and Warburg, 1991.

Britton, Stephen G. "The Political Economy of Tourism in the Third World." *Annals of Tourism Research* 9 (1982): 331–58.

———. "Tourism, Capital, and Place: Towards a Critical Geography of Tourism." *Environment and Planning D: Space and Society* 9 (1991): 451–78.

Brohman, John. "New Directions in Tourism for Third World Development." *Annals of Tourism Research* 23, no. 1 (1996): 48–70.

Brown, Dona. *Inventing New England: Regional Tourism in the Nineteenth Century.* Washington, D.C.: Smithsonian Institution Press, 1995.

Brynen, Rex. "Economic Crisis and Post-rentier Democratization in the Arab World: The Case of Jordan." *Canadian Journal of Political Science* 25, no. 1 (March 1992): 69–97.

———. "The Politics of Monarchical Liberalism: Jordan." In *Political Liberalization and Democratization in the Arab World,* vol. 2, *Comparative Experiences,* ed. Rex Brynen, Bahgat Korany, and Paul Nobel, 71–100. Boulder, Colo.: Lynne Rienner, 1998.

Buck-Morss, Susan. "Envisioning Capital: Political Economy on Display." *Critical Inquiry* 21 (Winter 1995): 435–67.

Burckhardt, John Lewis. *Travels in Syria and the Holy Land*. London: John Murray, 1822.

Burgat, François, and William Dowell. *The Islamic Movement in North Africa*. Austin: Center for Middle East Studies, University of Texas at Austin, 1993.

Burkart, A. J., and S. Medlik. *Tourism: Past, Present, and Future*. London: Heinemann, 1981.

Buzard, James. *The Beaten Track: European Tourism, Literature, and the Ways to Culture, 1800–1918*. Oxford: Clarendon Press, 1993.

Carroll, Katherine Blue. *Business as Usual? Economic Reform in Jordan*. Lanham, Md.: Lexington Books, 2003.

Cassarino, Jean-Pierre. "The EU-Tunisian Association Agreement and Tunisia's Structural Reform Program." *Middle East Journal* 53, no. 1 (Winter 1999): 59–74.

Cazes, Georges. "Le tourisme international en Thaïlande et en Tunisie: Les impacts et les risques d'un developpement mal maitrise." *Travaux de l'Institut de Géographie de Reims,* no. 53–54 (1983).

Chaabane, Sadok. *Ben Ali et la Voie Pluraliste en Tunisie*. Tunis: Ceres Editions, 1996.

Charmes, Jacques. "Secteur non structuré, politique économique et structuration sociale en Tunisie, 1970–1985." In *Tunisie au Présent: Une modernité au-dessus de tout soupçon?* ed. Michel Camau. Paris: Éditions du Centre Nationale de la Recherche Scientifique, 1987.

Chatelard, Géraldine. "Conflicts of Interest over the Wadi Musa Reserve: Were They Avoidable? A Socio-political Critique." *Nomadic Peoples* 7, no. 1 (2003): 138–58.

Chaudhry, Kiren Aziz. *The Price of Wealth: Economies and Institutions in the Middle East*. Ithaca, N.Y.: Cornell University Press, 1997.

Chemonics International. "Jordan Sustainable Tourism Development/ SITES, Final Report." Washington, D.C.: Chemonics International, 1997.

Christopher, Warren. *In the Stream of History: Shaping Foreign Policy for a New Era*. Stanford, Calif.: Stanford University Press, 1998.

Clancy, Michael. "Commodity Chains, Services, and Development: Theory and Preliminary Evidence from the Tourism Industry." *Review of International Political Economy* 5, no. 1 (Spring 1998): 122–48.

———. *Exporting Paradise: Tourism and Development in Mexico*. Amsterdam: Pergamon, 2001.

———. "Tourism and Development: Evidence from Mexico." *Annals of Tourism Research* 26, no. 1 (1998): 1–20.

Clawson, Patrick. "Tourism Cooperation in the Levant." Washington Institute Policy Focus Research Memorandum no. 26 (May 1994).

Clawson, Patrick L., and Howard Rosen. *The Economic Consequences of Peace for Israel, the Palestinians, and Jordan.* Policy Papers, no. 25. Washington, D.C.: Washington Institute for Near East Policy, 1991.

Commission National Sectorielle du Tourisme et du Thermalisme (CNSTT). *L'Evolution du Tourisme en Tunisie, Retrospective (1961–1971).* Tunis: CNSTT, 1972.

Connolly, William E. "Speed, Concentric Cultures, and Cosmopolitianism." *Political Theory* 28, no. 5 (October 2000): 596–618.

Crick, Malcolm. "Representations of International Tourism in the Social Sciences: Sun, Sex, Sights, Savings, and Servility." *Annual Review of Anthropology* 18 (1989): 307–44.

Culler, Jonathan. "The Semiotics of Tourism." In *Framing the Sign: Criticism and Its Institutions,* 153–67. Oxford: Blackwell, 1988.

Daher, Rami Farouk. "Tourism, Heritage, and Urban Transformations in Jordan and Lebanon." In *Tourism in the Middle East: Continuity, Change, and Transformation,* ed. Rami Farouk Daher, 263–307. Clevendon, UK: Channel View Publications, 2006.

———, ed. *Tourism in the Middle East: Continuity, Change, and Transformation.* Clevendon, UK: Channel View Publications, 2006.

———. "Urban Regeneration/Heritage Tourism Endeavours: The Case of Salt, Jordan." *International Journal of Heritage Studies* 11, no. 4 (September 2005): 289–308.

D'Amore, Louis J. "Tourism: A Vital Force of Peace." *The Futurist,* May–June 1988, 23–28.

David, Steven R. "Explaining Third World Alignment." *World Politics* 45, no. 3 (Summer 1991): 233–56.

Davidson, William D., and Joseph V. Montville. "Foreign Policy According to Freud." *Foreign Policy* 45 (Winter 1981–82): 145–57.

Davis, Mike. "Fear and Money in Dubai." *New Left Review* 41 (September–October 2006): 47–68.

Day, Arthur R. *Troubles on the East Bank: Jordan and the Prospects for Peace.* New York: Council on Foreign Relations, 1986.

de Kadt, Emanuel, ed. *Tourism: Passport to Development?* New York: Oxford University Press, 1979.

Deleuze, Gilles, and Félix Guattari. *A Thousand Plateaus: Capitalism and Schizophrenia.* Trans. Brian Massumi. Minneapolis: University of Minnesota Press, 1987.

Denoeux, Guilain. "La Tunisie de Ben Ali et ses paradoxes." *Maghreb Machrek,* no. 166 (October–December 1999): 32–52.

Diamond, J. "Tourism's Role in Economic Development: The Case Reexamined." *Economic Development and Cultural Change* 25 (1977): 539–53.

Dillman, Bradford. "Facing the Market in North Africa." *Middle East Journal 55*, no. 2 (Spring 2001): 198–215.

Dimassi, Hassine. "La crise économique en Tunisie: Une crise de régulation." *Maghreb-Machrek*, no. 103 (March 1984): 57–69.

Dimassi, Hassine, and Hédi Zaiem. "L'Industrie: Mythe et stratégies." In *Tunisie au présent: Une modernité au-dessus de tout soupçon?* ed. Michel Camau, 163–79. Paris: Éditions du Centre Nationale de la Recherche Scientifique, 1987.

Ding, Haihua, and Eric S. Koenig. "Boundary Dispute concerning the Taba Area. 27 ILM 1421 (1988)." *American Journal of International Law 83*, no. 3 (July 1989): 590–95.

Disney, Nigel. "Review of *Hyena's Sun (Soleil des Hyenes)*." *MERIP Reports*, no. 66 (April 1978): 22.

Drake, Laura. "Arab-Israeli Relations in a New Middle East Order: The Politics of Economic Cooperation." In *The Political Economy of Middle East Peace*, ed. J. W. Wright. London: Routledge, 1999.

Dunn, Ross E. *The Adventures of Ibn Battuta: A Muslim Traveler of the 14th Century*. Berkeley: University of California Press, 1996.

———."International Migrations of Literate Muslims in the Later Middle Period: The Case of Ibn Battuta." In *Golden Roads: Migration, Pilgrimage, and Travel in Medieval and Modern Islam*, ed. Ian Richard Netton, 75–85. Chippenham, UK: Curzon Press, 1993.

Dunning, J. H., and G. McQueen. "Multinational Corporations in the International Hotel Industry." *Annals of Tourism Research 9*, no. 1 (1982): 69–90.

Economist Intelligence Unit (EIU). "North Africa." *International Tourism Quarterly*, no. 4 (1972).

———. "The Role of Tourism in Economic Development: Is It a Benefit or a Burden?" *International Tourism Quarterly*, no. 2 (1973): 53–68.

———. "Tunisia." *International Tourism Report* 4 (October 1988).

EcoPeace. "The Gulf of Aqaba: The Pearl of the Red Sea." East Jerusalem: Friends of the Earth Middle East, 1995.

Edwards, Mike. "Tunisia: Sea, Sand, Success." *National Geographic* 157, no. 2 (February 1980): 184–217.

Ehteshami, Anoushiravan. *Globalization and Geopolitics in the Middle East*. London: Routledge, 2007.

Elsheshtawy, Yasser. "Redrawing Boundaries: Dubai, an Emerging Global City." In *Planning Middle Eastern Cities: An Urban Kaleidoscope in a Globalizing World*, ed. Yasser Elsheshtawy, 169–99. London: Routledge, 2004.

Endy, Christopher. *Cold War Holidays: American Tourism in France*. Chapel Hill: University of North Carolina Press, 2004.

Esposito, John L., and John O. Voll. *Makers of Contemporary Islam*. Oxford: Oxford University Press, 2001.

Euben, Roxanne L. *Journeys to the Other Shore: Muslim and Western Travelers in Search of Knowledge.* Princeton, N.J.: Princeton University Press, 2006.

Evans, Peter. *Dependent Development: The Alliance of Multinational, State, and Local Capital in Brazil.* Princeton, N.J.: Princeton University Press, 1979.

———. "Foreign Capital and the Third World State." In *Understanding Political Development,* ed. Myron Weiner and Samuel P. Huntington, 319–52. Boston: Little, Brown, 1987.

Export and Finance Bank. "Tourism Sector Report," June 20. Amman, Jordan: Investment Banking Unit, 2004.

Fakhoury, Leen. "Reuse of the Vernacular Built Environment in Tourism Development Projects in Jordan." *Traditional Dwellings and Settlements Working Paper Series* 107 (1998): 1–27.

Falise, M., and P. Masson. "La politique de développement technologique en Tunisie." *Annuaire de l'Afrique du Nord* 15 (1976): 161–74.

Findlay, Allan. "Tunisia: The Vicissitudes of Economic Development." In *North Africa,* ed. R. Lawless and A. Findlay, 217–40. London: Croom Helm, 1984.

Fineberg, Adam. "Regional Cooperation in the Tourism Industry." *Israel/Palestine: Issues in Conflict, Issues for Cooperation* 2, no. 6 (August 1993).

Fischbach, Michael R. *State, Society, and Land in Jordan.* Leiden: Brill, 2000.

Flanagan, Maurice. "Long-Haul Hubs and the Future of Air Transport." In *The Travel and Tourism Competitiveness Report 2007,* ed. Jennifer Blanke and Thea Chiesa, 95–106. Geneva: World Economic Forum, 2007.

Fliegel, Lisa. "In Search of a Jordanian Architectural Style." *New Middle East Magazine,* June–July 1994.

Friedman, Thomas L. *The Lexus and the Olive Tree: Understanding Globalization.* New York: Farrar, Straus, and Giroux, 1999.

Fröbel, Folker, Jürgen Heinrichs, and Otto Kreye. *The New International Division of Labour: Structural Unemployment in Industrialised Countries and Industrialisation in Developing Countries.* Cambridge: Cambridge University Press, 1980.

Furlough, Ellen. "Une leçon des choses: Tourism, Empire, and the Nation in Interwar France." *French Historical Studies* 25, no. 3 (Summer 2002): 441–73.

Furlough, Ellen, and Rosemary Wakeman. "La Grande Motte: Regional Development, Tourism, and the State." In *Being Elsewhere: Tourism, Consumer Culture, and Identity in Modern Europe and North America,* ed. Shelley Baranowski and Ellen Furlough, 345–72. Ann Arbor: University of Michigan Press, 2001.

Gant, Robert, and José Smith. "Tourism and National Development Planning in Tunisia." *Tourism Management* 13, no. 3 (September 1992): 331–36.

Gelbman, Alon. "Border Tourism in Israel: Conflict, Peace, Fear, and Hope." *Tourism Geographies* 10, no. 1 (May 2008): 193–213.

Gendzier, Irene L. *Notes from the Minefield: United States Intervention in Lebanon and the Middle East, 1945–1958*. Boulder, Colo.: Westview Press, 1999.

Geyer, Georgie Anne. *Tunisia: A Journey through a Country That Works*. London: Stacey International Publishers, 2004.

Gilpin, Robert. *Global Political Economy: Understanding the International Economic Order*. Princeton, N.J.: Princeton University Press, 2001.

Goldstone, Patricia. *Making the World Safe for Tourism*. New Haven, Conn.: Yale University Press, 2001.

Gradus, Yehuda. "Is Eilat-Aqaba a Bi-national City? Can Economic Opportunities Overcome the Barriers of Politics and Psychology?" *GeoJournal* 54 (2001): 85–99.

Gray, H. Peter. "The Contributions of Economics to Tourism." *Annals of Tourism Research* 9, no. 1 (1982): 105–25.

Gray, Matthew. "Development Strategies and the Political Economy of Tourism in Contemporary Jordan." In *Jordan in Transition, 1990–2000*, ed. George Joffé, 308–29. London: C. Hurst, 2001.

———. "Economic Reform, Privatization, and Tourism in Egypt." *Middle Eastern Studies* 34, no. 2 (April 1998): 91–112.

———. "The Political Economy of Tourism in Syria: State, Society, and Economic Liberalization." *Arab Studies Quarterly* 19, no. 2 (Spring 1997): 57–73

Greene, Joseph A. "Tourism and Archaeology." In *The Oxford Encyclopedia of Archaeology in the Near East,* ed. Eric M. Meyers and American Schools of Oriental Research, 222–26. New York: Oxford University Press, 1997.

Greenwood, Scott. "Jordan, the Al-Aqsa Intifada, and America's 'War on Terror.'" *Middle East Policy* 10, no. 3 (Fall 2003): 90–111.

Gregory, Derek. "Colonial Nostalgia and Cultures of Travel: Spaces of Constructed Visibility in Egypt." In *Consuming Tradition, Manufacturing Heritage,* ed. Nezar Alsayyad, 111–51. London: Routledge, 2001.

———. *The Colonial Present: Afghanistan, Iraq, Palestine*. Malden, Mass.: Blackwell, 2004.

Grissa, Abdelsatar. "The Tunisian State Enterprises and Privatization Policy." In *Tunisia: The Political Economy of Reform,* ed. I. William Zartman. Boulder, Colo.: Lynne Rienner, 1991.

Group Huit. "The Sociocultural Effects of Tourism in Tunisia: A Case

Study of Sousse." In *Tourism: Passport to Development?* ed. Emanuel de Kadt, 285–304. New York: Oxford University Press, 1979.

Hadidi, Adnan. "Conservation and Tourism in Petra and Jerash." In *Conservation and Tourism,* 108–112. London: Heritage Trust, 1985.

Hamdi, Mohamed Elhachmi. *The Politicisation of Islam: A Case Study of Tunisia.* Boulder, Colo.: Westview Press, 1998.

Hamil, Jim. *Mediterranean Textiles and Clothings.* Special Report no. 1121. London: Economist Intelligence Unit, 1989.

———. "Multinational Activity in the Mediterranean Rim Textile and Clothing Industry." In *Multinational Enterprises in Less Developed Countries,* ed. Peter J. Buckley and Jeremy Clegg. New York: St. Martin's Press, 1991.

Hammond, Philip C. "Petra: Myth and Reality." *ARAMCO World* 42, no. 5 (September–October 1991): 32–41.

Hammudeh, Musa. "Tourism Industry." In *Business and Investment in Jordan: Industry, Trade and Services,* ed. Wahib Shair, Ibrahim Badran, Ali Dajani, Moussa Hamoudeh, and Zeid Hamzah, 89–117. Amman: Steering Committee and Allied Accountants, 1995.

Hamouda, M. L. "Quelques aspects economiques de tourisme en Tunisie." *Revue Tunisienne de Sciences Sociales,* no. 22 (1970): 185–201.

Hannigan, John. *Fantasy City: Pleasure and Profit in the Postmodern Metropolis.* London: Routledge, 1998.

Hanouz, Margareta, and Tarik Yousef. "Assessing Competitiveness in the Arab World." In *The Arab World Competitiveness Report 2007.* Geneva: World Economic Forum, 2007.

Harb, Mona. "Pious Entertainment in Beirut: Al-Saha Traditional Village." *ISIM Review* 17 (2006): 10–11.

Harik, Iliya. "Privatization and Development in Tunisia." In *Privatization and Liberalization in the Middle East,* ed. Iliya Harik and Denis J. Sullivan, 210–32. Bloomington: Indiana University Press, 1992.

Harknett, Richard J., and Jefferey A. VanDenBerg. "Alignment Theory and Interrelated Threats: Jordan and the Persian Gulf War." *Security Studies* 6, no. 3 (Spring 1997): 112–53.

Harrison, David. "Tourism, Capitalism, and Development in Less Developed Countries." In *Capitalism and Development,* ed. Leslie Sklair, 232–57. London: Routledge, 1994.

Harvey, David. "The Art of Rent: Globalization and the Commodification of Culture." In *Spaces of Capital: Towards a Critical Geography,* 394–411. New York: Routledge, 2001.

———. *The Condition of Postmodernity: An Enquiry into the Origins of Cultural Change.* Oxford: Basil Blackwell, 1989.

———. *The Urban Experience.* Baltimore: Johns Hopkins University Press, 1989.

———. "A View from Federal Hill." In *Spaces of Capital: Towards a Critical Geography,* 128–57. New York: Routledge, 2001.

Hassan Bin Talal. "Jordan and the Peace Process." *Middle East Policy* 3, no. 3 (1994): 31–40.

Hazbun, Waleed. "The East as an Exhibit: Thomas Cook & Son and the Origins of the International Tourism Economy in Egypt." In *The Business of Tourism: Place, Faith, and History,* ed. Philip Scranton and Janet Davidson, 3–33. Philadelphia: University of Pennsylvania Press, 2007.

———. "Globalization, Reterritorialization, and the Political Economy of Tourism Development in the Middle East." *Geopolitics* 9, no. 2 (Summer 2004): 310–41.

———. "Mapping the Landscape of the 'New Middle East': The Politics of Tourism Development and the Peace Process in Jordan." In *Jordan in Transition, 1990–2000,* ed. George Joffé, 330–45. New York: Palgrave, 2002.

———. "Rethinking Anti-colonial Movements and the Political Economy of Decolonization: The Case of Tunisia." *Arab Studies Quarterly* 16, no. 1 (Winter 1994): 77–106.

Held, David, Anthony McGrew, David Goldbatt, and Jonathan Perraton. *Global Transformations: Politics, Economics and Culture.* Stanford, Calif.: Stanford University Press, 1999.

Henderson, Jeffrey, Peter Dicken, Martin Hess, Neil Coe, and Henry Wai-chung Yeung. "Global Production Networks and Analysis of Economic Development." *Review of International Political Economy* 9, no. 3 (August 2002): 436–64.

Henderson, Joan. "Tourism in Dubai: Overcoming Barriers to Destination Development." *International Journal of Tourism Research* 8 (2006): 87–99.

Henry, Clement M. *Challenges of Global Capital Markets to Information-Shy Regimes: The Case of Tunisia.* Occasional Papers, no. 19. Abu Dhabi: Emirates Center for Strategic Studies and Research, 1998.

Henry, Clement M., and Robert Springborg. *Globalization and the Politics of Development in the Middle East.* Cambridge: Cambridge University Press, 2001.

Hirschman, Albert O. "The Rise and Decline of Development Economics." In *Essays in Trespassing.* Cambridge: Cambridge University Press, 1981.

Hopkins, Michael. *Tunisia to 1993: Steering for Stability.* Special Report no. 1132. London: Economist Intelligence Unit, 1989.

Hopkins, Nicholas S. "Tunisia: An Open and Shut Case." *Social Problems* 28, no. 4 (April 1981).

Human Rights Watch. *False Freedom: Online Censorship in the Middle East and North Africa.* Washington, D.C.: Human Rights Watch, 2005.

Hussein ibn Talal. *Uneasy Lies the Head*. New York: Random House, 1962.

Huxley, Frederick C. "Development in Hammam Sousse, Tunisia: Change, Continuity, and Challenge." In *Anthropology and Development in North Africa and the Middle East,* ed. Muneera Salem-Murdock and Michael M. Horowitz. Boulder, Colo.: Westview Press, 1990.

Huybrechts, Eric. "Beirut: Building Regional Circuits." In *Global Networks, Linked Cities,* ed. Saskia Sassen, 237–46. London: Routledge, 2002.

International Monetary Fund (IMF). *Tunisia: Recent Economic Developments*. Staff Country Report no. 00/37. Washington, D.C.: International Monetary Fund, 2000.

Ioannides, Dimitri. "Strengthening the Ties between Tourism and Economic Geography: A Theoretical Agenda." *Professional Geographer* 47, no. 1 (1995): 49–60.

Israel, Government of. "Chapter 7: Tourism Development Options." In *Development Options for Cooperation: The Middle East/East Mediterranean Region: 1996 Version IV.* Jerusalem: Ministry of Foreign Affairs, Ministry of Finance, 1995.

Jbili, Abdelali, and Klaus Enders. "The Association Agreement between Tunisia and the European Union." *Finance and Development,* September 1996, 18–20.

Jedidi, Mohamed. "L'Expansion du tourise en Tunisie et ses problems." *Revue Tunisienne de Géographie,* no. 18 (1990): 149–80.

Jenner, Paul, and Christine Smith. *Tourism in the Mediterranean.* Research Report. London: Economist Intelligence Unit, 1993.

Jilani, Amor. "The Tunisian-European Association Agreement: Towards Founding a Euro-Mediterranean Zone." In *Regional Economic Cooperation in the Mediterranean,* ed. Olaf Köndgen, 51–55. Amman: Konrad Adenauer Foundation, 1997.

Joffé, George, ed. *Perspectives on Development: The Euro-Mediterranean Partnerships.* London: Frank Cass, 1999.

Jones, Jeremy. "Dubai: The Airport State." In *Negotiating Change: The New Politics of the Middle East,* 180–205. London: I. B. Tauris, 2007.

Jordan, Central Bank of. *Yearly Statistical Series (1964–1993).* Amman: Department of Research and Studies, Central Bank of Jordan, 1994.

Jordan, Hashemite Kingdom of. *Aqaba: An Overview of Projects.* Amman: Ministry of Planning, 1995.

———. *Dead Sea Tourist Area.* Amman: Ministry of Planning, 1995.

———. *Jordan: A Winning Business Destination, "Tourism Sector."* Amman: Ministry of Planning, 1997.

———. *Jordan Diary.* Amman: International Press Office, the Royal Hashemite Court, 1998.

———. *Jordan's Development Showcases: The JRV and Aqaba*. Amman: Ministry of Planning, 1995.

———. *National Tourism Strategy, 2004–2010*. Amman: Ministry of Tourism and Antiquities, 2004.

———. *Tourism Infrastructure*. Amman: Ministry of Planning, 1995.

Jordan Valley Authority (JVA). *Tourism Development Project of the East Coast of the Dead Sea (SPA), Part Four: Market Evaluation and Assessment, Suweimeh and Zara Development Areas*. Amman: Jordan Valley Authority/Sigma Consulting Engineers/Tourisme et Hotellerie Sauer Int., 1996.

Judd, Dennis R. "Constructing the Tourist Bubble." In *The Tourist City*, ed. Dennis R. Judd and Susan S. Fainstein, 35–53. New Haven, Conn.: Yale University Press, 1999.

———. "Visitors and the Spatial Ecology of the City." In *Cities and Visitors*, ed. Lily M. Hoffman, Susan S. Fainstein, and Dennis R. Judd, 23–38. Malden, Mass.: Blackwell, 2003.

Judd, Dennis R., and Susan S. Fainstein, eds. *The Tourist City*. New Haven, Conn.: Yale University Press, 1999.

Kagermeier, Andeas. "Le développement de nouvelles zones touristiques en Tunisie: L'example de Tabarka." *Revue Tunisienne de Géographie*, no. 31 (2000).

———. "New Touristic Centres in Peripheral Regions of the Maghreb: Their Development and Economic Importance in Tunisia and Morocco." *Arab World Geographer* 4, no. 2 (Summer 2001): 104–16.

Kamelgarn, Daniel. "Tunisie (1970–1977), le developpement d'un capitalisme dependant." *Peuples Méditerranées* 4 (1978): 113–45.

Kanna, Ahmed. "Dubai in a Jagged World." *Middle East Report* 243 (Summer 2007): 22–29.

———. "The 'State Philosophical' in the 'Land without Philosophy': Shopping Malls, Interior Cities, and the Image of Utopia in Dubai." *Traditional Dwellings and Settlements Review* 16, no. 2 (2005): 59–73.

Kaplan, Caren. *Questions of Travel: Postmodern Discourses of Displacement*. Durham, N.C.: Duke University Press, 1996.

Kassab, Suzanne. "On Two Conceptions of Globalization: The Debate around the Reconstruction of Beirut." In *Space, Culture, and Power: New Identities in Globalizing Cities*, ed. Ayse Oncu and Petra Weyland, 42–55. London: Zed Books, 1997.

Katodrytis, George. "Metropolitan Dubai and the Rise of Architectural Fantasy." *Bidoun* 4 (Spring 2005).

Katz, Kimberly. "Holy Places and National Spaces: Jordan and Islamic Jerusalem, 1948–1967." Paper presented at the Conference on the Social History of Jordan, March 24–26, 1998, Amman, Jordan.

Sponsored by Al-Urdun Al-Jadid Research Center and the University of Jordan.

Katzenstein, Peter J., ed. *The Culture of National Security: Norms and Identity in World Politics.* New York: Columbia University Press, 1996.

Kaye, Dalia Dassa. *Beyond the Handshake: Multilateral Cooperation in the Arab-Israeli Peace Process, 1991–1996.* New York: Columbia University Press, 2001.

Keck, Margaret E., and Kathryn Sikkink. *Activists beyond Borders: Advocacy Networks in International Politics.* Ithaca, N.Y.: Cornell University Press, 1998.

Keller, William W., and Louis W. Pauly. "Globalization at Bay." *Current History,* November 1997, 370–76.

Kelly, Majorie. "Jordan's Potential Tourism Development." *Annals of Tourism Research* 25, no. 4 (1998): 904–18.

Kemp, A., and U. Ben-Eliezer. "Dramatizing Sovereignty: The Construction of Territorial Dispute in the Israeli-Egyptian Border at Taba." *Political Geography* 19 (2000): 315–44.

Keohane, Robert O. *Power and Governance in a Partially Globalized World.* New York: Routledge, 2002.

Keshavarzian, Arang. *Bazaar and State in Iran.* Cambridge: Cambridge University Press, 2007.

Khalaf, Samir. *Civil and Uncivil Violence in Lebanon.* New York: Columbia University Press, 2002.

Khaled, Leila. *My People Shall Live.* Toronto: NC Press, 1975.

Khashan, Hilal. "The Levant: Yes to Treaties, No to Normalization." *Middle East Quarterly,* June 1995.

Khouri, Rami. *The Jordan Valley: Life and Society below Sea Level.* London: Longman, 1981.

King, Robert J. "The Political Logic of Economic Reform in Tunisia." In *Economic Crisis and Political Change in North Africa,* ed. Azzedine Layachi, 107–28. Westport, Conn.: Praeger, 1998.

Kjorlien, Michele L. "Peace Monitor: Jordanian-Israeli Track." *Journal of Palestine Studies* 31, no. 1 (Autumn 2001).

Koolhaas, Rem, Mitra Khoubrou, and Ole Bouman, eds. *Al Manakh: Analysis of Developments along the Gulf.* Amsterdam: Archis Foundation, 2007.

Kornbluth, Danishai. "Jordan and the Anti-normalization Campaign, 1994–2001." *Terrorism and Political Violence* 14, no. 3 (August 2002): 80–108.

Kotkin, Joel. *The New Geography.* New York: Random House, 2000.

Kovach, George S. *A Tourism Plan of Action for Jordan.* Amman: Communications Media Center, United States Operations Mission/Jordan, 1959.

Krasner, Stephen D. *Structural Conflict: The Third World against Global Liberalism*. Berkeley: University of California Press, 1985.

Krugman, Paul. *Development, Geography, and Economic Theory*. Cambridge, Mass.: MIT Press, 1995.

Lanfant, Marie-Françoise. "Introduction: Tourism in the Process of Internationalization." *International Social Science Journal* 32 (November 1980): 14–43.

Lash, Scott, and John Urry. *Economies of Signs and Space*. London: Sage, 1994.

Lasta, Zohra. "Aspects et problems du tourisme dans las ville de Tunis." *Revue Tunisienne de Géographie* no. 21–22 (1992): 120–54.

Lavie, Smadar. "Sinai for the Coffee Table: Birds, Bedouin, and Desert Wanderlust." *MERIP Reports*, no. 150 (January–February 1988): 40–44.

Laws, Eric. *Tourism Destination Management: Issues, Analysis, and Policies*. London: Routledge, 1995.

Layne, Linda. *Home and Homeland: The Dialogics of Tribal and National Identities in Jordan*. Princeton, N.J.: Princeton University Press, 1994.

Lesch, Ann Mosely. "The Egyptian-Israel Accord to Submit the Dispute over Taba to International Arbitration." In *The Middle East and North Africa: Essays in Honor of J. C. Hurewitz*, ed. Reeva S. Simon, 95–118. New York: Columbia University Press, 1990.

Lijphart, Arend. "Tourist Traffic and the Integration Potential." *Journal of Common Market Studies* 2, no. 3 (March 1964): 251–62.

Lipietz, Alain. *Mirages and Miracles: The Crisis of Global Fordism*. London: Verso, 1987.

Llena, Claude. "Tozeur, ravagée par le tourisme." *Le Monde Diplomatique*, July 2004.

Lobban, Richard A. "Responding to Middle Eastern Urban Poverty: The Informal Economy in Tunis." In *Population, Poverty, and Politics in Middle Eastern Cities*, ed. Michael E. Bonie, 85–112. Gainesville: University Press of Florida, 1997.

Löfgren, Orvar. *On Holiday: A History of Vacationing*. Berkeley: University of California Press, 1999.

L'Officiel du Tourisme en Tunisie. El Manar II, Tunisia: MarCom Editions, 1996.

Lucas, Russell E. *Institutions and the Politics of Survival in Jordan: Domestic Responses to External Challenges, 1988–2001*. Albany: State University of New York Press, 2005.

———. "Jordan: The Death of Normalization with Israel." *Middle East Journal* 58, no. 1 (Winter 2004): 93–111.

Lynch, Marc. "Jordan's Identity and Interests." In *Identity and Foreign Policy in the Middle East*, ed. Shibley Telhami and Michael N. Barnett, 26–57. Ithaca, N.Y.: Cornell University Press, 2002.

———. *State Interests and Public Spheres: The International Politics of Jordan's Identity.* New York: Columbia University Press, 1999.

———. *Voices of the New Arab Public.* New York: Columbia University Press, 2006.

MacCannell, Dean. *The Tourist: A New Theory of the Leisure Class.* New ed. Berkeley: University of California Press, 1999.

Maffi, Irene. "De l'usage de l'histoire par le pouvoir en Jordanie: Les musée et la construction de l'identité nationale à partir de 1967." *Jordanies,* no. 5–6 (June–December 1998): 84–99.

Majali, Abdul Salam, Jawad A. Anani, and Munther J. Haddadin. *Peacemaking: The Inside Story of the 1994 Jordanian-Israeli Treaty.* Norman: University of Oklahoma Press, 2006.

Mansfeld, Yoel. "Acquired Tourism Deficiency Syndrome: Planning and Developing Tourism in Israel." In *Mediterranean Tourism: Facets of Socioeconomic Development and Cultural Change,* ed. Yiorgos Apostolopoulos, Philippos Loukissas, and Lila Leontidou, 159–78. London: Routledge, 2001.

Marchal, Roland. "Dubai: Global City and Transnational Hub." In *Transnational Connections and the Arab Gulf,* ed. Madawi Al-Rasheed, 93–100. London: Routledge, 2005.

Martin, Lisa L. "The Leverage of Economic Theories: Explaining Governance in an Internationalized Industry." In *Governance in a Global Economy: Political Authority in Transition,* ed. Miles Kahler and David A. Lake, 33–59. Princeton, N.J.: Princeton University Press, 2003.

Massad, Joseph A. *Colonial Effects: The Making of National Identity in Jordan.* New York: Columbia University Press, 2001.

Matthews, Harry G. *International Tourism: A Political and Social Analysis.* Cambridge: Schenkman, 1978.

Matthews, Harry G., and Linda K. Richter. "Political Science and Tourism." *Annals of Tourism Research* 18 (1991): 120–35.

McBride, E. "Burj Al Arab." *Architecture* 89, no. 8 (2000): 116–27.

Meier, Gerald M., ed. *Leading Issues in Economic Development.* New York: Oxford University Press, 1976.

Meital, Yoram. "The Economic Relations between Israel and Egypt: Tourism, 1979–1984." In *Economic Cooperation in the Middle East,* ed. Gideon Fishelson, 283–301. Boulder, Colo.: Westview Press, 1989.

Memmi, Albert. "Jews, Tunisians, and Frenchmen." *Literary Review* 41, no. 2 (Winter 1998): 223–27.

Menicucci, Garay. "Review of *Bezness.*" *Middle East Report,* no. 192 (January–February 1995): 30–31.

Migdal, Joel S. *Strong Societies and Weak States: State-Society Relations and State Capabilities in the Third World.* Princeton, N.J.: Princeton University Press, 1988.

Ministere de L'Economie Nationale. *VIème Plan de Developpement Economique et Social, 1982–1986: Le Tourism.* Tunis: Republique Tunisienne, 1982.

Ministere du Tourisme et de L'Artisanat. *VIIIème Plan, 1992–1996: Rapport definitif de la Commission Sectorielle du Tourism, du Themalisme et de L'Artisanat.* Tunis: Republique Tunisienne, 1991.

Miossec, Jean-Marie. "La croissance du tourisme en Tunisie." *L'Information Géographique,* no. 4 (September–October 1972): 169–78.

———. "Le tourism en Tunisie: Un pays en développement dans l'espace touristique international (résumé de thèse)." *Les Cahiers d'URBAMA,* no. 13 (1997): 116–22.

Mitchell, Timothy. "Nationalism, Imperialism, Economism: A Comment on Habermas." *Public Culture* 10, no. 2 (1998).

———. *Rule of Experts: Egypt, Techno-politics, Modernity.* Berkeley: University of California Press, 2002.

———. "Worlds Apart: An Egyptian Village and the International Tourism Industry." *Middle East Report,* no. 196 (September–October 1995): 8–11.

Mody, Ashoka, and David Wheeler. *Automation and World Competition: New Technologies, Industrial Location, and Trade.* New York: St. Martin's Press, 1990.

Moore, Clement Henry. "Tunisia and Bourguibisme: Twenty Years of Crisis." *Third World Quarterly* 10 (1988): 176–90.

Moore, Pete W. *Doing Business in the Middle East: Politics and Economic Crisis in Jordan and Kuwait.* Cambridge: Cambridge University Press, 2004.

Morgan, Michael. "Homogeneous Products: The Future of Established Resorts." In *Global Tourism,* ed. William F. Theobald, 317–36. Oxford: Butterworth-Heinemann, 1998.

Morris, Peter, and Daniel Jacobs. *Tunisia: The Rough Guide.* 4th ed. London: Rough Guides, 1995.

MOTA/Dar Al-Handasah. *Petra Priority Action Plan Study: Phase One Report, Outline Development and Growth Scenario—Petra Region.* Vol. 1, *Existing Conditions.* Amman: Ministry of Tourism and Antiquities, the Hashemite Kingdom of Jordan/Dar Al-Handasah, 1996.

———. *Petra Priority Action Plan Study: Phase Two Report, Urban Development Plans.* Amman: Ministry of Tourism and Antiquities, the Hashemite Kingdom of Jordan/Dar Al-Handasah, 1999.

———. *Petra Priority Action Plan Study: Phase Three Report (Additional Items), Tourist Park Zone, Industrial Area, Elgee Traditional Village.* Amman: Ministry of Tourism and Antiquities, the Hashemite Kingdom of Jordan/Dar Al-Handasah, 1996.

MOTA/JICA. *The Study on the Tourism Development in the Hashemite Kingdom of Jordan.* Amman: Ministry of Tourism and Antiquities

(MOTA), the Hashemite Kingdom of Jordan and the Japan International Cooperation Agency, 1996.

Moudoud, Ezzeddine. "Les stratégies de relocalisation des firms multinationales." *Revue d'Économie Politique* 99, no. 1 (January–February 1989): 96–122.

———. *Modernization, the State, and Regional Disparity in Developing Countries: Tunisia in Historical Perspective, 1881–1982.* Boulder, Colo.: Westview Press, 1989.

Moussalli, Ahmad S. "Globalization and the Nation State in the Arab World." *MESA Bulletin* 32 (1998): 11–14.

Mowforth, Martin, and Ian Munt. *Tourism and Sustainability: New Tourism in the Third World.* London: Routledge, 1998.

Mufti, Malik. "Elite Bargains and the Onset of Political Liberalization in Jordan." *Comparative Political Studies* 32, no. 1 (February 1999): 100–129.

———. "Jordanian Foreign Policy: State Interests and Dynastic Ambitions." Paper presented at the Politique et Etat en Jordanie, 1946–96 conference, Institut du Monde Arabe, Paris, June 24–25, 1997.

Murphy, Emma C. *Economic and Political Change in Tunisia: From Bourguiba to Ben Ali.* Hampshire: Macmillan, 1999.

———. "Economic Reform and the State in Tunisia." In *The State and Global Change: The Political Economy of Transition in the Middle East and North Africa,* ed. Hassan Hakimian and Ziba Moshaver, 135–55. Surrey: Curzon Press, 2001.

Mzabi, Hassouna. *La croissance urbanie accélérée à Jerba et ses conséquences sur la vie de relations avec L'Extérieur.* Géographie, vol. 7. Tunis: Publications de L'Université de Tunis, Faculté des Lettres et Sciences Humaines de Tunis, 1978.

———. "Le tourisme en Tunisie." *Cahiers de Tunisie,* no. 101–2 (1978): 217–28.

Newman, David. "Citizenship, Identity, and Location: The Changing Discourse of Israeli Geopolitics." In *Geopolitical Traditions: A Century of Geopolitical Thought,* ed. Klaus Dodds and David Atkinson, 302–31. London: Routledge, 2000.

———. "Geopolitics Renaissant: Territory, Sovereignty, and the World Political Map." In *Boundaries, Territory, and Postmodernity,* ed. David Newman, 1–16. London: Frank Cass, 1999.

Nicholson-Lord, David. "The Politics of Travel: Is Tourism Just Colonialism in Another Guise?" *The Nation,* October 6, 1997, 11–18.

Noy, Chaim, and Erik Cohen. "Introduction: Backpacking as a Rite of Passage in Israel." In *Israeli Backpackers,* ed. Chaim Noy and Erik Cohen. Albany: State University of New York Press, 2005.

Nsour, Maen F. "Arab-Israeli Economic Relations and Relative Gains

Concerns." In *Review Essays in Israel Studies,* ed. Laura Zittrain Eisenberg and Neil Caplan, 283–307. Albany: State University of New York Press, 2000.

Odeh, Hanna S. *Economic Development in Jordan: 1954–1971.* Amman: Hashemite Kingdom of Jordan, Ministry of Culture and Information, 1972.

Office National du Tourisme Tunisien (ONTT). *Le tourisme Tunisien en chiffres.* Tunis: Office National du Tourisme Tunisien, Various Years.

———. *Le VIIème Plan: Le developpement du secteur touristique, bilan et perspectives.* Tunis: Office National du Tourisme Tunisien, 1986.

———. *Organisation et Fonctionnement.* Tunis: Office National du Tourisme et du Thermalisme, 1975.

———. *Realisations du IVème Plan (1973–1976) et orientations generales du Vème Plan (1977–1981).* Tunis: Office National du Tourisme Tunisien, 1975.

Organization for European Economic Co-operation (OEEC). *Tourism and European Recovery.* Paris: Organization for European Economic Co-operation, 1951.

Okruhlik, Gwenn. "Image, Imagination, and Place: The Political Economy of Tourism in Saudi Arabia." In *Iran, Iraq, and the Arab Gulf States,* ed. Joseph A. Kechichian, 111–29. London: Palgrave, 2001.

Ó Tuathail, Gearóid. *Critical Geopolitics: The Politics of Writing Global Space.* Minneapolis: University of Minnesota Press, 1996.

Ó Tuathail, Gearóid, and Timothy W. Luke. "Present at the (Dis)integration: Deterritorialization and Reterritorialization in the New Wor(l)d Order." *Annals of the Association of American Geographers* 84, no. 3 (1994): 381–98.

Pacione, Michael. "City Profile: Dubai." *Cities* 22, no. 3 (2005): 255–65.

Pannell, Kerr & Forester. *The Future Course of Tourism in the Hashemite Kingdom of Jordan: Phase I Report: Planning Parameters.* Washington, D.C.: KPF, 1986.

Pascoe, David. *Airspaces.* London: Reaktion, 2001.

Pattullo, Polly. *Last Resorts: The Cost of Tourism in the Caribbean.* London: Cassell, 1996.

Paul, Jim. "States of Emergency: The Riots in Tunisia and Morocco." *MERIP Reports,* no. 127 (October 1984): 3–6.

Pearce, Douglas. *Tourist Development.* 2nd ed. Harlow: Longman, 1989.

Peres, Shimon. *Battling for Peace: A Memoir.* New York: Random House, 1995.

Peres, Shimon, with Arye Naor. *The New Middle East.* New York: Henry Holt, 1993.

Perkins, Kenneth J. *A History of Modern Tunisia.* Cambridge: Cambridge University Press, 2004.

Piore, Michael J., and Charles F. Sabel. *The Second Industrial Divide: Possibilities for Prosperity.* New York: Basic Books, 1984.

Piro, Timothy. *The Political Economy of Market Reform in Jordan.* Lanham, Md.: Rowman and Littlefield, 1998.

Pizam, Abraham. "Does Tourism Promote Peace and Understanding between Unfriendly Nations?" In *Tourism, Crime, and International Security,* ed. A. Pizzam and Y. Mansfeld, 203–13. London: John Wiley and Sons, 1996.

Pleumarom, Anita. "The Political Economy of Tourism." *Ecologist* 24, no. 4 (July–August 1994): 142–48.

Poon, Auliana. "Flexible Specialization and Small Size: The Case of Caribbean Tourism." *World Development* 18, no. 1 (1990): 109–23.

———. *Tourism, Technology, and Competitive Strategies.* Wallingford, Conn.: CAB International, 1993.

Porter, P., and E. Sheppard. "Tourism and Development." In *A World of Difference: Society, Nature, Development,* 540–52. New York: Guilford Press, 1998.

Puig, Nicolas. "Nouvelles sociabilitiés dans le Sud: Territoires et forms d'organisation collective à Tozeur." *Maghreb Machrek,* no. 157 (July–September 1997): 78–89.

Rabinowitz, Dan. "Postnational Palestine/Israel? Globalization, Diaspora, Transnationalism, and the Israeli-Palestinian Conflict." *Critical Inquiry* 26, no. 4 (Summer 2000): 757–72.

Rabinowitz, Dan, and Khawla Abu-Baker. *Coffins on Our Shoulders: The Experience of the Palestinian Citizens of Israel.* Berkeley: University of California Press, 2005.

Richards, Alan, and John Waterbury. *A Political Economy of the Middle East.* 2nd ed. Boulder, Colo.: Westview Press, 1998.

Richter, Linda K. *The Politics of Tourism in Asia.* Honolulu: University of Hawaii Press, 1989.

———. "Tourism Politics and Political Science: A Case of Not So Benign Neglect." *Annals of Tourism Research* 10 (1983): 313–35.

Richter, Linda K., and W. L. Waugh. "Terrorism and Tourism as Logical Companions." *Tourism Management* 7 (December 1986): 230–38.

Ritter, Wigand. "Tourism in the United Arab Emirates." *Arabian Gulf Studies* 37 (1985): 165–99.

Rosenau, James N. *Along the Domestic-Foreign Frontier: Exploring Governance in a Turbulent World.* Cambridge: Cambridge University Press, 1997.

———. *Distance Proximities: Dynamics beyond Globalization.* Princeton, N.J.: Princeton University Press, 2003.

Rosenstein-Rodan, Paul N. "Problems of Industrialization of Eastern and South-Eastern Europe." *Economic Journal* 53 (June–September 1943): 202–11.

———. "The Theory of the 'Big Push.'" In *Leading Issues in Economic Development*, ed. Gerald M. Meier, 632–36. New York: Oxford University Press, 1976.

Ross, Dennis. *The Missing Peace*. New York: Farrar Straus Giroux, 2004.

Royal Society for the Conservation of Nature (RSCN). *Conservation of the Dana Wildlands and Institutional Strengthening of the RSCN*. Amman: World Bank/UNDP, 1997.

———. *Socio-economic Development for Nature Conservation*. Amman: USAID, 2000.

Russell, Kenneth W. "Ethnohistory of the Bedul Bedouin of Petra." *Annual of the Department of Antiquties of Jordan (ADAJ)* 27 (1993): 15–35.

Ryan, Curtis R. "Jordan in the Middle East Peace Process: From War to Peace with Israel." In *The Middle East Peace Process: Interdisciplinary Perspectives*, ed. Ilan Peleg, 161–77. Albany: State University of New York Press, 1998.

———. *Jordan in Transition: from Hussein to Abdullah*. Boulder, Colo.: Lynne Rienner, 2002.

Sabel, Charles F. "Learning by Monitoring: The Institutions of Economic Development." In *Handbook of Economic Sociology*, ed. Neil Smelser and Richard Swedberg. Princeton, N.J.: Princeton-Sage, 1993.

Said, Edward W. "The Arab Right Wing." In *Reaction and Counter-revolution in the Contemporary Arab World*, ed. Association of Arab-American University Graduates. AAUG Information Paper no. 21. Detroit: AAUG, 1978.

———. *Orientalism*. New York: Vintage Books, 1979.

Saihi, Tahar. "La Tunisie et les nouveaux marchés touristique." Paper presented at "Le tourism tunisien face aux défis de l'an 2000," colloquium sponsored by Centre de Recheres et d'Études Adminstratives and *Information Touristique*, May 19, 1989, Tunis.

Salem, Ali. *A Drive to Israel: An Egyptian Meets His Neighbor*. Trans. Robert J. Silverman. Tel Aviv, Israel: Moshe Dayan Center for Middle Eastern and African Studies, Tel Aviv University. English translation of essays published in 1994 in *Al-Akhbar Al-Youm* (Cairo), 2003.

Salem, Norma. "Tunisia." In *The Politics of Islamic Revivalism: Diversity and Unity*, ed. Shireen T. Hunter, 148–70. Bloomington: Indiana University Press, 1988.

Sampler, Jeffrey, and Saeb Eigner. *Sand to Silicon: Achieving Rapid Growth, Lessons from Dubai*. London: Profile Books, 2003.

Sampson, Anthony. *Empires of the Sky: The Politics, Contests, and Cartels of World Airlines*. New York: Random House, 1984.

Sassen, Saskia. *The Global City: New York, London, Tokyo*. Princeton, N.J.: Princeton University Press, 2001.

———. *Globalization and Its Discontents*. New York: New Press, 1998.

Satloff, Robert B. "Jordan's Great Gamble: Economic Crisis and Political

Reform." In *The Politics of Economic Reform in the Middle East,* ed.
Henri J. Barkey, 129–52. New York: St. Martin's Press, 1992.

———. "The Path to Peace." *Foreign Policy,* no. 100 (Fall 1995): 109–15.

———. *Troubles on the East Bank: Challenges to the Domestic Stability of Jordan.* New York: Praeger, 1986.

Saxenian, Annalee. *Regional Advantage: Culture and Competition in Silicon Valley and Route 128.* Cambridge, Mass.: Harvard University Press, 1994.

Scham, Paul L., and Russell E. Lucas. "'Normalization' and 'Anti-normalization' in Jordan: The Public Debate." *Middle East Review of International Affairs* 5, no. 3 (September 2001): 54–70.

Scholte, Jan Aart. *Globalization: A Critical Introduction.* New York: Palgrave, 2000.

Scott, Allen J. "The Cultural Economy: Geography and the Creative Field." *Media, Culture, and Society* 21 (1999): 807–17.

———. *Regions and the World Economy: The Coming Shape of Global Production, Competition, and Political Order.* Oxford: Oxford University Press, 1998.

Scott, James C. *Seeing like a State: How Certain Schemes to Improve the Human Condition Have Failed.* New Haven, Conn.: Yale University Press, 1998.

Seddon, David. "Riot and Rebellion in North Africa." In *Power and Stability in the Middle East,* ed. Berch Berberoglu, 114–35. London: Zed Press, 1989.

———. "Winter of Discontent: Economic Crisis in Tunisia and Morocco." *MERIP Reports,* no. 127 (October 1984): 7–16.

Sethom, Noureddine. *L'Industrie et le tourisme en Tunisie: Etude de géographie du développement.* Géographie, vols. 31–32. Tunis: Publications de la Faculté des sciences sociales et humaines de Tunis, Deuxieme serie, Université de Tunis, 1992.

———. "L'Industrie et le tourisme en Tunisie: Problematique du development." *Revue Tunisienne de Géographie,* no. 18 (1990): 237–60.

———. *L'Influence de Tourisme sur l'économie et la vie régionales dans la Zone de Nabeul-Hammamet.* Tunis: Publications de la Faculté des Lettres et Sciences Humaines de Tunis–Étude de Géographie économique, Université de Tunis, 1979.

Shafir, Gershon, and Yoav Peled. "Peace and Profits: The Globalization of Israeli Business and the Peace Process." In *The New Israel: Peacemaking and Liberalization,* ed. Gershon Shafir and Yoav Peled, 243–64. Boulder, Colo.: Westview Press, 2000.

Shahin, Emad Eldin. *Political Assent: Contemporary Islamic Movements in North Africa.* Boulder, Colo.: Westview Press, 1997.

Shapiro, Michael J. *Violent Cartographies: Mapping Cultures of War.* Minneapolis: University of Minnesota Press, 1997.

Sharp, James. "The Port El Kantaoui Tourist Complex and Its Regional Consequences." In *Field Studies in Tunisia,* ed. Ray Harris and Dick Lawless, 88–96. Durham, UK: Department of Geography, University of Durham, 1981.

Sharpley, Richard, and David J. Telfer, eds. *Tourism and Development: Concepts and Issues.* Clevendon, UK: Channel View Publications, 2002.

Shlaim, Avi. *The Iron Wall: Israel and the Arab World.* New York: Norton, 2001.

Short, John Rennie. *Global Dimensions: Space, Place, and the Contemporary World.* London: Reaktion, 2001.

Shoup, John. "The Impact of Tourism on the Bedouin of Petra." *Middle East Journal* 39, no. 2 (Spring 1985): 227–91.

Signoles, Pierre. *L'Espace Tunisien: Capital et Etat-Région.* Fascicule de Recherches no. 15 (Tome II). Tours: Centre d'Etudes et de Recherches URBAMA, 1985.

Simms, Steven, and Deborah Kooring. "The Bedul Bedouin of Petra, Jordan: Traditions, Tourism and an Uncertain Future." *Cultural Survival Quarterly* 19, no. 4 (Winter 1996): 22–25.

Simonis, Damien, and Hugh Finlay. *Jordan and Syria: A Lonely Planet Travel Survival Kit.* Hawthorn, UK: Lonely Planet Publications, 1997.

Sinclair, M. Thea. "Tourism and Economic Development: A Survey." *Journal of Development Studies* 34, no. 5 (June 1998): 1–51.

Sinclair, M. T., and V. Bote Gómez. "Tourism, the Spanish Economy, and the Balance of Payments." In *Tourism in Spain: Critical Perspectives,* ed. M. Barke, M. Newton, and J. Tower. Wallingford, Conn.: CAB International, 1996.

Smaoui, Ahmed. "Tourism and Employment in Tunisia." In *Tourism: Passport to Development?* ed. Emanuel de Kadt, 101–10. New York: Oxford University Press, 1979.

Smith, Valene L., ed. *Hosts and Guests: The Anthropology of Tourism.* Oxford: Basil Blackwell, 1978; 2nd ed., Philadelphia: University of Pennsylvania Press, 1989.

Sowers, Jeannie. "Nature Reserves and Authoritarian Rule in Egypt." *Journal of Environment and Development,* December 2007.

Stanley, Bruce. "Middle East City Networks and the 'New Urbanism.'" *Cities* 22, no. 3 (2005): 189–99.

Stein, Rebecca Luna. "'First Contact' and Other Israeli Fictions: Tourism, Globalization, and the Middle East Peace Process." *Public Culture* 14, no. 3 (2002): 515–43.

———. "Itineraries of Peace: Remapping Israeli and Palestinian Tourism." *Middle East Report,* no. 196 (September–October 1995): 16–19.

Steiner, Christian. "Contributing to Vulnerability or Stability? Strategies of Trans-national Tourism Companies in the Arab World after 9/11."

Paper presented at the Middle East Studies Association (MESA) Meeting, San Francisco, 2004.

———. "Tourism, Poverty Reduction, and the Political Economy: Egyptian Perspectives on Tourism's Economic Benefits in a Semi-rentier State." *Tourism and Hospitality Planning and Development* 3, no. 6 (December 2006): 161–77.

Stock, Robert. "Political and Social Contributions of International Tourism to the Development of Israel." *Annals of Tourism Research* 5 (October–December 1977): 30–42.

Storper, Michael. *The Regional World: Territorial Development in a Global Economy*. New York: Guilford Press, 1997.

———. "Territories, Flows, and Hierarchies in the Global Economy." In *Spaces of Globalization: Reasserting the Power of the Local*, ed. Kevin R. Cox, 19–44. New York: Guilford Press, 1997.

Strange, Susan. *The Retreat of the State: The Diffusion of Power in the World Economy*. Cambridge: Cambridge University Press, 1996.

Summer, Doris. "The Neoliberalization of Urban Space: Transnational Investment Networks and the Circulation of Urban Images, Beirut and Amman." *Villes et Territoires du Moyen-Orient,* no. 2 (May 2006): 1–9.

Susser, Asher. "Jordan." In *Middle East Contemporary Survey,* vol. 19, *1995,* ed. Bruce Maddy-Weitzman. Tel Aviv: Moshe Dayan Center for Middle Eastern and African Studies, Tel Aviv University, 1997.

———. "Jordan." In *Middle East Contemporary Survey,* vol. 20, *1996,* ed. Bruce Maddy-Weitzman, 405–56. Tel Aviv: Moshe Dayan Center for Middle Eastern and African Studies, Tel Aviv University, 1998.

———. "Jordan." In *Middle East Contemporary Survey,* vol. 22, *1998,* ed. Bruce Maddy-Weitzman. Tel Aviv: Moshe Dayan Center for Middle Eastern and African Studies, Tel Aviv University, 2000.

Tajina, Mohamed Aziz. "Le tourisme Saharien et son impact sur le developpement regional du Sud-Tunisien." *Cahiers de CERES, Serie Sociologie,* no. 18 (1991): 137–87.

Teller, Matthew. *Jordan: The Rough Guide*. London: Rough Guides, 1998.

TERPLAN. *How to Plan Tourism? An Example from Tunisia*. Prague: Czechoslovak Institute for Regional Planning, 1970.

Testas, Abdelaziz. "The Contribution of EU Investment to Tunisia's Economic Development." *Journal of North African Studies* 5, no. 2 (Summer 2000): 9–24.

Torres, Rebecca. "Cancun's Tourism Development from a Fordist Spectrum of Analysis." *Tourism Studies* 2, no. 1 (2002): 87–116.

Tukan, Jafar. "Architecture and Society." Paper presented at the Conference on the Social History of Jordan, March 24–26, 1998, Amman, Jordan. Sponsored by Al-Urdun Al-Jadid Research Center and the University of Jordan.

Tunisian External Communication Agency. *Tunisia, 1992–1996: The Development Strategy.* Tunis: Tunisian External Communication Agency, 1994.

Tunisian Secretariat of State for Information. *Tunisia Moves Ahead.* Tunis: CERES Productions, 1976.

Turner, Louis. "The International Division of Leisure: Tourism and the Third World." *World Development* 4, no. 3 (March 1976): 253–60.

Turner, Louis, and John Ash. *The Golden Hordes: International Tourism and the Pleasure Periphery.* London: Constable, 1975.

Twite, Robin, and Gershon Baskin, eds. *The Conversion of Dreams: The Development of Tourism in the Middle East.* Jerusalem: Israel/Palestine Center for Research and Information, 1994.

UNESCO/SECA. "Jordan: Petra National Park Management Plan." Paris: UNESCO, Cultural Heritage Division and Société d'Eco-Aménagement (SECA), 1994.

United Nations (UN). *Transnational Corporations in International Tourism.* New York: United Nations, 1982.

UNWTO. *See* World Tourism Organization.

Urry, John. "The Tourist Gaze 'Revisited.'" *American Behavioral Scientist* 36, no. 2 (November 1992): 172–96.

U.S. Agency for International Development (USAID). "Jordan 1993 Tourism Strategy." Included as attachment 5 as part of USAID Project Identification Document: Jordan Tourism Development Project, Project no. 278-0291, May 17, 1993, Chemonics International, prepared by Thomas G. Lloyd, 1993.

———. "Jordan Tourism Development Project: Contingency Planning Strategies." Amman, Jordan: Prepared by Thomas G. Lloyd, Chemonics International for USAID, 1994.

———. "Tourism Marketing Strategy." Technical Feasibility Studies Project V, Project no. 278-0291, September 28, 1993, Chemonics International, prepared by Thomas G. Lloyd, 1993.

U.S. Department of Commerce. *Doing Business in Tunisia.* Washington, D.C.: U.S. Commerical Service, 2004.

U.S. Department of State. "Fact Sheet: Mid-East-Mediterranean Travel and Tourism Association." Washington, D.C.: U.S. Department of State, Bureau of Public Affairs, 1995.

U.S. National Park Service. *Master Plan for the Protection and Use of Petra National Park.* Amman: USAID/Jordan, 1968.

US/ICOMOS. "Management Analysis and Recommendations for the Petra World Heritage Site." Amman, Jordan: United States Committee of the International Council on Monuments, 1996.

Vasile, Elizabeth. "Devotion as Distinction, Piety as Power: Religious Revival and the Transformation of Space in the Illegal Settlements of Tunis." In *Population, Poverty, and Politics in Middle Eastern Cities,* ed. Michael E. Bonie, 113–40. Gainesville: University Press of Florida, 1997.

———. "Re-turning Home: Transnational Movements and Transformation of Landscape and Culture in the Marginal Communities of Tunis." *Antipode* 29, no. 2 (1997): 177–96.

Vitalis, Robert. "The Middle East on the Edge of the Pleasure Periphery." *Middle East Report,* no. 196 (September–October 1995): 2–7.

Wahab, Salah. "Tourism and Terrorism: Synthesis of the Problem with Emphasis on Egypt." In *Tourism, Crime, and International Security,* ed. A. Pizzam and Y. Mansfeld, 175–86. London: John Wiley and Sons, 1996.

Wall, Nelson C. *A Study of the Rural Small Industry Problems and Potentials Associated with Rural Development in the Southern Siliana Area of Tunisia.* International Programs Division, Economic Development Laboratory, Georgia Institute of Technology: Prepared for the Ministry of Planning, Republic of Tunisia, and USAID, Mission to Tunisia, 1977.

Waltz, Susan E. "Islamist Appeal in Tunisia." *Middle East Journal* 40, no. 4 (Autumn 1986): 651–70.

Waterbury, John. "From Social Contracts to Extraction Contracts: The Political Economy of Authoritarianism and Democracy." In *Islam, Democracy, and the State in North Africa,* ed. John P. Entelis, 141–76. Bloomington: Indiana University Press, 1997.

Waters, Somerset R. "The American Tourist." *Annals of the American Academy of Political and Social Science* 368 (November 1966): 109–18.

Weiss, Linda. "Globalization and the Myth of the Powerless State." *New Left Review,* no. 225 (September–October 1997): 3–27.

Wendt, Alexander. *Social Theory of International Politics.* London: Cambridge University Press, 1999.

White, Gregory. *A Comparative Political Economy of Tunisia and Morocco: On the Outside of Europe Looking In.* Albany: State University of New York Press, 2001.

Williams, Allan M., and Gareth Shaw. "Introduction: Tourism and Uneven Economic Development." In *Tourism and Economic Development: European Perspectives,* ed. Allan M. Williams and Gareth Shaw, 1–16. Chichester, UK: John Wiley and Sons, 1998.

Winckler, Onn. "The Economic Factor of the Middle East Peace Process: The Jordanian Case." In *The Jordanian-Palestinian-Israeli Triangle: Smoothing the Path to Peace,* ed. Joseph Ginat and Onn Winckler. Sussex, UK: Sussex Academic Press, 1998.

Winckler, Onn, and Gad G. Gilbar. "The Development of the Tourism Industry in Jordan." In *The Jordanian-Palestinian-Israeli Triangle: Smoothing the Path to Peace,* ed. Joseph Ginat and Onn Winckler, 178–95. Sussex, UK: Sussex Academic Press, 1998.

World Bank. *Cultural Heritage and Development: A Framework for Action in the Middle East and North Africa.* Washington, D.C.: World Bank, 2001.

———. *Middle East and North Africa Economic Developments and Prospects 2005.* Washington, D.C.: World Bank, 2005.

———. *Peace and the Jordanian Economy.* Washington, D.C.: World Bank, 1994.

———. "Project Appraisal Document on a Proposed Loan to the Republic of Tunisia for a Cultural Heritage Project." Washington, D.C.: World Bank, 2001.

———. *Tunisia's Global Integration and Sustainable Development: Strategic Choices for the 21st Century.* Washington, D.C.: World Bank, 1996.

———. *World Tables.* Baltimore: Johns Hopkins University Press, various issues.

World Tourism Organization (UNWTO). *Inbound Tourism to the Middle East and North Africa.* Madrid: World Tourism Organization, 2003.

———. *Tourism Highlights 2006.* Madrid: World Tourism Organization, 2006.

———. *Tourism Market Trends: Middle East.* Madrid: World Tourism Organization, 2003.

———. *Yearbook of Tourism Statistics.* Madrid: World Tourism Organization, 1999.

Wynn, L. L. *Pyramids and Nightclubs.* Austin: University of Texas Press, 2007.

Yadgar, Yaacov. "A Myth of Peace: 'The Vision of the New Middle East' and Its Transformations in the Israeli Political and Public Spheres." *Journal of Peace Research* 43, no. 3 (2006): 297–312.

Zaiem, Med Hédi. "Les forces sociales en Tunisie et les mutations internationales." In *Le maghreb face aux mutations internationales,* ed. Abdelbaki Hermassi. Carthage: Beït Al-Hikma, 1993.

Zamiti, Khalil. "Le fonds de solidarité nationale: Pour une approche sociologique du politque." *Annuaire de l'Afrique du Nord* 35 (1996): 705–12.

Zartman, William I., ed. *Tunisia: The Political Economy of Reform.* Boulder, Colo.: Lynne Rienner, 1991.

Zunes, Stephen. "The Israeli-Jordanian Agreement: Peace or Pax Americana?" *Middle East Policy* 3, no. 4 (April 1995).

Index

Abdullah I bin al Hussein, (King Abdullah I), 82, 145; assassination, 83

Abdullah II bin al Hussein (King Abdullah II), 187–88; facilitation of entry procedures to Jordan, 200; Jordan First policy, 187; unilateral dependence on the United States, 187

Abou Nawas, 28–29, 32, 33

Abu Dhabi, 202

actor-network theory, 239n6

aerodrome of revolution, 85

Afghanistan: U.S.-led war in, 190

Aga Khan Trust for Culture (Egypt), 202

Agence de Mise en Valeur du Patrimoine et de la Promotion Culturelle (Tunisia), 69

Agence Foncière Touristique (Tunisia), 24, 54, 59

agency: actors in host countries, xxxiii; actors in the Middle East, xiv, xl, 195; Egyptians (nineteenth century), 228; global actors, xxxi

airline hijacking, 79, 85, 260n178

airlines, xxi, xix; Air Arabia, 205; charter, 8–9; CIA-sponsored, 84; Egyptian, 98, 120, 257n79; Emirates, 205; Gulf-owned, 28, 204–5; Jordanian, 79, 84, 119–20, 135; low-cost, 205; PanAm, 28; Qatar, 205; TWA, 28, 260n178

airports: in Dubai, 214; Eilat-Aqaba Peace Airport, 120, 137, 170–71; in Jordan, 86; in Tunisia, 23, 59, 65

air travel: between Egypt and Israel, 98, 120, 257n79; global geography of, 205; impact of 9/11 on, 190; between Jordan and Israel, 119–20; luxury, 205; rise of global, xxii–xxiii; to Tunisia, 23

Albright, Madeleine, 139

Algeria: civil war, 73

ecotourism (nature-based tourism), 44, 120, 229–30, 274n126; Dubai, 212; Israeli-occupied Sinai, 94, 256n59; Israel-Jordan border, 268n150; Jordan, 201–2, 230; Libya, 203; Oman, 203

Egypt: airlines, 98, 120, 257n79; cold peace with Israel, 98; cultures of travel in, 271n28; Jews who trace their roots to, 97, 232–33; maritime tourism route between Jordan and, 200–201; Husni Mubarak, 96; normalization concessions to Israel, 99; political violence in, 189–90, 194; politicization of tourism flows between Israel and, 79, 93–96, 257n78; pyramids, xxxiv; and realist-territorial geopolitical imaginary, 95–96, 100; territorial disputes between Israel and, 97; tourism arrivals, 98,193; U.S. aid to, 95. See also Salem, Ali; Taba

Ehteshami, Anoushiravan, 213

Eilat, 96–99, 120. See also Peace Airport; Taba

Emir Abdullah. See Abdullah I bin al Hussein

employment: tourism-related in the global economy, xviii; in tourism sector (Jordan), 138, 164; in tourism sector (Tunisia), 26, 38, 40–41, 61, 65, 69

English Patient, The, 61; and tourism marketing in Tunisia, 61–62

entrepreneurs, tourism: creation of a new class of, in Tunisia, 26; in Jordan, 92

Euben, Roxanne, 225

Europe: American tourism to,

xviii; post–World War II tourism development in, xviii

European Union, xxviii, 102; association agreement with Tunisia, 74; Mediterranean Barcelona declaration, 74

Evans, Peter, 20–21

exotification: cultural, 5; tourism and, 18, 58

experience of place: commodification of, xix, xxi–xxii, xxxiii–xxxv, 58–59, 143, 165, 167, 195–96; as definition of tourism, xix; and deterritorialization, xxxiii–xxxiv; hybrid, 229; and Islamic tourism, 225, 228; manufactured, 58, 215–16, 218; and tourist travel, xxii–xxiii, 7, 58. See also tourism

external economies (externalities), xxxiv, 71–72, 142; negative, 216; positive, xxix, xxxiv–xxxvi, 30–31, 33, 57, 65, 127–28, 166–67, 204, 216, 228, 242n53. See also locational economies; rent creation; rents

external image. See image, external; tourist image

fadayeen (Palestinian guerilla movement), 85

Fanik, Fahd, 89

Fanon, Frantz, 5

film: and Jordan's tourist image, 92; location shooting as tourism market niche, 202; and Tunisia's tourist image, 61–63

flexible production systems. See under Fordism

Fordism: crisis of, 64; definition of, 243n7; end of Keynesianism,

Waleed Hazbun is assistant professor of political science at Johns Hopkins University.

www.ingramcontent.com/pod-product-compliance
Lightning Source LLC
Chambersburg PA
CBHW020654270326
41928CB00005B/111